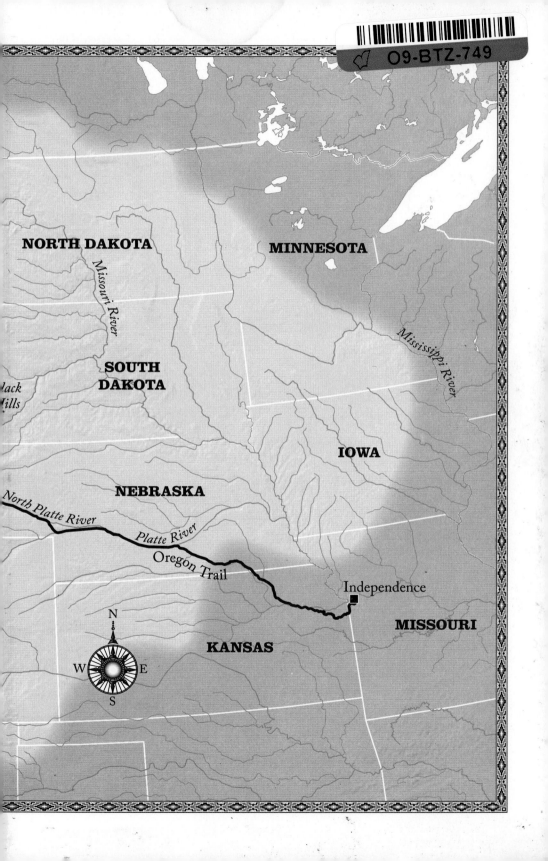

NORTH DAKOTA

MINNESOTA

Missouri River

SOUTH
DAKOTA

Mississippi River

Black
Hills

IOWA

NEBRASKA

North Platte River

Platte River

Oregon Trail

Independence

MISSOURI

N

W   E

S

KANSAS

THE HEART OF
EVERYTHING THAT IS

The Untold Story of Red Cloud, An American Legend

BOB DRURY & TOM CLAVIN

SIMON & SCHUSTER

NEW YORK LONDON TORONTO SYDNEY NEW DELHI

Simon & Schuster
1230 Avenue of the Americas
New York, NY 10020

First Simon & Schuster hardcover edition November 2013

SIMON & SCHUSTER and colophon are registered
trademarks of Simon & Schuster, Inc.

For information about special discounts for bulk purchases,
please contact Simon & Schuster Special Sales at
1-866-506-1949 or business@simonandschuster.com.

The Simon & Schuster Speakers Bureau can bring authors to your live event.
For more information or to book an event contact the
Simon & Schuster Speakers Bureau at 1-866-248-3049
or visit our website at www.simonspeakers.com.

Designed by Ruth Lee-Mui

Maps by Paul J. Pugliese

Manufactured in the United States of America

1   3   5   7   9   10   8   6   4   2

Library of Congress Cataloging-in-Publication Data
Drury, Bob.
The heart of everything that is : the untold story of Red Cloud,
an American legend / Bob Drury and Tom Clavin.
1. Red Cloud, 1822–1909.   2. Oglala Indians—King and rulers—Biography.
3. Red Cloud's War, 1866–1867.   4. Oglala Indians—Government relations.
5. Oglala Indians—History.   I. Title.
E99.O3R3725   2013
978.004'9752—dc23
[B]
2013003200

ISBN 978-1-4516-5466-0
ISBN 978-1-4516-5470-7 (ebook)

For Rita Olsen McDonald
—rfxd

For the Red Cloud family and residents of the Pine Ridge Reservation
—T.C.

CONTENTS

THE HEART OF
EVERYTHING THAT IS

PAHA SAPA

The Bluecoats, many of them veterans of the Civil War, had survived the most brutal deprivations—the "Hornet's Nest" at Shiloh, Stonewall Jackson's "River of Death" on the banks of the Chickahominy, the bloody Sunken Road at Antietam. They had held firm to cover the retreat at Bull Run and stood with Kit Carson at Valverde Ford. But the onset of the winter of 1866 was introducing them to a new kind of hardship as they broke trail through the rugged Powder River Country, the only sounds the creak of their frozen tack and the moan of the north wind as it tore through the stunted branches of scrub oak that choked the river corridors.

It was November 2, and it had taken the sixty-three officers and enlisted men of Company C of the 2nd U.S. Cavalry more than a month to traverse the nearly 700 miles from the flatlands of eastern Nebraska to the head of the Bozeman Trail in south-central Wyoming. They had traced the great bend of the North Platte across gale-scoured plains, climbed onto mile-high prairie whose altitude made their lungs wheeze and their heads ache, and forded more than two dozen ice-crusted rivers and streams. Now, veering west from the South Powder, they disappeared into the rolling buttes that buckled and folded to the northern horizon. The riders were still a day's journey from their destination, the isolated Fort Phil Kearny, a seventeen-acre redoubt on the fork of Little Piney Creek and Big Piney Creek just shy of the Montana border. With their black woolen sack coats cinched tight and their greasy kepis and Hardees pulled low against their foreheads, from a twilit distance the party could well have been mistaken for a column of wizened buffalo picking its way through the rugged Dakota Territory.* Along the trail they had passed a great many grave sites holding the remains of white men and women murdered by Indians.

The soldiers, reinforcements from the East, were unaccustomed to the ferocity of the *poudrerie* whiteouts that funneled down from the Canadian Plains. Though the biting northers had left the tops of the surrounding foothills and tabletops bald and brown, Company C's horses and wagon mules pushed through creek bottoms and coulees piled high with snowdrifts that sometimes reached their withers. That night they bivouacked in a narrow gulch, where a spinney of bare serviceberry trees formed a windbreak. Above them loomed the east face of the Bighorn Mountains, a 12,000-foot fortress of granite that few whites had ever seen. Platoon sergeants hobbled horses, posted pickets, and passed the word that fires could be lit for cooking. The men huddled close to the flames and methodically spooned up a supper of beans, coffee, molar-cracking hardtack, and sowbelly remaindered from the Civil War. Company C was nominally under the command of Lieutenant Horatio Stowe Bingham, a gaunt, hawk-nosed Québécois who had fought with the 1st Minnesota Volunteers from Bull Run to Antietam, where he had been wounded. But every enlisted man recognized that the most senior officer accompanying them, the coal-eyed Captain William Judd Fetterman, was the man who would

---

*The word "buffalo," a bastardization, was applied to the immense herds of "boeufs" first encountered by French trappers on the North American Plains, around 1635. In 1774 the animals were officially classified as "American bison" in order to taxonomically distinguish them from African and Asian buffalo species. Because across the prairies of the old West American bison were referred to as buffalo, that is the designation we have chosen for this book.

lead them on their paramount mission: to find, capture, or kill the great Oglala Sioux warrior chief Red Cloud.

For more than a year Red Cloud had directed an army of over 3,000 Sioux, Northern Cheyenne, and Arapaho warriors on a campaign across a territory that spanned a swath of land twice the size of Texas. It was the first time the United States had been confronted by an enemy using the kind of guerrilla warfare that had helped secure its own existence a century earlier, although this irony went largely unappreciated in dusty western duty barracks or eastern boardrooms where railroad barons, mining magnates, and ambitious politicians plotted to create an empire. Red Cloud's fighters had ambushed and burned wagon trains, killed and mutilated civilians, and outwitted and outfought government troops in a series of bloody raids that had shaken the U.S. Army's general command. The fact that a heathen "headman" had rallied and coordinated so large a multitribal force was in itself a surprise to the Americans, whose racial prejudices were emblematic of the era. But that Red Cloud had managed to wield enough strength of purpose to maintain authority over his squabbling warriors and notoriously ill-disciplined fighters came as an even greater shock.

As was the white man's wont since the annihilation of the Indian confederacies and nations east of the Mississippi, when he could not acquire Native lands through fraud and bribery, he relied on force. Thus at the first sign of hostilities on the Northern Plains the powers in Washington had authorized the Army to crush the hostiles. If that did not work, it was to buy them off. One year earlier, in the summer of 1865, government negotiators had followed up a failed punitive expedition against Red Cloud and his allies with the offer of yet another in a succession of treaties, this one ceding the vast Powder River Country as inviolable Indian land. Yet again gifts of blankets, sugar, tobacco, and coffee were proffered while promises of independence were read aloud. In exchange the whites had asked—again—only for unimpeded passage along the wagon trail that veined the dun-colored prairie. Many chiefs and subchiefs had "touched the pen" at a ceremony on the same grasslands of southern Wyoming where, fourteen years earlier, the United States had signed its first formal pact with the Western Sioux. Now, as he had in 1851, Red Cloud refused. He argued at council fires that to allow "this dangerous snake in our midst . . . and give up our sacred graves to be plowed under for corn" would lead to the destruction of his people.

"The White Man lies and steals," the Oglala warrior chief warned his Indian brethren, and he was not wrong. "My lodges were many, but now they are few. The White Man wants all. The White Man must fight, and the Indian will die where his fathers died."

By November 1866 the forty-five-year-old Red Cloud was at the pinnacle of his considerable power, and the war parties he recruited were driven by equal measures of desperation, revenge, and overinflated self-confidence in their military mastery of the High Plains. The nomadic lifestyle they had followed for centuries was being inexorably altered by the white invasion, and they sensed that their only salvation was to make a stand here, now; otherwise, they would be doomed to extermination. Red Cloud's warnings would prove prescient: the mid-1860s were a psychological turning point in white-Indian relations in the nation's midsection. Earlier European colonialism had involved not only the destruction of Native peoples, but also a paternalistic veneration—partly influenced by James Fenimore Cooper—of the cultures of the "Noble Savages . . . their fate decreed by a heartless federal government whose deliberate policy was to kill as many as possible in needless wars."

Now, however, Cooper's romanticism was a receding memory, a newly muscular America replacing it with a post–Civil War vision of Manifest Destiny. The old attitudes were reconfigured with cruel clarity, particularly among westerners. Even whites who had once considered Indians the equivalent of wayward children—naifs like Thomas Gainsborough's English rustics, to be "civilized" with Bibles and plows—were beginning to view them as a subhuman race to be exterminated or swept onto reservations by the tide of progress. By the summer of 1866 the United States had broken the previous year's flimsy treaty and constructed three forts along the 535-mile Bozeman Trail, which bisected the rich Powder River basin—an area delineated by the Platte River in the south, the Bighorns to the west, the wild Yellowstone River in the north, and, in the east, the sacred Black Hills: to the Sioux, *Paha Sapa*, "The Heart of Everything That Is."

Moreover, a much more immediate motivation for what newspapers would soon refer to as Red Cloud's War propelled the politicians in Washington. Four years earlier, in 1862, gold had been discovered in great quantities in the craggy mountain canyons of western Montana—gold now needed to fund Reconstruction and pay down the skyrocketing interest on the national debt. Nearly half a decade of civil war had left the Union on the verge of bankruptcy, and the government depended on the thousands of placermen and panners who had already made their way to the shanty boomtowns of Montana's "Fourteen-Mile City" via a serpentine route that skirted the western flank of the Bighorns and Sioux territory. But the most direct path to the fields ran directly through Red Cloud's land, which had been ceded to his people by treaty.

Small trains of miners and emigrants had already begun picking their way through this country, pioneers with hard bark who had no use for either American treaties or Indian traditions. Facing persistent attack, they were not shy in their disdain for laws that blocked their passage. The gold hand Frank Elliott spoke for most when he wrote to his father back east, "They will make many a poor white man bite the dust since they spare neither women or children. Something has to be done immediately. I tell you we are getting hostile. The Indians have to be chastised & we are going to give them the best in the shop." Federal officials wrung their hands over such attitudes, claiming that they lacked sufficient military force to rein in the white interlopers. Few politicians, however, had any real desire to do so. As a result, any treaty boundary lines that existed on paper dissolved on the ground.

This enormous pressure created tension from saloons to statehouses and forced General of the Army Ulysses S. Grant to send troops to reopen the Bozeman Trail. The wagon route, whose wheel ruts are still visible in places today, had been blazed in 1863 by the adventurers John Bozeman and John Jacobs and traced ancient buffalo and Indian paths. It angled north by northwest from the long-established Oregon Trail, and coursed directly through the heart of hallowed Indian hunting grounds teeming with fat prairie chickens, grouse, and quail; with wolves and grizzlies; and with great herds of elk, mule deer, and pronghorn antelope. The land was bountiful to the tribes. But above all, this was one of the last redoubts of the great northern herd of the sacred buffalo, millions upon millions of which migrated through the territory. It was the buffalo—the animal itself and what it represented to Indian culture—for which Red Cloud fought. And no American statesman or soldier had counted on the cunning and flint of the elusive Sioux chief in defense of his people's culture. In just a few months in the summer and fall of 1866 Red Cloud had proved the equal of history's great guerrilla tacticians.

From literally the first day European emigrants set foot on the New World's fatal shores,* whites and Indians had engaged in bloody, one-sided, and near-constant combat. Four centuries of these wars of conquest had combined with starvation and disease to result in the relocation, if not the extinction, of perhaps half of North America's pre-Columbian population. Gone or penned up on hard land were the Pequots and the Cherokee, the Iroquois and Choctaw, the Delaware and Seminoles and Hurons and Shawnee. With few exceptions the newcomers accomplished this with such relative ease that by the mid-nineteenth century a flabby complacency toward fighting the Indians had set in. This arrogance was exacerbated in the post–Civil War era. As the historian Christopher Morton notes, "Imagine: soldiers who had recently outfought Stonewall Jackson, J. E. B. Stuart, and the great Robert E. Lee are shipped west. It is described to them that they'll see a few Indians here, a few Indians there. Scraggly. Lice-ridden. Bows and arrows against rifles. Naturally they have no idea what they're getting into."

Thus from the outset of Red Cloud's War the U.S. Army's field commanders failed to recognize that this was a new kind of Indian conflict. For all their historic ruthlessness, the tribes had always lacked long-range planning, and their habitual reluctance to press a military advantage had ultimately led to their defeat and subjugation. Yet here was a military

---

*On April 21, 1607, Captain Christopher Newport led about twenty of the first permanent English settlers ashore near what was to become Virginia's Jamestown colony. They explored for nearly eight hours without seeing another human being. On their way back to the boat that had taken them ashore they were ambushed, with two men wounded by arrows. The incident is described on page 135 of a book edited by Colonel Matthew Moten, *Between War and Peace*.

campaign, as described by the historian Grace Raymond Hebard, led by "a strategic chief who was learning to follow up a victory, an art heretofore unknown to the red men." It was not unusual for Red Cloud to confound his pursuers by planning and executing simultaneous attacks on civilian wagon trains and Army supply columns separated by hundreds of miles. Nor was Red Cloud afraid to confront U.S. soldiers—and their deafening mountain howitzer, "the gun that shoots twice"—within shouting distance of their isolated stockades.

Sioux braves slithering on their bellies through the saltbush and silver sage came within a few yards of sentries in guard towers before shooting them off their posts; soldiers assigned to hunt, fetch water, and chop wood were harassed almost daily by hails of arrows fired from sheer cutbanks and hidden glens; dispatch riders simply disappeared into the emptiness of the rolling prairie with alarming regularity. It was like a fatal game, and thus by ones and twos the bulk of the undermanned and outgunned 2nd Battalion of the 18th U.S. Infantry Regiment stationed at Fort Phil Kearny was depleted. The cavalry of Company C was riding to their rescue.

The infantry battalion—eight companies of approximately 100 men each spread among three Bozeman Trail forts—was under the command of the forty-two-year-old Colonel Henry Beebee Carrington, a politically connected midwesterner who through four bloody years of civil war had never fired a shot in anger. His stooped posture and graying hair betrayed the vestiges of a sickly youth; his deep-set rheumy eyes appeared to be permanently weeping; Red Cloud and the Plains Indians had taken to referring to him derisively as the "Little White Chief." Carrington had chosen as his headquarters Fort Phil Kearny in Wyoming, about midway between Reno Station, sixty miles to the south, and Fort C. F. Smith, a further ninety miles to the northwest across the Montana border. He had begun construction on the post in July 1866, and during the compound's first six months of existence he recorded over fifty "hostile demonstrations," resulting in the deaths of 154 soldiers, scouts, settlers, and miners, as well as the theft of 800 head of livestock. Carrington's impotence in the face of this creeping if deadly harassment—"Scarcely a day or night passes without attempts to steal stock or surprise pickets" was typical of the tone of his pleading dispatches—led to constant requests for more soldiers, better mounts, and modern, breech-loading rifles to replace his troop's cumbersome, antiquated muzzle-loaders. For various reasons his petitions went largely unheeded.

Yet, surprisingly, in neither his official reports nor his personal journals did Carrington much note the devastating psychological toll Indian warfare was taking on his troops. The Natives' astonishing capacity for cruelty was like nothing the whites had ever experienced. The Plains Indians had honed their war ethic for centuries, and their martial logic was not only fairly straightforward, but accepted by all tribes without challenge—no quarter asked, none given; to every enemy, death, the slower and more excruciating the better. A defeated Crow, Pawnee, Cheyenne, Shoshone, or Sioux not immediately killed in battle would be subjected to unimaginable torments for as long as he could stand the pain. Women of all ages were tortured to death, but not before being raped—unless they were young enough to be raped and then taken as captive slaves or hostages to be traded for trinkets, whiskey, or guns. Crying babies were a burden on the trail, so they were summarily killed, by spear, by war club, or by banging their soft skulls against rocks or trees so as not to waste arrows. On occasion, in order to replenish their gene pool—or particularly after the tribes recognized the value of white hostages—preteens of both sexes were spared execution, if not pitiless treatment. This was merely the way of life and death to the Indian: *vae victis,* woe to the conquered. All expected similar treatment should they fall. But it was incomprehensibly immoral to the Anglo-European soldiers and settlers for whom memories of the Roman Colosseum, the barbarities of the Crusades, and the dungeons of the Inquisition had long since faded.

Even Carrington's most hardened veterans, their steel forged in the carnage of the Civil War, were literally sickened by what newspapers from New York to San Francisco euphemistically referred to as Indian "atrocities" and, in the case of women, "depredations." Captured whites were scalped, skinned, and roasted alive over their own campfires, shrieking in agony as Indians yelped and danced about them like the bloody-eyed Achilles celebrating over the fallen Hector. Men's penises were hacked off and shoved down their throats and women were flogged with deer-hide quirts while being gang-raped. Afterward their breasts, vaginas, and even pregnant wombs were sliced away and laid out on the buffalo grass. Carrington's patrols rode often to the rescue, but almost always too late, finding victims whose eyeballs had been gouged out and left perched on rocks, or the burned carcasses of men and women bound together by their own steaming entrails ripped from their insides while they were still conscious. The Indians, inured to this torture ethos, naturally fought one another to their last breath. The whites were at first astonished by this persistence, and most of the soldiers of the 18th Infantry had long since made unofficial pacts never to be taken alive.

Captain Fetterman, the relentless and adaptive Civil War hero, was charged with ending this Hobbesian dystopia. The Army's general staff considered Fetterman a new breed of Indian fighter, and as such he carried orders to Fort Phil Kearny installing him as second in command to Carrington, his old regimental commander. The final instructions he received before his departure from Omaha had been terse: "Indian warfare in the Powder River Country can be successfully ended once and for all by engaging in open battle with the Indians during the winter." These orders underlined the War Department's undisguised position that previous campaigns against Red Cloud, if indeed they could be called such, had stalled owing to a combination of incompetence and the American field commanders' aversion to cold-weather combat. In truth, even newcomers to the frontier such as Carrington soon learned that giving chase with horses, infantry, and supply trains consistently bogged down in deep snow was fruitless. But the eastern generals, who had conducted the majority of their Civil War marches in the South, were ignorant of Plains weather, and Washington expected the Army to drain this blood-soaked western swamp.

In the summer of 1866 the new commander of the Military Division of the Missouri, General William Tecumseh Sherman, undertook two long inspection tours of his vast western defenses. On the trail he became even more convinced that his troops' failure to apprehend or kill Red Cloud stemmed from reluctance to meet savagery with savagery. The craggy forty-six-year-old Sherman was already an expert on human misery, and he held no illusions that peace between the white and red races could be achieved. In his typical brusque view, all Indians should be either killed outright or confined to reservations of the Army's choosing. He had an eye toward the transcontinental railroad—whose tracks already extended 100 miles west of Omaha—and his genocidal judgments were succinct. "We are not going to let a few thieving, ragged Indians check and stop progress," he wrote to his old commander General Grant. "We must act with vindictive earnestness against the Sioux, even to their extermination—men, women and children."

Sherman recognized that the piecemeal destruction of the eastern tribes had been a centuries-long process, and was still continuing to some extent. He also understood that this slow, systematic eradication would not work in a West bursting with natural resources the United States needed immediately. The raw frontier he was charged with taming was too vast, and on his circuitous inspection tours he spent long, gritty days in the saddle, traveling (it seemed to him) to Creation and back. Wherever he rode he had been made to feel like a visitor, or worse, an interloper, by warriors who shadowed his every move, just out of rifle range, over hills, through ravines, and along alkaline creek beds. Finally, during a brief two-day stopover at Nebraska's Fort Kearney,* Carrington informed him, with no apparent attempt at irony, "Where you have been, General, is only a fraction of Red Cloud's country."

This caught Sherman's attention. Red Cloud's country? Over the past four years so many good men, in President Lincoln's words, gave the last full measure of devotion to preserve the Union. And a heathen considered this land *his country*? Carrington's choice of words was just another manifestation of the white-red cultural divide, however. Red Cloud no more considered the Powder River territory "his country," in the American sense of the phrase, than he would claim ownership of the moon and the stars. At best he was fighting to preserve *a* country that the *Wakan Tanka*, the Great Spirit, had provided for Indians' use. That Washington had

---

*Fort Kearney, in south-central Nebraska, was named for the Mexican War hero General Stephen W. Kearny. Its name was misspelled with an extra "e" in so many official government documents that this became recognized as the standard spelling. Fort Phil Kearny along the Bozeman Trail in Wyoming was named after the Civil War general Philip Kearny, Stephen Kearny's nephew.

deigned to cede to his tribe the right to occupy it in a succession of treaties and "friendship pacts" dating to 1825 only proved how confused these
whites were about the grand scheme of the universe. Unlike the conciliatory Indian headmen who a year earlier were willing to cease hostilities in
exchange for "protection" and "trade rights," Red Cloud was making war
to halt the increasing intrusion of whites into Sioux hunting grounds—no
more, no less.

The simplicity of this oft-stated purpose eluded Sherman. The general
was a manic-depressive whose mental illness had forced him to temporarily relieve himself of command in the early stages of the Civil War—this
relief, when discovered by the wire services, had prompted the headline
"General William T. Sherman Insane." Now his inner demons were made
terrifyingly manifest by a scalping, torturing tribe of "savages" his troops
could not even find, much less kill. It came as a further blow to his fragile
ego when, during a stopover at Fort Laramie, an officer produced a primitive map that displayed all the territory Red Cloud and the Western Sioux
had secured over the past two decades. This largely uncharted expanse of
primeval forests, undulating prairie, sun-baked tableland, cloud-shrouded
peaks, and ice-blue kettle lakes encompassed 740,000 square miles, extending south from the Canadian border into Colorado and Nebraska,
and west from the Minnesota frontier to the Great Salt Lake in Utah.
It was bisected by over a dozen major rivers and numberless creeks and
streams flowing out of the Rockies and Black Hills, and was home to an
abundance of tribes that the Sioux had either conquered or reduced to
vassal status.

In all, this cruel and mysterious territory of far horizons accounted for
one-fifth of what would one day become the contiguous United States.
No one tribe had ever before or would ever again reign over so much
open country. It was not long after seeing the map that Sherman ordered
his subordinates in Omaha to put this house in order. They, in turn, summoned Captain Fetterman. It was an obvious selection.

While Colonel Carrington had been the nominal commander of Ohio's
18th Regiment during the war, it was the robust Fetterman who had
earned the unit's battle honors and field promotions. He was an enigmatic

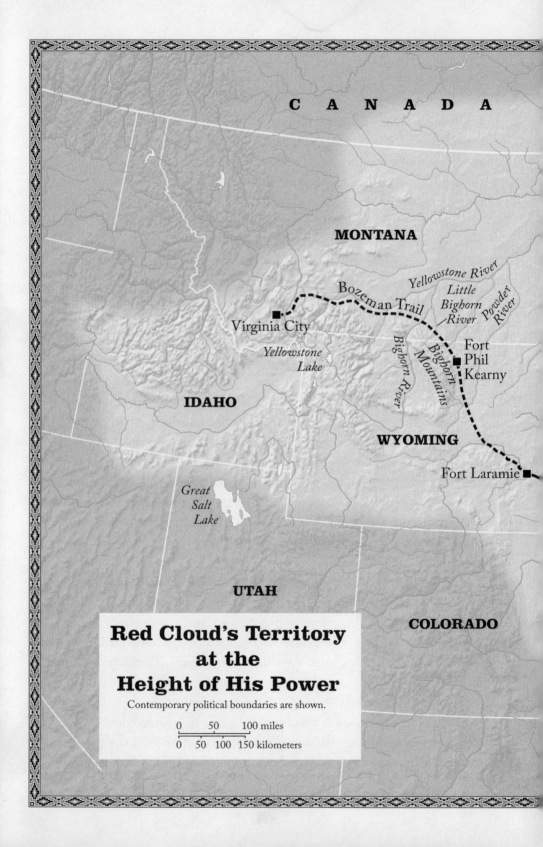

C A N A D A

MONTANA

Yellowstone River

Bozeman Trail

Little
Bighorn
River

Powder
River

Virginia City

Yellowstone
Lake

Bighorn River

Bighorn
Mountains

Fort
Phil
Kearny

IDAHO

WYOMING

Fort Laramie

Great
Salt
Lake

UTAH

COLORADO

Red Cloud's Territory at the Height of His Power

Contemporary political boundaries are shown.

0   50   100 miles

0   50   100   150 kilometers

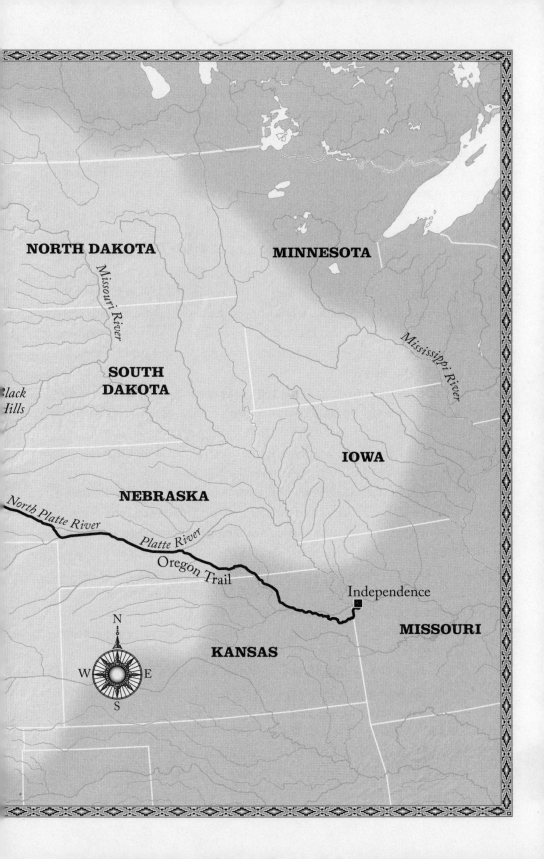

man whose wild, dark muttonchops and smoldering glare belied a graceful and refined sociability, and there was no questioning Fetterman's bravery. He had been cited for his leadership during the storming of Corinth, at "Hell's Half Acre" at Stones River, and at the fiery siege of Atlanta, and he was an officer who inspired lifelong loyalty in his troops. Carrington, on the other hand, was an administrator at heart, and not unaware of the snide comparisons with Fetterman whispered by both his superiors and his hot-blooded junior officers. "Few came [to Fort Phil Kearny] from Omaha or Laramie without prejudice, believing I was not doing enough fighting," he was to testify before a congressional commission investigating the failures of Red Cloud's War. Yet as confident as Sherman and his generals were that Fetterman would bring the fight to the enemy, Carrington believed that he had learned all too well in his six months among the Sioux that the strategies and tactics of Manassas and Bull Run would not apply to the far West.

The Indians were too clever for that. Despite the Army's overwhelming numbers, massed formations and set-piece engagements were simply foreign to the tribal mind-set of raid, feint, and parry. In Fetterman, Carrington sensed an officer too enamored of what one longtime frontier scout dismissed as "these damn paper-collar soldiers." Given the eventual outcome (and a mighty public relations campaign), Carrington's discretion was considered the more sound policy well into the twentieth century, while Grant's, Sherman's, and particularly Fetterman's strategy was judged as lacking. Despite his gleaming Civil War record, Fetterman was soon enough to be vilified as too clever by half: the wrong man at the wrong place in the wrong job. He was, it would be said in hindsight, a soldier who understood little about Red Cloud and less about Indian warfare, and a conventional wisdom developed that attributed his spectacular downfall to his hubris.

This counterfactual locomotive would be stoked by the memoirs of Carrington's successive wives, each of whom exalted and exonerated her husband at the expense of Fetterman. Carrington himself, who lived long enough into the Gilded Age to attend memorial anniversaries of Red Cloud's War, was also so keen to rehabilitate his public image that he must shoulder blame for the vilification of his subordinate. But if, as is said, survivors write history, it was primarily the Carrington women—aided and abetted by a lingering Victorian reluctance to call a lady a liar—who painted Fetterman as "an arrogant fool blindly leading his men to their deaths."

As it was, in that first week of November 1866, on the same night that Captain Fetterman and Company C of the 2nd Battalion bedded down in a snowbound gulch one day's ride from Fort Phil Kearny, eighty miles to the north thousands of hostiles from over 1,800 Sioux, Cheyenne, and Arapaho lodges had come together for a war council. There, on the sandy banks of Goose Creek where it flowed into the icy Tongue, Red Cloud gathered his warrior societies about him to finalize his plans to drive the white man from the Powder River Country and defeat the mighty United States in the only war the nation would ever lose to an Indian army. The great chief summoned the spirits of his dead forefathers to weave a tale of Indian survival, of Indian hope, of Indian victory. He insisted that the red man had been granted this land by the Great Spirit, as a birthright that had been theirs forever and would be theirs forevermore, in this life or the next. When he finished his speech more Indians spoke, and the campfires were banked before the pipe was passed and the war dance begun. And then, through billows of blue tobacco haze, Red Cloud retired to a warrior lodge erected in a copse of cedars along the river's edge. There he laid out for his battle commanders his strategy for the final destruction of the white interlopers and their forts in the Powder River Country.

So it occurred that preconceived history was bent, that the United States would lose a war, and that the fate of Captain Fetterman and the Bluecoats of the 2nd Battalion of the 18th Infantry Regiment of the United States Army was sealed.

 ❖ Part I ❖

THE PRAIRIE

East of the Mississippi civilization stood on three legs—land, water and timber. West of the Mississippi not one but two of those legs were withdrawn—water and timber. Civilization was left on one leg—land. It is a small wonder that it toppled over in temporary failure.

—Walter Prescott Webb, *The Great Plains*

FIRST CONTACT

It was a pageant unlike anything seen before in the West.

In the first week of September 1851, the largest gathering of Indians ever assembled descended on the lush grasslands on the outskirts of Fort Laramie in present-day southeastern Wyoming. They arrived from every compass point: Sioux, Arapaho, and Cheyenne from the North Platte and South Platte corridors; Arikara, Assiniboin, Mandan, and Minnitarees riding southwest from the far reaches of the Upper Missouri; Blackfeet and Shoshones from deep in the Rockies, the latter escorted down onto the flatlands under a white flag of truce held aloft by the mountain man Jim Bridger; and finally the stately Crows, completing an 800-mile trek from the buckling Yellowstone bluffs. All together more than 10,000 men, women, and children from more than a dozen sovereign tribes were represented—allies, vassals, mortal enemies. Clad in their most ornamental buckskins and blankets, riding their finest warhorses, ribbons and feathers flying, they had arrived to hear representatives from the Great Father in Washington make the case for peace—peace not only between the red man and the encroaching whites, but among the Indians themselves.

The environs of the weathered stockade on the eastern slope of the Rockies were a natural setting for such a powwow, a council that the United States deemed crucial to its westward expansion. Fort Laramie, established seventeen years earlier as a lonely vanguard post in the center of the vast wilderness, bisected what was to become known as the Oregon Trail. Over those years it had evolved from an isolated trading post into a lively marketplace that attracted fur traders and whiskey peddlers from St. Louis; Indians from across the Plains hawking buffalo robes; and horse traders like the legendary Kit Carson, who drove herds of New Mexican ponies up from the Arkansas River to sell at auction. Two years earlier, in 1849, the Army had purchased the dilapidated fort from the American Fur Company for $4,000, renamed and refurbished it, and installed within its log and adobe walls a small company of mounted riflemen—between 20 and 100 men, depending on the season and the whim of the general staff—as a way of regulating and protecting the increased flow of miners, homesteaders, and entrepreneurs westering through the Powder River Country.

The trails opened by the first frontier explorers in the 1820s and 1830s had initially drawn scientists, missionaries, and even wealthy sportsmen to the pristine territory on the far side of the Missouri River. On their return to the East these men spun beautiful, if fabulous, tales about the glories of the new Eden beyond the Big Muddy. Their stories were lapped up by newspapermen. In 1846 one New York City penny paper, noting the arrival in Manhattan of two British aristocrats recently returned from an "extended buffalo hunting tour in Oregon and the Wild West," used the terms "wonders," "agreeable," "grand," "glowing," and "magnificent" in one paragraph alone to describe the wild country. "The fisheries are spoken of as the best in the country," the article concluded, "and only equaled by the rare facilities for agriculture." This sort of breathless advertising naturally roiled the imagination of thousands of small farmers and urban dwellers who were eager to begin life anew in paradise—provided a family or its extended clan could scrape together the $400 needed to outfit a wagon with stock and provisions. Many could. The general course of the Oregon Trail, a new wagon road branching off from the older, more established Santa Fe Trail in Kansas, had been mapped and described by the explorer

John Frémont in 1842. The rutted route worked its way northwest over the Rockies at the South Pass, and it soon surpassed the Santa Fe Trail as a symbol of the nation's expansion.

Emigrant traffic was unobtrusive at first. For most of the 1840s the High Plains tribes remained too busy warring against one another to bother to molest the small caravans of prairie schooners that snaked across the Plains making twenty miles a day. These wagons, much smaller and lighter than those depicted in Hollywood films, had hickory bows positioned across hardwood frames that supported their cloth canopies. And, again, unlike the wagons in movies, they were pulled not by horses, but by stronger, sturdier oxen—and by mules, the more sure-footed, though sterile, offspring of a jackass and a horse mare. On the occasions when the wagons did arouse Indians' curiosity, their owners could usually pass freely after paying a small tariff of coffee or refined sugar, which the Indians considered a particular delicacy.

Still, to the Sioux in particular, the white travelers were an odd lot, "totally out of their element; bewildered and amazed, like a troop of schoolboys lost in the woods," wrote Francis Parkman, the explorer who traveled west from New England in the 1840s to live among the tribes. Not all were as naive, or unlucky, as the ill-fated Donner Party, destined to be trapped in the killing snowdrifts of the Sierra Nevada during the winter of 1846–47. Yet in his later years Red Cloud recalled watching in befuddlement as the hapless pioneers—blithely overconfident if under-outfitted and pathetically unprepared for the harsh, treeless prairie—burned expensive steamer trunks, chiffoniers, and even an occasional pipe organ for cook fires and littered the wheatgrass and fox sedge with goose-feather mattresses, grandfather clocks, and portable sawmills, in belated attempts to lighten the load on axles made from young, green wood that too often snapped hauling such extravagances.

Prior to the purchase of Fort Laramie what little policing was called for across the uncharted western territories was carried out by a small battalion of Missouri mounted volunteers who were stationed at Fort Kearney in the Nebraska Territory, 400 miles east of the Wyoming border. With the discovery of gold at Sutter's Mill in California in 1848, however, what had begun as a trickle swelled to a torrent. In 1850 alone an estimated 55,000 California-bound forty-niners and Mormons seeking refuge in Utah formed a nearly endless chain of wagons trespassing across Indian lands. They killed buffalo, fouled scarce water holes, denuded pasturage, and, most distressingly, spread diseases such as cholera, "the killing bile scourge," from which the Indians had no immunity.

This increased traffic resulted in so many Indian attacks that by 1851 westward travelers were literally passing the skulls and bones of their predecessors. In a diary entry, one teenage girl describes burying her murdered father on the banks of the Green River in a coffin dug out of the trunk of a western river birch. "But next year emigrants found his bleaching bones, as the Indians had disinterred the remains." A conservative estimate of trailside deaths for 1850 alone is 5,000, meaning that among the optimistic souls departing St. Louis to start a new and better life, one in eleven never made it past the Rockies. Such numbers drew Washington's attention, and the government found it necessary to reach out to the tribes, dominated by the Sioux, to come to some agreement regarding right of passage, for by the mid-nineteenth century the Sioux's jurisdiction and power were spreading like an oil slick across the Northern Plains.

In hindsight it seems inevitable that the most feared tribe in the territory would soon enough bump up against the continent's other burgeoning empire, the United States. The Western Sioux, however, had little comprehension of the enormous number of whites living east of the Mississippi, and considered themselves on an equal footing. This would soon enough change, but for now the Indian agent Thomas Fitzpatrick spent the summer crisscrossing the Plains from the Arkansas to the Yellowstone, spreading word of a grand treaty council, to be held near Fort Laramie in September, that would bring peace to the country once and for all.

It was not an easy sell. The western tribes had spent the better part of five decades raiding and fighting one another, and their running battles and blood feuds had altered the mosaic of the land. Rees hated Sioux, Sioux hated Shoshones, Shoshones hated Cheyenne, Cheyenne hated Pawnee. Almost everyone hated the Crows. Now they were being asked to suspend that history, to sit together and pass the pipe, to work out boundary agreements set by strange intruders from the East who spoke to them as if they were children. But Fitzpatrick, a former trapper and mountain man familiar with Native customs and mores, was respected among the clans. A tall, lank Irishman with a halo of thick, prematurely white hair, Fitzpatrick was an anomaly on the prairie: the intense Roman Catholic education he had received in County Cavan had made him something of a man of letters. But if the whites were impressed with his prose, it was his fighting ability that caught the Indians' attention. Called "Broken Hand" by nearly all the tribes, he had earned the sobriquet in a running battle with the Blackfeet during which he'd plunged his horse off a forty-foot cliff into the Yellowstone, shattered his left wrist when his rifle misfired, and still managed to kill several of his pursuers.

The Indians would listen to such a fighter—it was reported that shaking Fitzpatrick's good right hand was like grabbing a hickory stick wrapped in sandpaper—and in time he persuaded nearly every Head Man to at least hear out the government's plan. The Pawnee, by now living in mortal fear of the Sioux, were the only major tribe that refused to participate. The fact that Fitzpatrick also let it be known that he was in possession of $100,000 allotted by the U.S. Congress to procure gifts for any band willing to attend the council surely complemented his powers of persuasion. An additional enticement was the promised presence of the superintendent of Indian Affairs, Colonel David D. Mitchell, who, like Fitzpatrick, shared a long history with the Indians west of the Mississippi as a fur trapper and trader. Mitchell had served in his present position for a decade, and the Indians knew him and, somewhat, trusted him.

The Sioux were the first to arrive, their Head Men and warriors in full feathered headdresses according to their station and wealth, their vermilion-streaked cheeks a gaudy splash of color in the dusty flats. They were followed by younger braves arrayed in columns, and behind them the women and girls, bedecked in their best beads and shell-pendant earrings, with intricate porcupine quill work adorning their buckskin dresses. The women led the packhorses, which were dragging travois piled high with lodge skins, tepee poles, and small children. Among the Lakota bands was a twenty-year-old Hunkpapa from the Missouri River tribes named Sitting Bull, a fierce and outspoken leader of an elite warrior society, who, though still an obscure figure beyond his own tribe, was already warning against his people's growing dependence on the white man's trinkets and beads. Accounts differ, but some say that also present was the eleven-year-old son of an Oglala medicine man, later described by one biographer as "a bashful, girlish looking boy" so pale he was often mistaken for a white captive. His formal name was His Horse Stands In Sight, but he was usually called *Pehin Yuhana*, "Curly Hair," for the wavy locks he had inherited from his beautiful Miniconjou mother. He was still five years away from taking his nom de guerre, Crazy Horse. And astride a painted mustang was the most renowned warrior on the High Plains, the thirty-year-old Red Cloud.

At six feet, Red Cloud was tall for a Sioux, if not for most men of his era. His slender face was dominated by a beaked nose and a broad forehead, and the leathery skin around his ravaged brown eyes was prematurely creased, as if by parentheses, with age lines. Fond of accessories such as eagle feathers and ribbons, he carried himself with an erect, regal mien; and at such formal ceremonies his long, coarse black hair was almost always bear-greased and plaited around the wing bone of an eagle to signify elegance and propriety. A good, new rifle usually rested across his saddle pommel. On the whole he projected an aura of quiet dignity with an undercurrent of physical menace.

Red Cloud had been born nearby, just across present-day Wyoming's border with Nebraska, and he was familiar with the mesas, coulees, and streams surrounding Fort Laramie. His childhood had coincided with the beginnings of the seasonal Oglala migration south from the Black Hills after his people discovered the plentiful buffalo herds roaming the Republican River corridor, and he had helped drive out rival tribes who'd called the land home for generations, particularly the hated Kiowa. His Oglala band, the notorious and feared Bad Faces, was led by a venerable Head Man named Old Smoke, who had over the years become partial to the dry goods on offer at the white man's trading post—luxuries such as ribbons, combs, and mirrors that insinuated themselves into the Indian lifestyle. What cultural understanding the teenage Red Cloud gleaned from these light-skinned newcomers in their strange garments certainly came from these annual pilgrimages to what was then called Fort John. Now he had returned in quite a different capacity.

By this point in his life Red Cloud had served for almost a decade as the Bad Face *blotahunka*, a title bestowed on each band's head warrior. He was a combination of battle leader and police commissioner, and he commanded a select male society of soldiers and marshals known as *akicita*. Although the whites from the East probably had no idea that such a revered fighter was in their midst, most if not all of the Indians attending the council knew, respected, and feared him. It may be a stretch to say that Red Cloud was personally responsible for the rejection by the Pawnee of the Indian agent Fitzpatrick's invitation, but perhaps not too great a stretch, as Red Cloud had sent so many Pawnee to the Happy Hunting Ground. He had also slaughtered Crows, disemboweled Shoshones, and scalped Arikara, to the point where he and his Bad Faces were a sort of beacon for Lakota from other bands, who sought him out for the honor of riding and raiding with him. This was fairly unprecedented in Sioux culture. And though he had yet to do battle with whites, it is safe to assume that, given his innate intelligence, leadership, and farsightedness, rather than be intimidated by the 200 Bluecoats parading in their strange squares with modern Hawken rifles and mountain howitzers, Red Cloud was more likely studying this "great medicine." Again.

Six years earlier Red Cloud had attended another, smaller council on the Laramie Fork convened by the U.S. Army after a war had broken out between rival fur-trapping outfits vying to sell liquor to the Indians. The white man's "spirituous water," as the Indians called it, had then flooded the Powder River basin, and resulted in not only a flurry of attacks on emigrant wagon trains but an alarming series of deadly brawls among the Lakota themselves. The Army did not care much if Indians killed each other. But the raids on white trains could not be allowed. Colonel Stephen W. Kearny had cleaned out the whiskey sellers and parleyed for peace with the Sioux, although Kearny negotiated predominantly with a separate band called the Brules. This had left the young Red Cloud and his Oglala *akicita* free to study the martial drills that Kearny's commanders put their soldiers through every morning in an attempt to intimidate the Indians. And, now, here they were again, this time with a cannon. Red Cloud was glad to have the opportunity. He undoubtedly observed that though one shot from the big gun could tear up the earth and shatter trees, in the time it took the artillerymen to clean the barrel and reload, a small group of warriors on fast horses could wipe them all out.

The Sioux had been followed into Fort Laramie by the Cheyenne and Arapaho, and as the three tribes were allies they staked their lodges together and mingled freely. The whites grew tense on the second day of the council, however, when word reached the fort that the Sioux's ancient enemies the Shoshones were nearing the post. With each dust cloud that billowed over the horizon an Army bugler was ordered to sound "Boots and Saddles," and dragoons were put on alert to watch for any insult or affront that might spark a fight. Amazingly, there were no major incidents, although emotions ran high because of an incident that had occurred only days earlier.

It had happened before the trapper Bridger had met the main body of Shoshones to escort them into the camp. A small band of Shoshones, who were also known as the Snakes, had been attacked by the Cheyenne, who took two of their scalps. Though Sioux and Cheyenne leaders at Fort Laramie had given their word to refrain from violence during the treaty negotiations, Bridger remained leery. He was partial to the Snakes, having married into the tribe and lived with them on and off for some twenty years, and after the scalpings he had personally equipped their Head Man and some of his warriors with new rifles and ammunition. Despite the guns, the Shoshones approached the fort cautiously, Bridger and their chief riding a bit out in front of the slow-moving party. A ripple of excitement spread through the other Indian camps as they neared, and Sioux and Cheyenne women who had lost fathers, husbands, or sons in battles with the mountain Indians began to keen the shrill, broken tremolos of their death songs.

The Shoshones were right to be cautious. As the keening reached an eerie peak a young Sioux brave armed with a bow and a quiver of arrows leaped onto his pony and laid on the lash, spurring it to a gallop. He made for the Shoshone Head Man, who had apparently killed his father sometime before. Bridger had warned his corps of interpreters to be on the lookout for just such an act, and before the lone Sioux could get far he was intercepted, yanked from his saddle, and disarmed by a French-Canadian scout. Later that night Bridger held court at the fort's sutler's store (as was his wont), suggesting to off-duty soldiers in a language "very graphic and descriptive" that the Sioux were in fact lucky to escape a tussle.

"My chief would'er killed him quick," the mountain man said of the Sioux brave. "And then the fool Sioux would'er got their backs up, and there wouldn't have been room to camp 'round here for dead Sioux. You Dragoons acted nice, but you wouldn't have had no show if the fight had commenced. And I'll tell you another thing. The Sioux ain't gonna try it again. They see how the Snakes are armed. I got them guns for them, and they are good ones. Uncle Sam told 'um to come down here and they'd be safe. But they ain't takin' his word for it altogether."

Bridger was right; there would be no more incidents. The next day the entire Indian assembly and the various white commissioners and agents moved about thirty-five miles southeast of the fort to better pasturage near the confluence of the shallow Horse Creek and the North Platte. The Head Men rode with decorum, "while braves and boys dashed about, displaying their horsemanship and working off their surplus energy," according to one observer. All the while the companies of troopers positioned themselves between the traveling Sioux and Shoshones. The treaty council was scheduled to commence officially the next morning. It must have been a sight. Army engineers had erected a canvas-covered wooden amphitheater in rich bottomland twinkling with fireweed and silver sagebrush, and toward dusk a column of 1,000 Sioux warriors, four abreast on their war ponies, rode in shouting and singing. The confident Sioux then shocked the assemblage by inviting the Shoshones to a great feast of boiled dog. After the meal the two tribes were joined by the Cheyenne and Arapaho, and all danced and sang until dawn. There was no alcohol available; no one was killed.

The next morning tribal elders, conspicuously unarmed and clad in their finest ceremonial bighorn sheepskins and elk hides, approached a giant flagpole that the soldiers had improvised by lashing together the trunks of three lodgepole pines. The whites looked on as each elder in turn performed a sacred song and dance beneath the fluttering Stars and Stripes. The amphitheater had been left open facing east, and after the Head Men took their assigned seats the Indian agent Fitzpatrick had the awkward duty of informing the guests that the supply train hauling presents of tobacco, sugar, coffee, blankets, butcher knives, and bolts of cloth had been delayed leaving St. Louis. (He did not mention that the Army had misplaced the goods on a Missouri River steamboat landing.) There was some grumbling, but all in all the Indians took it well. No bands departed, and a large calumet of red pipestone with a three-foot stem was lighted and passed. As each Indian inhaled the mixture of Plains tobacco and bearberry kinnikinnick, he offered elaborate hand signals designed to pay homage to the Great Spirit and to attest that his heart was free from deceit.

Meanwhile, the vast prairie beyond this semicircle was a riot of activity. Indian women, naturally curious, made ceremonious trading visits to their tribal enemies' camps, while young braves staged manic horse races, gambled on archery and knife-throwing contests, and flirted with maidens wearing their most colorful toggery. Reported a correspondent for the *Missouri Republican* in the stilted journalese of the era, "The belles (and there are Indian as well as civilized belles) were out in all they could raise in finery and costume. And the way they flaunted, tittered, talked and made efforts to show off to the best advantage before the bucks justly entitled them to the civilized appellation we have given them."

Farther off, on the lush grasslands past the hundreds of lodges that had blossomed like prairie chickweed, preteen boys from each tribe stood sentry over herds of mustangs stretching to the horizon. They eyed one another warily, no doubt recognizing ponies stolen over the years. There were perhaps 2 million wild mustangs loose on the Great Plains at the time, and most tribes were adept at rounding them up and breaking them. Yet the Indians had an extraordinary facility for horse theft, so they preferred to increase their herds by means of raids, and this set off a roundelay of horseflesh in which it was not unusual for a remuda to pass from Sioux to Crows to Blackfeet to Nez Percé and back to the Sioux. Often an Indian would end up stealing a horse that had been stolen from him months or even years earlier.

On the morning of September 8, a Monday, the tribal leaders were invited to the center of the circle, where the formal treaty ceremonies were to take place. What followed was "a sight presented of most thrilling interest," according to B. G. Brown, one of the secretaries at the conference. "Each nation approached with its own peculiar song or demonstration, and such a combination of rude, wild, and fantastic manners and dresses, never was witnessed. It is not probable that an opportunity will again be presented of seeing so many tribes assembled together displaying all the peculiarities of features, dress, equipment, and horses, and everything else, exhibiting their wild notions of elegance and propriety."

After this welcoming ceremony, Fitzpatrick strode to the center of the semicircle. He introduced a host of government commissioners, including Colonel Mitchell, who now lived in St. Louis and had traveled partway by steamboat up the Missouri. Framed by the Laramie Mountains scraping the western sky, Mitchell stated his purpose in clipped and concise sentences. Yes, he acknowledged, it was true that the white emigrants passing over Indian lands were thinning the buffalo droves. And, yes, their oxen and cattle were indeed consuming the grasses. For this, he said, the Great Father in Washington was prepared to make annual restitution in the form of hardware, foodstuffs, domestic animals, and agricultural equipment to the Indians, $50,000 worth for each of the next fifty years. But both sides would have to bend, he emphasized, and in exchange for this the tribes must grant future travelers right of passage across the territory as well as allow the U.S. Army to erect way stations along the trails west. Finally, he said, the white man was here to help the Indians delineate, and learn to respect, sovereign territorial boundaries. Civilization was upon them whether they liked it or not, and the constant intertribal slaughter must cease. To that end Mitchell urged each nation to select one great chief with whom the United States could negotiate these terms.

As the interpreters relayed these proposals, it is not difficult to imagine the bemusement with which they were greeted by warriors like Red Cloud, who possessed a judicious sense of what not to believe. Why did these confused whites not just tell the wind to stop blowing, the rivers to cease flowing? Red Cloud, the Sioux, and all the western tribes were accustomed to going where they wanted when they wanted, and taking what they wanted on the strength of their courage and cunning. And though perhaps unaware of the vast number of Americans living far to the east, Red Cloud and the rest were more than familiar with the promises broken over and over by the white leaders in Washington. They had only to look south, where the dispossessed peoples from beyond the Mississippi had been forcibly transported to an official Indian Territory in what was now Oklahoma. These forlorn tribes lived in a squalid homeland of the uprooted, scratching out a living on hard dirt, awaiting government handouts like beggars. Worse, the handouts rarely came. This was the future that the Great Father envisioned for the proud Sioux? These naive whites were funny, if nothing else.

The topper was their final demand. The idea that any one Head Man, no matter how well regarded by the tribe, could speak for every brave in every band was incomprehensible to the Sioux. For centuries their culture had consisted of fluid, haphazard tribal groups further splintered by the overlapping structures of extended families, warrior societies, and clans. Only in buffalo hunts and formal warfare could leaders impose any kind of discipline on their followers, and even then only rarely. How could the whites not see that one "chief," or two, or even a dozen could not possibly rule these tangled relationships? Why not appoint a king of the world?

Even the men—and they were always men—looked on as leaders were never granted absolute authority, most especially over the warrior class, the *akicita*. The Sioux political ethos, with its extreme family loyalties, worked naturally against any one man's rising to authoritarian tribal status. Eighteen hundred years earlier Plutarch had described the Greek concept of democratic government as the individual being responsible to the group, and the group responsible to its core principles. This would have struck a nineteenth-century Native American as lunacy, as culturally foreign as the frenzied Sun Dance or the art of scalp-taking would have been in Buckingham Palace or the court at Versailles. So despite the whites' determination to designate a succession of notable Indians as "tribal chiefs" with whom the United States could negotiate treaties, the point was academic. Besides, most white soldiers and frontiersmen had a difficult enough time physically distinguishing a hostile Sioux from, say, a friendly Delaware. To delineate the subtle power shifts of the Indians' political, religious, and military societies was beyond their capacity. Nor did they much try.

Nonetheless, when Mitchell nominated a compliant Head Man with whom he had once traded extensively and peaceably, the Indians essentially shrugged and played along, anxious for their gifts. Given past experience, they were also fairly certain that the white men had no intention of keeping their promises. So as they awaited the wagon train from St. Louis they held councils of their own and devised entertainments. One of these included a demonstration few whites had ever seen and lived to tell about.

On the afternoon of the fourth day a troop of about 100 Cheyenne Dog Soldiers armed with guns, lances, and bows and arrows rode onto the treaty grounds to reenact a battle charge. The braves, wearing only loincloths and parfleche moccasins, were painted in their fiercest war colors, and their horses' manes and tails were dusted and beribboned. On the animals' flanks, etched in red ocher, were symbols enumerating each fighter's coups—enemies killed, scalps taken, horses stolen. What at first appeared to the whites as nothing more than a haphazard, if clumsy, stampede evolved as if by magic into a disciplined martial drill, with the Cheyenne horsemen dismounting and remounting efficiently and precisely as they circled and charged. The white onlookers, the soldiers in particular, were stunned—and apprehensive. These warriors had been bested by the Sioux? It was a lesson the next generation of Army Indian fighters would forget at their peril.

More than a week was spent on such entertainments and continuous feasts as the Indians awaited the *wakpamni*—the great distribution of bribes. There were a few surprises. At one shared meal the Cheyenne atoned for the recent killing of the two Shoshones by returning the scalps to the brothers of the victims, along with gifts of knives, blankets, and pieces of colored cloth. And the famous Belgian Jesuit priest Pierre-Jean De Smet wandered through the camps proselytizing, offering Mass, and, he claimed, baptizing 894 Indians and 61 "half-bloods." One of the bands he preached to was Red Cloud's. And though Father De Smet failed to convert the Bad Face *blotahunka,* Red Cloud was known for the rest of his life to "spout bits of Christian doctrine." It was from this gathering that De Smet bequeathed to us one of the more droll descriptions of the Indian love of boiled dog. "No epoch in Indian annals," he wrote, "shows a greater massacre of the canine race."

Meanwhile, as the days wore on, the grass for miles in every direction was clipped clean by the thousands of Indian ponies and the banks of Horse Creek and the North Platte were turned into stinking midden heaps. There was so much human waste that the Army troop moved its encampment two miles upriver to escape a stench one soldier described as "almost visible." When messengers finally brought news that the gift-laden caravan was a day away, Fitzpatrick and the superintendent of Indian Affairs, Mitchell, reassembled the tribal elders to ask if they had chosen chiefs to represent them. The Indians were sly. They had ridden hundreds of miles and delayed the fall buffalo hunt to receive presents. They were not going to depart empty-handed, even if avoiding it meant participating in a sham. They told the whites they had indeed selected emissaries, and several men from various tribes stepped forward. After the conditions of the original treaty terms were again read aloud and translated—including the unthinkable demand that the Sioux cede to the Crows the territory on either side of the Powder as it flowed north into the Yellowstone—a clever Arapaho Head Man named Cut Nose more or less spoke for all the tribes when he announced, "I would be glad if the whites would pick out a place for themselves and not come into our grounds. But if they must pass through our country, they should give us game for what they drive off."

The government delegates took such cryptic comments as acquiescence in all their demands. Though the savvy Plains veteran Fitzpatrick must have known better, he stood mute while the designated "chiefs" approached a table set up in the amphitheater. Like most Indians, the Sioux could neither read nor write, and so could not sign or print their own names. The government had obligingly worked out a practice for them: when a Head Man agreed to a treaty, he would step up to a table where a scribe sat, accept a token blanket or string of glass beads, and with one or two fingers touch the top of an offered fountain pen. The scribe would then add the name of the Indian to the document. It was a useless ceremony, as the Indians had no real understanding of what they were agreeing to or, more accurately, giving away. In any case the U.S. government usually had no intention of living up to its end of the bargain. Nevertheless, one by one they made their marks next to their names. Of the two Sioux "chiefs" who touched the pen, neither was from the Oglala tribe, let alone from Red Cloud's Bad Face band. One was from the Brule band of the Lakota—a strong, pioneering people, but martially no match for the Oglalas. The other represented a small contingent of the Missouri River

Sioux. Although we cannot guess at what went through Red Cloud's mind as he and Old Smoke stood and watched, both knew that real power flowed not from an inkwell, but from an otter-skin quiver or, better yet, from the muzzle of a gun.

So on the final day of the council what was known to history as the Horse Creek Treaty was signed to ensure a "lasting peace on the Plains forevermore." After the signing ceremony the wagon train pulled into camp and formed a corral, and a final grand feast followed the distribution of gifts. Besides the usual allotments of coffee, sugar, and tobacco, sheets of thin brass were distributed; the Sioux, ever vain, liked to cut these into doubloon-sized ovals and weave them through their hair. Head Men and esteemed braves were also presented with commemorative medals featuring a likeness of the Great Father, President Millard Fillmore; and with U.S. Army general officers' uniforms, including ceremonial swords and red sashes. Many Indians wore these uniforms the next day—this was probably their first encounter with pants—as the tribes dispersed to the four corners of the territory from which they had arrived.

The 1851 Horse Creek agreement was the most sweeping official treaty the Western Sioux had ever signed with representatives of the United States. It would, perforce, also be the first to be broken. Luckily for historians, a long-lost autobiography that Red Cloud dictated in his old age supplies a rare look into this era from the Sioux perspective. Even so late in his life, long past the era of the great Indian wars, Red Cloud seemed to fear some form of retribution, and his book barely touches on his interactions with the whites; when it does, the few passages are so opaque as to render his true feelings nearly impenetrable. Regarding the Horse Creek council, however, he does hint that some of the older (and weaker) Head Men who camped that September on the North Platte were intrigued by the idea of the white and red man bound forever in peace. What can definitely be inferred from Red Cloud's writings, however, is that he had no intention of abiding by the treaty. The Lakota were the strongest and most feared tribe on the High Plains. And within the Lakota, Red Cloud's Oglalas vied for primacy.

In interpreting Red Cloud's life and times in the context of the Horse Creek Treaty, one might—*might*—grant that he could have lived without actively attacking the emigrant trains and provoking war with the United States, at least for the moment (but subsequent events make this a ticklish argument). One could even make the case that despite his peoples' deep political tradition of near-fanatical individualism, he may have even acceded to the concept of a single Sioux "chief," most likely because it would have been himself.

But no one, certainly not Red Cloud, could possibly have imagined him a bottled spider confined to a specific territory, no matter how large or how bountiful. The idea of Red Cloud prohibited from leading raids, from stealing horses, from taking scalps—the very exploits for which he was already renowned—was inimical to his nature. Such adventures had been the essence of the Sioux ethos since time immemorial. And if Red Cloud was anything, he was a creature of the myths and legends of his forebears, connected to those ghosts by what a future American president, on whom he would one day wage war, referred to as the mystic chords of memory.

GUNS AND BADLANDS

The first French explorers to make contact with the Sioux in the mid-1600s noted with not a little horror the tribe's fierce and utter barbarism. The Europeans had long since adapted and reconciled themselves to the New World's Stone Age cultures. But the Sioux's vicious raids on their Algonquin neighbors to the north and east—and the sheer joy the Sioux took in tearing their enemies limb from limb with rocks, clubs, sharpened sticks, and flint knives—called to mind nothing so much as Dark Age memories of Norse berserks or marauding Huns. Watching these battles as spectators, the European newcomers had no idea that the savagery was actually a finely tuned conceit. To the Sioux, war was the reason for living, and though their raids and ambushes were of course made to establish territory and gain booty, more important was the chance for an individual warrior to give vent, in public, to an aggressiveness prized by the tribe's ethos.

A Sioux brave would wager his last breath against the most courageous adversaries, and no matter the outcome, he won. A good death did honor to an entire life, and thus on the battlefield and afterward he was an exhibitionist with no sense of modesty. When he took a scalp, hacked off a hand, gouged out an eye, or severed a penis, he screamed at the top of his lungs to proclaim his own greatness. Later, when he handed the scalp to his woman, she too sang his glory while dancing with the bloody skull piece suspended from a pole.

Such behavior was alien enough to baffle seventeenth-century Europeans. Whites observed a tribe that hunted and grubbed for a living with flint arrows and stone tools and exhibited no artistic tendencies other than painting their bodies and faces with hideous designs in preparation for battle. The Sioux did not weave baskets or fabrics, bake pottery, or make jewelry. They disdained farming and constructed no permanent lodges. And with no pack animals available on the continent—unlike the horse, mule, camel, or ox, the buffalo could not be bred to be harnessed or yoked—Native American animal husbandry had lagged about four millennia behind the rest of the world. Also, as other tribes took their first, tentative steps into modernity, this cultural leap seemed impossible for the hunter-gatherer Sioux. Had some of their historical contemporaries— the imperious Aztecs, the sophisticated Cherokee, the politically savvy Iroquois—been aware of their existence, they would probably have considered the Sioux laughable or subhuman. But the Sioux could fight, and the fires of their blood-feud memories were banked and stoked until the day they died.

The Sioux, like all American Indians, are descendents of Asian nomads who crossed the thousand-mile Bering Land Bridge in various migrations between 16,500 and 5,000 BC. There is archaeological evidence to suggest that the first pre-Columbian peoples to strike south from Beringia and into what is now the great, grassy, Northern Plains of the United States did so about 12,000 years ago, trailing and stalking the migratory routes of the great herds of mastodons, woolly mammoths, and a giant form of bison that had gone extinct by the time the Europeans arrived. These hunters, who devised their first bows and arrows around the time Jesus was preaching in Judaea, rapidly spread east and west to the shores of the Atlantic and Pacific, through Central America, and across the Isthmus of Panama. Linguists hypothesize that the wandering proto-Sioux bands originated somewhere in the southeastern United States, perhaps in the Carolinas or near the Gulf of Mexico.

By the 1500s the Sioux were again on the move, pushing up the Mississippi River Valley and settling near the river's headwaters in the forests of northern Minnesota. At the time, as today, the region was laced by a network of intersecting streams, marshes, and lakes, and the development of the birch bark canoe allowed separate bands not only to gather and consume wild rice from still waters, but to stake out individual territories.

Theirs was a patriarchal society with tribal affiliation passed from father to son, a simple solution for men fathering children with multiple wives from different bands. Leaders—called "Head Men" and "Big Bellies"—were for the most part chosen on merit. In some cases a chief would create an inside track for his favorite son, but even then the inheritor would have to earn the band's loyalty on the strength of his wisdom, his personality, and above all his martial ability. And if an ordinary brave was not pleased with a new chief, he had the option of persuading any followers to strike out with him and form a new band with himself as Head Man.

Perhaps influenced by the seven stars of the Big Dipper—the "Carrier" that conveyed the souls of the dead to the Milky Way, which the Sioux called the "Road of the Spirits"—the tribe attributed mystical qualities to the number seven. It was the hostile Chippewa who dubbed these peoples "Sioux," or "Little Snakes." The Sioux referred to themselves as *Otchenti Chakowin*, the "People of the Seven Council Fires," those tribes being the Sissetons, Yanktons, Yanktonais, Santees, Leaf Santees, Blewakantonwans, and Lakota/Dakotas.* Each tribe in turn usually consisted of seven bands, and with minor dialectical differences they all spoke the same language. The seven council fires thus served to validate the cohesion of the peoples as a single, united nation.

Early New France officials and traders valued the North American

---

*The last are a single tribe, but differentiated by one branch's substitution of the letter "D" for "L"; these were also known as Tetons, which translates roughly as "Allies." This is only a dialectical difference, not a political one. Various Sioux political subdivisions are split to this day over the pronunciation of "Lakota," "Dakota," and "Nakota," but they all consider themselves part of the same tribe. For the purpose of narrative cohesion, we will refer to the Oglalas, Brules, Hunkpapas, Miniconjous, Sans Arcs, Two Kettles, and Blackfeet Sioux—not to be confused with the Blackfeet mountain tribe—as "Lakota."

Indians' hides and pelts, and pursued a social policy of benign neglect toward the tribes. Though the Europeans would occasionally attempt to agitate the Indians as a buffer against probes from the nascent Spanish empire far to the southwest, for the most part they left the "nations" to their own political and military customs. As a result, for over a century the savage Sioux generally had their way with their Algonquin neighbors. That balance of power shifted abruptly around 1660, when English trading ships sailed into Hudson Bay offering muzzle-loading, smoothbore flintlock muskets and steel knives in exchange for furs. The bay bordered the homeland of the Cree, an Algonquin people, and they were the first Native Americans to obtain this new weaponry. The journals of British sailors record great numbers of Cree paddling out to their flotillas in canoes piled high with furs and skins; the braves returned to the Cree villages bearing crates of guns, powder, and ball.

With the aid of their Algonquin cousins the Chippewa as well as a renegade band of Sioux called the Assiniboines, the newly armed Cree took bloody revenge on the People of the Seven Council Fires, who had terrorized them for generations. They drove the Sioux from their forested hunting grounds into swampy wastelands, where they could only grub for acorns, roots, and edible plants. And still the Algonquins hunted them like small game. The Scottish explorer Alexander Mackenzie, who was knighted for being the first man to traverse Canada to the Pacific Ocean, remarked that these forlorn Sioux were so skittish that the mere sight of strange spires of campfire smoke would drive them deeper into the swamps and marshes.

As best historians, ethnologists, and paleoanthropologists can tell, the Indians who would eventually become known as the Western Sioux split from their woodland eastern cousins sometime around 1700. These breakaway tribes subsequently splintered into many smaller bands as they conquered or subjugated a host of peoples during their migration west by southwest onto the buffalo ranges. Of course, the Sioux were not alone in these territorial shifts; the European invasion and subsequent expansion sparked chain-reaction movements all over the continent, and tribal borders were in a state of flux. A few years earlier the powerful Iroquois had overrun the Ohio Valley and did much the same, first to the Hurons and then to the Eries, driving them farther and farther west. And, now, tribe by tribe, the Algonquins with their modern weapons were in turn forcing the Sioux out of their fetid marshlands and onto the tall-grass prairies west of the Mississippi. French trappers and *voyageurs* were virtually the only chroniclers of these great migratory shifts, and they recorded that the Yanktonais tribe of Sioux moved west first, followed by the Lakota faction of the Tetons, who were in turn trailed by the Yanktons.

By the early eighteenth century the People of the Seven Council Fires found themselves far to the west and south of their old hunting grounds, and it was here, at the elbow bend of the Minnesota River in southwestern Minnesota—where the watercourse makes a hard northeast turn toward the Mississippi—that a further fragmentation of these tribes took place. As each tribe reached this crucial geographic boundary the same scene was played out. After council parleys that invariably led to squabbles, the elder, more conservative tribal leaders opted to follow the Minnesota River northwest to its headwaters, keeping to the more forested country. Younger clans, meanwhile, forded the river and plunged into the prairie, which seemed endless but eventually rose to the Black Hills and, beyond, the Rockies. Thus was born the Western Sioux nation.

Modern Americans living in an irrigated and fertilized West would find it difficult to visualize the stark contrast in the early eighteenth century between the green, forested land and what lay beyond when it more or less ceased to exist around the ninety-fifth meridian west—a line running a roughly southerly course from modern-day Minneapolis to San Antonio. The sere, harsh, timberless prairie that stretched westward from that line was as great a barrier as any ocean. Even the grass bending and rising uniformly with the wind gave an impression of waves rolling in from the sea. The country was bisected in places by lonely rivers and creeks, but it had almost no natural lakes and even fewer aquifers, so the land was prone to vast dust storms in summer and blizzards beyond the imagination of most easterners in winter. The decision to venture into this emptiness called for either extreme courage or supreme foolhardiness. The Sioux had ample streaks of both.

Not long after the Lakota group opted to ford the Minnesota, it fractured naturally into the seemingly requisite seven factions, led by the pioneering Brules and Oglalas,* the tribe in which Red Cloud would be raised. At around the same time, English traders from the Hudson's Bay Company were also migrating south to the confluence of the Minnesota and Mississippi Rivers, near modern-day Saint Paul. There, beginning in the eighteenth century, they began holding annual trade fairs. This nascent commerce was the start of a cultural entanglement that through disease and alcohol would kill more Plains Indians than all the battles with whites combined. It was also at these fairs that Western Sioux bearing buffalo robes for trade finally began to arm themselves with guns and steel knives. A familiar pattern repeated itself as they moved onto the prairie. Just as the Chippewa and the Cree had pushed the Sioux west, so the Sioux with their muskets would defeat or shoulder aside each successive Plains tribe with which they came into contact.

Though the Sioux were to become its most vicious practitioners, warfare among Indians was simply a way of life. Nearly every tribe called itself "The People" and harbored deep suspicion and hatred toward outsiders with whom it competed for game and plunders. Death arrived swiftly and often in the violent thrust and parry of aggression and defense, abetted by a culture that revolved around a quest to avenge insults and injuries real and perceived. Yet it was rare for Indians to set out to conquer a territory in the European sense of the idea. The Sioux were that rarity, and as they spread west a northern branch of the Cheyenne was the first to fall. These Cheyenne, having been similarly mauled by armed Cree to their north, packed up and walked west across the Missouri River. This Sioux triumph was followed in rapid succession by the defeat of the weak Iowas and Otoes. Both of these farming tribes retreated farther west in hopes of allying with the more numerous Omaha, who occupied the territory south of the Great Bend of the Missouri. But the Omaha, like the Cheyenne, Otoes, and Iowas before them, lacked firearms. The Sioux slaughtered them at every turn. The survivors of all three tribes fled into the eastern

---

*The Siouwan word *Oglala* roughly translates as "scattered peoples" or "divided peoples." The name Brule—from *brûlé,* meaning burnt in French—was probably bestowed on the group by late-seventeenth-century fur traders mistranslating "burnt thighs" from Siouwan dialect, although some linguists give the literal meaning of the word as "stinky feet."

Missouri floodplain, with the savvy Otoes crossing the river to decamp in southern Nebraska.

Precisely how many years or decades it took the various bands of Western Sioux to reach the Missouri, and in what order they did so, is lost to history. What is known is that before the arrival of the white man, all Eastern Sioux tribes had conducted annual summer hunting parties across the Minnesota River to track the buffalo through the tall grass around what today is the Minnesota–South Dakota border. By 1725, however, these lands were largely denuded of game; this suggests that it was the relocated Western Sioux who had scoured them clean. Further, sometime in the late 1720s or early 1730s reports from French explorers and trappers indicated that the Iowas, Otoes, and Omaha were again on the move, retreating north from their fixed locations in the fertile bottomland of Nebraska and moving up into the inhospitable wastes of the northern Dakota Territory. Although the reason for this migration is unclear, historians reasonably speculate that once again they were fleeing the Western Sioux.

By the mid-eighteenth century the Oglala and Brule bands of Lakota had tracked the buffalo herds up onto the windswept flatiron plateau that the French called the Coteau des Prairies. This 100-by-200-mile pipestone escarpment, carved by retreating glaciers and rising gradually to 900 feet, is sharply defined on modern satellite imaging maps. Shaped like an arrowhead pointing north, it fans south from North Dakota through South Dakota, through Minnesota, and into northern Iowa. As the Sioux were still without horses, they transported their smallish lodgepoles and tepee skins across these rocky highlands on the backs of their dogs, women, and children—including girls as young as six or seven. Progress was naturally slow, perhaps five to six miles a day, and their westward movement was delayed even more by the annual trek from the treeless Plains back to their old territory to acquire more weapons and ammunition at the English trade fairs, which by now had moved to the wooded headwaters of the Minnesota River.

Even as the bloody French and Indian War raged along the Atlantic seaboard, the Western Sioux returned to these fairs for guns, allowing the seven Lakota bands to exchange goods and news with their eastern kinsmen. Intermarriage was common among the tribes and bands, as was the baffling swiftness with which each group might change its name. (Thus the people Lewis and Clark chronicled in their journals as the Teton Saone—most likely a collective name bestowed on all Lakota who lagged behind their westward-driving cousins—turn up as the Hunkpapas two decades later.) Most modern historians, for clarity's sake, have settled on the seven Lakota bands that we noted earlier: the Oglalas, Brules, Miniconjous, Sans Arcs,* Two Kettles, Hunkpapas, and Blackfoot-Sioux. It was also around this time that the Lakota had their first encounter with Indians who owned horses, the Arikara.

The Sioux were certainly aware of the existence of the horse. Although they had no formal written tradition, since at least the early seventeenth century various bands had kept and passed down pictographic "Winter Counts," a sort of snapshot chronicle of the most important events of any given year—eclipses, raids, droughts—etched into a deerskin or buffalo hide. The Lakota Winter Count of 1624 included a rough outline of the mustang that had been introduced to the western hemisphere by the Spanish a century earlier. But the Arikara, or Rees, were the first people the Sioux had ever seen incorporate the animal into their culture.

The Arikara were a semiagricultural people who lived in fixed villages of earth lodges strung like beads along the Upper Missouri near present-day Pierre, South Dakota. Their compounds were fortified by wide ditches, earthen walls, and in some cases even cedar log stockades. And despite the haughty Sioux's disdain for these "dirt eaters," they were a hardy tribe known to ride their tough little ponies on buffalo hunts as far west as the Black Hills, an island of trees in a sea of grass 135 miles away. The Arikara had probably acquired their mounts, as well as some Spanish-made saber blades, in trade with the southern Kiowa, who prized the corn, squash, and beans of the Arikara. And though the Sioux coveted their horses, the Rees had numbers on their side. Their total population of

---

*The Sans Arcs were said to have acquired their name after following the order of one of their hermaphrodite priests to lay aside their bows and arrows while he performed a sacred ceremony. In the middle of this rite enemies attacked, routing the weaponless tribe.

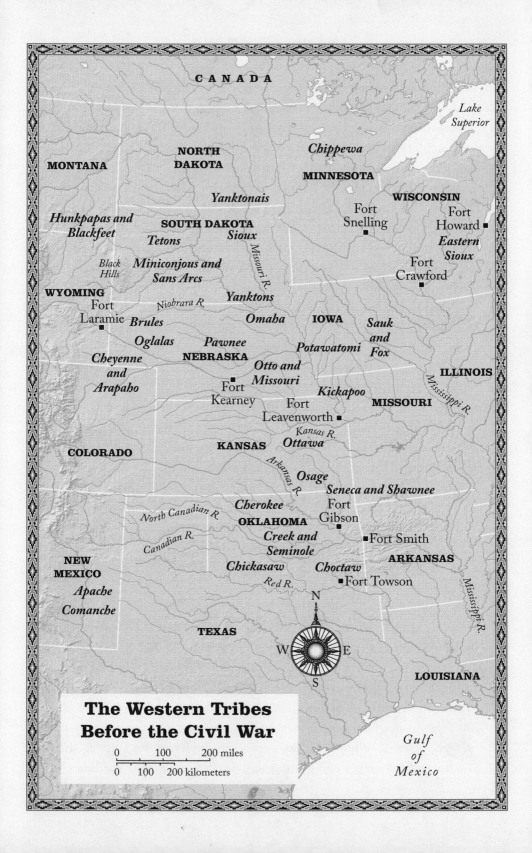

The Western Tribes Before the Civil War

perhaps 20,000, including 4,000 warriors, was nearly double that of all the wandering bands of Lakota put together.

Apparently sensing that they had nothing to fear from these emaciated newcomers from the east adrift on the High Plains, the Arikara initially took pity on the Lakota. After all, the Arikara had horses with which to not only ride down buffalo, but also overwhelm slow, pedestrian enemies. They also had attached the Spanish steel blades to the tips of their heavy, fourteen-foot buffalo lances, so no mangy band of itinerants on foot was any match for them. This overconfidence led them to accept some Brules and Oglalas into their villages and, in effect, provide them with handouts of corn, dried pumpkins, and even a few old horses. This was a mistake.

Despite their strong mounts and steel, the Arikara did not have guns. And though their settlements were too well fortified for the Lakotas to storm, raiding parties of 20 to 100 Sioux began roaming around the edges of their villages, burning their cornfields, and running down and scalping any Rees who ventured beyond the walls and moats. The Sioux also managed to steal a few horses. In the end, however, it was smallpox that doomed the Arikara. Three great epidemics, caused by tainted European blankets, swept through their settlements in the last quarter of the eighteenth century. The tribe was so severely weakened that by 1795 even its fortified villages afforded little safety against the marauding Sioux. What was left of the broken tribe fled north, abandoning the Missouri watershed below the river's Great Bend, virtually beckoning someone to claim the land. The peoples soon to be known as Red Cloud's Sioux, who to this point, culturally, continued to have at least one foot in Minnesota, happily complied.

In the second half of the eighteenth century sketchy reports began reaching English traders on the Missouri about a tectonic shift in the balance of power on the prairie. The little information we have about this period comes almost exclusively from the Lakota Winter Counts, which allow various interpretations at best, and only wild guesses at worst. In this case they do not help much. It remains a mystery, for example, why the formerly forest-dwelling Oglalas apparently preferred to keep as their base the scrubby country in present-day South Dakota near the brackish water of the aptly named Bad River. Early French trappers, the first whites to set eyes on this landscape, aptly christened it *Mauvaises Terres*. The Sioux agreed, naming it *mako sica*, "land bad," and one wonders what went through their minds as they traversed the most desolate, and weirdest, geographic formation in the United States.

To call the Badlands a moonscape does an injustice to the moon. Situated in southwestern South Dakota, some forty-five miles due east of present-day Rapid City, this stark, treeless mash-up of slate-gray gullies, buttes, canyons, plateaus, and towering hoodoos was once the western-most bed of North America's Great Inland Sea, a shallow body of water that connected the Arctic Ocean to the Gulf of Mexico 65 million to 80 million years ago and split the continent roughly in half. Millions of years later a dome of molten rock ruptured the earth's crust on the western edge of this sea and gave rise, first, to the towering granite outcroppings of the Rockies and, later, to the Black Hills. The land to the east of these mountain ranges crumpled and folded in on itself in a chain reaction, and the Inland Sea drained.

Rivers and creeks streaming out of the mountains spread mud, gravel, and sand across the Badlands, which was transformed over millennia from a lush, semitropical ecosystem into a dry geological wasteland. Northern winds and diminished rainfall combined with frost and flash floods to further erode the soft, sedimentary rock and volcanic ash, leaving exposed in the sharp ridges and nobs the fossil remains of the Inland Sea's eerie creatures—protoalligators, giant sharks, and predatory marine reptiles such as the toothy mosasaur, which grew up to fifty feet long. What the Sioux made of the petrified bones of these fantastical creatures littering the dynamic sweep and complications of the landscape no one knows.

The "Badlands Wall," which runs sixty miles on a rough east-west line, delineates the upper and the lower prairie, and to the naked eye this harsh vista would appear to offer nothing but misery and slow death to any human foolish enough to enter. But the Sioux were no ordinary people. They were quick to recognize that the sixty or more varieties of mixed short grasses growing on the eastern rim of the Badlands were prime fodder for buffalo, antelope, and mule deer (as well as for the millions of prairie dogs that in turn provided food for wolves, foxes, rattlesnakes, coyotes, black-footed ferrets, hawks, and eagles). And though bighorn sheep weighing up to forty pounds would be hunted to extermination there by the mid-1920s (they were reintroduced into Badlands National Park in 1964), these food sources would have been plentiful enough for the Oglalas, who now thought of themselves as a sovereign tribe.

Before they acquired horses, the Oglalas took advantage of the Badlands' topography by posting scouts on its high, eerie rock spires to spot buffalo herds drifting like a dark cloud's shadow across the prairie below. As the animals' eyesight was poor, a herd could be approached carefully and quietly from downwind, and on a signal from these lookouts a hunting party would form a semicircle behind the buffalo and, whooping and waving blankets, stampede them over a cliff like a stream of water. The men would then sing the buffalo song as the entire band made camp next to the pile of dead and dying creatures. As every American schoolchild has since come to learn, no part of the dead beast was wasted.

Religious ceremonies were attached to the butchering of each section of the animal, from the skull to the pancreas; and the fatty meat was divided out, usually in accordance with tribal seniority. The savory tongue and liver—sliced warm from the writhing buffalo and flavored with bile dripped from the gallbladder—were awarded to the bravest hunters, and the tanned hides that were not set aside for robes were sewn into buckskins, leggings, and moccasins (and, later, tack and saddles). The horns were used to carry crushed herbal medicines, and the bones were fashioned into tools ranging from sewing needles to war clubs. The coarse, matted hair was twisted into ropes; the bladders were set aside for water storage; the sinews were made into bowstrings; and the inch-thick skin on the side of the buffalo's neck was set out to bake in the sun before being cut into shields that could stop an arrow and deflect a musket ball. At night, the band would roast a portion of the succulent marrow over fires fueled by bricks of dried buffalo dung, the smoke of which seasoned the meal with a bitter tang. The leaner meat was mixed with marrow grease and seeded chokecherries and pounded into a nutritious concoction called pemmican, a staple of western Indians.

Back east the buffalo was best known for providing the tens of thousands of lap robes that warmed New Englanders and Midwesterners through sleety winters. The tanning process that created these blankets—always performed by women, who sang their own buffalo song—was backbreaking. First the stinking hides were pinned taut to the ground and thoroughly scraped with flint knives or elk's antlers to remove the flesh. Then a mixture of jellied buffalo brains and liver was rubbed into the fleshy side until it penetrated the pores. After being left for several days to dry in the sun, the hides were carried to a nearby river or stream and washed until somewhat pliable. They were then tied to poles with rawhide thongs and stretched taut again. Any stray fleck of meat still attached was eliminated by an elk antler or a fleshing flint, and more jellied buffalo brains were rubbed in. After several days, when the gooey brains had been sufficiently absorbed, women or girls would grab either end of the hide and draw it back and forth around a small tree for hours, as if operating a large two-person saw. When the end product was soft enough to fold, it was a buffalo robe.

The historian Royal Brown Hassrick does not exaggerate when he notes in his classic study, *The Sioux*, that once the Lakota moved out of the forests and into the heart of the great northern buffalo range, "their way of life burst into magnificence." And for a brief period in early spring the earth around their camps near the Badlands exploded in a glorious green, and the air was perfumed with clusters of blooming elephant head, larkspur, and wild crocus that lent a magenta-streaked patina to the new buds of dog ash, cottonwood, and river willow sprouting along streambeds roaring with clean, cold snowmelt.

But the vibrant display was short-lived. By late May streams and creeks were already drying into mud wallows, and the plant life had withered to a dingy brown that provided excellent kindling for the ubiquitous prairie fires ignited by lightning strikes. Yet the Sioux even learned to use this to their advantage. The succession of fires that swept the area left large swaths of the land covered in ash. The Oglalas welcomed these fast-moving walls of flame that danced into and out of sandstone arroyos and consumed the grassy bases of sand hills. The drought-resistant native grasses had roots that grew as deep as twenty-four inches, holding them steady in the soil and allowing for rapid regrowth. Within a few days tender green shoots would push up through the blackened wasteland to attract packs of hungry animals. These included herds of the perpetually astonished-looking pronghorn antelope, the Lakota meat of preference after buffalo. Though these antelope could run at nearly fifty miles per hour and were the fastest animals on the North American continent, they were surprisingly easy to hunt. The Indians would merely cut armfuls of sagebrush, hold the branches before their chests and faces, and slowly walk to within arrow distance before loosing their volleys. Perhaps this accounted for the animals' apparent astonishment.

The Oglalas' chosen territory may have been high, dry, and windswept—they mocked their Brule cousins as *Kutawichasha*, or soft and indolent "Lowland Folk" who lingered in the more hospitable south—but it provided them with what they needed to fill their bellies and to keep warm in winter. This, in turn, allowed them the luxury of more time to form raiding parties that prowled the prairie in every direction until the "savage" Sioux became known, and feared, across the High Plains. All this fighting, however, was merely a prelude to one overarching aim—control of the isolated, 6,000-square-mile mountain range rising to the west like a giant green fortress, known to all as the Black Hills.

THE BLACK HILLS
AND BEYOND

Today on the Pine Ridge Indian Reservation the descendants of Red Cloud tell a story, probably apocryphal but powerful and perhaps steeped in some greater truth. It is about a chance meeting in Washington between a resentful Red Cloud and an Army officer who had served on the frontier. Red Cloud, by then a great Lakota Chief, had already driven the Bluecoats from Sioux territory, burned their forts, and secured the Black Hills for his people. He had then been persuaded, in 1870, to travel to Washington, where he assumed he would arrive as a dignitary. But the U.S. government had an ulterior motive.

With the Montana mines nearly played out, old rumors of gold in the Black Hills had begun to simmer again, like water coming to a boil. As far back as 1823 the Bible-thumping mountain man Jedediah Smith had reported great veins of gold running through the hills, but Smith was killed by Comanche on the Cimarron soon afterward, and no one was certain exactly where he had seen the ore. Given the size of the range, any exploratory expedition to discover America's next great strike would have to be fairly large—large enough to attract the Indians' notice. The politicians and generals hoped that on the long journey east Red Cloud would be intimidated by the size, strength, and modernity of the nation. They wanted him to think twice before fomenting a second war over any white intrusion into his territory.

As the tale goes, one evening Red Cloud attended a White House reception given by President Ulysses S. Grant, and found himself in conversation with the bitter officer. Trying to explain the mystical hold that *Paha Sapa* had on his people, he told the officer, "My ancestors' bones lie in the Black Hills."

"Horseshit," the officer replied. "Your people have been there no more than a couple of generations. They come from Minnesota, and you were born in Nebraska. You took that land from the Crows. And do you know why you took that land from the Crows? Because you could.

"And do you know why we will take that land from you? Because we can."

It is said that years later, as an old man, Red Cloud recounted this exchange to his lifelong campfire companion Sam Deon, a white trapper and trader who became the conduit through which the great chief told his life story. What the officer would never have been able to understand, Red Cloud told Deon, was how in the time before time began, the goddess Ite, the mother of the four winds in Sioux myth, conspired with the trickster god Inktomi to create the "Buffalo nation" of Siouan peoples. Together these deities delivered the Sioux nation up from a subterranean netherworld and onto the surface of an earth teeming with game. And what portal did the gods choose for this deliverance? The mystical "breathing" Wind Cave of the Black Hills. This, Red Cloud said, was the reason why the Sioux revere the mountain range.

In reality the Wind Cave of the Black Hills is a 132-mile series of honeycombed underground tunnels composed of thin, calcite fins—one of the longest caverns in the world. Because of its deep passageways and the smallness of its only mouth, the Wind Cave reacts inversely to outside air pressures. Thus it seems to "exhale" when the outside air pressure is low, and to "inhale" when the pressure is high. Red Cloud and his people believed that the ancient gods delivered their ancestors from this cave. Today, standing before the cavern's eight-by-ten-foot entrance, one still gets the sense that the cave is alive and "breathing." And though no one will ever know for certain who was the first Sioux to "discover" the Black Hills, the Oglala Winter Count of 1775–76 depicts a Head Man named Standing Bull feeling the breath of the Wind Cave the summer before America's Founding Fathers signed the Declaration of Independence.

By the late 1700s the Lakota, led by the Oglalas and Brules, had pushed farther and farther west across the South Dakota prairie. As the tall grass shortened to sparse sedge and greasewood and finally disappeared altogether across tracts like the Badlands, the lush slopes of the Black Hills swelling on the western horizon must have indeed appeared a godsend. It was also around this time that the pioneering Oglalas and Brules ceased their annual treks back to Minnesota to exchange robes and hides for weapons. Sensing a captive and untapped market, British merchants—now outnumbering the French on the North American continent by four to one—established a new location for the annual trade fair on the Great Bend of the Missouri near its confluence with the James River.

When not fighting rival tribes, the Lakota became, in a sense, middlemen between the English traders to the northeast and the Plains Indians to the west and south. They were careful to restrict the flow of bartered goods to the white man's foods and his ribbons, his blankets and glass beads, while keeping for themselves his flintlocks, ammunition, and steel knives as well as iron kettles, which could be broken apart to make arrowheads. Whenever possible the Lakota bundled the European goods to exchange with the horse tribes for mustangs, the most prized commodity on the Plains. But by now their warlike reputation preceded them, and their rivals were not naive. The animals remained hard to come by. So despite their steady accumulation of arms, the Sioux were still on foot: slow, plodding travelers, lugging whatever belongings their women, children, and dog travois could carry. And then, seemingly out of the blue, they acquired their first pony herds.

Fossil remains attest to the presence of prehistoric protohorses on the North American prairie until the end of the Pleistocene epoch, 10,000 years ago. The earliest of these animals had toes instead of hooves and were the size of foxes. Succeeding iterations grew as large as collies. But, like the much larger mammoths and camels that also once roamed the Plains, this animal went extinct, and it was not until the Spanish introduced the modern horse onto the continent in the early 1500s that the stone canyons of the western hemisphere again echoed with thundering hooves. Despite the images carved into our subconscious by Hollywood Westerns, all American Indians, from Inuit to Iroquois to Inca, went on foot before encountering Europeans. Moreover, by one of history's chance quirks the breed introduced to the New World by the conquistadores was ideally suited to its new environment, and the Lakotas' extraordinary knack for taming and breeding the animal was an epochal moment in the timeline of the tribe and the American West.

Unlike the hulking, grain-fed steeds hitched to carts and plows across the middle and upper regions of Europe and ridden into battle from the Roncevaux Pass to Bosworth Field, the fleet Spanish mustang traced its lineage to animals that had once roamed the arid steppes of Central Asia. The breed took centuries to make its way to southern Europe via the Moorish invasions of Iberia, and along that journey it commingled with similar desert horses from the Middle East and North Africa to become a self-sufficient, intelligent animal quite at home in the dry, dusty climate of the Andalusian plain and, later, the North American West. The smallish mustang, usually no taller than five feet from hoof to shoulder, was easy to break and able to travel great distances without water. It prospered in the high, dry flatlands of Mexico, thriving on the spare clumps of grass, shrubs, and even weeds. It was also prolific. Within two decades of Hernán Cortés's conquest of Montezuma and the Aztec empire in 1519, the governor of the Northwest Frontier territory in New Spain, Francisco Vásquez de Coronado, rode north as far as Kansas in search of the "Seven Cities of Cíbola" with more than 1,000 horses—terrifying, alien creatures to the Indians.

The territory the Spanish conquered soon extended north from Mexico City through present-day New Mexico, Arizona, and California; and Coronado and the settlers of New Spain knew full well the spell their horses cast over the indigenous peoples whom they enslaved and converted by force. In the eyes of the Indians the horse endowed the European invaders with seemingly supernatural powers, and some tribes even believed that the mounted conquistadors were immortal. Given the inhumanity with which the colonial authorities treated their sullen Native subjects, the Spanish also recognized the consequences of allowing the Indians any modicum of freedom or self-government—and most particularly any familiarity with horsemanship. Thus whenever a tribe did resist, retribution was swift. In 1595, to take just one example, a Spanish military expedition of seventy men dispatched to punish a restive band of Pueblos slaughtered 800 men, women, and children and took another 500 prisoners. The right foot was severed from every male captive over the age of twenty-five, and males between the ages of twelve and twenty-five and females over the age of twenty were sentenced to slavery in the fields. It is little wonder the Indians lived in abject fear of the horse and its barbarous riders.

Meanwhile, although Coronado never found his "Seven Cities," along his trek north he met numerous American Plains Indians. His descriptions of these resourceful, dexterous peoples hint at his foreboding about their quite literal bloodthirstiness. Describing a buffalo hunt, Coronado wrote, "They cut the hide open at the back and pull it off at the joints, using a flint as large as a finger . . . with as much ease as if working with a good iron tool. They eat raw flesh and drink blood. When they kill a cow they empty a large gut and fill it with blood, and carry this around the neck to drink when they are thirsty. When they open the belly of a cow they squeeze out the chewed grass and drink the juice that remains behind because they say it contains the essence of the stomach."

Should these hardy people ever acquire mounts, Coronado recognized, they would constitute New Spain's greatest peril. Yet as hard as the Spanish tried, they could not completely fence off their proliferating stock. Southwestern Apache were the first to take advantage, running the animals off during raids on isolated rancheros and later capturing them at water holes and in box canyons. The Apache ate most of their catch, but they spared the strongest, equipping them with crude tack fashioned from buffalo hide and using them as transportation for more distant raids. The Apache never did learn to breed these partially broken mustangs; when they needed to replenish their herd they organized more raids. Now they were more mobile than any other tribe on the continent, and the radius and targets of their attacks expanded across the New Mexico territory. They fell hardest on their ancient enemies, the Pueblos.

The Pueblos had been forced more or less at gunpoint into a pact with the Spanish colonizers—in exchange for forced labor and desultory conversion to Catholicism, the Spanish would provide protection against the Apache. Once the Apache had horses, however, this proved an impossible commitment. Mounted raids on Pueblo communities increased, and before Spanish expeditions could be roused the Apache would vanish like ghosts into the frontier's Rembrandt gloom. The Apache raids grew more frequent and vicious, and in 1680 the Pueblos finally rose, emboldened by desperation and by a charismatic medicine man named Juan de Popé.

The ensuing massacre was retaliation for a century of cruelty. The Pueblos plundered Spanish haciendas, demolished government buildings, and took particular joy in destroying convents and churches and killing Franciscan priests, twenty of whom were captured in a churchyard and tortured to death, their bodies dumped in the charred husk of their chapel. The few Spanish who survived abandoned their livestock on a disorganized flight south to El Paso or to Mexico itself. Once New Mexico was cleared, the shaman Popé ordered his people to renounce the language, the religion, and even the crops of the colonizers. The Pueblos tore up fields of barley and wheat and slaughtered and ate the Spanish sheep and cattle. Because they had never developed the Apache taste for horseflesh, they merely flung open the corrals and allowed thousands of mustangs to run free across the Southern Plains. This has come to be known as North America's "Great Horse Dispersal," the seed of the transformation of the culture of the American West.

In the aftermath of this great escape, a combination of raiding and trading between tribes spread horse culture across the Plains. The Comanche, heretofore a primitive people barely scratching out an existence in the harsh Wind River country of west-central Wyoming, were drawn south to present-day West Texas by the lure of the wild herds. They were the first tribe to perfect horse-breeding techniques, including gelding, which had eluded the Apache. Soon the flow of horseflesh followed the ancient northerly trade routes. Within a century the Wichitas of Oklahoma were mounted; they were followed by the Kiowa of Kansas and the Pawnee of

Nebraska. The Ute, Southern Cheyenne, Arapaho, Blackfeet, and Crows, and the tribes of the Canadian prairie, all acquired mustangs. As did the Sioux. Although the westernmost Lakota, the Oglalas and Brules, had been in possession of a few staggering, worm-eaten nags stolen from old enemies like the Arikara, no one can say at what precise moment they encountered their first herds of wild mustangs—the *sungnuni glugluka*. It was probably sometime between 1770 and 1785. The western Lakota bands took to these stout little animals with their sleek necks and concave faces like no other people on the Northern Plains.

The Arikara, driven high up on the Missouri and decimated by small-pox epidemics, tried to thwart the burgeoning Sioux by allying with the Mandan. The partnership came to naught, as the horseless Mandan were ridden down and slaughtered by the score while the Arikara remained huddled behind their battlements, subject to constant Sioux raids. The newly mounted Lakota, imbued with an "arrogance born of successful conquest," spread south and farther west, and by 1803 had cleared the Kiowa from their traditional hunting grounds around the Black Hills and forced them to abandon their Missouri River Valley trade routes. Their old nemesis the Omaha, who had resettled in present-day northeastern Nebraska, had by now also obtained horses as well as guns from friendly Mississippi River tribes. Neither acquisition helped. When the Omaha tried to put up a fight, the Sioux crushed them.

The acquisition of horses did not alter the Sioux's nomadic hunter-gatherer culture so much as extend it, changing the dynamics of America's Northern Plains much as the invention of the stirrup had turned yurt-dwelling Mongols into the bloody scourge of Eurasia. The Cheyenne, who occupied land close to the Black Hills, have a traditional narrative, according to which the first Sioux they ever encountered were a greasy, lice-ridden band who arrived at one of their summer camps on foot, begging for food. This changed dramatically with the appearance of the wild herds. And besides naturally adding to the tribe's wealth and power, it also subtly affected ancient customs. As packhorses could pull much larger travois than dogs, for instance, the size of the Lakota elk-skin lodges doubled. And with greater contact with conquered tribes came the concept of decoration. Oglala and Brule wives and daughters began to adorn formerly bare tepees with pictures of the sun, moon, stars, buffalo, and of course horses, using pigments made from blood, sap, ground roots, dead insects, and urine. In recognition of the horse's transformation of their lifestyle Lakota braves even adopted a custom of dignified death for certain prized animals, letting older horses loose in secluded pastures to die instead of slaughtering them for food.

What would not be altered, however, was the tribe's all-consuming lust for battle honors. Some historians argue that the Great Horse Dispersal actually stunted Sioux society by preventing the tribe's progression into the "civilized" pursuit of agriculture, hierarchical organization, and social diversification. In other words, the arrival of the horse amplified the Stone Age culture of the Lakota. Now, dazzling Sioux war parties riding painted mounts rapidly and overwhelmingly extended their savage and relentless subjugation of neighboring tribes. Moreover, even when a Lakota rider was ambushed or outnumbered, the horse afforded a swift, heretofore un-imaginable means of escape. And there was no better hiding place than in the folds and crevasses of the sacred Black Hills.

The Oglala writer Luther Standing Bear once described the Black Hills as "a reclining female figure from whose breasts flowed life-giving forces, and to them the Lakota went as a child as to its mother's arms." The Crows and Cheyenne had temporarily blocked the route to this earth mother. That began to change in the late 1700s. The Oglala Winter Count of 1785–86 depicts the defeat of a large Crow party in a great battle. It was the beginning of the end for the Crows, who for years afterward could mount only a rearguard action as they retreated farther and farther northwest into the Rockies. Around the same time a combined Oglala-Brule force swept down on a Cheyenne camp south of the Black Hills to avenge a warrior killed in a horse raid. They massacred many Cheyenne and captured the settlement's tepees, weapons, and horses. Thereafter the Oglalas, the Brules, and even the Miniconjous, another Lakota tribe that had by this time forded the Missouri, all welcomed the Cheyenne as sub-ordinate allies.

It is difficult to explain what inspired the Western Sioux with such undying hatred for certain tribes, such as the Crows, Pawnee, and Kiowa, while at the same time they made tentative peace with others, such as the Cheyenne. Yet the Lakota seemed to tolerate the tall, stately Cheyenne more than any others despite the fact that the Cheyenne were distant cousins of the same Algonquins who had driven the Lakota out of Minnesota. One likely reason for this friendship was that, like the Lakota, the Cheyenne were fiercely opposed to white emigration. Another, and perhaps more important, reason was their access to horses through a long tradition of trading with tribes to the south, which the Sioux considered enemies. In any case, after a flurry of brutal early battles, the Sioux and Cheyenne settled into a partnership that would continue over the next century.

Meanwhile, as more of the Minnesota Sioux bands and tribes were drawn onto the Great Plains in the early 1800s by the estimated 60 million buffalo migrating across the prairie—more than eleven times the number of people living in the United States, according to the 1800 census—the Oglalas and Brules continued to lead the march west, their advance scouts sending back word of the rolling paradise of rivers and abundant game that lay on the other side of the Black Hills. According to the Winter Count of 1801, a combined Oglala-Brule raiding party that ventured to the head of the Powder River was set upon by the Crows, who in one of their rare victories killed thirty Sioux braves. Some historians believe that it was around this time that the Sioux collectively decided to abandon the arid, broken land east of the Black Hills and to make their home among the thick grasses and game herds of the Powder River Country of Wyoming and Nebraska.

This would take some effort. Although thoroughly outgunned, the Crows were richer in horses than the Sioux—a Crow brave was considered poor if he owned fewer than twenty horses, while a Lakota Head Man was considered wealthy if he owned thirty—and Crows were known to be capable of riding forty miles nonstop in twenty-four hours, thus perfecting the art of escape even while carrying captives. In fact, of all the Indians on the Plains, the Crows and their cousins the Gros Ventres were the only tribes who did not routinely torture and kill women and children prisoners. Infant mortality, high among all Plains Indians, was particularly severe among these rugged mountain tribes, and with their population

constantly in jeopardy, they made a habit of marrying their female prisoners and adopting the children. Crow warriors, as tall as the Cheyenne, also
had a physical trait that distinguished them from just about every other
tribe in the West, if not the continent. Given their diet, lifestyle, and,
at best, casual hygiene, most adult Indians had teeth like a crazy fence.
Contemporaneous accounts, however, describe the Crows' teeth as invariably straight, gleaming white, and remaining intact in their mouths into
old age.

And while the Sioux were to eventually push these fine-dentured people higher into the forested crags of the Bighorns and beyond, the Crows
were also blessed, or cursed, with memories as long as the Sioux's. Crow
fathers passed on to sons a burning hatred of the Sioux (as well as their
toadies the Cheyenne), while Sioux fathers instructed *their* sons in the
most excruciating tortures, to be reserved for Crow enemies. A favorite
was not only to gouge out a Crow's eyes and hack off his ears, arms, feet,
and penis, but also to punch a hole in his bladder and urinate or defecate
into it.

Indian torture rituals, as inconceivable as they were to most whites,
did have a purpose beyond inflicting excruciating pain. The majority of
tribes believed that all humans went to the same idyllic afterlife in the
exact physical condition in which they had died. This breathtaking arca-
dia, bursting with ponies and game and populated by unlimited comely
maidens, was a literal Happy Hunting Ground. But if the ghostly warrior had no eyes or tongue with which to see this paradise and taste its
fatty meat, if he had no feet with which to chase the game, no hands with
which to draw back a bowstring, no genitalia with which to satisfy his car-
nal desires, then one man's heaven had become another's hell. This belief
was universally accepted among the tribes, although the even more cruel
atrocities exchanged between Sioux and Crow were purely malicious.

For all the wonders of such an afterlife, however, both the Lakota and
the Crows recognized that on this earth their continual battles came down
to the acquisition and defense of the most desirable hunting grounds.
And as much as the Western Sioux hungered for the Crows' Powder River
Country, by the turn of the nineteenth century they were not yet strong
enough to take it and hold it. Instead they consolidated in the territory on

the buffalo feeding grounds to the east of the Black Hills across present-day South Dakota to such an extent that when Captain Meriwether Lewis and Lieutenant William Clark led an expedition that ascended the Missouri in the fall of 1804, the American explorers were amazed to find that so few Sioux had managed to amass such vast power and prestige.

Following a parley with the Oglalas on the Bad River, the Americans recorded in their journals that the entire tribe totaled sixty lodges containing 360 people, 120 of them warriors led by a chief named Stabber. Granted, not all seven of the Oglala bands may have been camped together, and to this day some historians dispute Lewis and Clark's census, finding it difficult to fathom how such a minuscule armed force could have routed the more numerous Arikara, Kiowa, Omaha, and lesser tribes while simultaneously enfolding the defeated Cheyenne into its orbit. The key word is "armed." The Sioux had the most, the best, and in some cases the only guns in any fight. And though the disparate Sioux bands and tribes operated as politically distinct entities, their shared language, myths, and culture provided a loose coherence that radiated power in all directions across the Plains.

To this point the Western Sioux's contact with whites had been limited to annual swap meets on the Missouri and occasional visits from mountain men. But following the War of 1812, French traders began to reassert themselves along the Big Muddy, establishing permanent posts on its Great Bend to barter with the Arikara and Mandan. The Lakota occasionally lingered along the river after the trading season to ambush French keelboats, and in the summer of 1807 a group of Oglalas fired on a small U.S. Army unit escorting home a Mandan chief who had accompanied Lewis and Clark to Washington. During the shoot-out an Oglala Head Man named Red Shirt was killed by an American ensign. Red Shirt could very well have been the first Sioux to die at the hands of a U.S. soldier. He would be far from the last.

Sometime in 1815 another momentous opportunity fell to the Lakota when the Cheyenne invited them to an annual horse-trading meet held on the North Platte in Nebraska, just south of the Wyoming border. The Cheyenne had been attending these all-Indian exchanges for decades, to

acquire not only mustangs but Spanish swords, knives, and bits of con-
quistador breastplates and helmets from Comanche, Kiowa, Arapaho, and
Plains Apache up from the Red River. But this was the Sioux's first venture into the verdant North Platte territory. The visit did not go as peacefully as the Cheyenne had hoped—a Brule brave split open a Kiowa's skull
with his war club, precipitating an all-out battle. But the Lakota liked
what they saw of the country. When the Lakota liked what they saw of a
country, it was not a good omen for the inhabitants.

At this time the Northern Plains contained several neutral zones that
separated the major hostile tribes from one another. These areas had no
fixed boundaries and were subject to continual mutations as the fortunes
of war ebbed and flowed. Four of them related to the Western Sioux—the
Yellowstone drainage of the Powder and Rosebud Rivers to the northwest, a loose demilitarized zone against the Crows; the western Laramie
Plains that kept the Ute at bay; the Republican River country along the
Kansas-Nebraska border contested by the Kiowa; and the region between
the forks of the South Platte and North Platte, east of which resided the
Pawnee. All Indians trod cautiously through these territories, usually only
in heavily armed hunting or war parties. So it was a sign of the Sioux's
growing dominance that by the spring of 1821 a band of Brules were
confident enough to stake camp on the stubby Nebraska panhandle in the
center of the fourth neutral zone, not far from the Colorado border along
a tributary of the North Platte called Blue Water Creek.

Among this band of Brules was a brave called Lone Man, whose
Oglala wife, Walks As She Thinks, was pregnant with her first child. In
early May some of the Sioux reported seeing a glowing red meteor streak
across the night sky above their camp. Several days later Walks As She
Thinks spread a brushed deerskin blanket over a bed of sand on the banks
of Blue Water Creek and gave birth to her first son. When Lone Man announced to the band that he had named the boy after the strange meteorological occurrence in order to appease the Great Sprit, the Brules agreed
that he had done a wise thing. This is how the child came to be called
Makhpiya-luta, or Red Cloud.

"RED CLOUD COMES!"

I n the spring of 1825, four years after Red Cloud's birth, Brigadier General Henry Atkinson led one of the earliest American military expeditions up the Missouri River. Atkinson, a decorated veteran of the War of 1812, departed St. Louis for the Yellowstone and was charged with securing treaties of "perpetual friendship" with as many of the Northern Plains tribes as possible. The 475 rifle-bearing soldiers from the 1st and 6th U.S. Infantry Regiments who sailed with him were blunt reminders to the Indians of the consequences of failing to grasp the import of this friendship.

The Sioux, eyeing the gun barrels that lined the deck of Atkinson's wheelboat, were no fools. When the general reached the Oglala camps in South Dakota they laid out a grand banquet of venison, antelope, and buffalo meat. Atkinson noted their extraordinary good health, and recorded the tribe's number at nearly 1,500, a fourfold increase from Lewis and Clark's estimate two decades earlier. This was probably an undercount, given that not every member of each Oglala band was present. A population explosion of such magnitude over so brief a period could be credited to a miscount by Lewis and Clark. More likely it indicated the beneficial influence of the horse. Not only had horses allowed the Indians to range farther after game to prevent winter shortfalls and ward off famine and nutritional diseases, but the packhorses had taken on the physical burdens that previously stunted or damaged the ovaries and wombs of women and girls of childbearing age. In addition, being able to act on their bold wanderlust had allowed them to avoid diseases such as smallpox and cholera, which had begun to afflict Indians living in fixed villages across the nation's massive midsection.

A more subtle purpose of Atkinson's excursion was to bind the tribes to licensed, regulated trade agreements with the burgeoning United States—as if the words "licensed" and "regulated" had any meaning in Native culture. Nevertheless, gifts were proffered and various Western Sioux Head Men—some actually chiefs, others put forward as a kind of joke on the Americans—touched the pen. For example, on July 26, 1825, the Hunkpapas "signed" a treaty that began: "For the purpose of perpetuating the friendship which has heretofore existed, as also to remove all future cause of discussion or dissension, as it respects trade and friendship between the United States and their citizens, and the Hunkpapas band of the Sioux tribe of Indians, the President of the United States of America, by Atkinson, of the United States Army, and Major Benjamin O'Fallon, Indian agent, with full powers and authority, specially appointed for that purpose, of the one part, and the undersigned Chiefs, Headmen, and Warriors of the said Hunkpapas band of Sioux Indians, on behalf of their band, of the other part." Even the most skilled interpreter could hardly have conveyed the sense of this to the Hunkpapas.

The United States may have been in its infancy, but even the Indians of the far West had by now heard stories about a government whose customary double standard ignored nearly all Native interests. They accepted General Atkinson's beads and blankets, nodded at his assurances, slyly inquired if he had guns for sale (he did not), and on his departure continued with their lives as if nothing had changed. They certainly had no idea that 1825 was also the year when Secretary of War James Barbour had begun to act on a concept of the forcible removal of the eastern tribes, first put forth by his predecessor, John C. Calhoun, to an "Indian Country" in modern Oklahoma, where "the future residence of these people will be forever undisturbed."

The more salient fact for Red Cloud that year was the death of his father, Lone Man. According to his incomplete autobiography as well as statements he made late in life, the cause of Lone Man's death was an addiction to what the white man called whiskey but was in reality a shuddering mixture of diluted grain alcohol, molasses, tobacco juice, and crushed red pepper. Red Cloud may have witnessed his father succumb to delirium tremens. Although historians do not take every word of Red Cloud's memoir as hard truth—his dictated account almost certainly smoothed the sharp edges of his savage youth—this particular assertion about his father's alcoholism seems reasonable and reliable, not least because the timing coincided with a trade war between Canadian and American merchants, who were flooding the Indian camps along the Missouri with cheap rotgut in order to attract business. Native Americans of the eighteenth and nineteenth centuries had no more immunity to alcohol than to smallpox, and if bringing whiskey to the negotiating table facilitated the one-sided deals, so much the better.

In any case, Lone Man's death left an impression. Red Cloud abhorred the distilled *mini wakan*—"the water that makes men crazy"—and its mongers for the rest of his life. Years later, after he had assumed tribal leadership, a whiskey trader rode into his camp in early April just as his band was breaking winter quarters. Red Cloud was not happy with this disruption, but despite his position as a Head Man he could not forbid his braves to indulge. All he could do was order the trader to set up temporary shop beyond the village boundaries. By early evening many of his men were drunk, and disputes broke out over real and perceived insults, fresh and ancient. Red Cloud bounded around the village extinguishing these small prairie fires until one drunken brave killed an elderly father in an argument over his daughter. Red Cloud exploded, and ordered the trader's wagon and tent burned and his barrels and kegs emptied onto the flames.

After Lone Man's death, Red Cloud's mother left the Brule camp and took him, his younger brother Big Spider, and an infant sister back to her original Oglala band, which was led by Old Smoke. He recognized her as a "sister," a term indicating that she was either his true sibling or a close cousin with the same status as a sister. Although he was by then in his early fifties, Old Smoke was still a vibrant war leader; he had been a Head Man for close to two decades, and his band was the largest, strongest, and most influential of all the Oglala tribes, if not of the Sioux nation. His willingness to take in Walks As She Thinks and her family proved most fortunate for her elder son. Fatherless boys, though not explicitly ostracized in the patriarchal Sioux society, nonetheless began life at a distinct social disadvantage. Red Cloud's burden was further lightened by having not one but two strong uncles who by all accounts cared greatly for him and his mother, brother, and sister.

Old Smoke's brother was a warrior named White Hawk, and there is evidence that he may have been the band's *blotahunka*, or chief protector. The Sioux set great store by inculcating in their children from infancy a respect for a reserved poise, and apparently White Hawk was crucial in teaching the young Red Cloud to control what he called the "unusually headstrong impulses" that in the future would establish his reputation for heartless cruelty. White Hawk was also responsible, along with Walks As She Thinks, for the child's education, and before Red Cloud was two years old both his mother and his uncle were interpreting for him the message to be found in every birdsong and the track of every animal, the significance of the eagle feather in a war bonnet, and the natural history of the tribe in relation to its surroundings. By the age of four he was sitting at council fires emulating the gravity of his elders.

As the Western Sioux's territorial ambitions expanded, so too had their political traditions, and the concept of tribal leadership had evolved since the bands departed Minnesota. Back in their old homeland along the Mississippi the Head Men of the Seven Council Fires were for the most part totemic figures, influential and certainly supported by their kinsmen, but wielding nothing close to absolute power. Since the Missouri crossings, however, a more hierarchical system of social organization had gradually taken hold. This was no doubt partly because of the decisions that needed to be made on a daily basis by a wandering, warlike people no longer tethered to set communities. No Head Man could as yet "order" any braves to obey his commands. (Nor would he ever be able to.) But as authority accrued to the best hunters, trackers, horsemen, and fighters, a sort of natural primacy was accorded certain men that would have been unrecognizable to their distant eastern cousins. Old Smoke was one of these men, and as his power grew so did the ambitions of his rivals.

When Red Cloud was thirteen years old he watched Old Smoke suppress his cousin Bull Bear's attempt to usurp his leadership. Bull Bear, by all accounts a canker of a man with a face like a clenched fist, had strength in numbers. But Old Smoke retained the loyalty of his brother White Hawk's less numerous but better-armed *akicita*. In the end, Bull Bear's followers thought better of challenging them. Under Lakota custom and with White Hawk's braves at his back, Old Smoke could have confiscated Bull Bear's horses and women as punishment for his mutinous insubordination. Instead he merely banished Bull Bear and his followers, greatly weakening his own band in the process.

Humiliated, Bull Bear threw dust in Old Smoke's face before riding out of camp. It was an act of disrespect Red Cloud never forgot. And though numerous explanations have been put forth for how around this time Old Smoke's people acquired a new name—some said it was because of their sullen, fierce demeanor; others said it was because of their penchant for cheating on their wives—Bull Bear's intemperate affront is the likely reason they became known as the *Ite Sica*, or "Bad Faces." The incident also gave Bull Bear's new band the name for which it would be known forevermore—the *Kiyuska*, or "Cutoffs."

Temporary winter settlements notwithstanding, the Lakotas rarely maintained residence in any one place, following the game along rivers that acted as natural highways, seeking fresh pasturage for their expanding herds of ponies, and camping along long-trod trails in places that had acquired mystical significance. As these journeys pushed the tribe farther and farther west by southwest out of South Dakota, life on the lush prairie offered Indian men and boys plenty of opportunity for self-reflection and long, metaphysical conversations deep into the night as the camp's women—closer to slaves than second-class citizens by modern standards of thinking—did most of the hard work. Red Cloud therefore had ample opportunity to absorb his uncles' wisdom and insights regarding the Sioux philosophy of existence.

The Sioux regarded the universe as a living and breathing—if mysterious—being. And though they recognized the passage of time as measured by the predictable movements of the sun, the moon, and the stars, to their eyes mankind was but a flickering flame in a strong wind; and their concepts of past, present, and future were blurred so that all three existed simultaneously, on separate planes. Whites steeped in Christian culture and Victorian science failed to comprehend this Indian cosmos, and often threw up their hands and resorted to the cliché of Indian spirituality as an amalgam of ignorance and superstition. This also contributed greatly to the white man's description of Indians as feral and nihilistic people utterly lacking personal discipline. There was, however, a precise structure underpinning Sioux religious beliefs, even if it remained largely unrecognizable to outsiders.

In brief, Sioux religious philosophy flowed from their recognition of what the famous Oglala holy man Black Elk described as the "Sacred Hoop" of life. That hoop consists of a series of concentric circles, divine rings, the smallest of which encompasses one's immediate family. The hoops then expand outward, growing ever larger to envelop extended clans, bands, tribes, entire peoples, the earth and all its living things, and finally the universe. It is a universe in which everything, from the clouds in the sky to the insects on the ground, is connected as a part of *Wakan Tanka.* So while whites viewed animals in terms of their usefulness as food or workers, the Sioux saw them as nearly equal, sentient beings. Thus the young Red Cloud learned from his elders, for instance, that running down a stray single buffalo that had escaped from one of their hunts was a question not of greed but of necessity, so the beast would not warn others of its kind away. This was the sort of knowledge and wisdom that dominated conversation in each tepee, and in this regard Red Cloud was fortunate to have Old Smoke as a kinsman.

The section of the Sioux tepee opposite the entrance is called the *catku,* and it was the place of honor where the head of the family slept, sat, and discussed matters of what can be called philosophy and politics. While the women and infants generally lived on the other side of the fire closer to the lodge's entrance, the eldest son sat with his father in the *catku* until about the age of six, learning and observing. The young Red Cloud occupied this position in Old Smoke's tent. In later years, Red Cloud and his closest kin often told stories about Old Smoke's habit of treating the boy as his own. It was in Old Smoke's *catku* that Red Cloud absorbed his first life lessons.

Given the makeup of Western Sioux bands at the time, Old Smoke's probably comprised a dozen or so extended families that, in the spirit of the Sacred Hoop, raised their children collectively. Whites were later shocked at the laxity with which the Sioux treated their children, especially their boys. Young males were continually showered with love, did nothing but play games, and were rarely punished for even the most obnoxious transgressions. (The Sioux were equally appalled when they saw white fathers on the emigrant trails beating their children in order to instill discipline.) Not incidentally, all the games Lakota boys played were intended to hone their tracking, hunting, and fighting skills, which provided the only means of social advancement in Sioux society.

Boys and young braves loved to gamble on pastimes involving clubs, sticks, and rocks that often knocked them silly. A version of "king of the hill" was popular—with the "attackers" issued shortened lances to count coup against the "king." There was one major difference from the game as we know it: Sioux boys played at night, when stealth was crucial. By the age of three or four, boys would be gathered in packs, presented with toy arrows and spears, and told to pick out an object—a rock, a tree—at a short distance and aim for it. The boy who came closest kept all the "weapons." As the boys grew, so did the distance from the targets until at around the age of twelve they were given otter or dogskin quivers and real bows constructed of strong, dried osage that could propel either flint or iron-tipped arrows completely through a buffalo, or a man.

Red Cloud, blessed with strength and coordination well beyond his contemporaries, excelled in these competitions. Perhaps because he was a child whose father had died not in battle or on the hunt but from whiskey, and he stood just outside the ring of light thrown by the lodge fires of boys with important fathers, it was always Red Cloud who hit hardest with the lance during "king of the hill," or laughed loudest while confiscating the other boys' toy weapons. Such was his temper that was he was sometimes warned by his uncles to curb his ruthless streak.

As soon as a Sioux boy was capable of straddling a pony, his father, an older brother, or—as in Red Cloud's case—an uncle would present him with a colt and its tack. He was instructed in the colt's care and feeding, and it was made clear to him that the precious horse was now his responsibility. Preteens learned rudimentary horsemanship through pony races—the sight of boys holding tight to reins as 850-pound animals nearly bounced them out of rough saddles was a near-daily occurrence—and as they grew older one of their paramount chores was caring for the family's herd. When a family was too poor to furnish a son with his own horse, his peers lent him a colt to break. This ensured that each male member of the band grew up with a thorough knowledge of martial horsemanship. The older the boys became, the more closely their horse games simulated raids and buffalo hunts. According to the few surviving accounts of Red Cloud's boyhood, he took naturally to this horse culture, and especially to the hunt.

The advantages the horse provided the Sioux in both hunting and warfare cannot be overstated. Once mounted, hunting parties could track, out-gallop, and kill buffalo along migratory routes never before accessible. Although the bands still occasionally drove an entire herd over a cliff when the opportunity presented itself, gone were the days when a party of hunters camouflaged in wolf skins were forced on their bellies to approach a single bull or cow, cull it from the herd, and bring it down with a volley of arrows. Now a solitary mounted brave, his pony stretched out and galloping belly low, rider and steed exhibiting an intimate kinetic grace, could do the work of a half-dozen men.

The buffalo hunt did not come naturally to the skittish mustang. A full-grown bull stood six feet tall at its shoulder, and was ten to twelve feet from nose to tail. With an average weight of just under 2,000 pounds—some bulls grew to 3,000—it was not averse to turning, standing, and fighting. The horse and rider who faced these beasts needed heart, agility, and stamina, but above all a reactive instinct acquired by years of practice. From birth a colt was accustomed to the scent of its prey by being smeared with buffalo fat and being swaddled in buffalo robes. When it was old enough to be broken, a snug cord fashioned from buffalo hair would be fitted over its muzzle and attached to leather reins made from buffalo sinews. Its owner would train it to charge by continually riding at full gallop in and among the tribe's horse herds, running as close astern as possible. When it was deemed ready to hunt, its ear would be split as a sign of respect and importance. Almost every Lakota family had at least one pony that was specifically groomed for buffalo hunting. Such was its worth that on the rare occasion when it was traded, it could bring between ten and thirty common horses in return.

The distribution of the slain buffalo's component parts also changed with the coming of the horse. Whereas hunting, particularly cliff-driving, had once been a group effort on foot, now the killer of a slain beast could be identified by the distinctive designs and fletching of the arrows that brought the animal down. Although the meat was still shared among the band, the hides were awarded to the clan of the arrows' owners, and this too marked a subtle change in tribal hierarchy. With individual hunters thus rewarded, competitive boys became even more anxious to prove their mettle, and by the time Sioux boys reached their early teens the most adept of them could bury two dozen arrows into a buffalo's short ribs with deadly accuracy in the time it took an American dragoon* to fire and reload his musket. One frontiersman watched an exhibition put on by Lakota boys and noted, "They could hit a button, pencil, or any small article at about thirty yards." Red Cloud developed this gift.

Early white observers of a Sioux buffalo chase described it as barely controlled chaos, with braves knocking one another out of the saddle helter-skelter. This was taken as just another example of the Indians' lack of discipline—a mistake, as whites had not been trained to detect the hunt's formal structure. The action was aggressively policed by *akicita* outriders, who would bring down any brave who got out ahead of the advancing line of attackers and spooked a drove prematurely. In later years Indians who had grown up riding with Red Cloud said there was nothing in life he enjoyed so much as the spirit and excitement of the buffalo run.

---

*"Dragoon" was derived from the "dragon guns" carried by legendary French mounted forces.

• • •

Where the buffalo ranged, Old Smoke and his band followed, usually breaking and making new summer camps at least once a week in order to find fresh pasturage. In his autobiography Red Cloud had little to report about his early youth. Perhaps he did not think his life important until he became a hunter and warrior. But according to Lakota custom, his uncles and mother undoubtedly steeped him in the topography and plant and animal life of the Powder River Country. Old Smoke's band would have roamed through all the major river valleys, from the Republican to the Yellowstone to the Missouri, and would have been familiar with the geographic nuances of Nebraska's Sand Hills, the Black Hills straddling what is today's South Dakota–Wyoming border, and even the Laramie Range on the eastern face of the Rockies. He would have been taught to recognize plants such as the special riverbank sage that warded off evil spirits, heed signs that buffalo were near, and learn to differentiate scat from a grizzly with a belly full of elk from the scat of a hungry bear that might be on the prowl for a Lakota horse. Becoming one with his physical environment was as natural a part of an Indian child's education as learning to read and write was to an American boy back east. And although the great American wagon migrations were still a decade off, Red Cloud acquired a rudimentary knowledge of the ways of the whites from Old Smoke's frequent layovers at the trading post that was to become Fort Laramie.

The mean, small structure, erected in 1834 and initially named Fort William, was the only American trading post west of the Missouri. Situated at the juncture of the Laramie and the North Platte in southeastern Wyoming, about midway between present-day Cheyenne and Casper, it was the brainchild of an Irish-born mountain man, Robert Campbell, and was named after his trigger-happy partner, William Sublette, who was said to have fled the mountains after initiating the slaughter of a band of peaceful Gros Ventres during the annual mountain man rendezvous of 1832. Campbell and Sublette had trapped in the Rockies for over a dozen years, and both recognized by the mid-1830s that the European craze for beaver hats was dying. The new money would be made in buffalo robes, and the two did a thriving business, especially with the Lakota, whose superior tanned hides of buffalo cows were craved by the merchants in St. Louis. (Bull hides were deemed of lesser quality.)

Fort William, protected by a fifteen-foot palisade of cottonwood logs and a cannon mounted in a blockhouse over the front gate, became a regular winter transit point for Indians meandering across the Powder River Country. White-Indian interactions were generally peaceable. Given their isolation and small numbers, the two mountain men and the few teamsters they employed did not have much of a choice. The Indians, meanwhile, not only wanted and needed the dry goods they imported, but saw no glory to be gained by wiping them out. They were, after all, merely whites. The Lakota, in any case, were still busy with the broader pursuits of their Plains expansionism, raiding and fighting the Crows, Ute, Pawnee, and Kiowa at every opportunity.

Once they took a territory, the Sioux patrolled it ruthlessly. This philosophy of security through aggression naturally filtered down to individuals, for whom military glory became a stepping-stone to leadership. It was impossible to become a Sioux leader without also being a distinguished warrior, and no one was more prepared to seize the mantle and the rewards that came with it than Red Cloud. The most important of these rewards was social advancement. "When I was young among our nation, I was poor," he told Sam Deon. "But from the wars with one nation or another, I raised myself to be a chief."

A warrior's vocation was the only path to success and stature for a fatherless boy, even a boy with powerful and respected uncles. Red Cloud was about sixteen years old when he joined his first raiding party. It was sometime in the late 1830s, and the Lakota were waging a war of attrition against the Pawnee, who dwelled in stationary earth lodges and whose territory in east-central Nebraska was dwindling precariously. One day after a rare unsuccessful raid on a Pawnee stronghold along the twisting Platte, word spread through the Oglala camp that Red Cloud's older cousin had been killed in the fight. The horror of losing a battle to the lowly Pawnee turned to cold fury, and Old Smoke organized an even larger retaliatory force from among several Lakota bands camping nearby. Red Cloud had always, if reluctantly, obeyed the pleas of his mother when she argued that he was too young to take part in these raids. Despite a Sioux woman's inferior status, Walks As She Thinks did speak with some authority due to her brothers' standing. But even the respect afforded Old Smoke and White Hawk could not alter the fact that Red Cloud's absence from the war parties was beginning to be remarked on.

When young warriors painted and dusted themselves and their horses for battle, an unofficial head count circulated through the camp as to who was riding and who was staying behind. Although there were many reasons for a man of fighting age to sit out a raid (usually having to do with omens), any young brave repeatedly failing to participate was said to have had his "heart fail him." Red Cloud was still on the cusp of war-party age, but perhaps he had heard this insinuation once too often. Or maybe his cousin's death was the spark. For whatever reason, on this day as the departing braves gathered at one end of the village a shout suddenly rose among the mothers, wives, and sisters gathered about the warriors. "He is coming."

"Who is coming?" someone called.

"Red Cloud," called another voice, and the crowd took up a chant. "Red Cloud comes! Red Cloud comes!"

He then appeared on his spotted pony, painted and feathered, leading a spare bay by a rope. Both horses wore ribbons entwined in their manes and tails.

Within moments the scouts had fanned out and the bulk of the party rode east down the North Platte. It took the Sioux ten days to reach the rough sand hills overlooking the Pawnee village. On the eleventh day they charged at dawn. One can imagine the terrifying, primal electricity that accompanied the roaring sound of battle. Elk-bone whistles shrieked. High-pitched war whoops cut the air. Lakota arrows and musket balls ripped through the blankets and skins hanging from the entrances to the earthen Pawnee lodges.

As their women and children fled, Pawnee fighters scrambled from their beds and poured through the camp on foot, loosing their arrows from taut bows and swinging their war clubs wildly above their heads. They made for their pasturage only to discover that Sioux scouts had driven off their horses. Though the Pawnee were known as efficient hand-to-hand fighters, they were now facing a mounted enemy, and the battle looked to be over almost before it began. The Sioux trampled through the camp, crushing men, women, and children under their horses' hooves, and it was only the fortuitous arrival of a large Pawnee hunting party that broke off the fighting.

The Sioux gathered up nearly 100 stolen horses and rode off, putting two solid days' distance between them and a token, weak pursuit. When they neared their own camp women and boys rode out to meet them and escort them into the village. Their ululation reached fever pitch as four warriors paraded from lodge to lodge lofting Pawnee scalps high on their spears. One of the four was Red Cloud. He had made his first kill.

It was a Lakota custom that when warriors returned from battle their closest kinswomen gathered about them, took the reins of their bridles, and led them to their lodges in a fawning procession. For Red Cloud, this task fell to his mother. When he and Walks As She Thinks reached their tepee the boy dismounted, entered, put away his weapons, and waited. Soon enough a young female cousin called at the entrance. She beckoned him to his uncle's lodge. Red Cloud rose, wrapped himself in a blanket, and strode through the camp. One can only imagine what was going through the young man's mind as veteran braves grunted and yipped in approval and young women stole peeks at the conquering hero.

When he reached Old Smoke's tepee he was fed a sumptuous meal and prompted to recount his performance, particularly the circumstances of his scalp-taking. He would tell the story many times that day, including during his first appearance in the soldier lodge, the village's largest, where warriors spun tales of battle in order that the narratives might become public property. Meanwhile, the fires in the tepees of the men who had not returned were doused, and in the surrounding hills the wails of their women echoed for hours as they cut their hair and flesh in mourning rituals, some even chopping off fingers.

The next morning, amid more feasting, a tall medicine pole was erected in the center of the camp, and at dusk ceremonial fires were lit in a circle around it. When the sun had set, a drumbeat announced the victory dance. For the next two days and nights the warriors danced without stopping; should one drop from exhaustion, another would take his place.

Those like Red Cloud who had killed an enemy used a tincture that was ground from manganese oxide to paint themselves black from head to toe as a show of menace. But the most important ceremony was saved for the end of the dance. It was then that the distribution of the Pawnee horses took place. Most were kept by their captors, but some were given to the tribe's old, poor, and infirm, and even to the *winkte*, the transvestites who had opted out of male Lakota society and lived on the edge of camp with the band's other dispossessed. That day Red Cloud proudly gave away the one pony he had made off with. Alas, he never mentioned the recipient. More important, he also learned a great lesson. He had witnessed this ceremony many times, but he now *felt* a true understanding of the Sioux concept of martial honor. Someone, for the first time, was in his debt.

After his first killing Red Cloud noted another important lesson— warriors who had physically struck an enemy without killing him, or "counted coup," were accorded the tribe's highest respect, more so than those who had taken scalps. Among the western tribes it was understood that the greatest courage was displayed by coming close enough to smell a man's hot breath while striking, or "quirting," him and allowing him to live. The theory was that in so doing a brave took a greater chance of being killed himself. Such was Red Cloud's intuitive intellect that as a teenager he was beginning to comprehend how the ancient customs could be used, even by a fatherless boy, to accrue power. It was the opening of Red Cloud's strategic and tactical mind, and he stored this memory for use during the rest of his life, beginning with an incident only a few months later.

COUNTING COUP

I t was the winter after Red Cloud's first kill, and Old Smoke's Bad Faces had staked camp in a small cottonwood valley close to where the Laramie flows into the North Platte near the Nebraska-Wyoming border. Though the season was waning, it had been an unusually severe March, with successive storms rolling down from the north. Under the cover of one of these spring blizzards a raiding party of fourteen Crows, on foot and far from their Montana homeland, had closed to within about ten miles of the Sioux pony herd when they were spotted by a lone Oglala brave out hunting deer. Their plan had been good. The Crows were just unlucky. And now they were doomed.

The mounted Sioux hunter raced back to camp, and that night a party of fifty to sixty braves, including Red Cloud, rode out to ambush them. They circled around behind the Crows, and by dawn they had the raiders, still unaware of their predicament, trapped near the mouth of a tight canyon. The Sioux charged, their gunshots and battle cries echoing off the defile's granite walls. The Crows, weak from their trek, outnumbered, and caught completely by surprise, recognized at once their hopeless situation. They knelt in the snow, drew their blankets over their heads, and sang their death songs. Red Cloud, the first of the attackers to reach them, drew his bow, slowed his horse, and ostentatiously struck three of the Crows in the back of the head. He then rode off a bit and turned to watch his tribesmen annihilate the intruders.

The victory banquet that night was a muted affair. The Bad Faces well understood that little glory had been achieved by massacring enemies who refused to fight back. Only one young brave was singled out to be celebrated, for he had struck the Crows while they were still alive and armed. As Red Cloud had anticipated, his stature within the tribe soared that night. He was a quick learner, and the Crow coup notwithstanding, a quicker killer.

In later years, when old Sioux who had ridden with Red Cloud reminisced, they invariably recalled three traits the young brave always exhibited. The first, surprisingly, was his grace. He rode, walked, and stalked like a panther, his every action shorn of extraneous movements. The second was his brutality; he was like flint, they said, hard and easily sparked. On one occasion he killed a Crow boy who was guarding a herd of ponies, and the next day he waited in ambush for the pursuing Crow chief, the boy's father, to kill him, too. On another he took obvious joy in jumping into a river to save a floundering Ute from drowning, only to drag him up onto the bank, knife him to death, and scalp him. The third trait was his arrogance, essential to any Sioux leader and exemplified by a famous story about the one and only time he allowed a captured enemy to live.

It occurred while Red Cloud was leading a horse raid against the Crows. Before reaching their camp he and his braves ambushed a small party of Blackfeet who had gotten there first. As the Blackfeet were escaping with a remuda of mustangs, the Oglalas captured one brave. They brought him to Red Cloud, who told the man that if he could withstand what would come next without uttering a single sound, he would live to see his family again. Red Cloud then handed his knife to his best friend, a Lakota brave named White Horse, who had recently lost a cousin in battle. He told White Horse to scalp the man alive. Two Lakota took hold of the Blackfoot's arms as Red Cloud stood before him, his heavy war club raised. White Horse walked behind the Blackfoot, grabbed his braid, and took the scalp at its roots. The Indian, his body trembling, blood running down his face, never made a noise. Red Cloud, true to his word, told him to return to his village and tell his people that it was the Lakota warrior Red Cloud who had done this to him. Red Cloud had intuited that the Blackfoot would withstand the agony in silence, and as much as he coveted an enemy's scalp, it was more important at this stage that rival tribes learned, and feared, his name.

By the time Red Cloud reached his late teens his fighting qualities—reckless bravery, stealth, strength, and imperviousness to personal danger—had been established and were merely being honed and perfected. He once single-handedly killed four Pawnee in battle, and his ruthless massacres of men and boys—Arikara, Snakes, Gros Ventres, and Crows—were becoming legendary. He was a living embodiment of the maxim that war is the best teacher of war; in his case, too much was never enough. Moreover, as a striving young brave he did not spare himself the self-inflicted pain common in Sioux warrior culture. There were numerous self-torture and vision-fasting purification rites that Lakota fighting men undertook, but none was as notorious—or as fearsome and unfathomable to whites—as the annual Sun Dance ceremony.

In the Sioux ethos this fortnight-long ritual, usually held in July before the late-summer raiding season—the "Moon of the Ripening Chokecherries"—offered the penultimate physical sacrifice to the "great mystery" of the universe; and it is likely that Red Cloud performed his own Sun Dance purification around this time. Sioux braves (and, in a few rare cases, women) believed that only by subjecting the body to excruciating physical suffering could an individual release the spirit imprisoned in the flesh and come to understand the true meaning of life. This was no mere quest for spiritual enlightenment. It was the key, the Sioux believed, to gaining a physical edge, to avoiding bad luck and illness, and to ensuring success during the hunt and in battle. Warriors like Red Cloud felt that the Sun Dance ceremony made them much harder to kill. Some whites who observed or heard of the ceremony judged the tribe to be "masochists." But to all the participants the rituals of the Sun Dance celebration were the price paid by those who hoped to become tribal leaders.

The Sun Dance was always voluntary, and whenever possible it was performed in the shadow of *Mato Paha:* Bear Butte, the majestic

1,200-foot stone edifice in present-day western South Dakota long revered as a holy place by both the Lakota and the Cheyenne. The ceremony was initiated by a warrior through a simple vow to a celestial deity to exchange his suffering for heavenly protection. Much as modern prizefighters have seconds, a young Lakota, typically in his late teens or early twenties, would approach older men who had undergone the ordeal to help guide him through it. The dance was generally held in public, sometimes in a specific lodge set up for the occasion, but more often in the center of the village. There a painted pole made from the trunk of a forked cottonwood, representing the Tree of Life, was erected beneath an arbor. The acolyte believed that this symbolic tree connected him to his creator. The older men would pierce either side of the Sun Dancer's breasts, and sometimes the back flesh near the wing bones, and push wooden skewers through the cuts. Then they looped rawhide thongs over the exposed ends of the skewers and tied the free ends of the lines to the center pole. In extreme cases heavy buffalo skulls would be hung from the incisions in the back.

As medicine men uttered prayers and female relatives trilled and wailed to a steady drumbeat, the Sun Dancer gyrated around the pole, going through a series of ancient dance steps, for twenty-four hours. The ceremony ended in one of two ways. Either the dancer would fling himself backward from the pole, ripping his own flesh, or his older mentors would seize him and yank him back hard. In either instance the result was the same. The skewers would burst from his chest and back and the odd, ragged bits of flesh would be trimmed away with a ceremonial knife and laid at the foot of the pole as an offering to the sun.

For Red Cloud, the Sun Dance had multiple purposes. The most fundamental was that as a Sioux warrior he needed all the celestial help he could get. But he also saw the sacrifice as another rung on the ladder to tribal acceptance and prominence, for aside from his fighting skills he was also beginning to exhibit cunning resourcefulness. This pragmatism may have been innate, or the young brave may have gone out of his way to demonstrate it to his peers as a sign that he was capable of one day becoming their chief. What was becoming undeniable, however, was that he had the best qualities of a warrior chief.

Once, while still a teenager, Red Cloud joined a large party on a raid into Crow lands. Resting by day and riding by night, traversing only the rugged ravines and wooded creek bottoms that provided cover in enemy territory, the Sioux took twice the usual time to cover the distance. After two weeks of riding they reached a spot close to where Rosebud Creek empties into the Yellowstone. Red Cloud, impatient with the cautious pace set by the expedition's leaders—two prominent warriors named Old-Man-Afraid-Of-His-Horses* and Brave Bear—diplomatically suggested that they were in fact much closer to the Crow encampment than they realized. The two elder men disagreed, and Red Cloud did not argue. He was learning to control his temper, to refrain from blurting out an insult that might make him an enemy for life. Instead, he waited for his tribesmen to retire for a rare night's rest, then donned a thick pair of moccasins and sneaked away on foot with a trusted friend.

The two walked for ten miles, picking their way through thick copses of lodgepole pine and blue spruce, before they heard a faint sound, perhaps a horse's whinny. They settled on a ridgeline to await the dawn. At the first streaks of light in the east they saw below them a herd of fifty Crow mustangs quietly feeding on a small, grassy plateau. The remuda was guarded by a lone sentry who was sleeping with his back against a tree. There was no Crow village in sight. They crawled down to the herd, caught two fine horses, and mounted. Red Cloud signaled to his friend to lead the herd in the direction of the Bad Face camp, and rode his own horse toward the sleeping Crow. When he was only a few yards from the sentry he raised his war club and broke into a gallop. The horse's pounding hooves awakened the Crow, who ducked seconds before Red Cloud's club slammed into the tree where the man's head had been.

The terrified Crow took off at a sprint. Red Cloud, still mounted, calmly retrieved an arrow from his quiver, nocked it, and sent it into the man's back. He trotted up to the writhing body, dismounted, grabbed the

*Whites sometimes translated this name as "Man Even Whose Horses Are Feared." Yet given the Sioux's subtle humor and their habit of passing names from fathers to sons, it is more likely that the name Old-Man-Afraid-Of-His-Horses was bestowed on a grandfather in the late eighteenth century, when the tribe was acquiring its first wild mustangs and just learning, sometimes awkwardly, how to break them.

victim's own knife from his belt, and stabbed him to death before scalping him.

The ride back to the Sioux camp was far from triumphant. Red Cloud warned his companion that they might be in trouble and were likely to be subjected to the whipping that usually accompanied the "soldiering of a delinquent." When they were met on the trail by the Lakota raiding party, several *akicita* indeed charged them, with quirts raised. But at commands from Brave Bear and Old-Man-Afraid-Of-His-Horses they halted, and Red Cloud (who was obviously the instigator) was ordered to state his case. He related his adventure and showed them the scalp. He said that he would never have risked his tribesmen's lives if the Crow horses had been tethered near an enemy camp where warning cries could have been raised. He added that, judging by the horse tracks he had seen, he could indicate where the Crows kept an even larger herd. The two elders sent Red Cloud and his friend back to the temporary camp, deciding to reserve judgment, and punishment, until they followed up on this intelligence.

The next day, when the party returned with another 250 stolen mustangs that had been captured in a dawn raid on the Crow village—located exactly where Red Cloud had guessed—he was forgiven. He was also awarded half of the fifty horses he had taken. His fellow warriors took approving note. As a bonus, he was now a rich man.

It was not long after this episode that Red Cloud's uncle White Hawk, the Bad Faces' *blotahunka*, was killed—some say by the embittered Bull Bear—and his charismatic young nephew inherited the bleached white bull-hide buffalo shield signifying his rank. Red Cloud now commanded a select society charged with not only protecting the band from outside enemies but, as they had demonstrated during the Crow raid, acting as a sort of police force to maintain tribal discipline during buffalo hunts and amid the controlled chaos when the village moved from one pasturage to another. One autumn, while the band was camped in a timbered thicket on the Clear Fork of the Powder, Red Cloud led a party of about forty hunters out onto the buffalo grass to stock their winter larders. These hunts could be monthlong affairs, with the Indians moving every two or three days from one temporary campsite to the next as they followed the herd and burdened their packhorses with piles of hides and dried meat. On this occasion they were joined by a party of Cheyenne, who accompanied them back to the Clear Fork and staked their own winter camp about a mile away.

The next day a sobbing Bad Face woman came to the new *blotahunka* and told him that while gathering water she had been molested by a Cheyenne brave. Red Cloud questioned her, realized he knew who the man was, and gathered seven of his *akicita* to ride on the Cheyenne village. Aside from his gun, bow, and quiver of arrows, he also carried an old Spanish saber. What happened next was nearly unprecedented on the Plains. On reaching the village he ordered his men to form a circle around the Cheyenne brave's lodge, stepped inside alone, and began to club the man with the flat of the steel blade. The Cheyenne's howls and yelps, not to mention the presence of "foreign" warriors in the camp, naturally attracted attention. Soon a large group of armed Cheyenne had surrounded the Sioux. The *akicita* signed that Red Cloud was inside redressing a grievance, and that all should stand back. Astonishingly, the Cheyenne obeyed. Soon enough the cries from the tepee turned to whimpers, and Red Cloud stepped out. He wordlessly signaled his men to mount and led them out of the camp at a gallop.

This episode was extraordinary on several levels. As a general rule of the era, when Indians were angry enough to fight, they were angry enough to kill en masse; fistfights or gunfights between individuals from separate tribes were rare. And the fact that Red Cloud, of all people, had left the Cheyenne man alive seemed to run against the grain of his warrior's nature. But what is almost beyond comprehension is the fact that a band of Cheyenne, known for their courage as well as for their hair-trigger tempers, did not retaliate when a small party of Sioux rode into their camp and formed a human chain around one of their lodges while, inside, their tribesman was being beaten to a bloody pulp.

The only explanation was that the man executing the rough justice was Red Cloud, whose fame by now preceded him throughout the Powder River basin and beyond.

"PRINT THE LEGEND"

L arge raiding parties consisting of scores, and in some cases hundreds, of braves like the one that fell on the Crow village had been the modus operandi for excursions since the Sioux had walked out of the Minnesota forests. But by the early 1840s a new weapon, the Hawken rifle, had been introduced to the Plains, and it was rapidly changing the military equation among the tribes. Red Cloud was one of the first to recognize, and put to use, the gun's several advantages over the cumbersome Kentucky rifle, which had been in use since the Revolutionary War. The Hawken was light enough to carry easily whether one was on a horse or on foot; it fired a larger-caliber ball; and it was accurate to 400 yards—about four times the distance of the black-powder, muzzle-loading long rifle. Also, its firing mechanism had been tempered to avoid "flashes in the pan"—which occurred when the small charge of gunpowder in the priming pan failed to pass through the touch-hole and ignite the main, propelling charge, and which was a frustrating and often deadly characteristic of the older guns.

The Hawken, equipped with a rear "set trigger" and a front "hair trigger," had been manufactured in St. Louis by the German immigrant brothers Jacob and Samuel Hawken for over twenty years, and Indian fighters and mountain men such as Kit Carson and Jim Bridger had long carried it through the Rockies. There was even a rumor that toward the end of his life Daniel Boone, who admired the gun's curved maple cheek piece, had put away his famous Kentucky rifle in favor of an early version of the Hawken. But it had taken the increased trade between white pioneers and settlers traversing the Oregon and Mormon Trails for the gun to reach the Lakota.

It occurred to Red Cloud that the Hawken's lightness and accuracy from a distance—always complemented, of course, by arrows, lances, war clubs, and tomahawks—would make smaller raiding parties of ten to twelve men as effective as the large-scale undertakings of the past. Smaller forays would be able to travel through enemy territory with greater stealth, and they would increase a village's security by allowing more braves to remain in camp to guard the women, children, and horses. It was said that from the day the Bad Faces acquired a small cache of Hawkens, Red Cloud personally led every raid in this manner. So daring were his new tactics that Lakota from other bands began to arrive in his camp seeking to ride with him.

Yet as his fame among Indians grew—Red Cloud's name was by now synonymous with success—so too did jealousy and resentment. A particular rival was a Bad Face warrior named Black Eagle. Had Red Cloud been actively looking to secure his reputation, he could not have asked for a more perfect foil than this envious brave. By all accounts Black Eagle was handsome and virile, came from a respected family, and was a renowned tracker and hunter who had acquired numerous scalps and counted many coups. His insides must have twisted when he saw the son of an alcoholic Brule take what he considered his own natural place atop the Oglala pecking order. But Black Eagle bided his time and concealed his intentions until one day he asked to join a small party Red Cloud had personally chosen to lead into the Rocky Mountains on a horse raid against the Shoshones. Red Cloud, unaware of Black Eagle's simmering resentment, agreed.

The Lakota, so at home on the prairie, had many superstitions about the dark, ominous mountains that formed its western frontier, and it was highly uncomfortable journeying through them. Even the Black Hills were usually entered only for religious and purifying ceremonies, and when bands staked lodges near the sacred *Paha Sapa* they made certain to keep a respectful distance from the foreboding slopes. One of their favorite camping spots was on the indented oval of red sandstone shale that still circles the Black Hills' core. According to Indian lore, this slightly indented rock formation was the result of ancient races between huge, fierce Thunderbirds and giant mammals, from whose combined weight the track had sunk, while the land in the middle burst into flames out of which the mountains rose.

Now Red Cloud proposed to go into an even higher mountain range, where an expedition would confront not only attacks by human enemies like the Shoshones but also, perhaps, gargantuan mythical animals and spontaneous combustion. Thus it may have been no surprise to Red Cloud when, about 100 miles into the Bighorn range, one of his trusted lieutenants told him that Black Eagle was fomenting mutiny. Black Eagle grumbled and complained to the other braves that their party was lost and in effect begging to be ambushed. He was agitating for an immediate return to their village, knowing full well that in the Lakota scheme of honor such a retreat would have humiliated Red Cloud.

That night Red Cloud approached his eleven other raiders one by one to determine whom he could trust. When he discovered that Black Eagle had managed to convince only three braves, he gathered his seven loyal tribesmen and concocted a plan. The next morning he invited the entire group to accompany him to the top of a nearby peak, the tallest in the area, for the ostensible purpose of finding their bearings. When they finished the ascent Red Cloud's loyalists formed a ring around Black Eagle and the three other mutineers. Red Cloud then strode into the circle. He pointed to the east, turned to Black Eagle, and said, "Do you see that high blue ridge away yonder? At the foot of that mountain is our village. There is where the women are. Go. You cannot get lost. You can go back over the same trail you came. There is lots of game. Get some of your party to kill it for you. And when there is another war party to go out, you had better stay at home and send your women." Red Cloud had thrown down the most insulting gauntlet a Sioux could conceive. Black Eagle said nothing. He was outnumbered, and he knew it. He left with his followers.

The raid against the Shoshones was a wild success. The eight remaining Bad Faces captured sixty horses and Red Cloud added a Shoshone scalp to his growing collection. As the party wound out of the Rockies they also killed enough elk and deer to feed the entire camp. Not even a mountain lion's attack on one of their packhorses piled high with venison could dim their spirits. A day out of the Bad Face camp an outrider galloped up to them. It was a relieved Big Spider, who said Black Eagle was still spreading rumors: that Red Cloud was lost in the mountains, that he had been ambushed, that he had probably been killed. Red Cloud's return a day later must have been triumphant, but in his memoirs he records only that on entering the camp he distributed the horses and meat and ordered a giant feast prepared. Oddly, Red Cloud took no punitive action against the traitorous Black Eagle, who, given the outcome of the raid, might have been expected to gather his followers and leave the Bad Face camp to start his own band as Bull Bear had done. Perhaps Red Cloud was content to let Black Eagle stew in his own humiliation; or it may have been that Black Eagle's influential family intervened. In any case, the fact that Black Eagle suffered no consequences indicates that he and Red Cloud were more or less equal in social stature. And soon thereafter, Black Eagle again attempted to alter the equilibrium.

The new attempt occurred during a hiatus in Red Cloud's horse theft. The Bad Faces had staked lodges on a broad plateau in southeastern Wyoming among a cluster of rust-colored hills known as the Rawhide Buttes. Over millennia the North Platte had cut a narrow, winding channel through these granite knobs, forming sheer rock walls rising to 100 feet on both banks. At a bend in the river a small valley angled gently from these cliffs, its carpet of wild bluegrass sprinkled with patches of fireweed, sticky geranium, and alpine forget-me-not. It was late summer, game was plentiful, songbirds nested in the saltbush, and soft warm breezes caressed the valley. Red Cloud was understandably loath to stir himself to raid and fight, although he eagerly joined hunting parties riding out for buffalo, elk, and deer. Because of his absence from horse raids, however, the gifts of stolen mustangs he habitually spread around the village had fallen off precipitously. Perhaps valuing this booty more than their pleasant surroundings, his tribesmen had begun to complain.

Black Eagle sensed an opportunity. Determined to emulate Red Cloud's new, targeted raiding tactics, he recruited eight volunteers to join him and a medicine man priest (as opposed to a medicine man doctor) on an expedition into Crow territory. The priest, however, warned him that the number ten was a bad omen, and Black Eagle spent several days trying to persuade Red Cloud's old friend White Horse—the brave who had scalped the Blackfoot alive—to join him. White Horse rejected the offers until one night Red Cloud encouraged him to go along as a spy. White Horse rode out with Black Eagle's expedition the next morning.

Several weeks passed before Black Eagle's straggling braves were spotted returning through the sun-slant of a late September afternoon. Five were mounted and five were on foot. One was missing. That night they all told a story of having been ambushed by a large war party of Crows, who had killed a Bad Face brave named Red Deer during, they said, a heroic standoff. The Crows had then stolen their horses. Although the raiders were perfunctorily celebrated for their narrow escape, something in their narrative did not ring true. It was as if schoolchildren were reciting a lesson by rote.

Late that night White Horse visited Red Cloud's lodge and over a pipe related the true story. There was no large mass of Crows, he said; there had been just a small hunting party, which had stumbled on their encampment at night. The Oglalas had stupidly boxed themselves into a narrow gorge ringed by thick growths of bur oak, and the sentries Black Eagle had posted to guard the horses at the mouth of the gorge were either incompetent or asleep. In the mad chase to recover the stolen animals—with everyone on foot except White Horse, who had slept next to his hobbled horse a little apart from the others—someone from their own contingent, no one was certain who, had in the dark mistaken Red Deer for a Crow and shot him dead. His face had been mutilated, and Black Eagle himself was about to take Red Deer's scalp before someone recognized that the body was wearing Sioux moccasins. They entombed Red Deer in the crook of a white spruce tree, and all except White Horse,

who still had his pony, took turns riding home on four mustangs that belonged to Crow scouts who had picketed their animals unwisely.

Red Cloud took in this information almost wordlessly, speaking only
to assure a shaken White Horse that he was not to blame for Red Deer's
death. The next day, as Red Cloud circled through the camp, rumors were
already spreading that there was something off about the tale Black Eagle
and his party had told. Red Cloud heard whispers, some alleging abject
cowardice, that were even more sordid than the truth. Yet instead of confronting Black Eagle and exposing him as a fraud and a liar, Red Cloud
found it wiser to let people's imagination do the job for him. White Horse
had also informed him that it was the priest who had concocted the cover
story, but now the medicine man was having second thoughts about continuing the lie. Red Cloud quietly pulled the priest aside. What passed
between them remains unknown, yet from then on the priest not only said
no more about the episode but was seen riding through camp on one of
Red Cloud's finest horses.

This was just another example of how the young man's political savvy
was keeping pace with his image as a warrior. More than 100 years later
the Hollywood director John Ford, famous for his panoramic Westerns,
articulated a similar strategy for demeaning a rival in his film *The Man
Who Shot Liberty Valance:* "When the legend becomes fact, print the legend." For Red Cloud, a variation of this maxim would prove a valuable
learning tool on his way to acquiring political power. For Black Eagle, it
was the end of his hopes of ever becoming a Head Man.

Although few whites on the continent were aware of it, a seminal moment
in the chronology of the American West occurred on the High Plains
sometime in the early 1840s. Red Cloud was either twenty or twenty-
one. (The Indians were not sticklers for dates; credible historical sources
place the event sometime during the winter of 1841–42.) The Bad Faces
had staked winter lodges on the Laramie plain along Chugwater Creek,
and camping not far off was Old Smoke's antagonist Bull Bear and his
Kiyuska. Since their contentious split, Bull Bear's pugnacious reputation
had attracted many warriors—more than were drawn to any other band—
and a council of Oglala elders had selected him as a sort of Head Man for

the entire tribe. The electors respected Old Smoke. In his youth he had
been hard as bur oak. But they were hesitant to bestow such an honor,
and the challenges that came with it, on a man who was now in his sixties
and had grown corpulent and jovial. There was also an ugly memory to
consider.

Some years back white traders near Fort Laramie had begun to treat
Old Smoke as the "chief" of the Oglalas. This nettled Bull Bear, who had
ridden up to Old Smoke's tepee in the Bad Face camp and challenged
him to a fight. When Old Smoke failed to come out of his lodge and
meet him, Bull Bear slit the throat of the "chief's" favorite horse. None of
this sat well with Red Cloud. But given Sioux mores and his own lack of
stature at the time, there was little he could do about it. Undoubtedly the
elders took this into account when they named Bull Bear as their leader.

Now, before hunkering down for that winter of 1841–42, Red Cloud
had led a small party on one last autumn raid into Ute country in present-
day Utah and western Colorado. On his return to Chugwater—leading
a string of stolen ponies, and with the requisite Ute scalp affixed to his
lance—he learned that in his absence a Bad Face brave had run off with
a *Kiyuska* girl, and the girl's father, an ally of Bull Bear's, was demanding
retribution from the Bad Faces. Red Cloud must have thought this rich.
"Stealing" a woman was a rather mundane fact of life among the Lakota—
particularly if the woman was not averse to being "stolen," as seemed to
be the case here—and the blustery, bellowing Bull Bear was notorious
for taking any young maiden that he fancied, with no thought of recom-
pense. Nevertheless, the insolent and more numerous *Kiyuska* were not in
the habit of letting pass what they perceived as an insult, and Bull Bear
was certain to view any transgression, however minor, as an attack on his
primacy. Red Cloud was told that Bull Bear was personally plotting a
showdown.

In theory, the same Lakota council of elders who had chosen Bull
Bear as Head Man would rule on disputes such as this. The *Kiyuska*
leader, however, had demonstrated that he was not a man to stand on
ceremony. Each band's warrior class was in effect the essence of its Head
Man's authority, and Bull Bear had formed blood ties to numerous Oglala
braves since his split with Old Smoke. Over time he had also developed a

dangerous taste for the white man's alcohol, which occasioned his band's frequent stopovers at the Fort Laramie trading post. Bull Bear's well-known affinity is probably the reason white whiskey traders passed near the *Kiyuska* lodges a few days after Red Cloud's return from the Ute raid. This accelerated the showdown. Yet again the wheel of fortune was oiled by whiskey.

After draining several jugs of *mini wakan,* Bull Bear and his braves rode to the Bad Face camp. The first person they encountered was the father of the brave who had run off with the *Kiyuska* girl. The circumstances are unclear, but the man may have gone out to meet Bull Bear specifically to make amends for his son's transgression. Bull Bear shot him dead. At the report of the rifle, a dozen Bad Faces, including Red Cloud, poured from the warriors' lodge. Rifle volleys and arrows were exchanged, and one shot grazed Bull Bear's leg, knocking him from his saddle. As he sat dazed on the ground, half drunk, blood seeping from his thigh, Red Cloud rushed to him. He shouted, "You are the cause of this," hefted a rifle, and put a bullet in his brain.

Bull Bear died instantly. His death was an unenviable example and an awful warning. And though it was generally felt that he had improved the world by taking leave of it, after the gun smoke cleared the Oglala elders once again found themselves trying to maintain a fragile peace between the Bad Faces and *Kiyuska.* In the end the fact that the *Kiyuska* remained the more numerous tribe swung the selection, and the council elected Bull Bear's son, who was also named Bull Bear but now took the name Whirl-wind, to succeed his father as Head Man.

It was a watershed in Sioux history. Though Whirlwind may have been the titular Head Man, it was evident to all that Red Cloud, barely out of his teens, had become the de facto warrior chief of the Oglala tribe—and, by extension, of the Western Sioux nation.

Part II

THE INVASION

Bring me men to match my mountains
Bring me men to match my plains
Men with empires in their purpose
And new eras in their brains.

—Sam Walter Foss, *The Coming American*

OLD GABE

A charcoal-hued pictograph from the Lakota Winter Count of 1851 is roughly interpreted as meaning "The Big Issue." This translation surely had more to do with the gifts spread among the Indians at the Horse Creek Council than with the actual treaty signed. Neither side would pay much heed to that. The Army tried to use the pact as a carrot, though with so few troops stationed west of the Missouri its stick was weak and hollow. The Indians, equally cynical, leveraged it to cadge as many more "presents" as possible, including a shipment of cattle, the "spotted buffalo," delivered as part of the government's promised annuity. A few Indians developed a taste for the white man's beef, although most still preferred what they considered the real thing. In reality, both sides recognized the pantomime, as did the United States Congress, which voted soon after to reduce annuity payments from fifty to ten years, with a murky codicil stipulating that, at the discretion of the president, the annuity deliveries could be extended if the tribes behaved.

In his autobiography Red Cloud does not reveal his thoughts as he, Old Smoke, and the Bad Faces rode north from Horse Creek through the lowering haze of that September morning in 1851. Despite the

proscriptions in the Horse Creek Treaty, Red Cloud soon enough returned to the lifestyle of all Western Sioux braves intent on earning
glory—hunting buffalo, stealing horses, counting coup, warring on other
tribes. One suspects that thereafter he gave the grand assembly little more
than a passing thought except, perhaps, as a reminder of the plentiful
Hawkens and deadly cannons the white soldiers possessed. With his keen
eye for weapons, he also surely noticed that a few of the American officers
wore a new type of weapon strapped to their legs, a revolver that fired six
times without having to be reloaded. Red Cloud possessed forethought
unusual in an Indian, and the possibility must have crossed his mind that
one day he might have to look down the barrels of those guns.

At the same moment another man, a white man whose actions were
more germane to the treaty council, also rode off from Horse Creek. He
had no idea that his life was to become intertwined with Red Cloud's and
with the brutal Indian wars destined to reshape the American landscape.
This was the mountain man Jim Bridger. It is difficult to fathom why,
today, Bridger's adventures and accomplishments have faded from our
national consciousness. For a great portion of the nineteenth century his
name was synonymous with the opening of the West—thanks in no small
part to a semiaquatic rodent whose pelt, when blocked into a hat, became
a *de rigueur* clothing accessory in European courts, theaters, and gentle-
men's clubs.

Through much of the eighteenth and nineteenth centuries the beaver was
to European fashion what bread and circuses were to the Roman mob. The
wool felt of *Castor canadensis* so dominated European markets for men's
hats that between 1700 and 1770 English milliners exported over 21 million of these hats to the Continent alone. By 1820 that figure had nearly
doubled; the Old World species of the animal had been hunted close to
extinction, and its North American cousin, at least east of the Mississippi,
had fared little better. Stepping into this commercial vacuum were the
many fur companies of the American West.

Semiaquatic beavers prefer to build their dens, called "lodges," in
climates made cold either by latitude or by elevation. The New World
had plenty of each type, and it is estimated that in the 1600s as many as

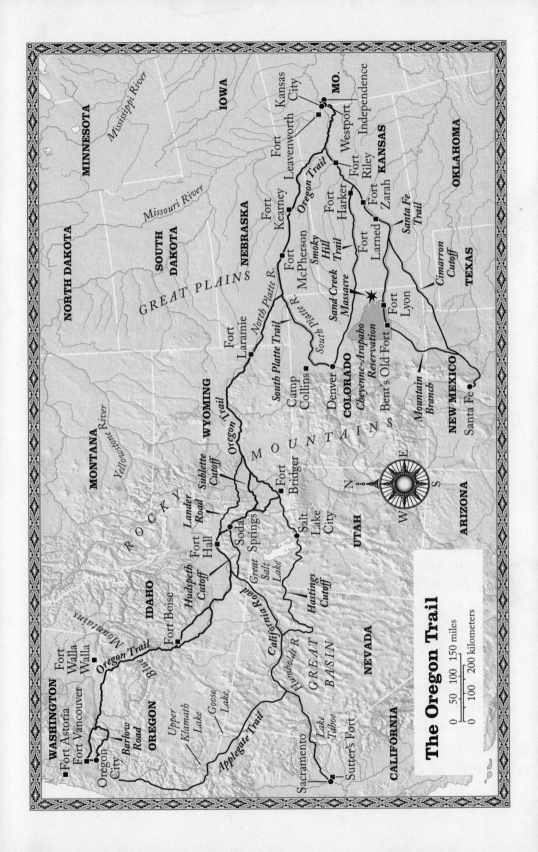

The Oregon Trail

400 million beavers populated the continent, with a beaver dam every half mile on every stream, in every watershed, in North America. And though the beaver market thrived along the continent's rocky spine from Vancouver to Taos, the western trapping trade was initially centered more or less along the river corridors to the east and south of the Black Hills—close enough to the American Fur Company's outposts on the Missouri for Indians to exchange their furs for weapons, beads, and blankets. With adult beavers weighing up to forty pounds and St. Louis newspapers advertising pelts at $8 a pound—$154 in current, inflation-adjusted dollars—it was only a matter of time before the white man jumped into the game. So while on the other side of the continent the American invasion of Ontario was turning into a disaster, in 1812 the Canadian Robert Stuart, a scout for John Jacob Astor's Pacific Fur Company, blazed what would come to be known as the Oregon Trail. Stuart, at the head of a party of trappers, forged a path from Fort Astoria on Oregon's Pacific coast through the Rocky Mountains and into southeastern Wyoming by way of the South Pass carved by the Sweetwater and the Platte.

Trapping in this same area a decade later, the French-Canadian Jacques La Ramée happened on a tributary of the North Platte so packed with beaver that it was said you could walk on their backs from one bank to the other without getting your boots wet. Not too much more is known about La Ramée, who was reportedly killed by Indians on the small river that was to posthumously bear the American version of his name, Laramie. (As do a city, a county, and six more geographic features in the present state of Wyoming: no small accomplishment for such a ghostly figure.) But the sleek pelts La Ramée and a few others like him shipped back to St. Louis inspired an industry led by a small band of hard, restless men willing to risk their lives beyond the fringe of civilization.

By 1824 brawling, bearded, buckskin-clad trappers had explored beyond *Paha Sapa*, across the Powder River Country, up into the Rockies, and over great tracts of deserts and alkali flats all the way to the Pacific. They spread through the ranges singly, in twos and threes, and in small brigades either as "free trappers" or as contract men tied to the established outfits or the new Rocky Mountain Fur Company. In their search for fresh fur fields they combed distant, isolated streams and river gorges, "rough and violent, making repeated falls, and rushing down long and furious rapids." Their payoff was beaver dams so thick "that one would back water to the falls above it for ten miles." Among them was a twenty-year-old Virginian named James Felix Bridger.

A young America craved heroes, and homegrown adventurers had fired the public imagination since the republic's inception. Lewis and Clark, the Bostonian circumnavigator Robert Gray, Zebulon Pike, and Daniel Boone were feted as demigods in their own lifetimes. Davy Crockett and Kit Carson were destined to join them. Of all these pioneers, however, none loomed larger than Bridger, who, ironically, felt a deep ambivalence toward the white civilization encroaching on the Indians. This sensitivity set him apart from his contemporaries. He would kill as ruthlessly as any other, but he also had a conscience that once prompted a warrant for his arrest on charges of consorting with and supplying arms to hostile tribes.

Bridger was born in 1804, the eldest son of a surveyor from Richmond who moved his wife and three children from Virginia to St. Louis two years before the British burned the nation's capital. The mean, rough river town took its toll; by Bridger's fourteenth birthday his parents and siblings were dead. He found work as a blacksmith's apprentice, and learned to handle guns, horses, and river craft well enough to be accepted two years later on a keelboat expedition seeking the source of the Missouri. Bridger was tall and spare at six feet, two inches, and his most striking features were his keen gray eyes set over cheekbones that seemed sharp enough to cut falling silk. He wore his mop of long brown hair, thick as otter fur, parted in the middle, and became known throughout his life for a kind, gentle disposition. His first taste of Indian fighting occurred on that keelboat journey, when his outfit was attacked on separate occasions by Arikara and Blackfeet. All told, eighteen whites were killed. The Holy Roller trapper Jedediah Smith, impressed by Bridger's poise, nicknamed him "Old Gabe" after the Archangel Gabriel—perhaps envisioning the lanky teenager standing tall atop the 7,242-foot Harney Peak, the Black Hills' highest summit, blasting his trumpet to signify the end of time, or at least the Indians' time. The nickname stuck for the rest of Bridger's life.

Afterward Bridger—an autodidact who spoke passable French, Spanish, and close to a dozen Indian tongues—joined two more river expeditions before his wanderlust took him into the mountains, where he hunted and trapped on both sides of the Continental Divide. In 1824, at the age of twenty, he led a small party up the Bear River in northern Utah to the lifeless shores of a briny body of water. Bridger thought he had reached a bay of the Pacific Ocean. Further surveillance determined that it had no outlet. He and his men had "discovered" the Great Salt Lake. Over the next three decades Bridger ranged from the Wasatch to the Yellowstone tracking beaver, otter, and grizzly. It was a prodigal, if perilous, lifestyle. In lean times he grubbed for roots and wild rosebuds and pricked the ears of his pack mules in order to drink their blood. When the beaver harvest was fat he awaited the caravans rolling in from St. Louis to the annual mountain man rendezvous, commonly held around Independence Day. There he would dance fandangos and get "womaned" while trading great packs of beaver pelts for rifles, gunpowder, and real whiskey, as opposed to the near-poison palmed off on the Indians.

In the 1830s one of the earliest congregations of missionaries trekking west encountered one of these rendezvous on the wild Wind River. A clergyman's horrified wife provided a vivid snapshot of the "scandalous" incident. "Captain Bridger's Company comes in about ten o'clock with drums and firing—an apology for a scalp dance," she wrote. "Fifteen or twenty Mountain Men and Indians come to our tent with drumming, firing, and dancing. I should say they looked like emissaries of the devil, worshipping their own master. They had the scalp of a Blackfoot Indian, which they carried for a color, all rejoicing in the fate."

By this time Bridger was a legend even among the larger-than-life "French Indians" roaming the High Country. His bravery was unquestioned, and he was said to be the best shot, the savviest scout, the most formidable horseman, and, though functionally illiterate, the ablest interpreter in the Rockies. He took two arrows in the back in a fight with Blackfeet in 1832; his companions could extricate only one. Three years later, at a rendezvous on the Green River, a passing surgeon was enlisted to remove the other. The operation, witnessed by a Presbyterian missionary, illustrates the chilling realities of life on the frontier. Bridger fortified himself with several large swigs of raw alcohol before the doctor "extracted an iron arrow, three inches long, from the back of Capt. Bridger," wrote the Reverend Samuel Parker. "It was a difficult operation, because the arrow was hooked at the point by striking a large bone, and cartilaginous substance had grown around it." Two years later the American landscape artist Alfred J. Miller crossed paths with Bridger at the 1837 rendezvous and captured him in a watercolor. Bridger posed in a full suit of steel armor that had been presented to him by a Scottish hunter for whom he had once served as a guide.

Along the way "Old Gabe" formed, broke up, and re-formed partnerships and trapping companies with dozens of fellow mountain men, including Carson, "Broken Hand" Fitzpatrick, William Sublette, and the Irishman Robert Campbell, the last two the future cofounders of what would become Fort Laramie. Unlike the well-educated Fitzpatrick, most of these rough sojourners had little, if any, formal schooling, so their commercial success is all the more fascinating. Survival, however, required that their fighting ability far outweigh their business acumen. On one notable occasion a Ute raiding party made off with some of Bridger's and Fitzpatrick's mounts. For nearly a week the two led a party of trappers in pursuit through the rugged Uinta Mountains. When they finally came on the Indian camp, Fitzpatrick fronted a charge while Bridger sneaked through a thicket of willow and mountain juniper to flank the village. He successfully stole back their own horses as well as forty Indian ponies. Meanwhile Fitzpatrick and his men took six Ute scalps and escaped.

Despite these occasional skirmishes, however, in most cases the trappers adopted a live-and-let-live philosophy regarding the Indians— Bridger's paternal affection for the Shoshones at the Horse Creek Council is a prime example. They were also generally free of the racism that infected the flatlands, and many went native themselves in all but name, taking squaw wives and siring mixed-race families. Bridger was known to anger white traders by warning Indians away from blankets that he suspected were infected with smallpox, and his first wife, Cora, was the daughter of a Flathead chief. She bore him three children, but died in childbirth delivering their third, a daughter named Josephine. A year later his eldest daughter, Mary Ann, was captured and killed by a raiding party of Nez Percé. Even this did not affect his goodwill toward the tribes, which he sensed were destined to be exploited, if not exterminated, by his own countrymen.

Toward the late 1830s, after a 150-year heyday, the beaver trade collapsed when cheap silk imported by the British East India Company replaced beaver felt as the European hat material of choice. In 1840 the mountain men held their sixteenth and final rendezvous before disappearing into the gloaming corners of the West. It was a memorable affair. According to the well-traveled Father De Smet, when the fur traders convened near the Green River on June 30, 300 Shoshone warriors arrived at full gallop, "hideously painted, armed with their clubs, and covered all over with feathers, pearls, wolves' tails, teeth and claws of animals. Those who had wounds, and those who had killed the enemies of their tribe, displayed their scars ostentatiously and waved the scalps they had taken on the ends of poles. After riding a few times around the camp, uttering at intervals shouts of joy, they dismounted and all came to shake hands with the whites in sign of friendship."

And to bid one another farewell. What had once been a regiment of 3,000 trappers scouring the pine-bearded Rocky Mountain peaks dwindled to a few hundred forlorn wanderers, unfit for any other way of life, but still hoping to scrape out an existence above the clouds. Like Campbell and Sublette, however, Bridger had foreseen that the bottom would fall out of the beaver market and had hedged his bet by building his own, smaller stockade far to the west of Fort Laramie, on Blacks Fork of the Green River, near the present-day Utah border. It was the only river crossing for almost 400 miles, and he anticipated a surge of emigrants when he wrote that the rough picket fort "promises fairly" to become a strategic ford on the Oregon and California Trails. He had wagered well. Eventually even a Pony Express station was maintained at Fort Bridger.

Bridger was a mostly absentee owner of his river keep, leaving maintenance and day-to-day operations to a Spanish partner while he hired out as a scout on scientific, military, and commercial expeditions to Oregon, California, and present-day Mexico. In 1848 he was remarried, this time to a Ute woman, who also died in childbirth after giving him another daughter, Virginia. Two years later he took his third and final wife, the daughter of the Shoshone chief whom he would escort under the flag of truce to the Horse Creek Treaty Council. A year before that assembly, however, an Army topographical engineer, Captain Howard Stansbury, visited him at Fort Bridger. Stansbury was seeking a more direct route to Utah from the Missouri, and he asked for Bridger's help. The leathery mountain man is reported to have yanked a burned stick from his cooking fire and scraped it along a slab of slate, drawing a trail of nearly 1,000 miles that climbed and descended the Rockies and crossed four major rivers and numerous creeks before finally skirting the southern terminus of the Black Hills. The next morning he packed his mules and led Stansbury along this trace. The captain mapped the route with geodetic and astronomical equipment, and the Union Pacific Railroad was soon to follow the same line, which led through what is still called Bridger's Pass, bisecting the Continental Divide.

The orphaned teenager who had once answered a newspaper advertisement for keelboat hands had grown into a mountain man "with one third of the continent imprinted on his brain." The breadth and depth of his knowledge about the territory and its tribes had not gone unnoticed by the Army, and Stansbury's successful railroad survey reinforced Bridger's reputation as a good fellow to have along in a tight spot. Someone in the federal government's bureaucracy surely made a mental note that this was a fellow who might be of future service to the United States. It did not hurt that for all his affection for Indians, Bridger had never really cared much for the Sioux.

THE GLORY ROAD

At the same time that trappers roamed the High Country amassing and losing small fortunes, the Lakota were spilling farther and farther west into the country bordering the Rockies. This territorial expansion naturally escalated their deadly tangles with the mountain tribes and, parenthetically, foreshadowed a subtle shift in their dynamics with the whites. To this point in Sioux history, both in Minnesota and on the High Plains, their only real contact with the white race had been with traders considered too few and inconsequential to be of concern. But the mountain men had formed ties, in many cases blood ties, with the Shoshones, Nez Percé, and Crows, and nearly always took their side in bloody skirmishes with the Plains Indians. The Western Sioux suffered considerable losses from the guns of the sharpshooting trappers, and some Lakota advocated driving all whites—trappers and traders alike—from the Powder River Country.

But the majority of the bands had become too dependent on the wares on offer at places like Campbell's and Sublette's market post, particularly the addictive goods: coffee, tobacco plugs, and another form of cheap, laudanum-laced wheat liquor called Taos Lightning. They had begun to import these from New Mexico via the Santa Fe Trail, the west's first, thin ribbon of commerce, made famous by Kit Carson. Indians who were friendly with the traders, including Old Smoke's and Red Cloud's Bad Faces, at first defended them. They argued that to place traders on the same level as the trappers was akin to, say, treating a Cheyenne like a Pawnee. Even the collapse of the beaver market seemed a good omen, as it meant fewer of the hairy white men standing between them and their mountain enemies. When Lakota began dropping dead from laudanum overdoses, however, antiwhite rumblings intensified.

More ominous was the depletion of the vast northern buffalo herds that had once blanketed the Plains from the Upper Arkansas to the Missouri Breaks. Early American explorers reported riding from sunup to sundown through a single grazing drove, and one frontiersman spotted a herd that, he estimated, measured seventy by thirty miles. Though still numbering upward of 25 million to 30 million, nearly double the 17 million Americans counted in the 1840 U.S. census, the animals had begun to recede into smaller and smaller pockets. The decline was still imperceptible to most whites, but the Indians felt it, and feared it—although they do not seem to have considered that, because of their own growing dependence on the white man's trade, especially his alcohol, they were complicit.

As early as 1832 the peripatetic western painter George Catlin reported passing through Fort Pierre on the Upper Missouri and watching a St. Louis keelboat merchant off-load a hull full of whiskey and announce that he would take salted buffalo tongues in kind. The Indians—Catlin does not name their tribe, but given the location they were probably a band of Sioux—formed a hunting party, slaughtered 1,500 buffalo, and sliced out their tongues in a remarkable day's work. So great was their thirst, however, that they left the meat and skins littering the prairie for the wolves to pick over. Before they became enmeshed in the Americans' commerce, such mass killings would have been unthinkable.

In 1841 the "Missouri Frenchman" Pierre Chouteau of the St. Louis Missouri Fur Company purchased Fort William from the mountain men Campbell and Sublette, renamed it Fort John, and expanded the old post. A fifteen-foot adobe wall was constructed around the half-acre courtyard, and living quarters, warehouses, and a crude blacksmith's shop were added.

Two cannon towers, called bastions, were positioned on opposite corners of the stockade, and a set of large double gates lent the structure an air of menace. All this would serve as a template for dozens of Hollywood directors. In that same year the Bidwell-Bartleson party became the first wagon train to push off from what would soon become the eastern anchor of the Oregon Trail in Independence, Missouri, the portal of American westward expansion built on a site that the angel Moroni informed Joseph Smith had once been the Garden of Eden. The Bidwell-Bartleson caravan made for California, and it was guided by Thomas Fitzpatrick, who stopped at Fort John to reprovision. It had a mere eighty travelers, including the wandering Jesuit Father De Smet. Though it may have been a small affair, its importance was not.

By the time Chouteau sold the fort to the government eight years later, the United States was a changed country, its domain having increased by 66 percent. Two decades earlier, with the Regular Army capped at 6,000 men, the future president Colonel Zachary Taylor had in essence declared the end of war on the North American continent—"The ax, pick, saw, and trowel has become more the implement of the American soldier than the cannon, musket, or sword." That was before the annexation of Texas in 1845, the negotiations with Great Britain a year later that set the present-day U.S.-Canadian border at the forty-ninth parallel, and Mexico's ceding of Alta California and most of the Southwest in the Treaty of Guadalupe Hidalgo—a concession made possible in large part when Taylor (now a general) routed Generalísimo Santa Anna's army at the Battle of Buena Vista.

That treaty, which cleaved Mexico nearly in half and added 1.2 million square miles of new land to the United States, was signed just before John Sutter lifted several flakes of gold from the mountain stream over which he was constructing a sawmill. America's victory in its first war of foreign intervention meant that no longer would the nation's vast, barren midsection need to serve as a convenient buffer—a perpetual wilderness designated as the "Permanent Indian Frontier"—to hold off foreign powers such as Russia, Great Britain, or Mexico; and settlers from the East and miners from the West began to fill the Great Plains and the intermountain West. The void on the nation's map was taking shape. Indians, meanwhile, sensed a gradual invasion of their territory that gave no indication of ebbing.

What had begun as a trickle turned into a wave of homesteaders bound for Oregon's lush Willamette River Valley; miners bound for the gold fields of California; and, after the murder of Joseph Smith, Mormons bound for the sweeping vistas that wound down into the Salt Lake country. When Smith's successor Brigham Young decided to flee west with his flock, the first Mormon wagon train moved up the Platte in the spring of 1847 on the parallel Mormon Trail, a route that merged with the Oregon Trail at Fort John before crossing the mountains. By late summer of that year the broad, harsh Salt Lake Valley was already being irrigated, fenced, and farmed despite the fact that the land was still technically, if precariously, a part of Mexico. The next season three more Mormon trains of nearly 800 wagons, with Young himself in the van of the slow procession, transported 2,400 Latter-day Saints from Nebraska to Utah.

The Lakota, in particular the Oglalas, were initially helpless in the face of this onslaught. Red Cloud's killing of Bull Bear had divided the tribe physically as well as emotionally, and those who were now called the "Bear People" had drifted southeast to Nebraska to hunt with the Southern Cheyenne while the "Smoke People" generally staked camps farther north on the Clear Fork of the Powder, and often as far east as the White. When bands from either faction made the trek to what they had known as Fort William, they were shocked by its transformation. A company of the 6th U.S. Infantry consisting of about fifty officers and enlisted men was now permanently bivouacked at Campbell's and Sublette's once-sleepy trading post. Before the Indians' eyes Fort Laramie had become the Bluecoats' main command and logistics center in the West, an oasis within which travelers could resupply, find decent medical care, purchase fresh horses, and hire scouts to guide them over the Rockies. When the soldiers—"Walk a Heaps," to the Lakota—were not drilling or taking target practice, they enlarged the fort's kitchens, warehouses, and corrals; added enlisted men's and officers' quarters; and even constructed a schoolhouse and a wooden bridge spanning the Laramie River, a mud wallow for most of the year but an unfordable torrent of mountain melt in the spring. From 1849 to 1851 more than 20,000 wagons trailing over 140,000 head of livestock passed through Fort Laramie, an "Ellis Island of the West" in the center of Lakota land. The Indians seethed.

To the Mormons and homesteaders, who had dubbed the Oregon Trail the "Glory Road," the route may have been a godsend: a pathway across the High Plains that led to the promised land. But to the Indians it was a trail rife with pestilence. They believed that these insolent *Meneaska* were infecting their country not only spiritually, but also—by intention—with actual, fatal diseases. The Indians' anger and bloodshed spiked, and emigrants' journals from the era are filled with entries describing all manner of "provocations," from stolen oxen to gruesome killings. Even intertribal fights occasionally spilled over. On May 18, 1849, a newspaper, the *St. Louis Republican,* printed a letter from a gold miner whose wagon train had been intercepted by a small band of Pawnee fleeing a larger party of Sioux. The Pawnee begged for sanctuary. The whites refused and stood by, watching as the Sioux killed and scalped every Pawnee save one squaw and her young son.

The sullen "savages," another emigrant wrote, were now "foes on every hand, subtle as the devil himself." Sioux braves lurked in butte breaks and amid the papery leaves of thick stands of cottonwoods and gambel oaks, from which they rode down on small parties unlucky enough to have been separated from the main wagon train. At night they sneaked into white camps to drive off horses and cows and steal metal cookware. They were constantly on the lookout for any pioneer too careless with his weapon. Should he lay his rifle down for even a moment to hitch his oxen team, or to fill his water barrel from a stream, the rifle would be gone, and perhaps him with it if no one stood lookout. And so ended the days of informal tolls of sugar and coffee in exchange for unmolested passage across the prairie.

Though Red Cloud never admitted making any of these early raids on the emigrant trains—and historians generally take him at his word—tension was nearing the breaking point. Oddly, the last people to notice this were the soldiers deployed to Fort Laramie, who remained rather oblivious of the Indians' growing rancor. The enlisted men's biggest complaint was the mind-numbing monotony of their daily routines such as putting up hay and chopping firewood in blowtorch summer winds, and cutting tons of ice blocks from the North Platte and Laramie and hauling them to the post's icehouse through the raw Plains winter. The only diversion was dropping by the sutler's store, which was run by former trappers, in hopes of meeting civilians laying in provisions and bearing news from the East. A highlight was the arrival of a mountain man wintering over before finding work as a scout in the spring. To sit by a roaring fire, whiskey jar in hand, and listen to the likes of Jim Bridger or Tom Fitzpatrick spin yarns of taking down an angry grizzly or escaping a Nez Percé ambush was tantamount, on the frontier, to attending a performance at the Royal Albert Hall by the "Swedish nightingale," Jenny Lind. The adventure stories of derring-do over high passes, through deep canyons, and across sere deserts might as well have been tales from another planet to the Bluecoats, almost all of them easterners and many of them European-born. (There was a distinct whiff of the peat bog among the enlistees; company rosters were larded with names such as McQuiery, Condon, Doyle, Grady, and Haggerty.)

But for the most part deployment to the fort was a monotonous, back-breaking grind, and the soldiers would do almost anything to have their names dropped from the daily rolls of wood-chopping and ice-cutting: "fatigue work" assigned by the sergeants. This included volunteering for field service, which meant accompanying Army freight and mail wagons across the prairie. In the early days of Fort Laramie the notion of an Indian attack on a well-armed Army unit, no matter how small, seemed almost absurd. Soon enough, however, the same soldiers who had once angled for escort duties would yearn for the carefree days of wielding axes and ice cutters. They would also have their own war stories to swap with the likes of "Broken Hand" and "Old Gabe."

PRETTY OWL AND PINE LEAF

The four pillars of Sioux leadership—acknowledged by the tribe to this day—are bravery, fortitude, generosity, and wisdom. Time and again Red Cloud exhibited each. Yet, traditionally, the Lakota also considered lesser factors when weighing the attributes of an aspiring Head Man. One was the patronage of important religious medicine men. Red Cloud was a crafty enough politician to recognize this, and his gifts of horses to the shamans and vision diviners as well as the lavish piles of meat his hunting forays provided to the entire band—with holy men usually receiving the choicest cuts—were more than enough to sway ecumenical opinion.

The second factor was a trickier business. It involved paternal lineage and prestige, specifically the membership of a man's father in important fraternal societies. In *The Sioux,* Hassrick notes Red Cloud's "unexcelled" war record, "unparalleled" brilliance as a leader, and unequalled diplomatic "finesse," only to conclude, trenchantly, that in spite of these qualities, Red Cloud "was never able to command the kind of reverence among the Sioux which someone from an important family might have received." Among the Oglalas, even Red Cloud's strong maternal bloodline could not completely erase the memory of his alcoholic Brule father.

He would always lack the cachet of a Head Man like Whirlwind, son of Bull Bear.

A stoic, Red Cloud faced and accepted this prejudice while doing his best to overcome it. He joined numerous warrior societies, and went out of his way to aid the weak, the poor, and the old among his band in particular and the tribe in general. Around 1850, as he turned twenty-nine, he also calculated the advantage of marrying into the right family in order to seal power alliances, even if it meant abandoning his one true love—to her tragedy and his horror.

A Sioux man could take as many wives as he could afford—the bride price, a kind of reverse dowry, always involved the transfer of property, usually horses. Aside from his Brule lineage, Red Cloud's desirability as a son-in-law was manifest, and the parents of the tribe's most eligible maidens knew it. He was also in love with two women whom he intended to marry. The only question was which he would wed first. It was a social formality among the Lakota that a man wait at least a month or two before marrying again, which meant that the first wife would always hold a slight edge in status. Red Cloud had set his sights on two women from within his Bad Face band. He was more attracted to a girl named Pine Leaf—and events would prove that she was hopelessly in love with him as well—but Pine Leaf's family did not have the prestige of another young Oglala woman, Pretty Owl. In the end, he chose Pretty Owl to become his first wife, with every intention of bringing Pine Leaf into his tepee when the proper amount of time had passed.

Red Cloud's courtship of Pretty Owl was the talk of the camp. While his mother, sister, and aunts began construction of a honeymoon lodge sewn from tanned elk skins, his older male relatives entered into negotiations with Pretty Owl's father. As a result of these negotiations, Red Cloud tethered four fine mustangs to Pretty Owl's lodge early one spring morning. The horses were a splendid matrimonial gift, and the people of the camp gathered about waiting for Pretty Owl and her father to come out and inspect them, as was the custom. When, by noon, no one from her family had so much as pulled back the flap of their tepee, Red Cloud arrived with four more ponies, all better than the first. He left the eight horses for review.

Eight beautiful mounts were a grand—actually an excessive—bride price, even for a family as well connected as Pretty Owl's. By late afternoon, however, they remained unaccepted. The crowd began to buzz over the rejection. Some thought Red Cloud a fool, whose obvious desperation to climb the social ladder led him to waste his resources on such a fickle family. Others whispered that Pretty Owl was behind the public humiliation; she knew that Red Cloud's heart favored Pine Leaf, and this was her way of making him pay. There was a puzzled murmur when Red Cloud arrived for a third time, with four more ponies. These included a mustang everyone knew to be his favorite racing horse. He tethered them and left. And there the twelve animals stood until sundown, when a glowing Pretty Owl, a spot of vermilion on each cheek, came out of the tepee beside her father. He looked over the ponies casually and nodded to his daughter, who began to untie them. This signaled acceptance, and the crowd erupted in whoops and hollers.

Two days of feasting and dancing ensued. The Bad Face village was enthralled by the pageantry—but there was at least one exception. Several times during the festivities Red Cloud caught glimpses of a subdued Pine Leaf lurking in the flickering shadows beyond the bonfire. He vowed to himself to slip away and tell her that he loved her, and that he would soon take her as his second bride. The opportunity never arrived. On the second night of feasting Pretty Owl's father led her to the center of the camp. She was clad in a tunic of brushed deerskin that had been bleached white by a scouring with prairie clay. A medicine man presided over the ceremony: Red Cloud pledged his troth by withdrawing the ramrod from his Hawken and tapping it on Pretty Owl's shoulder, symbolically counting coup. "You are mine," he told his new wife. The two retired to their lodge in the shadow of a large tree, set a little apart from the village on a rolling swale carpeted by threadleaf sedge and wild blue flax.

The next morning at dawn the groom stepped from his tepee into a gray mist. He carried a rawhide lariat, intending to ride into the surrounding hills to gather his horses. When he passed the single tree near his honeymoon lodge he froze. Hanging from a low branch, a rope around her neck, was Pine Leaf. Her face was bloated and distorted; her bulging eyes were open. She seemed to stare accusingly at the man who had thrown her over. For perhaps the only time in his life, Red Cloud fell into shock. He mechanically threw his blanket over Pine Leaf's head and walked to her father's lodge to inform him. Then he returned to his mother's tepee; lowered himself into her bed, facedown; and did not move.

Pretty Owl fled to her father's tepee and was not present when Pine Leaf's family arrived to cut her down. Wails and moans echoed through the village, gradually superseded by the angry cries of Pine Leaf's male relatives as they slashed Red Cloud's honeymoon lodge to pieces. Still he did not stir from his mother's bed. None of his friends moved to stop the razing of his tepee, although a few did surreptitiously retrieve his rifle and bow. Soon the torn elk skins littered the sedge, and the small mob's energy was spent. That afternoon Red Cloud and Pretty Owl watched from a respectful distance as Pine Leaf's body was carried on a travois to the top of a boulder-crowned butte and lifted onto a scaffold. Plates of food and a jug of water were laid by her side, and her favorite pony was shot and arranged beneath her to accompany her into the afterlife. A large quilt of tanned skins was draped over the grave site.

A short time later, their grief assuaged, Pine Leaf's clan apologized to Red Cloud and Pretty Owl for having been impetuous and repaid them with gifts of horses. The clan even built them another elk skin tepee. But the incident left a deep impression. Red Cloud fathered five children with Pretty Owl—and probably more with other Sioux women—but he always insisted that he remained "monogamous" for the rest of his life, an oddity in Sioux culture, in fealty to the tragic memory of his first love, Pine Leaf.

Whether Red Cloud was unlucky in love is debatable; he and Pretty Owl remained married for fifty-nine years, and she was present at his deathbed. More important, despite now being in league with her powerful relatives, he was fortunate in another matter, one over which he had no control—specifically, to have been born at the right moment in Sioux history. The mid-nineteenth century was an opportune time for a striving Oglala brave from the wrong family to buck the ancient traditions. The Western Sioux had put up a putative united front at the Horse Creek Council, largely for the benefit of their white audience. But the Lakota were in fact facing their greatest existential crisis since stepping out onto the prairie.

The buffalo herds were shrinking, the Army presence on their lands was multiplying, and the emigrant trains were transmitting diseases that felled entire villages. The Oglalas in particular were so splintered that the northern "Smoke People" and the "Bear People," now hunting as far south as the Arkansas, were nearly separate tribes. The growing autonomy of each served only to weaken the other.

From the white point of view—which was always confused, at best, by the dizzying particulars of Indian hierarchy—Red Cloud was too young and obscure to be considered a "chief" as long as stalwarts like Old Smoke, Whirlwind, and Old-Man-Afraid-Of-His-Horses still held that position. The Indians, however, looked at tribal leadership more obliquely. Red Cloud was undoubtedly the most feared warrior on the High Plains. And though his rank as a *blotahunka* was, officially, below that of Old Smoke or Whirlwind, in troubled times a warrior's prominence was elevated, in spirit if not in fact. The U.S. government, through a process of natural selection, would one day recognize Red Cloud as "chief" of the Lakota. But long before that, there was a sense among his people that he was their spiritual and martial leader.

And if Red Cloud literally had to fight to maintain that position, he would happily do so. There were certainly enough opportunities for a man with his wolfish ambition, as the worsening scarcity of the buffalo led to even more competition between the western nations. It also did not hurt that he had acquired a reputation for supernatural powers. The truth was that Red Cloud worked hard to hone his craft as warrior, hunter, and scout. He taught himself to cut trails by prowling alone, barefoot, over the trackless western prairie through pitch-dark nights, the better to "feel" where an enemy might have trod. And he became so attuned to natural phenomena that he could "smell" water from even the tiniest shift in wind currents. These were talents few white men ever acquired.

There had been minor roadblocks, both emotional and physical, to his growing legend. Close friends noticed that Pine Leaf's suicide had smothered any vestigial joy in his already somewhat dour personality. And, during a horse raid, not long after the killing of Bull Bear, he had taken a Pawnee arrow that passed clean through his body. But he had recovered swiftly from that wound, and this was much remarked on by friend and foe alike, as was the general good health and good fortune of those who rode with him. And because of his prowess at finding game it was rumored that he could talk to animals, and sometimes even take their form. Most amazingly, simultaneous Red Cloud "sightings" at impossible distances led to reports that he could either fly or be present in two places at once. Whether or not he cultivated this mystique, it elevated his prestige among a people who set great store by charms, spells, omens, and dreams, and who envisioned only a diaphanous curtain separating the human and spirit worlds. The Crows, perhaps the most superstitious tribe in the West, certainly believed in this Sioux warrior's mystical powers.

A few summers after the Horse Creek Council the Bad Faces were hunting perilously close to Crow country, camped on crumpled, loamy black earth along a turbid river called the Little Missouri. The water was flowing taupe with runoff one night when a Crow raiding party struck the Oglala pasturage and made off with nearly 100 ponies. The next morning Red Cloud recruited fifteen to twenty *akicita* and lit out after the Crows. They rode west for three hard days and nights before locating the enemy camp spread over the pleated flats where Rosebud Creek flows into the Yellowstone in present-day Montana. The Bad Faces hobbled their mounts and crawled through the dark on their bellies toward the Crow herd, springing from the thick saw grass at dawn and killing and scalping most of the young sentries. By the time the alarm was raised Red Cloud was leading his braves east at a gallop, stampeding not only the stolen Oglala ponies but an additional 100 or so Crow mounts.

The surprise factor gave the Bad Faces a tentative head start, but from the higher limestone bluffs they could see that a large party of Crows, too many to take on, had wrangled spare horses and were flying after them. It was in such situations that the genius of Red Cloud—and perhaps his renown as a flying shape-shifter—blossomed. At dusk the Sioux reached a tableland scarred by a maze of crooked double-back trails. Red Cloud instructed six of his warriors to keep the stolen herd moving east at a leisurely gait while he and the rest laid false tracks through the breaks. He also turned over his headdress to one of the departing Bad Faces. As he expected, when the Crows reached a high point leading into the tableland they spotted the remuda moving slowly across the distant prairie, escorted by only a few riders—one of whom, judging by his feathers, was Red Cloud. But given the unhurried pace and the confusing tracks, they suspected an ambush. They proceeded warily.

While they picked their way through the rocky goosenecks, expecting a surprise attack around every outcropping, Red Cloud and his braves caught up to the herd and helped drive them back to the Little Missouri. He suggested to Old Smoke that they dismantle the lodges and disperse. But first he instructed the band to gather all the old and lame horses destined to be "given to the moon." Having rounded up fifty or so of these animals, he gathered them into a small valley and had a sort of Potemkin Village of tattered lodges skins erected to give the impression that someone was guarding them. Then he and a small party again rode west, careful to avoid the oncoming Crows.

The Crows reached the decoy village that night and crept past the tepees, not realizing that these were unoccupied. Then they spotted the animals. They took the bait, stampeding the ponies and riding breakneck through the dark. It was only at dawn that they realized the herd they had stolen back consisted of old, worthless horseflesh. A few had even died from exhaustion during the escape. When the humiliated Crows gazed up at an eastern height they were greeted by the sight of Red Cloud and his Bad Faces framed by the rising sun, mooning them in mockery.

Red Cloud did not go out of his way to suppress the rumors of his preternatural capabilities, because if such a reputation aided him in his battles against enemies, and in accruing even greater honors, such was the way of the Sacred Hoop. On the other hand, not every fight he picked was intended as a strategic maneuver to enhance his tribal standing. Sometimes it just felt good and natural to go out and steal horses. If he took some scalps in the process, so much the better.

Thus one midsummer day when life in the Bad Face camp grew too monotonous for the *blotahunka* and a group of restless warriors, they decided that it had been far too long since they had raided the Arikara. Red Cloud and twenty-three braves rode off toward the faraway Upper Missouri. By the 1850s nothing was left of the once mighty Arikara except a pathetic tribe in a single earth-lodge village abutting the Missouri in a forlorn corner of present-day North Dakota. Red Cloud's raiding party traversed over 150 miles before reaching the big river, where they spied a cluster of tepees set in a stand of willow extending down to the water's pebbly banks. The Bad Faces recognized the lodges as belonging to Gros Ventres, usually a much hardier foe than the Arikara. But a Sioux brave could resist anything except temptation, and the sight of a large pony herd feeding along the braided streambeds emptying into the river determined their decision. Moreover, these were not the mighty Gros Ventres of the mountains, but merely their river-dwelling cousins. The prairie-hardened Lakota looked down on such bottom-dwelling "mosquito eaters" with a contempt customarily reserved for cowards and whites. They counted the lodges, and estimated between thirty and forty fighting men—versus twenty-four Oglala warriors. On its face, a Sioux rout.

It took the Bad Faces several hours to creep through a marshy gully until they were behind the village. At noon they charged, on foot, screaming, eagle feathers streaming. The barrels of their Hawkens blew fire, and arrows whistled. But these mosquito eaters could fight. They streamed from their lodges and formed a skirmish line that not only held but repulsed the Bad Faces, driving them north against the river. There they mustered again and charged at a full run. Once more the Gros Ventres stood their ground, their long rifles and arrows knocking down four Oglala braves. On the next retreat Red Cloud's party managed to cut 100 or so ponies from the enemy herd. One Oglala had been killed, three more had been slightly wounded, and a healthy remuda was in their possession. They counted it a good day's work, found a ford, crossed the river, and rode south.

That night Red Cloud, satisfied that they were not being pursued, laid his dead compatriot to rest in the branches of a large elm and split his command. Ten braves, including the three wounded, were sent to escort the stolen herd back to Old Smoke's summer camp on Heart Creek. The remaining thirteen would follow Red Cloud south along the Missouri until they came on their original target, the Arikara village. They found it the next afternoon, nestled between an overhanging shale promontory and the river. They climbed the escarpment to scout their attack.

Hollywood movies have not accustomed us to envision Indians, particularly western Indians, living in houses. But as the Sioux peered down on the Arikara village the tableau resembled a medieval European hamlet more closely than what we have come to expect of a North American Indian camp. The Arikara lived in round lodges constructed from woven and plaited willow branches anchored by thick cottonwood beams. Over this infrastructure was daubed, inside and out, a wet, mortar-like mixture of prairie grass and mud that dried into effective weather stripping. A single opening not far up the oval roof served as both chimney and window, and larger structures were often divided into family living quarters and indoor stables for cherished mounts. Unlike the majority of western tribes, the Arikara also built corrals to pen their ponies at night. In spite of their recent hard times, the tribe had always been, and remained, good horsemen. This accounted for the Sioux's interest. The Arikara were also known for their strange little boats—made of buffalo bull hides stretched tight over rounded frameworks of willow branches—that they sailed in lieu of canoes. They were expert at navigating these unstable tubs across rivers and surging creeks. From his perch on the butte Red Cloud could see a small flotilla of the craft beached on a sandy shoal at the far end of the camp.

The Arikara village conformed to the mud-yellow river flats in two elongated crescents, with an open space, like a main street, running between them. A good-size corral made from interlaced sagebrush protruded from one end. The effect was that of a series of giant anthills girding a dusty town square. Nothing seemed amiss or suspicious as dusk deepened into night and the Rees brought in their herd. Still, as a precaution the Sioux waited until midnight before mounting and moving out. Crouched low in their saddles, they dropped down the butte in single file, Red Cloud in the lead. The plan, which indicates that they were not looking for a fight, was to smash open the Arikara corral and stampede the horses. Once again in defiance of our cinematic preconceptions, rarely did Indians fight from horseback; even on the vast Plains they preferred to sneak up on an enemy on foot. The Bad Faces moved to within an arrow's flight of the corral when two rows of Rees rose from the tall grass on either side of their column and opened fire with rifles and bows.

Red Cloud realized immediately that the Rees had been alerted to their presence by the Gros Ventres. In the pandemonium he and the brave behind him lost control of their mounts, which bolted down the corridor and through an opening in the Arikara corral. The two men dropped to the ground and mixed with the herd. But the volleys of gunshots had agitated the remuda, and several of the horses were rearing and bucking. The last Red Cloud saw of his companion, the brave was clutching the tail of a horse that broke through the sage fence and galloped downriver.

Within moments the gunfire behind Red Cloud subsided, the rifle reports becoming more spaced. He could sense that the fight had moved from the river and up onto the bluffs. The Arikara did not know he was here. It would not be long, however, before they returned to check on their herd. Now or never. Red Cloud squatted low, dipping beneath the mustangs' bellies and crawling around the skittering hooves until he reached the corner of the corral closest to the village. He pinned his rifle against his leg, threw his blanket over his head, and stepped boldly into the main thoroughfare that ran between the earth mounds. There was no moon, and lights from the chimney-windows cast eerie shadows as he walked toward the water. He passed several people, including men with weapons, who took no notice. Once, a woman carrying water addressed him in the Arikara tongue, which he did not understand. He grunted in response. The smell of the rushing river in the night air, thrillingly sweet and fresh, filled his nostrils. He was a few yards away from the bank. He forced himself not to run.

He scrambled down the crumbling bank and was about to swim for it when he remembered the boats. He made for them, cut one loose, pushed it out into the current, and tumbled inside. It was like riding a teacup circling a bathtub drain. The shooting had stopped completely now, and he could see torches nearing the spot on the riverbank where the tribe moored their craft. But they must not have missed the boat he stole. No one followed him.

There was a single paddle in the boat, and he used it to propel himself down the main channel and push off from shoals. He drifted all night on the swift current and at dawn steered into a narrow creek on the west side of the river shaded by dusky box elders. The stream fed down from a pocket ravine enclosed by walls of fine-grained yellow sandstone. He was hungry, and he took a chance, tying up and exploring the valley floor. There was no game, but he spooked a small flock of prairie chickens and shot one off a tree branch. He plucked its feathers with rough abandon, as if killing it for a second time; sliced out the entrails; and ate the bird raw. He crawled into the brush beside the boat and lay flat. He was certain his friends were dead.

When Red Cloud awoke it was nearly sundown. He pushed back into the river and for four days repeated this pattern: drifting by night and hunting, eating, and sleeping by day. Early on the fourth night he thought he heard drumbeats carrying up the river corridor. He paddled to the bank and moved cautiously, grabbing overhanging reeds and tree roots hand over hand to slow his progress against the rough current. He heard a dog bark, then another. He tied up and crawled to the edge of an Indian camp. He burrowed into a nook of butterfly weeds just outside the firelight to listen for voices coming from the tepees. Presently he heard one, an old man haranguing a woman. He was speaking the Sioux tongue. Red Cloud stood and strode into the open. He assumed he had found a band of eastern Lakota: Hunkpapas or Miniconjous, perhaps even an adventuresome Yankton clan that ordinarily roamed farther to the east. He was instead surprised to find himself surrounded by Brules, their astonishment at the sight of the mighty Red Cloud in their midst equal to his own relief and delight.

For days the Brules feted Red Cloud as he told and retold the story of the fight with the Gros Ventres, the trap set by the Arikara, and his miraculous escape by the river. Finally they supplied him with horses and provisions, and selected two young braves to escort him home. Five days later he rode into Old Smoke's camp, to the shock and jubilation of Pretty Owl and the Bad Faces, who had supposed him dead. Of the fourteen warriors who had been ambushed by the Arikara, he was the seventh to straggle in. Although two more survivors arrived the following day, one died almost immediately from his wounds. No more followed. The brave Red Cloud had last seen gripping the tail of the runaway Arikara horse did not return. Red Cloud himself had suffered no visible injury. His legend grew.

Few of these constant intertribal raids and fights were ever reported to eastern authorities, although government Indian agents in the West knew full well that the Indians' adherence to the articles of the Horse Creek Treaty had lasted about as long as it took for the ink to dry. But the agents stood to lose too much power and wealth if Washington were to understand this. In some cases the Lakota even implored the Indian agents to inform the Great Father that they no longer wished to be held to the pact, that they neither wanted nor needed the American gifts if accepting them meant having to cease their raids on the Arikara and Pawnee or, more gallingly, ceding any land to the hated Crows. The Hunkpapas, a tribe being squeezed by sodbusters pushing up the Missouri and egged on to retaliate by the charismatic young warrior-mystic Sitting Bull, were most adamant in this regard. They refused to have anything to do with the Indian agent assigned to their tribe, and warned him to stay out of their territory if he valued his scalp.

In their reports to St. Louis and Washington, however, the agents never mentioned any of this. Instead they found more tractable, mostly alcoholic Head Men loosely associated with the Hunkpapas to sign the receipts for any commodities delivered according to the treaty—but not without first taking their own hefty cut of the grain, cattle, and tools. Unlike Sitting Bull's people far to the northeast, Red Cloud continued the ancient warring rituals without much government interference, although he and Old Smoke could not completely disentangle the Bad Faces from the growing white presence clogging the Oregon Trail. The Oglalas continued to be mesmerized by the mysterious lure of these queer strangers with their funny clothes, odd body odors, and bald, vulture-like heads.* Whether or not the Indians connected the cross-cultural pollination that accompanied these interactions with the ravaging diseases and cheap whiskey carried by the newcomers, it was happening, and there was no stopping it.

Old Smoke and Red Cloud had for the most part managed to keep their band as far north on both sides of the Black Hills as possible during the worst of the cholera, measles, and smallpox outbreaks. But many other Sioux bands were decimated, particularly those roaming west of Fort Laramie, where word of the rampant epidemics was slower to arrive. On one of his surveying expeditions, the same Captain Stansbury who had sought Jim Bridger's assistance in laying out the railroad route observed lodge after lodge filled with Lakota corpses lying in their own watery bile.

---

*Most pure-blood Native Americans, like Australian Aborigines, lack the gene that causes baldness.

Red Cloud is reported to have personally devised a remedy for cholera, a concoction of boiled red cedar leaves that apparently had some effect on the dehydrated and dying, although not nearly enough. Evidently there were Bad Faces who had become too dependent not only on the white man's liquor, gleaming metal cook pots, tobacco, and glass beads, but also, now, on his medicine. They were left to beg for such goods by the side of the increasingly rutted "Glory Road," usually to no avail.

These outbreaks were one reason the Western Sioux initially welcomed the arrival of U.S. troops at Fort Laramie. The Indians believed (insanely, in hindsight) that the soldiers had been dispatched to police and control, if not curtail altogether, the prairie schooners slithering through their country like a long white snake. They ultimately realized, with astonishment, that the exact opposite was true. The Bluecoats and their officers cared not a whit for the Natives. They were there to serve the emigrants, at any cost. In this they were complicit with the traders in requiring trumped-up Head Men with whom they could do business. And if a true leader such as Red Cloud refused to allow his people to visit the Army-backed trading posts, they could easily find another, more pliable "chief."

Few details from the Indian perspective have emerged about the hazy years immediately prior to and after the Horse Creek Treaty Council. What is known is that at some point—no one is certain precisely when—the Army selected an elderly, obscure Brule Head Man named Conquering Bear to represent the Lakota as just such a "chief." The decision was undoubtedly a sop to the trading post operators, as Conquering Bear and his band were regular visitors to the private stores and warehouses that had begun to bloom like sage stalks around the soldiers' stockade. Conquering Bear's elevation, however, further divided the Western Sioux. As always, the Indians could not conceive of a single man making decisions for all seven Lakota tribes. And even if the idea had any validity—which it did not—if there was going to be a single Head Man to represent the Western Sioux, why choose one so far past his fighting prime?

The eastern Lakota—the Miniconjous, Hunkpapas, Sans Arcs, Two Kettles, and Blackfeet Sioux—for the most part ignored Conquering Bear's appointment, or saw it as a good joke on the crazy whites. But the Oglalas, in closer contact with the Americans, were astounded and angry.

This was more than just an insult; it was a clear erosion of their autonomy. Whirlwind, Head Man of the Oglala Bear People, had inherited many of his father's bullying and obnoxious traits, and he nearly sparked an intertribal war by initially refusing to recognize Conquering Bear's chieftaincy. He eventually thought better of alienating the more numerous Brules, however, and relented. And Red Cloud, despite his reputation, was not yet even thirty years old and could not have expected to be handed so lofty a position. Still, this second snub to his mentor Old Smoke—first by the Oglala council of elders after the killing of Bull Bear, and now by the heedless whites—sat in his stomach like broken glass. By now Old Smoke was in his early seventies, but unlike the old women of his tribe—"ugly as Macbeth's witches," according to the historian Francis Parkman, who visited the tribe around this time—the Head Man of the Bad Faces was by all accounts still large, strong, and wily.

Conquering Bear, however, remained a "chief" in name only among most Brules, further proof to the tribes that accommodation with the United States was a fool's game. The newcomers took, and took, and then demanded more. As the Lakota-born historian Joseph M. Marshall III wryly notes, "The whites had one truth and the Lakotas another." Further hostilities, if not all-out war, with the land-grabbing whites must have seemed inevitable to the Western Sioux. For the astute Red Cloud it was merely a question of when and how. It would take a concerted strategy—never an Indian strong point—to defeat these invaders, as well as a true sense of unity among the squabbling tribes. This, too, was a doubtful proposition. Thus it no doubt occurred to Red Cloud that his best strategy was to stall for time. He was still young and held no official tribal leadership position. If the goal was to check the American flood tide, there was no way, right now, that the Indians could challenge the might of the U.S. Army. He knew well that aside from his own relatively well armed *akicita*, perhaps one in a hundred Sioux braves owned a gun that worked. As it turned out, when the first deadly shots were loosed in what would become the decades-long Indian wars on the High Plains, it was the soldiers who fired them.

A BLOOD-TINGED SEASON

I n June 1853 nearly 2,000 Sioux and Cheyenne arrived at Fort Laramie to stake their lodges amid the ripening blades of blue grama extending like a thick, manicured lawn in all directions from the white man's lonely outpost. The Lakota contingent included large delegations of Brules and Oglalas, among them the Bad Faces, as well as a small band of Miniconjous down from the Upper Missouri. All were awaiting delivery of the promised government annuity. The fort, never fully manned to begin with, was garrisoned by only thirty or so soldiers, as a good third of the 6th Infantry had completed their tours and been discharged at the spring thaw, despite the fact that their replacements had not yet arrived. The post was also missing a detachment of mounted infantry that had been deployed to escort one of the summer's first Mormon wagon trains rolling into the territory.

It had been a glorious spring, and on the brisk, clear morning of June 15 several Miniconjou braves asked to join a boatload of emigrants who were being ferried across the swift-running North Platte, nearly bursting its banks with snowmelt. The leader of a small squad of Bluecoats assisting the emigrants refused the request, a small scuffle ensued, and a

Miniconjou fired a shot, freezing the Indian dogs frolicking in the prairie grass. The musket ball missed its mark, and the offending brave disappeared into a ravine intersecting the prairie.

This seemingly irrational provocation had become familiar Miniconjou behavior since the death of their longtime Head Man, The One Horn. He was by all accounts a strong and judicious chief, wary and wise in the ways of the whites. He was also a handsome man, if we judge by the three Catlin paintings for which he sat, with a broad forehead, sharp cheekbones, a Roman nose, and piercing oval eyes. But when illness took his favorite young wife, so heavy was his grief that in a kind of ritual suicide he attacked a bull buffalo, alone, on foot, with only a knife. The two-horned animal gored The One Horn to death. Since then, observed the fur trader Edwin Denig, the tribe had fractured into several "quarrelsome and predatory" factions of "murderous character" toward the whites.

The soldiers stationed at Fort Laramie were certainly aware of this "Miniconjou problem," and later that afternoon a platoon of twenty-three dragoons led by a callow second lieutenant named Hugh Fleming rode to the Miniconjous' isolated camp and shot to death at least five braves. It is not known if the troublemaker was among them. Word spread among the Lakota, and war councils were convened. The Oglala Head Man Old-Man-Afraid-Of-His-Horses was able to persuade his furious tribesmen—including an influential medicine man who was the father of the eleven-year-old Crazy Horse—not to retaliate. Still, members of the arriving Mormon train could feel the tension. "The Indians no more look smiling, but have a stern solumn [sic] look," a homesteader's wife noted in her diary. "We feel this evening that we are in danger. We pray the kind Father to keep us safe this night."

Her prayer was answered, but not those of another emigrant family camped farther away from the main body of wagons. That night a party of Sioux crept up to their isolated encampment and killed a husband and wife and their two children. When news of these "most terrible butcheries" reached the fort another squad of enraged soldiers galloped out of the gates and fired on the first Indians they saw, killing one and wounding another. This led to an age-old Indian conflict—again young warriors thirsted for vengeance; again older and wiser heads counseled caution.

It is not difficult to imagine the soldiers' shooting spree as the visceral response of resentful, ill-disciplined, and possibly drunken troops isolated in hostile territory. Personal revenge has occurred in armies throughout history, and these overreactions foreshadowed American atrocities at Sand Creek, at Biscari, at My Lai, at Abu Ghraib. Moreover, the few officers stationed at Fort Laramie were young and inexperienced, unable to control their enlisted men, most of whom considered the Indians subhuman. The instigator of the killings was not even a soldier, but a hard-drinking half-blood interpreter named Wyuse, employed by the Army. Small, swarthy, and foul-tempered, Wyuse was the son of a French trader and a woman from the conquered Iowas, and he had a searing hatred for the Sioux. One of the soldiers who fell under his sway was the shavetail Second Lieutenant John Grattan, a twenty-four-year-old eager to prove his mettle in battle against the Indians—to "see the elephant," in a colloquial phrase that was to become popular during the Civil War. A recent West Point graduate, Grattan drank to excess and boasted incessantly about "cracking it to the Sioux." He became a constant drinking partner of the scheming interpreter Wyuse.

Before more blood ran, two companies of mounted riflemen that were returning to the United States from the Oregon Territory arrived at Fort Laramie. So too did the trusted government Indian agent "Broken Hand" Fitzpatrick. Fitzpatrick persuaded the veteran cavalry commander from Oregon to linger, and between his straightforward apologies to the Miniconjous, his long-standing friendship with several Lakota Head Men, and the overwhelming firepower of the Oregon contingent, a fight was averted. The unusually punctual arrival of the annuity train served to ease the tension—for the moment. The continuous beat of war drums provided the sound track for the restless winter that followed as Lakota Head Men and war chiefs rode to and from one another's camps to discuss the growing difficulties with the arrogant whites, particularly the murderous soldiers, and to argue over possible solutions.

The Miniconjous were bent on vengeance. Their sentiments were echoed, not surprisingly, by Sitting Bull and the Hunkpapas. The headstrong Sitting Bull, now thirty-two, had counted his first coup at the age of fourteen, when he'd disobeyed his father and joined a raiding party against the Crows. He had since grown into a skilled fighter as well as a holy *wicasa wakan,* or "vision seeker," who had performed the Sun Dance numerous times. His voice carried weight, but not enough to convince the Oglalas and Brules—who were much more familiar with the Army's firepower and who urged accommodation. In the end, the old "chief" Conquering Bear, perhaps wiser than some gave him credit for being, proposed a radical solution. The Lakota, he said, should petition the Great Father in Washington to reconsider his policy of stationing such small, ill-trained, poorly led, and easily spooked garrisons in the middle of a territory granted to the Western Sioux by the white man's own treaty.

Red Cloud was not happy with this compromise, which he perceived as a groveling response. His influence over the Lakota would carry much greater force a decade hence, but now he remained silent as he went along with the plan with a mixture of disappointment and anger. Given the apparent timidity of so many of the Sioux Head Men, as well as their inability to reach a consensus, a part of him recognized that this was not the politic moment to speak up for Indian provocations. As it happened, the blood-tinged events of the following summer proved beyond his control.

In August 1854, the Lakota returned to the grasslands on the North Platte, again in anticipation of the Army freight wagons hauling the seasonal annuity. This time they staked camp a cautious distance south of Fort Laramie. The post's duty roster had increased to forty troopers and two officers—the twenty-eight-year-old garrison commander Fleming, since promoted to first lieutenant, and his hard-charging subordinate Grattan. The same small band of Miniconjous were again present; they had the foresight to camp close to a large contingent of Brules. One afternoon a Mormon wagon train was passing nearby when a worn-out, footsore cow broke its tether and wandered in among the Miniconjou lodges. A pack of dogs cornered the lame animal in a dry arroyo, from where its terrified owner dared not retrieve it. A Miniconjou man shot the cow, butchered it, and shared the stringy meat with his band.

In the white man's eyes, Conquering Bear was still the "chief" of all the Lakota, and when word of this seemingly inconsequential event reached him he sensed trouble. He acted immediately to head it off by riding into

Fort Laramie and offering payment for the cow. Lieutenant Fleming in-
stead insisted that the offending Miniconjou turn himself in. Conquering
Bear was incredulous. Not only was the scrawny animal not worth a fight,
Conquering Bear was also acting in accordance with the document he and
the Army officials had signed three years earlier. A provision of the Horse
Creek Treaty stated that in the case of an Indian offense against a white
civilian, the offending tribe, through its chief, should offer satisfaction.
Conquering Bear suggested they wait for the arrival of the Indian agent
Fitzpatrick, who usually came to the post around this time of the year. The
Lakota, he said, would abide by whatever compensation "Broken Hand"
deemed fair. Lieutenant Fleming was surely aware that Fitzpatrick had
died of pneumonia six months earlier in Washington while on a mission
to plead the Indians' case. Whether or not he informed Conquering Bear
of this remains unrecorded. In any case the Head Man's attempted compromise failed to mollify Fleming and the Mormons, who were obviously
itching for a fight.

In a last-ditch effort at reconciliation, Conquering Bear told Fleming
that he would try to persuade the offending Miniconjou to turn himself in. This was an extraordinary offer, and Conquering Bear must have
known it was useless. No Indian, and especially no Sioux, would willingly
allow himself to be taken to the Bluecoat jail. An Indian would rather die
fighting. Conquering Bear's incredible offer indicates that he was aware
of what could happen if the soldiers provoked another confrontation. But
young Fleming was in a lather. The next morning, egged on by Grattan,
Fleming ordered his subordinate to lead a troop to the Brule-Miniconjou
village and seize the cow-killer. In hindsight more than 150 years later,
what followed is no surprise. But no Army officer serving on the godforsaken western frontier in the 1850s, let alone an officious graduate of
the Military Academy, could be faulted for such hubris. In Grattan's view
the white race would always trump the red, no matter the numerical odds.
It was his Christian God's intended order of things.

Grattan requisitioned a twelve-pound field piece and a snub-nosed
mountain howitzer, and called for volunteers. All forty infantrymen
stepped forward. He selected twenty-nine to mount up. He also summoned the interpreter Wyuse, who was so drunk he had to be lifted onto

his saddle. Along the trail this motley cavalcade halted at a small trading post operated by a stout little "Missouri Frenchman" named James Bordeaux. Grattan tried to convince the veteran trapper to join him. But Bordeaux, who had married a Brule, was too wise in the ways of the Indians. He knew that when they drove their herds in from the grasslands they were preparing for a fight. He eyed the clusters of mounted Sioux flanking the troop on the red-earth bluffs overlooking the rutted road—including, by his own admission, Red Cloud's Bad Faces—and declined to join the soldiers. Bordeaux did offer Grattan one piece of advice: gag your drunken interpreter.

Between the gates of Fort Laramie and Grattan's destination stood at least 300 Oglala lodges, another 200 Brule lodges, and finally the 20 Miniconjou lodges next to a smaller contingent of 80 Brule tepees. Five thousand Indians. Twelve hundred warriors. Still, on nearing the Miniconjou camp, Wyuse galloped ahead roaring insults and threatening to eat the heart of every Lakota before sundown.

Conquering Bear, again exhibiting a jarring independence, attempted one final intercession. He met Grattan at the edge of the Miniconjou camp as the officer positioned his artillery and asked him to hold the guns while he made a last appeal to the offending man who had killed the cow. Later, there were reports that the half-blood Wyuse intentionally mistranslated these last words. In any case, as the old chief rode away Grattan lost what little patience he had started with, particularly after seeing half a dozen Indians leave a tepee and begin to prime their muskets. He ordered his men to form a skirmish line. One went a step further, aimed his rifle, and fired. A brave tipped over dead. At this Grattan ordered a volley loosed into the village. The rifle reports surprised Conquering Bear, who turned and tried to wave Grattan off. The old man was standing tall in the center of the camp, exhorting his tribesmen not to return fire, when the howitzers boomed and another rifle volley echoed. Grapeshot splintered several lodgepoles, and Conquering Bear fell, mortally wounded.

It was over in minutes. Rifle balls and clouds of arrows as thick as black flies sailed into the American line. Grattan and most of his men were killed on the spot. A few wounded Bluecoats managed to swing up onto horses or crawl into the artillery wagon to try to flee back up the trail. One, punctured by seven arrow and musket holes, made it as far as Bordeaux's trading post, where he staggered inside and hid in a closet. He later died from his wounds. The rest were engulfed by Brules and Miniconjous galloping up the road and a separate wave of Oglalas led by Red Cloud and his *akicita* sweeping down from the bluffs. The soldiers were dead by the time the whirling dust clouds kicked up by the horses had settled. Odds are Red Cloud killed his first white man that day.

Wyuse darted into an empty tepee, a "death lodge" whose owner had been buried a few days earlier. The Lakota found him and dragged him out. He writhed in the dirt and wailed for mercy as they sliced out his forked tongue and replaced it with his severed penis. When what was left of his body had ceased twitching, two Oglala boys ran up to his corpse and offered him the ultimate Sioux insult by jerking up their breechcloths and waggling their own penises before his empty eyes. One of them was the fair-skinned Crazy Horse.

After the soldiers' bodies were stripped of uniforms, boots, guns, and ammunition, the customary orgy of atrocities ensued. Scalps were collected and limbs hacked away. Some of the bodies were flayed and skinned, others rolled into a roaring bonfire. Grattan, pierced by twenty arrows, died splayed across his cannon; his boots were filled with manure and shoved down the big gun's barrel. Back at Fort Laramie, Fleming and his remaining ten infantrymen could only await the same fate. They were too distant to have heard Grattan's first rifle volley. But when the sound of cannon fire confirmed that a fight had begun they hurried the emigrants and their livestock into the stockade and barred the double gates. When no one from Grattan's troop returned they prepared for the inevitable attack.

Meanwhile, when the last of Grattan's dead Bluecoats had been picked over and chopped to pieces, the Lakota warriors and their Cheyenne allies gathered at Bordeaux's trading post. The Brules had carried the bleeding, unconscious Conquering Bear to the mean adobe structure, and while the life oozed from his body their bloodlust ran hot. Some Head Men, predominantly Oglalas, urged temperance, and it is a measure of their authority and their powers of persuasion that a war party did not immediately start up the trail to storm the fort. Yet with most warriors still arguing for a fight, Bordeaux suddenly materialized among them like a ghost. At the snap of the first shots he had climbed onto his roof, flattened himself, and watched the slaughter. Now he clambered down to address the seething warriors. He knew well that he was arguing for his own life.

Bordeaux told the Indians that if they overran the fort more white troops would come: hundreds, thousands, with their long knives and their guns that shoot twice. The Indians, both the guilty and the innocent, would be hunted to the four corners of the earth. He coaxed and he wheedled. He drained his stock of trade goods, bestowing gifts on important fighters. As the western sky purpled to the color of a mussel shell and then to sooty black, he talked in a voice that became increasingly hoarse, imploring the Head Men to consider their responsibilities to their tribes, to their bands, to their women, and to their children. When the first rays of sunrise glinted off the dew-flecked branches of a nearby stand of dog ash the Indians were still, amazingly, listening to Bordeaux's exhortations.

Bordeaux later testified that when the Indians rode off, not to attack the fort but instead to plunder the nearby American Fur Company warehouse, he collapsed in an exhausted, trembling heap onto the beaten brown grass. The man had previously carried a reputation as something of a coward, stemming from an incident years earlier when he managed what was then still called Fort John and had refused to engage in a rifle duel with a drunken mountain man. When the trapper called him out from the front steps of his own bunkhouse, Bordeaux refused to leave his bedroom until the man sobered up and departed, and such was his humiliation that even his squaw wife had been disgusted with him. On this night he erased that stigma forever.

By the time the tribes broke camp the next morning the story of the "Grattan Massacre" was already curdling. It was now the devious Conquering Bear who had lured the innocent soldiers into a trap. The *Council Bluffs* (Iowa) *Bugle* reported that Grattan was attempting a peaceful parley with the Indians when Conquering Bear poked him with a lance, "calling him a squaw and a coward, and charged him with being afraid to fight." Lieutenant Fleming went along with the lie, his career and reputation at stake. The white traders, who should have known better, said nothing. No doubt their government shipping contracts influenced their silence.

Messengers were sent east with news that the Western Sioux nation had risen, and frenzied calls for a retaliatory Army force reverberated from the Platte to the Missouri and, eventually, on to the Potomac. White attitudes hardened. When the rare voice was raised asking why, if the Sioux had taken to the warpath, there had been no follow-up raids on trading posts or emigrant trains, it was shouted down with the all-purpose charge "Indian lover."

In November a small party of Brules from Conquering Bear's clan did in fact attack a mail coach on the Oregon Trail south of Fort Laramie. The raiders were led by a half-Brule warrior named Spotted Tail, a famous fighter who, though two years younger than Red Cloud, led his band's *akicita* and was said to have already taken more than a hundred scalps. Spotted Tail ordered the two coach drivers and a luckless passenger killed and mutilated, and a strongbox containing $20,000 in gold coins was taken. (This incident, four score and nine years later, gave the writer Ernest Haycox and director John Ford the germ of an idea for a movie about an embezzling banker's stagecoach being stalked by hostile Indians.)

Later that winter Spotted Tail sent out emissaries carrying the war pipe. Some Miniconjous and Hunkpapas, including Sitting Bull's clan, were receptive. But on the whole the outriders returned frustrated. Most of Conquering Bear's Brule kinsmen and nearly all of the Oglalas, including Red Cloud and the Bad Faces, considered the fight with Grattan a one-off affair in which revenge had been taken. The Indians' considerations, however, as usual mattered little. Calls to avenge the "murders" of young Grattan and his men spread like ripples on a lake all the way to the Capitol, where the causes, and repercussions, of their deaths were debated in Congress. Moreover, the St. Louis shipping companies, spooked by the mail coach raid and the missing strongbox cache, used the atrocities to lobby politicians and reporters for more federal troops to clean out the "savage" menace. Indian agents, silent at first but now sensing their gravy train departing, protested. It was too late. The government's hand had been forced.

A LONE STRANGER

A sense of foreboding spread across the High Plains in the wake of the Grattan affair just as, in the early summer of 1855, Red Cloud was granted the highest social and political honor extended to a Sioux warrior. After long years of striving he was finally asked to become a part of what passed for the aboriginal Lakota aristocracy, in an elaborate public "Pipe Dance" ritual called the *hunka*. The ceremony was attended by all the Oglala bands save one, Whirlwind's *Kiyuska*, reaffirming their reputation as the "Cutoffs." Though Old Smoke was still alive and hearty, this was the clearest signal yet that the tribe considered Red Cloud a future Head Man. Ironically, the ceremony did not occur before an embarrassing military setback.

Following the spring buffalo hunt the Bad Faces had staked camp in northern Nebraska along the Niobrara, a shallow, braided river that meanders across willowed sandbars snagged with driftwood to its confluence with the Missouri. The men of the village, as usual, lounged around the cook fires fashioning new bow staves and arrows or dozing in the shade of lean-tos attached to their lodgepoles while women and girls repaired tools, butchered meat, and tanned buffalo robes. One day a party of their old enemies the Poncas swept through the camp, killed two Sioux, and escaped unscathed with a number of ponies. The Poncas, a small, agricultural tribe even in their heyday, had been pushed out of the Ohio River Valley more than 150 years earlier by the Iroquois, and in their much diminished condition had laid claim to the nearly 600 miles of the Niobrara River corridor as their new territory—until the Western Sioux descended on them and overwhelmed them in a short war in the early 1800s. Since that defeat the Poncas, their strength recorded by Lewis and Clark (and probably undercounted) at less than 200 men, women, and children, had been further reduced by a smallpox epidemic. By the mid-nineteenth century they were bottled up on a small piece of land where the Niobrara empties into the Missouri, tending tiny plots of maize and other vegetable gardens. That they had dared to raid the Bad Faces and succeeded was not only a wonder but an embarrassment, exacerbated when the small group of pursuing *akicita* led by Red Cloud failed to find them.

It was therefore a chastened band of Bad Faces who broke camp soon after and moved north toward the White River in South Dakota where the *hunka* ceremony was to be held. But the incident with the Poncas was soon forgotten as they joined the entire Oglala tribe on rolling bluestem grassland along the banks of the White in preparation for the Pipe Dance. In essence, the ritual that followed, while not officially anointing Red Cloud as Old Smoke's successor, certainly made him eligible. Given his modest heritage, even a few decades earlier this would have seemed impossible. But these were desperate times for the Western Sioux, and Red Cloud's martial prowess and wealth of horses allowed for such an exception. It was a good political start for the thirty-four-year-old *blotahunka*, and the pageant itself offers a rare insight into the similarities between the Sioux religious liturgy and allegedly more civilized Christian rites.

After several days of feasting, tribal elders planted a three-foot-wide tree stump gilded with gypsum, a sacred mineral, in the center of the vast area to serve as an "altar." The Oglalas—men, women, and children— encircled this holy table, leaving openings on opposite ends. Through the eastern portal marched the tribe's Head Men and shamans adorned in their most lavish finery, feathers, and paint. Simultaneously, a procession of supplicants, including Red Cloud, entered from the west, naked except for small breechcloths. At a signal from a sacred drum the Head Men, according to seniority, peeled off from the shamans and formed a line that wound past the altar and in front of the candidates. Each Head Man placed his palm on each applicant's forehead as a symbol of his worthiness and submission to the Great Spirit. Then, still in single file, the older men returned to the east side of the altar, took up a gourd of water, and again approached the applicants, one standing before each applicant to wash first his face, then his hands, then his feet.

When the Head Men had returned to their original positions the shamans stepped forward, one by one, performing ancient, elaborate dance steps and flourishing a single eagle feather in the direction of the four compass points. Each laid his right palm flat on the symbolic stump, and with his left hand pointed to the sun while vowing to the Great Spirit that his heart was pure. He emphasized that he had never lied to injure his people, nor ever spilled the blood of any tribesman. He intoned that he expected the same from the men who were about to join the leadership class. This shaman then moved to the other side of the altar, removed a small bag of paint from his belt, and proceeded to daub the face of the first candidate. While that was occurring, another shaman moved to the stump in the same manner and made the same vows; and by the time the first had moved on to paint the next face, the second was painting the first candidate's hands and arms.

And so it went with a third shaman, who spread paint over the legs of the applicants from knees to feet. A fourth shaman followed, anointing each candidate's face and head with holy oil. Finally, the tribe's most celebrated priest stepped forward. After making the by-now familiar vows at the altar, he swept his hands over the heads of the acolytes and in a voice that all the tribe could hear issued a sermon driving home the great duties and responsibilities the electees owed to the Siouan peoples by virtue of their new, exalted position.

When these ministrations were complete, the Head Men took their new brethren by the hands and led them into a semicircle on the east side of the altar. The high priest then removed from his pouch a handful of downy eagle feathers, which had been plucked from the underside of the bird's wing, and attached one to each man's head. The ceremony was complete; the men had been elevated to the chieftain class. As the tribe's best dancers burst from the crowd to gyrate around the holy tree stump, another round of feasting began.

When Red Cloud later recounted this ceremony, he described it as one of the proudest moments of his life. Yet his joy, he wrote, was not for himself. Not only had the ritual promoted individual warriors into an elevated class; it also redounded to their male children. This meant that his only son, Jack Red Cloud—the fourth of five children he would sire with Pretty Owl—would not have to suffer the hereditary prejudices that had stood in his own path to leadership. Of course, if the whites had their way in that summer of 1855, his hopes and dreams for his son would be of no consequence.

While the Oglalas were gathered for the Pipe Dance their cousins were busy. The Brules in particular, coalescing behind the charismatic Spotted Tail, stepped up their raids to steal livestock from the emigrant trains— abetted later in the summer by Oglala bands returning from the *hunka*. Spotted Tail had taken his name as a boy when a trapper presented him with the gift of a raccoon tail, and he wore the talisman on every raid. It became a familiar sight to whites traveling the "Glory Road"; sometimes their last. Similarly, in June 1855 a group of Miniconjous waylaid a wagon train passing through a tight ravine on the trail. When the wagon master rode out to mollify them with the usual gifts of sugar and coffee, they shot him through the heart. A few days later the same Indians, eighteen braves in all, swooped down on another train and ran off sixteen horses. During the melee an oxcart became separated from the main body; the Indians surrounded it and relentlessly thrust their lances into a man and woman until their organs seeped out and spilled onto the prairie. A group of horrified Oglala Head Men later returned the stolen stock, and even organized a general Lakota offensive against the Omaha in hopes of distracting the bloodthirsty Miniconjou braves. But the damage had been done. That August, a year to the day of the Grattan massacre, a new Indian agent named Thomas Twiss rode into Fort Laramie.

Twiss, a lean, ambitious West Point honors graduate, had been personally recruited for this position by the veteran Indian fighter Colonel

William Selby Harney. Harney, with his plump cheeks and snowy whiskers, resembled a uniformed Father Christmas. But his jolly countenance was deceiving. He had once been chased out of St. Louis by a mob after he'd beaten to death a female slave who had lost his house keys. And he hated Indians and enjoyed killing them, either in the field or at the end of a rope on the gallows. He had led troops against the Sauk in the Black Hawk War and against the Seminoles during Andrew Jackson's Everglades campaign—where his buffoonish negligence resulted in the massacre of an entire detachment of dragoons. He himself had escaped by capering through the Florida bush wearing only his underwear. The resultant embarrassment increased Harney's fervor to slay red people; and during the Mexican War his overzealous pursuit of the Comanche—as opposed to engaging Santa Anna's troops—enraged the commander of the U.S. forces, General Winfield Scott, who relieved him of command. But the Harneys were Tennessee neighbors of the family of President James K. Polk, who reinstated the colonel. Now the War Department decided that Harney and his agent Twiss were just the men to put down an as-yet-nonexistent Sioux uprising in the High Plains.

Twiss's first official proclamation was to declare the nearby North Platte a literal "deadline." He dispatched riders to inform the Lakota and their allies that any Indians found north of the winding tributary would be considered hostile and killed on the spot. Though this applied to much of the prime buffalo range, many Brules and almost all the Oglalas rode south and made camp near the post. In his typical coy fashion, Red Cloud never mentions in his memoir whether he obeyed Twiss's order, and there are no witnesses to his presence at Fort Laramie that summer. He does hint throughout his book, however, that in a pinch he often found it convenient to be off hunting or raiding in the no-man's-land west of the fort, and it is not difficult to imagine him, at this stage in his life, thumbing his nose at the Indian agent's proclamation by doing just that.

The tribes and bands of Oglalas and Brules who did "come in" initially staked separate camps on either side of Fort Laramie, but Twiss eventually forced them to combine their 400 lodges into one huge village thirty-five miles north of the stockade. When the Indian agent felt he had a quorum he rode out to address the Head Men. He told them that he knew the names of the Brules who had attacked the mail coach and promised that they would face swift and certain justice, as would any Indian who left this safe harbor and recrossed the North Platte. As Twiss spoke, Colonel Harney's combined column of 600 infantry and cavalry troops had already begun a stealthy march out of Fort Leavenworth in eastern Kansas, bound for Sioux territory.

This turn of events spelled disaster for a Brule band led by a Head Man named Little Thunder. Though of the same tribe as Conquering Bear, Little Thunder was not overtly associated with Spotted Tail or the slain chief's clan. He had even taken the French trader Bordeaux's side against attacking Fort Laramie after the fight with Grattan. Bordeaux now tried to return the favor by sending runners to Little Thunder's camp, urging him to return before Harney's force found him. But Little Thunder was overconfident about his friendship with the whites—it is what had led him to disregarded Twiss's edict in the first place. Moreover, his buffalo hunt along Blue Water Creek, not far from where Red Cloud was born, was proving a spectacular success. He told Bordeaux's messengers that his people were still following the herd across the vast corduroy plain in order to lay in winter meat. When the hunt was complete, he added, he would come in.

In late August Little Thunder's sparse band was joined by an even smaller group of Oglalas that included Crazy Horse's family. All told, about 250 Indians had made camp in a narrow swale along Blue Water Creek—which the whites called Ash Creek—several miles north of the North Platte. Some of the boys, including Crazy Horse, were out scouting the droves, but Little Thunder had posted no sentries in the juniper-flecked hills that overlooked his encampment. He was not hard to find, and on September 2, one of Harney's Pawnee scouts found him. The colonel arranged his line of attack by sundown, and at dawn marched his infantry through the tall saw grass lining the natural defilade carved by the stream. His final instructions to his men were to spare not "one of those damned red sons of bitches." By the time the Indians spotted them it was too late.

Little Thunder and several warriors rode out, unarmed, to parley. The Head Man signed this intention to Harney's scout. But it was an old

Indian trick for a leader to buy time while his people broke down their lodges and slipped away. On the colonel's command the infantrymen shouldered their rifles and advanced in a quick march. The Indians turned and galloped off, only to run headlong into Harney's cavalry sweeping down the creek. What ensued became known as the Battle of Ash Creek.

It was a mad scene. The Army pincers closed, regimental bugles blared, and battle guidons snapped as bullets and arrows flew. Cavalry horses panted and snorted, and booming howitzers sent grapeshot ripping through tepees. Braves taken by surprise picked up tomahawks, spears, and war clubs and shrieked as they threw themselves at the American lines. They were cut down by rifle fire. Women and children screamed, dogs yelped, and the hooves of racing Indian ponies echoed from bare ocher buttes and cracked, dusty coulees soon pocked with scarlet pools of blood. The running fight, if it can be called that, covered five miles before it was over. One of Harney's company commanders noted drily in his journal, "There was much slaughter in the pursuit." And the young topographical engineer Gouverneur Kemble Warren, who was riding with the troop—and who would be better known in later years as the Union general who arranged the last-minute defense of Little Round Top at the Battle of Gettysburg—recorded "the heart-rending sight—wounded women and children crying and moaning, horribly mangled by the bullets."

Eighty-six Lakota men, women, and children were killed. The soldiers, bent on revenge for Grattan, scalped most of the bodies and mutilated the pubic areas of the women, whose vaginas were hacked out as trophies. Another seventy women and children were captured. Harney's losses were negligible—four killed and seven wounded. When the abandoned Indian campsite was searched, soldiers found papers taken from the mail coach (but not the gold coins), the scalps of two white women, and clothing identified as belonging to Grattan's troops. Although a popular Army marching song* celebrating Little Thunder's death was composed soon

---

*We did not make a blunder,
  We rubbed out Little Thunder,
  And we sent him to the other side of Jordan.

afterward, the Brule Head Man had in fact escaped. (He was, ironically, killed by his own people ten years later for fraternizing with whites.)

After the Battle of Ash Creek the Lakota called Harney "Women Killer." (While technically correct, this seems a bit precious given the Sioux's own rules of engagement.) After Harney had force-marched his captives to Fort Laramie, the officers were allowed to select the prettiest for themselves, with the rest "shared out among the soldiers." A year later half-breed "war orphans" ran thick at the fort, including an infant girl alleged to have been fathered by Harney himself. Between amorous interludes the colonel rode out to the Lakota camp and demanded the surrender of Spotted Tail and the others who had raided the mail coach. In what would have been an unthinkable act prior to Ash Creek, several Head Men persuaded the responsible Brules to turn themselves in for the good of the tribe. Spotted Tail and his retinue arrived at the fort the next day, unarmed, in their finest battle raiment, singing their death songs. Watching closely as they surrendered was the young Crazy Horse. He knew Spotted Tail well. His father was married to two of the great warrior's sisters.

Inexplicably, instead of being hanged, Spotted Tail and the rest were taken in chains to Fort Kearney on the Lower Platte, where for two years they were employed as scouts. The Lakota, Red Cloud in particular, were astounded. Friendly Indians had been slaughtered while hostile braves were housed and fed. The whites seemed truly crazy—but they also possessed overpowering strength of arms, and Harney made certain the Indians recognized it. He established Fort Grattan at the mouth of Ash Creek and garrisoned it with a company of the 6th Infantry. He then spent most of the autumn of 1855 on a leisurely march through the heart of Western Sioux territory, from Fort Laramie to Fort Pierre on the Upper Missouri. It was an affront, a challenge to any and all to come out and fight. No one dared. A year later, testifying at a government hearing investigating the Blue Water Creek engagement, Harney apologized to the panel (but, notably, not to the Indians) for his attack on Little Thunder's people. He stated that when he moved up the "Glory Road" that September he had been "very mad," and anxious to strike the first camp of Indians he could find on the wrong side of the North Platte.

As word of Harney's testimony circulated among the Lakota they gave him a new nickname—"Mad Bear." The Indians suffered another indignity in March 1856 when Harney summoned the Lakota Head Men from their winter camps to a council. He demanded that they return any property and livestock stolen from whites and end all harassment of emigrants along the Oregon Trail—a virtual surrender of the once buffalo-rich Platte River Valley—and added that the United States now also officially considered the path of Harney's diagonal march from Fort Laramie to Fort Pierre as inviolable American land. He promised that the same consequences that had befallen Little Thunder would be meted out to any Indian harassing travelers along this new road. And there, in an unmarked grave, the skeletal remains of the Horse Creek Treaty were buried.

It was as if a veil had fallen from the eyes of the Lakota. Why it had taken so long is impossible to say. For nearly four decades they had put up with traders, trappers, soldiers, and emigrants trespassing on their lands. They had been literally sickened to death by white interlopers, and when they protested they had been given promises that the whites never intended to keep. They had watched the buffalo herds recede as homesteaders advanced along the Missouri. They had seen the whites turn on a Head Man they themselves had appointed and kill him over an old cow, friendly tribes attacked by soldiers, and their women and children murdered, captured, and raped. The trapper-trader Edwin Denig, traveling among the Lakota at the time and not particularly favorably inclined toward the "heathens," nonetheless feared their imminent destruction. "They are split into different factions following different leaders, and through want of game and unity of purpose are fast verging toward dissolution," he wrote in 1856. "Their ultimate destination will no doubt be to become a set of outlaws, hanging around the emigrant road, stealing horses, killing stragglers and committing other depredations until the Government is obliged to use measures for their entire extermination. It cannot be otherwise. It is the fate of circumstances which, however to be regretted, will become unavoidable."

Denig may have overestimated the disastrous effects American guns and germs had on the Indians—he put the entire Oglala population in 1856 at somewhat less than 700, but just a year earlier the Indian agent

Twiss had counted 450 Oglala lodges with a population closer to 2,000. Denig's prophecy would also prove faulty—the Lakota may have been down, but they were not out. In retrospect, it seems unlikely that a stray cow would become the impetus for a series of events that tipped the High Plains toward three decades of conflict. Yet there it was. Something big, the Western Sioux had finally recognized, something momentous never before considered, must be done.

Camped somewhere deep in an impenetrable crag of the immense Powder River Country during the late autumn of 1856, more than likely in the shadow of the sacred Black Hills, one imagines the thirty-five-year-old Red Cloud stepping from his tepee to listen to the bugle of a bull elk in its seasonal rut. Around him women haul water from a crystalline stream as cottonwood smoke rises from scores of cook fires and coils toward a sky the color of brushed aluminum. The wind sighs, and a smile creases his face as he observes a pack of mounted teenagers collect wagers in preparation for the Moccasin Game, or perhaps a rough round of Shinny. His gaze follows the grace and dexterity of one boy in particular, a slender sixteen-year-old with lupine eyes. The boy is Crazy Horse, and the war leader of the Bad Faces makes a mental note to keep tabs on this one.

All is well for the moment in Red Cloud's small world. But as he strolls through the village he spots movement atop a distant sandstone mesa. He catches a glint of the sun's last rays reflected, he knows, by a saddle pommel plated with Mexican silver, and he understands that the horse's owner is an Indian. Gradually the dark speck comes into focus, a single approaching rider, and Red Cloud recognizes the distinctive raised cantle and raven-feathered arrow fletchings—three at the top, three at the bottom, tied with sinew—favored by the Brules. Within moments the lone visitor dismounts before Old Smoke's lodge, and Red Cloud joins his tribesmen already gathered as the Head Man pulls back the flap of his tepee and signals them to enter.

Inside, seated by a wood fire, the Brule stranger eagerly accepts a bowl of dog stew seasoned with prairie turnip and wild artichoke and wordlessly consumes his meal before pulling from his buckskin blouse a long object wrapped in a wolf's pelt. It is a pipe, as Red Cloud knows before it is even unwrapped. But it is not the war pipe he is anticipating. This sacred pipe indicates a greater matter, one that Red Cloud has never before encountered. Enjoy your winter camp, the messenger reports, and make your spring buffalo hunt. But come the next summer hard decisions must be made.

As the stranger continues Red Cloud realizes that, for the first time in his life, for the first time since the Western Sioux ventured out onto the High Plains, all the Lakota have been summoned to a grand tribal council. It is there that they will formulate a united resistance against the mounting white threat.

SAMUEL COLT'S INVENTION

In August 1857 more Lakota congregated along the placid Belle Fourche River than had attended the Horse Creek Treaty Council six years earlier. For 10,000 years bands of indigenous North Americans had made pilgrimages to this holy ground in present-day western South Dakota where the stark Bear Butte loomed high over the riverbanks. To the Cheyenne this igneous rock was the sacred "Giving Hill," the height from which the Great Spirit had imparted the "sweet medicine" of life to the tribe; and this belief influenced later Sioux arrivals, who considered remains of an ancient volcanic eruption a holy place of meditation despite placing their own origin myth farther south, in the Black Hills. But never before had the Western Sioux come together at Bear Butte, or anywhere on the Plains, as a single people.

To this gathering had arrived not only Oglalas, Miniconjous, and Brules but the wild northern tribes—the Sans Arcs, Blackfeet Sioux, Two Kettles, and Hunkpapas—who set a tone of defiance. By some estimates as many as 10,000 Indians were present, more than three-quarters of the total population of Western Sioux, convened under a domed blue sky to fashion a "national" policy for dealing with the American aggressors. The

Lakota had finally recognized their mistake in not challenging General Harney when he invaded their country, and they vowed that this would be the last in a half century's worth of accommodations.

The lodges were arranged in a huge oval around the southern rim of the barren stone tower, and as young men raced horses, gambled, and purified themselves in preparation for a multitribal Sun Dance, women gossiped and girls preened for boys running among tepees gawking at heroes they knew only from legend. Here was the fierce Hump, the mighty Blackfoot whose future was said to have been foretold when as a boy he strayed into a cave and stared down a great gray wolf. Hump was conferring with his handsome tribesman Long Mandan, whose clear, wide-set eyes sparkled above scythe-like cheekbones. Young and old alike tilted their heads to gawk at the seven-foot Miniconjou fighter Touch The Clouds, who walked in the manner of a praying mantis, lifting his legs so high that he appeared to be using them as feelers. Packs of snapping dogs followed the fierce Hunkpapa "shirt wearer," Four Horns, who wore a necklace of raw meat strung across his hair-fringed tunic and was accompanied nearly everywhere he went by his nephew Sitting Bull. In each lodge they visited, these two proselytized for war against the whites.

Revered members of the western Oglala bands such as Red Cloud and the father and son Old-Man-Afraid-Of-His-Horses and Young-Man-Afraid-Of-His-Horses—the father striding through the camps with a regal mien befitting a man acknowledged by many as the successor to the slain Conquering Bear—introduced themselves to eastern counterparts such as the seasoned fighter Crow Feather of the Sans Arcs. And Crazy Horse, now nearly seventeen, was reunited with his family, including his younger half brother Little Hawk, whose adventuresome raids on the Crows had already inspired jubilant brave-heart songs. It was reported that of all the maidens vying to catch the eye of Crazy Horse, he was most attracted to a raven-haired beauty named Black Buffalo Woman, niece of Pretty Owl and Red Cloud. This infatuation would not end well.

Over many council fires and private feasts the Americans were, figuratively, put on trial. Militants like Red Cloud and Sitting Bull lobbied separately and together for immediate raids against Army detachments and emigrant wagon trains. Moderates such as

Old-Man-Afraid-Of-His-Horses and a Hunkpapa Head Man named Bears Ribs urged forbearance, arguing that the whites seemed content to have secured their "holy road." The moderates would fight if they must, they said, but why disturb a hornet's nest? Red Cloud and his allies countered that it was only a matter of time before these white wasps again flew as a swarm in search of larger Indian orchards. When had the Indian, Red Cloud asked, ever known the whites to be satisfied with the lands that they already possessed?

Despite these tactical disagreements, one unifying strategic goal did emerge—continued protection, by force if necessary, of the sanctity of the most sacred Black Hills. Oaths were sworn to defend the cherished *Paha Sapa* from all white intrusions; and the festivities remained generally upbeat and positive, the only shadow cast by the pale boy with the curly hair—the precocious Crazy Horse. He had spent the spring and early summer wandering from Montana to Kansas with his best friend, Young-Man-Afraid-Of-His-Horses. They had visited bands from numerous tribes, and at the Bear Butte Council Crazy Horse told a disheartening tale.

A month earlier he had joined a Cheyenne camp staked well below the Platte, on the banks of the Smoky Hill River south of the Republican—coincidentally, this would be the site of General George Armstrong Custer's first Indian campaign a decade later. There he was befriended by a medicine man called Ice. It was from Ice, he said, that he began to learn the ways of the Cheyenne, who, if possible, hated the whites even more than the Sioux did. Ice's people had carried out several successful raids on small detachments of soldiers crossing the Kansas Plains, but had been taken aback by the small guns the Bluecoats now carried that fired multiple rounds without having to be reloaded after each shot. These were the revolvers Red Cloud had seen at Horse Creek. But neither he nor any of the other Indians present at Bear Butte that summer were aware that their world was in the process of an irrevocable evolution, and that a driving force behind this change was emanating from, of all places, an industrial city far to the east in a state called Connecticut.

The inventor of these mysterious weapons, Samuel Colt, had taken a roundabout journey to fame. Colt's fascination with guns began when he

was a child living in Hartford and his maternal grandfather, a former officer in the Continental Army, bequeathed him a flintlock pistol. As Colt
grew older he became familiar with a cumbersome multibarreled handgun
called a "pepperbox revolver," which required the shooter to manually
rotate its cylinder, like a pepper grinder, after each discharge. Then, when
he went to sea in 1830 at the age of sixteen, on a brig bound for Calcutta,
he observed that the spokes in the ship's wheel, no matter in what direction it was spun, always synchronized with a clutch to hold the wheel in
place. He became transfixed by the idea of applying that technology to a
handgun. Using scraps from the ship's store, he built a wooden model of
a five-shot revolver based on the movement of the brig's wheel: a cocking
hammer would rotate the cylinder, and a pawl would lock it in place on
the tooth of a circular gear.

Back in the United States two years later, Colt secured American and
European patents for his invention, founded the Patent Arms Manufacturing Company in Paterson, New Jersey, and set about raising funds. He
was spectacularly inept. He toured the eastern United States and Canada
with what can best be described as a carnival act: his demonstrations
incorporated nitrous oxide, wax sculptures, and fireworks. He presented
theatrical speeches and gave elaborate dinner parties awash in alcohol to
which he invited wealthy businessmen and military officers in hopes of
luring investors and securing Army contracts. Colt's problem was that he
usually ended up outdrinking them all. Although his sales spiked briefly
when the Army ordered a consignment of five-shot Colts during the Second Seminole War, it was not enough to keep the firm afloat. In 1842, the
assets of the Patent Arms Manufacturing Company were sold at public
auction in New York City.

Colt tried his hand at other inventions—underwater electrical deto-
nators and, in partnership with Samuel Morse, a cable waterproofing
company to run undersea telegraph lines. But their genius was ahead of its
time, and Colt returned to his revolver. While tinkering with its original
design he scraped together the money to hire a New York gunsmith to
begin a limited production run—and then lightning struck in the form of
a veteran of the Seminole War named Samuel Walker. One day Walker
knocked on Colt's door with an order for 1,000 guns. Walker had recently

been promoted to captain in the Texas Rangers, and his Ranger company had used the five-shot Patent Colt with great success against marauding Comanche. Now he proposed adding a sixth round to the cylinder. Their collaboration produced the Walker Colt, the template for a generation of western handguns.

At the urging of General Sam Houston, President James Polk approved succeeding versions of Colt's handgun, most famously the Navy Revolver, as the official sidearm of the U.S. Army. It would be said after the Civil War that "Abe Lincoln may have freed all men, but Sam Colt made them equal." By then, Colt and Walker were both dead—Walker was killed in a skirmish during the Mexican War, in 1847; and Colt, wealthy beyond description, died of gout in 1862 at only forty-seven. But their revolver lived on, and Red Cloud, always enamored of new weapons, took a particular interest as Crazy Horse continued his story of the white soldiers and the magic guns.

Not long after one of their raids, the boy said, the Cheyenne learned that the Bluecoats were assembling a large retaliatory force to ride on their camp along the Smoky Hill. There was much debate among the Dog Soldiers about how best to face these new weapons until the medicine man Ice gathered the band's warriors and led them to a small lake near the village. The Cheyenne set even more store by charms and omens than did the Sioux, and Crazy Horse had watched as Ice taught the braves his medicine songs and told them to immerse their hands in the lake water while they sang and he danced. Satisfied with the ritual, he instructed a few of the cleansed Dog Soldiers to extend their arms, palms out. He then handed a rifle to another brave and ordered him to shoot. The bullets bounced off their hands.* The Cheyenne, mystically inured against the white man's balls and bullets, were now not only eager but frenzied for a fight.

Soon enough, in mid-July, they got their wish when about 300 Dog Soldiers rode out to face an equal number of Bluecoats of the 1st U.S.

---

*Stephen E. Ambrose, in *Crazy Horse and Custer*, proposes an explanation of this "miracle": the shells may have been underloaded with gunpowder, perhaps on Ice's secret instructions.

Cavalry under the command of Colonel E. V. "Bull Head" Sumner. It was an extraordinary scene, possibly the only classic "European" battle formation the Indians ever displayed on the American Plains. They rode from the west into a tight valley bounded by the Solomon River to the north and a string of high bluffs to the south. Sumner must have been shocked. The Indians' martial attributes—their speed, their stealth, their ability to surprise—were considered skulking and sneaky by American Army officers. Yet here was an enemy line as worthy of attack as any Hussar light cavalry. Sumner ordered his mounted skirmishers into three rows and cantered up the valley from the east. The Cheyenne raced their horses wildly in circles in order to give them a second wind, and then re-formed and loped easily toward the Americans.

Now the U.S. cavalrymen became confused. The few Indians who had long rifles held them at their sides, barrels pointed to the ground, while the rest kept their arrows in their quivers. At Ice's signal the Cheyenne horsemen extended their arms, palms out, and awaited the usual fusillade. But no guns sounded. Sumner had inexplicably ordered his troops to sling their carbines and unsheathe their three-foot-long "Old Wristbreaker" sabers. Sumner's instructions were pure chance. Never before or afterward was a saber charge recorded in the long history of the Indian wars. At the sight of the long knives descending on them the Cheyenne panicked. Their medicine had not prepared them for swords. Some turned and fled, while others dashed toward the river or up into the bluffs. It was a demoralizing rout. Only four braves were killed, and the women and children managed to flee, but the Americans captured the entire Cheyenne camp as well as the Indians' herd of packhorses and mules. On the American side, the "battle" was notable for drawing first blood from the young Lieutenant James Ewell Brown "Jeb" Stuart, who suffered a slight wound from a bullet to his chest.

The memory of the defeat, Crazy Horse told his Sioux brethren, had rested heavily on his mind since the day after the fight, when he and Young-Man-Afraid-Of-His-Horses packed up and rode north toward Bear Butte. Now he vowed, along with many others, to avenge it. To Red Cloud this account of the guns that fired six times must have seemed ominous. Whatever trepidation he felt, however, may have been overridden by the decisions made by the Lakota Head Men at Bear Butte. By the time the thousands of Indian ponies had reduced the prairie grass to nubs in all directions it was decided that each tribe would stake out its own, new hunting ground to develop and defend. "Thus," writes the Sioux historian Robert W. Larson, "those Oglalas who had followed Old Smoke chose the Powder River."

A BRIEF RESPITE

B y mid-century the era of the Oglalas' annual spring buffalo hunt from the Black Hills east to the Missouri had long ended. White settlers had converted the fertile floodplain along the Big Muddy in the state of Iowa and in the Kansas, Nebraska, and Dakota Territories into one long string of farms and small communities, and by 1857 nearly two dozen steamboats were in regular service between St. Louis and Sioux City. With the homesteaders hemming the Lakota in from the east while Army troops stepped up patrols along the Oregon Trail to the south, the Western Sioux had no choice but to forge north and west, deeper into the rich buffalo grounds bordering the Yellowstone and Bighorn ranges on lands held by the Crows, the Shoshones, the Nez Percé, and the northern Arapaho.

Ironically, despite their haphazard approach to a unified "war" on the whites, in the years following the Bear Butte gathering this migratory shift allowed most of the Oglalas to give the Americans a wide enough berth that their culture experienced a minor but flourishing mini-renaissance, evoking memories of the fat and happy early 1800s. The Powder River Country had the most unspoiled hunting grounds in North America, and as Oglala society grew wealthier and stronger, so too did Red Cloud's grip on power. Warriors from disparate Oglala bands now vied to ride with him against the Crows and other enemies, and each fighting season he attracted greater numbers of Brules, Miniconjous, and even Sans Arcs and Hunkpapas to join his far-reaching expeditions. These companions included Crazy Horse.

Because of the new geographic reality, Red Cloud's martial leadership also took on a new form and function. No longer could he afford to lead a few braves on raids merely for glory and plunder; his war parties for the first time now also hunted for Indian "intruders" to expel from the Western Sioux's burgeoning empire. This often meant deviating from the traditional Lakota method of prairie warfare on open, flat terrain. On one occasion, for instance, his scouts picked up fresh Shoshone moccasin tracks hugging the base of the Bighorns in northern Wyoming. Red Cloud and about seventy-five braves caught up to the Shoshones and chased them back into the mountains. In the old days, that would have been warning enough. Not now. Red Cloud ordered his Sioux to dismount and hitch their horses, and they pursued the Shoshones on foot up the steep pitch. A running high country battle through thick whitebark pine and blue spruce ensued—a fight a Mohawk, a Choctaw, or even a Minnesota Sioux might have felt more comfortable engaging in than a Plains Lakota. When the Shoshones disappeared behind a circular wall of boulders that formed a natural fortress on top of a rocky promenade, Red Cloud's braves surrounded them.

For a day and night the Lakota besieged the Shoshones, feinting, charging, being beaten back, each side's sharpshooters firing whenever an enemy exposed himself. Occasionally a Sioux arrow would lodge in a Shoshone's head as it was raised over the top of the wall. For the most part, however, the Shoshones holding the high ground got the better of the fight. One defender in particular seemed to have the best shooting eye— he had killed at least one Bad Face and wounded several others—and Red Cloud, crouched behind a tree perhaps 100 yards downslope, studied the shooter's pattern. He observed that the enemy would jump onto the stone barricade, aim his long rifle, and fire in a nearly continuous motion before ducking back down for cover. Red Cloud also noticed that the Shoshone shot from behind the same rock each time.

Red Cloud hatched his plan and signaled to one of his braves to dash for a nearby boulder. As he expected, the sharpshooting Shoshone showed himself. Red Cloud stood, and in an electrifying display of accuracy, shot him dead. The Shoshone toppled forward, outside the fortress, and a shrieking Red Cloud tore up the mountain brandishing his tomahawk. He reached the man, scalped him, and hacked off his right arm at the shoulder. He then crawled to and fro along the outside of the wall, raising the severed arm at intervals and shouting for the cowardly enemies to come out and fight like men.

But the Bad Faces, still mired in the ways of prairie warfare, failed to press their psychological advantage. So excited were those guarding the rear of the makeshift fort that they abandoned their positions to crowd below Red Cloud and whoop him on. This left open a back door through which most of the Shoshones escaped into the forest. Red Cloud was furious. But all he could do was file away the episode and ensure that it never happened again. The Oglala war party climbed down the mountain, retrieved their horses, and rode back and forth along the foot of the range for three days as a signal to any Indians who might be watching that this was now Lakota land. This, too, was something new.

Meanwhile, far to the south, General Harney's clearance of the Platte River corridor provided a freeway for the thousands of emigrants still driving west. Among these were motley bands of Mormon "handcart pioneers," who formed a nearly continuous stream into the Salt Lake Valley. Many of the converts to the Church of Jesus Christ of Latter-day Saints were recent northern European immigrants who could not afford to pay $300 to $500 for a prairie schooner and a mule or oxen team. Those families, disproportionately Danish and Swedish and speaking little or no English, instead loaded up their earthly possessions into pushcarts that could be purchased in Iowa City for as little as $10. These sturdy contraptions—a simple bed of hickory or oak laid over thin iron wheels— could haul up to 500 pounds, and between 1856 and 1860 nearly 3,000 Mormons walked west from the United States into the New Zion, pushing and pulling their humble handcarts.

Those numbers multiplied nearly exponentially when gold was discovered in 1858 on Cheyenne and southern Arapaho lands along Cherry Creek, the future site of Denver. The area around Pikes Peak came to resemble an ant colony, with 100,000 pitmen and placermen swarming over the hills and dales. So safe had the Oregon Trail become that by 1860 the newly formed Pony Express began carrying mail along a 2,000-mile route between St. Joseph, Missouri, and Sacramento, California, completing the circuit in ten days during good weather and fourteen in the dead of winter. The small, wiry Express riders, many of them still in their teens, sparked a trend in publishing circles back east, their roughneck adventures filling "true" dime novels and early pulp magazines. The romance lasted longer than the endeavor. Less than two years later the swashbuckling operation was shut down when the Western Union Telegraph Company finished stringing its lines. The railroad was also coming: industry executives were already dusting off Captain Stansbury's old surveys in preparation for laying track.

Most of the Indians these emigrants saw before reaching the Rockies were bands of "tame" Oglalas and Brules—"Laramie Loafers," the Bluecoats called them with a sneer—who scratched out a living begging and scavenging along the trails west. There was much to scavenge, for it is doubtful that by the early 1860s Red Cloud would have recognized the Platte River Valley of his youth. The route was now littered with broken-down wagons and handcarts, empty food tins, and clothes worn to rags, while the cottonwood and chokecherry trees that had once lined every creek and streambed had been burned for countless cooking fires. The buffalo had disappeared, having lost the battle for the corridor's already scarce water and vegetation to the 100,000 head of cattle and 50,000 sheep that passed through the territory annually. And the Oregon Trail itself had been transformed into "a swath of stinking refuse," its very air soured by the rotting carcasses of worn-out horses, mules, oxen, and sheep mixing with the half-buried corpses of humans struck down by heat, exhaustion, or disease, their bones dug up and picked over by gray wolves and coyotes.

The increased traffic proved beneficial for traders, blacksmiths, innkeepers, hostlers, and even a few professional gamblers who set up shop along the route—as well as for some of the old mountain men whose financial opportunities skyrocketed with the need for guides and scouts. As late as 1852 Jim Bridger had been sighted still trapping in the Rockies, probably as much for sport as need, since his cedar log fort on the Blacks Fork of the Green River in central Utah was doing a thriving business as a layover near the "California ferry," which put off at the head of the western trails. But Bridger's legendary intimacy with the Indians, particularly the Ute and his wife's Shoshone tribe, made him a marked man.

Unlike the Lakota, the mountain tribes stood in the way of the Mormons' expansion. Brigham Young, by now governor of the Utah Territory, had turned the Salt Lake Valley into his own semiautonomous fiefdom, which he named Deseret, and in July 1853 a full-scale war broke out between the Ute and the Latter-day Saints. Both sides committed the usual atrocities and Young, suspicious of Bridger's loyalties and envious of his real estate holdings, used the bloodletting as an excuse to issue a territorial proclamation forbidding all trade with any of the tribes. The following month at a Mormon town hall meeting Bridger was accused of having "stirred up the Indians to commit depredations upon our people." It was alleged that he had supplied the Shoshones with powder and lead—the very act with which he had kept the peace, and for which he had been lauded, at the Horse Creek Council two years earlier. "Old Gabe" was tried and found guilty in absentia at a secret hearing, and a posse of 150 "avenging angels" was dispatched from Provo to arrest him. Indians warned him and he eluded the riders, taking his family east to Fort Laramie. When the Mormons reached his stockade they burned his copious stocks of whiskey and rum and seized the fort and livestock. They never returned them.

From Wyoming, Bridger meandered farther east until finally, after having been away for thirty years, he arrived back home in St. Louis. His fame had preceded him, and he was mobbed by reporters and well-wishers wherever he went. He purchased a large farmstead just outside the city, but plowing, planting, and reaping were not in his blood. Through the remainder of the decade he found steady employment, at $5 a day, guiding various kinds of expeditions. He took part in a congressional scientific survey seeking the source of the Yellowstone, and discovered a mountain pass that shortened the route between Denver and Salt Lake City for the overland mail coach—today's U.S. Route 40. He achieved some measure of revenge on the Latter-day Saints by guiding 2,500 federal troops into Salt Lake City during the "Mormon War," fought over Brigham Young's theocratic rebellion of 1857–58. And in one of the more bizarre chapters of his life he contracted with a wealthy, dissolute Irish peer, Sir St. George Gore, as a scout for Gore's hunting safari. Bridger spent the better part of two years wandering the High Plains with Gore—the eighth baronet of Manor Gore, near Sligo—mostly trying to prevent his self-indulgent employer and a retinue of beaters, skinners, wranglers, chefs, and sommeliers from wandering into Lakota territory.

He was not often successful. Gore killed animals on a whim at an astounding pace, and toward the end of his wanton holiday he and Bridger crossed paths with U.S. Army captain Randolph B. Marcy, fresh from his discovery of the headwaters of the Red River. Marcy recorded that among Gore's voluminous antelope, deer, and elk trophies were the coats of 41 grizzly bears and 2,500 buffalo skins. It took six wagons and twenty-one carts to haul all this. Since Bridger professed to care deeply for the welfare of the Indians, it is difficult to explain why he did not recognize that such indiscriminate slaughter might antagonize the Western Sioux.

But if Bridger did not notice, Red Cloud surely did. The great *blotahunka* was now Head Man of the Bad Face Oglalas in all but name, because at age eighty-two, Old Smoke had faded into senescence to enjoy the December of his long life. Though greenhorn Army officers deployed to Fort Laramie after the Mormon War continued to recognize the more pliant Old-Man-Afraid-Of-His-Horses as "chief" of the Sioux—Red Cloud's name had yet to appear in any official government reports—most Lakota, including those from the far Missouri River regions east of the Black Hills, considered Red Cloud their martial and spiritual leader.

This primacy, however, also carried a heavy responsibility. The history of the white incursion had demonstrated that individual bands could not stand alone against the might of the American Army. But could a multitribal alliance actually be formed to battle the intruders? And if so, what were its chances of prevailing? Of one fact Red Cloud was certain— large-scale engagements against the Bluecoats where the two sides were of equal numbers were essentially suicide missions. The only way to fight them was to gather enough of the squabbling Sioux under one banner and use overwhelming force against any smaller targets that presented themselves. Barring that, or perhaps in addition to that, the Indians would need to rely on stealthy hit-and-run tactics, where the chance of casualties was low. They would use their knowledge of the country to run off Army remudas and beef herds, and starve the Bluecoats out of their isolated forts. It would be a war of decoy and ambush, of fighting from bluff to butte and from coulee to creek bed—in short, a guerrilla war before it was actually known as such. It was, Red Cloud recognized, the Indians' only recourse.

Yet how to rouse his disparate peoples, particularly his own tribesmen? Despite the occasional incursions by insatiable white hunters guided by the likes of Bridger, the Lakota cultural and political revival in the years following the Bear Butte assembly had ushered in a period of quiescence. With their enemies, particularly the Crows, cleared from the mile-high Powder River Country, the Lakota were free to roam an immense short-grass prairie bursting with buffalo, antelope, elk, deer, and bighorn sheep and crossed by abundant sources of sweet water flowing out of pine-shrouded ranges. During the broiling summer months cool mountain meadows awash with goldenrod and back-eyed Susans beckoned, and in winter the south face of the Black Hills constituted a gigantic windbreak against the numbing gales freighting down from the Canadian flats.

Moreover, just as Old-Man-Afraid-Of-His-Horses had argued at Bear Butte, the Bluecoats had not strayed far from their line of forts and mail stations along the Oregon Trail since General Harney's march. Even the secondary road Harney had blazed from Fort Laramie to Fort Pierre was now growing over; the ruts from the Army freight wagons were barely visible beneath carpets of white prairie clover and purple asters. Red Cloud still suspected that white expansion was not complete, that the trespassers would once more arrive in greater numbers to steal Lakota lands. Why they had not done so already remained a mystery.

Given the circumstances, it would be hard to make the case for war on the whites. As it was, Red Cloud and the Western Sioux had no way of knowing that, far to the east, two American armies were already preparing for an epic Civil War that would, at least temporarily, push the "Indian Problem" far down on the government's list of priorities.

THE DAKOTAS RISE

The distant echoes of the bombardment of Fort Sumter on April 12, 1861, reverberated well beyond the Mississippi. As one historian noted, "the frontier army suddenly ceased to protect the frontier." At the start of the hostilities, officers from southern states, who represented nearly a third of the Regular Army's officer corps, resigned en masse—313 threading home to fight for the Confederacy, including 182 of the Army's 184 West Point graduates. Most of the noncommissioned officers and enlisted men remained true to the Union, but they, too, rapidly disappeared from the Plains. Even the detachment at Fort Laramie, the western communications hub connecting the coasts, was reduced to a skeleton garrison of about 130 soldiers as battalions and regiments from across the West marched home. Chaos ensued as the sons of Virginia planters, Boston Brahmins, Iron Mountain dirt farmers, and Philadelphia steamfitters enlisted as volunteers and state militiamen trained in haste and then moved like chess pieces across a grand board. The few southern officers who did not relinquish their commissions were viewed with suspicion by the War Department—particularly the Tennesseean General Harney, who remained commander of the Northwest Territories.

In the years since the fight at Blue Water Creek and his "invasion" of the Lakota lands, Harney's bungling adventures had continued into the farcical. He still hunted Indians, seemingly for sport, but that had never bothered the authorities back east. It was only when, in 1859, he nearly set off a shooting war with Great Britain that his superiors thought to rein him in. This occurred during an inspection tour of the U.S.-Canadian borderlands, when his inept handling of a minor incident involving an "English" hog rooting through an American farmer's fields resulted in an armed standoff between Harney's troops and British Royal Marines. Diplomats were roused, cooler heads prevailed, and Harney was shuffled back into the nation's interior, where it was thought he could do no more lasting damage to either himself or the Union cause. But twelve months into the Civil War he was relieved of command by President Lincoln when rumors surfaced that he was secretly negotiating a western truce with Confederate authorities.

Harney denied the charge and set off for Washington to defend himself. But he somehow lost his way and made the error of passing through rebel-held territory, where he was captured and presented to General Robert E. Lee. Lee offered him a Confederate commission, which Harney to his credit declined, and he was released and allowed to complete his journey. On reaching Washington, however, Harney was quietly retired and whisked from the national stage.

Though happy to be rid of the murderous "Mad Bear," the Western Sioux made no concerted effort to exploit either Harney's absence or the War Between the States. Nevertheless, those who learned of its particulars took no small satisfaction in the great droves of white men slaughtering each other on faraway battlefields. This absence of tension, however, did not prevent rumors from reaching Washington of Confederate agents fomenting insurrection among the tribes, particularly the Sioux, the Cheyenne, and, farther south, the sullen peoples occupying the Indian Territory of present-day Oklahoma. In keeping with the government's usual incomprehension of Indian mores, particularly those of the Northern Plains tribes, none of the fearmongers gave a thought to why Indians would ever fight for a slaveholding republic that had facilitated the greatest deportation of Native Americans on the continent. In any case, the South lacked the means to incite such an uprising.

The exception was in Minnesota, where the war did, however tangen-
tially, facilitate a feral Indian conflict in the summer of 1862. It erupted,
and was put down, with brutal efficiency, but not before much blood—
most of it Indian, and innocent—was spilled.

For years small bands of renegade Dakotas—the closest eastern cousins
of the Lakota—had mounted scattered attacks on isolated homesteaders
in Minnesota. The most notorious occurred in 1857, when a Santee brave
named Scarlet Point led a war party that killed at least thirty whites near
one of Iowa's Okoboji lakes. Scarlet Point then crossed the Minnesota
border and raided several farmsteads in Jackson County before escaping
west. Yet despite the "Spirit Lake Massacre,"* as the incident came to be
known, the better-armed Minnesotans seemed willing to live with this
risk as long as the majority of the Indians kept to the reservations. Their
attitude changed in 1862.

The ember that ignited the Minnesota powder keg could be traced
back, as usual, to the government's broken promises. Four years earlier
Minnesota had become the thirty-second state admitted into the Union,
and in the summer of 1862 it was not lost on the Indians that the already
sparse population of just over 170,000† had been drained of young men,
many of whom were off fighting the Confederacy. Washington had signed
treaties with the Dakotas in 1851, and again in 1858, whereby the Sioux
ceded large blocks of rich bottomland in the southwest part of what was
then a territory in exchange for over $1.5 million and an annual allowance
of sundry trade goods. In addition, the Dakotas agreed to relocate to two
Indian agencies on the Upper Minnesota River; these consisted of a strip
of land about 20 miles wide and 150 miles long on either side of the river.
Like most of these pacts, the treaty was not worth the ink used to write it.

The Sioux soon realized they had been duped; they could not exist, let

---

*It should be noted that whites have always been much more inclined to affix the
term "massacre" to Indian atrocities while preferring to call their own victories, such as
the one at Blue Water Creek, "battles."
†Five American cities had a greater population than Minnesota, and three western
hubs—New Orleans, Cincinnati, and St. Louis—each contained nearly as many
people.

alone thrive, on their new reservations, and the promised government payments were not only smaller than they expected, but usually late—if they
arrived at all. Various Dakota Head Men tried every avenue short of war
to rectify the injustice, including making a trip to Washington with their
Indian agents to plead their cases. This, amazingly, resulted in two more
treaties in which the Indians agreed to hand over an additional 1 million
acres on the north side of the Minnesota River. Congress authorized a
payment of 30 cents an acre for the land but, like the earlier compensa-
tions, these funds disappeared. The Sioux were now desperate, and as their
plight worsened they enlisted the advocacy of a local Episcopal bishop, the
Reverend Henry Whipple, who wrote a heartfelt letter to President Lincoln on their behalf. Whipple denounced the local Indian agents as party
hacks and the entire U.S. Indian Office as a congeries of "inefficiency and
fraud." Nothing came of his intervention, and the Indians' contempt for
the white man's lies and deceit intensified.

A subsequent series of harsh winters and crop failures left the Dakotas
near starvation, and when in June 1862 the promised government annuity failed to arrive, they took advantage of the state militia's depletion
and rose. Nearly 5,000 Sioux descended on Indian agency warehouses
on the Upper Minnesota demanding provisions: pork, flour, tobacco, and
coffee. The cowed agents agreed, but of course there was not enough to
go around. A delegation of Dakotas then asked the local traders to extend them credit based on their government IOUs. A merchant named
Andrew Myrick summed up the whites' reaction, telling friends, "If they
are hungry, let them eat grass." As would become evident later, the Indians
knew of Myrick's remarks.

An uneasy month passed in the high north until, around noon on Sunday, August 17, four Dakota hunters who were returning to their lodges
on a rutted trail in south-central Minnesota stopped at a combination
store, inn, and post office operated by a man named Robinson Jones and
his family. One of the braves found a cache of hen eggs, smashed them,
and taunted his companions as cowards. Goaded into action, the other
three entered the Joneses' compound and demanded whiskey. Jones was
inside with his two adopted children: blond, fifteen-year-old Clara Wilson and her fifteen-month-old half-brother Joshua. His wife was half a

mile away, visiting at the home of her son Howard Baker, his wife, Clara, and her two young grandchildren. Also at the Baker homestead that day were a young couple who had stopped on their push west from Wisconsin: Viranus Webster and his wife (she is referred to in the accounts only as Webster's "new young wife").

When Jones refused the demand for liquor the Indians threatened him, and he burst out the back door and ran for the Baker homestead. Just as he was entering the house, the Dakotas caught him and clubbed him and his wife to death. Before Howard Baker and Viranus Webster could reach their rifles they were shot and killed. Their wives somehow managed to gather the two Baker children and escape into the woods. But when the Indians returned to the Jones compound they came upon the teenage Clara Wilson. They raped her and shot her to death. They were apparently unaware of the presence of her sleeping baby half-brother.

Word of the attack on Clara Wilson rattled the surrounding communities. Some whites, including Bishop Whipple, attempted to stem the reaction, but it was inevitable. The Dakota Sioux had murdered white adults and raped and killed a blond, angelic-looking teenage girl. Such atrocities always evoked hard and swift vengeance. Whipple's Indian counterpart was a Dakota Head Man named Little Crow, who that very night convened a tribal council and cautioned his people against fighting. Little Crow had been among the Indians who had journeyed to Washington, and he feared for the tribe's very existence in a war with America. "We are only little herds of buffaloes left scattered," he told the bands gathered around the council fire that night. "The white men are like locusts when they fly so thick that the whole sky is a snowstorm. You may kill one, two, ten, as many as the leaves in the forest, and their brothers will not miss them. Count your fingers all day long and white men with guns in their hands will come faster than you can count." But Little Crow could not deter his tribesmen, and with weary reluctance he assumed the role of war chief.

The next day painted war parties descended on white settlements and farms across western Minnesota and overran the government barns and warehouses of the lower Indian agency. The braves killed about twenty whites, including the contemptuous merchant Myrick, who tried to flee his store by jumping from a second-story window. He was run down and scalped before he could reach the forest, and his corpse's mouth was stuffed with grass. About 100 emboldened warriors next surrounded Fort Ridgely, a rickety log structure in the southwest corner of the state that had been constructed nine years earlier with no forethought of an Indian attack. Over 200 frightened civilians, mostly women and children, were gathered in the stockade, which was defended by a few farmers and twenty-two volunteer soldiers. But they possessed cannons, and even though the fort's commander, Lieutenant Thomas Gere, was bedridden with mumps, the powerful artillery allowed his troops to hold out for three days until reinforcements arrived.

It was the beginning of the end. Within weeks a large combined force of 1,500 from the Minnesota militia and the Regular Army—many of them paroled from Confederate prison camps specifically to return to Minnesota to fight Indians—routed the Dakotas at the Battle of Lake Wood. Afterward the soldiers scalped the enemy dead as their commander and the state's first governor, Colonel Henry Sibley, looked on admiringly. As Little Crow had predicted, the white men with guns were as numerous as the leaves in the forest. The fight went out of the Indians.

The Dakotas claimed they were promised leniency if they surrendered—"[Sibley] assured us that if we would do this we would only be held as prisoners of war for a short time," recalled the warrior Big Eagle. And increasingly large numbers turned themselves in, until the Army held 1,250 Indian men and boys in custody. But the military judicial commission appointed to try the Indians either knew nothing about or ignored Sibley's guaranty. Most of the Sioux were handed long prison terms, and 307 were convicted of murder, rape, or both, and sentenced to be hanged the day after Christmas. These sham proceedings were too much for even some vengeful whites, and several clergymen and muckraking newspaper editors began investigating and reporting the injustices. The din reached all the way to the White House, where President Lincoln commuted the death sentences of 268 men while personally writing on Executive Office stationary the names of the remaining 39 to be hanged. (One of these 39 would be granted a last-minute reprieve.) Little Crow remained at large until the following summer, when he was recognized by a white hunter who collected a bounty by shooting and killing him. His tanned scalp, skull, and wrist bones were put on public exhibition.

Estimates of the number of white civilians and soldiers killed in the "Dakota War" range as high as 800. Indian dead were undoubtedly much more numerous; no one bothered to count them. The war's impact on the eastern Sioux, however, went deeper than its death toll. The once mighty Dakotas were now a society in shards, "most of the six thousand former residents of the reservations either forced to flee westward to the plains, incarcerated, or executed," according to one historian. And as those renegades who did manage to reach the prairie related their stories, the entire bloody business left a palpable foreboding hanging over the Lakota camps of the Upper Missouri and the Powder River Country. The implications were not lost on Sam Deon, the thirty-four-year-old Québécois fur trader, when he arrived at Red Cloud's winter camp on the Belle Fourche in northern Wyoming on a bitter cold night not long afterward.

A short, wiry man who could speak several Sioux dialects fluently, Peter Abraham "Sam" Deon had set out from Montreal fifteen years earlier to make his fortune in the uncharted American West. Arriving in St. Louis via Boston and New Orleans, he found work almost immediately as an agent for the American Fur Company, and had since roamed extensively among the firm's Upper Missouri trading posts exchanging dry goods, blankets, tinned groceries, and guns for buffalo robes and beaver pelts. The ruddy-faced Deon—described in one Army officer's journal as "a jolly, royal, generous fellow; happy everywhere, and whom the very fact of existence filled with exuberance and joy"—was quick to accept the manners and psychology of the Sioux. He understood, for instance, that there was no such thing as a homogeneous "Indian," that each tribe had its own social, political, and martial mores, and that these indigenous people would never comprehend the workings of a capitalist free market. Accordingly, he knew enough to frame his transactions as an exchange of gifts. Moreover, during his High Plains circuits Deon had taken as his wife Red Cloud's maternal aunt Bega, later known as Mary Highwolf, and camped with her people often. He was as close to the great warrior chief as any white man could be, and over the course of their tentative friendship he had witnessed firsthand the maturation of the strapping young brave from a prideful, ambitious, and arrogant youth into a thoughtful and soft-spoken leader.

Unlike most whites, Deon understood perfectly the breadth of Red Cloud's influence not only over his own Oglala Bad Faces, but over all the Western Sioux. On this December night in 1862 he would also learn just how adept Red Cloud could be at sending a veiled message. A week earlier Deon had set out from his base at Fort Laramie, 150 miles to the south, leading a mule train of four high-sided Murphy wagons hauling over 10,000 pounds of trade goods. Like all white traders, Deon had his share of violent run-ins with the Plains peoples; he seemed to consider this the price of doing business. Yet for all his long good-fellowship with Red Cloud, he was savvy enough, after the Minnesota rising, to be wary. Red Cloud was fresh from a final victory over the Crow chief Little Rabbit, whom he had personally killed in a fight that marked the unofficial end of any Crow pretensions to the Powder River Country. The decisive generalship Red Cloud had displayed during the blood-soaked "Crow Wars" in the late 1850s and early 1860s not only added to his prestige among the Lakota, but also served to bring his name to the attention of soldiers still stationed in the West.

Though remaining proud of his ability to count coup and take scalps, Red Cloud had reached his early forties, an age when the role of leading war parties should naturally be relinquished to younger braves. He also recognized that he could do his people the most good by dedicating himself to formulating strategic tribal aims. He suspected that when the white Civil War ended, whichever side proved victorious would again set its sights on Lakota lands. This apprehension gnawed at him, and manifested itself most obviously in his muted celebration of his victory over the Crows. There was also another reason for the pall that seemed to hang over his village: as Deon's wagons rolled into view: the thirty-nine Dakota braves still awaited the gallows in a jail in Mankato, Minnesota, and Red Cloud and his people were aware of this. These hard feelings made Deon worried.

The trader and his teamsters understood just how vulnerable and isolated they were. Two years earlier the census had recorded over 31 million people in the United States, not counting Indians but including nearly 4 million slaves. Ninety percent lived east of the Mississippi. The boom-town of Denver had fewer than 5,000 inhabitants, and there were no white population centers of any significance at all west of the Black Hills until one crossed the Rockies and traveled another 1,000 miles to San Francisco. Moreover, the closest U.S. Army post to Red Cloud's winter camp—Fort Laramie, with not even 150 soldiers—was a six-day ride.

Given all this, Deon was not certain what kind of welcome he would receive, and was surprised when Red Cloud invited him and his men into the camp proper instead of ordering them to its edge, as was the usual trading custom. Even more shocking was the feast laid out for the whites—a meal of boiled venison, hominy, and strong roasted coffee. Though the teamsters eased themselves into the firelight as if entering a snake pit, after some friendly trading Deon was beckoned to attend a storytelling session in Red Cloud's lodge. He sat cross-legged as the great warrior stood to take the floor.

By all accounts the chief's heroic tales lacked any subtlety—like his deeds, they were straight to the point. This bluntness did not make them any less riveting. Tonight, perhaps with the fate of his thirty-nine con-demned Dakota kin on his mind, he began with a story of once having saved a fellow warrior's life during a raid on the Omaha.

It was a long-ago spring morning, Red Cloud began, and he was a young warrior with scant reputation, when Old Smoke's scouts spotted the gray plumes of many cook fires near the bluffs surrounding Prairie Creek in what is now central Nebraska. Red Cloud was a member of the war party sent out to investigate, and from the summit of a red sand hill they spied several hundred trespassing Omaha engaged in a raucous buffalo-hunt dance around a pole erected in the center of an encamp-ment. From the top of the pole flew an old, tattered Spanish flag. The Sioux charged immediately, their mounts thundering through the village and scattering the dancers. Red Cloud decided that depriving the Omaha of their pennant was more important than killing or counting coup, and he beckoned several Sioux braves to follow him as he broke off from the attack. But by the time he reached the center of the village the Omaha had organized a spirited defense, and what Red Cloud had perceived as a game of capture the flag suddenly turned serious. When he neared the sapling that flew the piece of cloth, arrows and a few balls from ancient muskets cut the air around him. He had raised his tomahawk and was about to hack off the top of the pole when one of his companions was shot. At that instant Red Cloud dropped the tomahawk and caught the brave by one hand before he hit the ground. Then another Sioux warrior grabbed the wounded man's other arm, and the three rode to safety.

Approving grunts filled the lodge, and Deon himself nodded in admiration. The white trader was well aware of the great value that all Indians placed on the rescue of a fallen comrade; it was considered the paramount act of bravery. He was looking forward to the probable denouement: perhaps Red Cloud had returned to the Omaha village to skewer and flay an enemy brave, or at least toss a writhing body onto a pile of roasting buffalo chips. Instead, Red Cloud abruptly fell silent and gestured to a very old man seated closest to the lodge fire. Via a series of hand gestures he indicated that he was now anxious for his friend Deon to hear the tales of the old days and old ways, and encouraged the old man to recount the Sioux origin story, "The Lost Children." The old man lifted his clay pipe, filled the wooden bowl with dried kinnikinnick, lit it with an ember, and drew in several puffs. He passed the pipe to his west, and began to speak.

What followed was a riveting tale of revenge, betrayal, heroism, and the sundering of the Sioux Nation into eastern and western branches. It involved mythical ancient battles and a band of Lakota children, mistakenly abandoned, who taught themselves to survive, alone, on the prairie. Although the children were initially angry enough to fight the elder kinsmen who had "lost" them, in the end both sides came to an agreement that if any Sioux tribe ever called for help, every other tribe was duty-bound to answer. And thus it had been, concluded the old man at the lodge fire, that the great Nation of the Seven Council Fires was divided into separate tribes, yet each tribe would forevermore remain loyal to its cousins.

By this point in time the great, grand oaths sworn at the Bear Butte gathering five years earlier were thought to have been forgotten by the Western Sioux. But this night, left unsaid but hovering over Red Cloud's lodge like smoke from the fire, was the moral of both stories. Red Cloud had made it clear to Sam Deon how he, his tribesmen, and by extension every Lakota warrior stalking the High Plains felt about the treacherous treatment of the Minnesota Dakotas at the hands of the white man.

Six days later, at 10:30 on a dull gray morning in faraway Mankato, the raucous cheering of a vast crowd of civilians and soldiers drowned out the death songs of the thirty-eight Dakotas who climbed the scaffold. (President Lincoln, as noted above, had commuted one man's sentence.) A moment later, according to one observer, the Indians' "lifeless bodies were left dangling between heaven and earth." It was the largest mass execution in American history.

Most died wearing war paint.

THE RESISTANCE

'Tis true they were a lawless brood,
But rough in form, nor mild in mood.

—Lord Byron, *The Bride of Abydos*

STRONG HEARTS

Traveling at 250 feet per second and deadly accurate to 100 yards, it produced a sound that was described variously as a shrieking whistle or a mere whisper on the wind. In either case soldiers on the frontier certainly heard it coming, even if there was no time to react. So it was that in all likelihood Lieutenant Caspar Collins, a musket ball already lodged in his hip, recognized the hiss of the arrow an instant before its cast-iron tip pierced his forehead, drilled through his skull, and exploded his prefrontal cortex. The last thing he saw was his cavalry troop being overrun by Indians.

Hundreds of Sioux and Cheyenne had poured from the ocher bluffs that overlooked the Army outpost known as Bridge Station, hard by the North Platte. They engulfed Collins's command in a matter of moments. One trooper inexplicably dismounted in a dusty washout, determined to fight on foot. He was dead nearly before his boots hit the ground. Another's horse was shot out from under him; wounded, he crawled on his hands and knees toward the 1,000-foot wooden span that led to the barricaded stockade on the far side of the river. Bluecoats on the battlements watched an Indian bury a tomahawk in his head. A third trooper fell with his mount, horse and rider both bristling with arrow shafts.

The last anyone saw of Lieutenant Collins, he was still in the saddle, blood streaming down his face, his hands squeezing the reins in a death grip as his horse reared and galloped into the center of the war party. Collins had been warned before leaving the fort that his was a suicide mission.

"I am not a coward," he had replied. "I know what it means to go out . . . but I've never disobeyed an order. I'm a soldier's son."

His body was never recovered.

It was July 26, 1865, and Collins was one of twenty-nine cavalrymen from Ohio and Kansas killed in a daylong series of running fights in east-central Wyoming that came to be known as the Battle of Red Buttes. How many Indians fell Red Cloud could not immediately determine, as half of his force had ridden off to attack a train of Army freight wagons making for the fort. What he did know was that he had, at long last, set out to avenge a lifetime's worth of lies, injustices, and broken promises. In the process, he had ordered the first shots fired in what would come to be known as Red Cloud's War. He had no idea that three long columns of Bluecoats would soon be mounted and moving toward him with orders to kill him and every male Indian over the age of twelve.

The events at Red Buttes had followed from the Dakota Uprising of 1862. Yet years before Collins's death at Bridge Station, Red Cloud had anticipated the war and its consequences, mentally sifting the possible outcomes like a placerman panning a mountain stream. While the Union and Confederate armies savaged each other in the east, the western side of the Mississippi had grown turbulent and vicious on both sides of the Oglalas' tranquil Powder River territory. In Colorado the Ute had taken to raiding and burning the overland stage stations leading into Denver, and in the northern Rockies the Shoshones and Bannocks had declared open hostilities on the gold seekers drilling more and deeper holes into their mountains. Across the Kansas-Nebraska frontier marauding Cheyenne Dog Soldiers were killing emigrants and homesteaders by the score and—in the worst affront to white sensibility—frequently kidnapping women and children. The Comanche and Kiowa had virtually closed the Santa

Fe Trail, and there were rumors of emissaries from those great southern confederacies traveling to the Oklahoma Territory to foment an Indian insurrection all across the Plains.

Meanwhile, Sitting Bull had soaked the Upper Missouri with tableland blood, for it was there that the most militant Minnesota Dakota renegades had allied with his feral Hunkpapas to terrorize traders and steamboat operators threshing the turbid waters of the frontier as well as the few dryland farmers and ranchers hardy enough to settle the country's most windswept prairie. Any Indian considered too friendly toward the Americans was also fair game. The Hunkpapa chief Bears Ribs, who had urged moderation on Red Cloud and others at the large war council at Bear Butte in 1857, was slain by the Lakota after repeatedly ignoring Sitting Bull's warnings to refuse the government's handouts of rotten seed corn and sacks of moldy flour. Bears Ribs's 250 ragged followers were left to wander through the desolate country alone; no other band was willing to take them in.

Even the hanging of the thirty-eight Dakota Sioux in Mankato had failed to still white fears, and from 1863 onward news of the Minnesota "massacres" spread panic among settlements up and down the Missouri. President Lincoln and his War Department were inundated with alarmist telegrams from western politicians demanding troops to quell a Sioux rebellion that, ironically, was still limited to Sitting Bull's distant corner of the Upper Missouri in present-day North Dakota. Nonetheless the government responded by constructing a series of new posts and fortified camps running from Omaha to Salt Lake City, including one above and four below Fort Laramie along the Oregon Trail. They not only were of little use—the hostiles were ghosts, everywhere and nowhere—but served to further inflame the western tribes. Through all of this, Red Cloud's Powder River Country constituted perhaps the only peaceful oasis in the West. The great Oglala warrior chief recognized that this was temporary.

Some historians have viewed the indigenous tribes' failure to take advantage of the American Civil War by acting collaboratively as the Indians' most serious military error. That reasoning is based on a false premise. It is generally assumed that the great migration of the Regular Army at the onset of the War Between the States emptied the West of troops for the duration of the conflict. This was true at first. But Lincoln's Treasury needed gold and silver from the mountain territories to pay for the war, and the president recognized that without military escorts many of the miners making for Montana, Colorado, Nevada, and Idaho would never get there alive. The Union also required a fair amount of firepower to ensure that the ore made it out safely. Indian attacks were not the only potential peril; the Cherry Creek gold strikes along the front range of the Rockies in Colorado were precariously close to the Confederate state of Texas. Thus the Army presence west of the Missouri gradually increased until, by 1865, it actually exceeded prewar numbers.

It was a tentative buildup. Twice during the summer of 1862 combined Hunkpapa-Dakota war parties ambushed cavalry detachments that were escorting wagon trains of miners to the gold camps of Virginia City in western Montana, already a boomtown rivaling Denver. During the second attack they harassed a company of Iowa volunteers nearly all the way back to Sioux City. But 1862 was also the year Lincoln and the Free-Soilers took advantage of the absence of the southern plantation owners from Congress to pass the Homestead Act. This meant that beginning January 1, 1863, any U.S. citizen—or *intended* citizen, including freed slaves and female heads of households—could take title to 160 acres of government land west of the Mississippi, provided he or she improved the property, lived on it for five consecutive years, and had never taken up arms against the United States. The filing cost was $18. The trails west, already swollen with fortune seekers, men (like Mark Twain) looking to avoid military service, and the over 300,000 deserters from the Union and Confederate Armies, were now filled with families lugging harrows, seed drills, and new steel plows that sliced open the prairie much more easily than wood or cast iron. All this combined with a succession of fabulous strikes from the Comstock Lode to the Boise Basin Rush to at least double the West's population.

These new voters, loyal Unionists, wanted roads and telegraph lines, stage and mail service, and above all protection against the Indians. Lincoln was a shrewd politician with an eye toward a second term. There was no question as to his response, and northern volunteers who had enlisted to fight Johnny Reb instead found themselves marching on what the newspapers called "red pagans." In August 1864 the dilettante

General Alfred Sully—a Philadelphia watercolorist and oil painter of some renown—led a column of 2,500 men into North Dakota and defeated Sitting Bull's Sioux on the Upper Knife in a vicious three-day battle. In the end the Hunkpapas and Dakotas had no answer for Sully's howitzers. The general personally ordered the bodies of three braves thought to have slain his aide-de-camp decapitated. Their severed heads were fixed on poles and left behind as a warning. It was a turning point, forcing the North Dakota hostiles to migrate southwest toward the Black Hills, inching the conflict closer to Red Cloud.

And as news of Sitting Bull's rebellion spread to the Powder River Country, small bands of wild Miniconjous, Sans Arcs, Blackfoot Sioux, and even some Oglalas began making raids of their own. The few miners foolhardy enough to make for Montana via Nebraska and Wyoming were scalped and dismembered, mail stages were destroyed, and Army supply wagons were looted and burned. A favorite Indian practice on discovery of a chest or barrel of bacon, a staple of frontier mess tents, was to lash a captured teamster to a wagon wheel, pile the rashers about him, and set the meat afire. One relief party of troops that arrived in the aftermath of such a scene was barely able to tell the seared human from the hog. Meanwhile there was little the scattered and limited frontier troopers could do but cock an ear from behind log and adobe fortifications and listen as Indians bayed like prairie wolves from distant buttes and mesas.

Among these Indians was Crazy Horse. By the start of the white man's Civil War the twenty-year-old Oglala's reputation had grown with every coup counted and every scalp taken during the Crow Wars. His raiding companions now included not only Bad Faces, but also Miniconjou braves from his mother's side of the family, and the legend of his one-man charges—which the Sioux called "dare rides"—was such that the number of horses shot out from under him became a standard joke among his fellow fighters. He was the incarnation of war, always personally in the forefront of raids and attacks, separated from his party by twenty to forty yards, a solitary whirlwind leading a line of warriors spread behind him like the wings of a hawk. "We know Crazy Horse better than you Sioux," a Crow fighter once told a Lakota. "Whenever we have a fight he is closer to us than he is to you."

Yet Crazy Horse was far from being what the Indians called a reckless "Black Heart," a suicidal warrior riding into battle alone with only a war club in his hands and a death song on his lips. His followers knew well what to expect when he led them on raids, as he always planned what military strategists today would call an exit strategy. His fellow fighters were also struck by his unusual habit of jumping from his pony during critical moments of a skirmish in order to gain a more stable position from which to nock his arrows. When he was not battling Crows there was no finer tracker or hunter among the Lakota, and he invariably felled the most cows during the semiannual buffalo hunts. But he also tended to ride off by himself and return with fat elk, deer, antelope, and waterfowl. As his Dream Spirit Guide instructed, he always distributed the best meats from his kills among families, clans, and villages of lesser means.

Crazy Horse had also discovered what the Indians called their personal "life path" when he was accepted into an Oglala soldier-society called the Strong Hearts. Inspired in part by tales of Sitting Bull's defiance, the Strong Hearts were repelled when many of their own tribe relied on trade with the Americans for food and clothing; they themselves adopted an ideology of complete separatism from white ways. They refused to eat beefsteak, bacon, or sugar; to drink coffee or whiskey; or to wear any garment not made from traditional skins. They also warned off less-militant bands they discovered trekking to Indian agencies or forts to trade for these items, threatening to kill the offenders' ponies if they continued.

Although Crazy Horse was generous to Lakota society's least favored members, since his rejection by Black Buffalo Woman he had by all accounts become a taciturn adult whose heart was said to be not much larger than the talismanic pebble he wore behind his ear. But he was also a deeply spiritual young man, and among the spartan Strong Hearts he found a true home. "[He] was good for nothing but to be a warrior," observed the half-blood interpreter Billy Garnett, who through his Oglala mother befriended Crazy Horse in the 1860s. Now, with their mountain enemies defeated, the Strong Hearts turned their attention to the whites. Each spring during the Civil War years they rode south from their camps along the Yellowstone as soon as the grass was up, separating into groups of ten or fewer, spreading out among the trails leading west and concealing themselves among thick groves of willows and in shadowed hollows. There they awaited opportunities to rustle stock or kill emigrant stragglers. They did not yet have the strength to take on the U.S. Army, but they were confident that the time would soon arrive.

Life may have seemed cheap to the settlers and emigrants on the High Plains, with hundreds of thousands lying dead on eastern battlefields, so the Army justifiably considered the Indian raids pinpricks. The government's strongest reaction was to ban the sale of guns and ammunition to any of the Powder River bands. Moreover, Crazy Horse and his Strong Hearts aside, through the first half of the 1860s Red Cloud and his people showed no inclination to disrupt the status quo. Relatively undisturbed in their new territory on the Upper Powder, free of the white man's debilitating whiskey and diseases, the Oglalas and their Brule cousins reveled in the return to a more pure and natural lifestyle, the open spaces of the high prairie corresponding to some mystical place within the Sacred Hoop. They passed the seasons hunting in the majestic, game-laden territory and making occasional raids on the increasingly beleaguered Crows and Shoshones—by now pushed almost beyond the Bighorns—before settling into cozy winter camps where the larders were piled high with venison and buffalo meat.

Even when, in 1861, a regiment of infantry and five companies of cavalry were deployed from California to Fort Laramie to protect the overland mail route along the Oregon Trail, the Bad Faces maintained a tentative peace with the soldiers. In fact, during that same year the eighty-seven-year-old Old Smoke and his family bade farewell to the band and "retired" to the outskirts of the fort to settle among the Laramie Loafers. There is even some indication that before his peaceful death in 1864 the venerable Oglala Head Man was persuaded by the local Indian agent to farm a small plot of land. More likely, as the Sioux historian George Hyde speculates, Old Smoke "gave permission for the women to try their hand at it." This Oglala-Brule idyll was of course destined to end violently. At the very moment that Red Cloud and his people were reacclimatizing themselves to the ancient Sioux traditions, 1,400 miles away a former assistant bank teller from Delaware was taking his first steps toward their epic showdown.

AN ARMY IN SHAMBLES

William Judd Fetterman had long harbored a desire for military service. Born in 1835 into a Cheshire, Connecticut, military family, Fetterman's mother died from complications during childbirth. He was orphaned at nine years old on the death of his father, Lieutenant George Fetterman. He went to live with his uncle William Bethel Judd, another Regular Army officer who served with distinction during the Mexican War. Bethel, like George Fetterman, had graduated from West Point, and the young Fetterman hoped to follow in their footsteps. But when he applied in 1853 he was rejected by the Military Academy's admissions board, for unknown reasons. Thereafter the eighteen-year-old grudgingly took up a career in banking, working in Rochester, New York, before moving to Delaware. In 1861 a second opportunity for military service arose with the expansion of the Army of the Republic at the outbreak of the Civil War. Fetterman, now twenty-six, jumped at the chance.

Fetterman secured a commission as a first lieutenant less than two months after rebel artillery shells tore into Fort Sumter, and in June 1861 he reported for duty at Camp Thomas in Columbus, Ohio. The depot had been established as the regimental headquarters of the 18th Ohio

Infantry under the command of another civilian who had volunteered for service, the Yale-educated abolitionist attorney Colonel Henry Beebee Carrington. Carrington was appointed to the position by his good friend Salmon P. Chase, a former governor of Ohio currently serving as Lincoln's treasury secretary. Fetterman arrived in Columbus just five days after Carrington, and together the two officers spent the next five months organizing and training the companies of raw volunteers. It was soon apparent that the physically frail Carrington's greatest assets were political and clerical. Fetterman, on the other hand, seemed a born field commander.

Theirs was the classic contrast: Cicero and Demosthenes, with the former moving men's minds while the latter made them get up and march. Yet this did not spark a rivalry; Carrington and Fetterman seemed to sense that they complemented each other's attributes, and their combined skills were necessary to turn the regiment into a trim, well-disciplined unit. They also became personal friends, with the thirty-seven-year-old Carrington's wife, Margaret, remarking in her journal on the younger officer's "refinement, gentlemanly manners, and adaption to social life" at the camp.

When Fetterman was promoted to captain, given command of the 18th's 100-man Company A, and ordered to the front in November 1861, Carrington remained at his desk in Ohio. In 1862, Fetterman led the company during its suicidal bayonet charge at Corinth, and soon thereafter he fought in the Battle of Stones River, a medieval slugfest that produced the highest percentage of casualties in the entire Civil War. It was noted in his record that he stood in the front lines alongside his enlisted men for the duration of this thirty-six-hour engagement. And though the regiment suffered over 50 percent casualties during the fight, Fetterman emerged without a wound.

Meanwhile, Carrington's knack for recruiting kept him in charge of training depots in Ohio and, later, Indiana, while Fetterman, serving under General Sherman throughout the Georgia campaign of 1864, was promoted to battalion commander. The 18th performed admirably during engagements at Kennesaw Mountain, at Peach Tree Creek, and at Jonesboro—despite suffering more casualties than any other regiment in the Regular Army—and Fetterman's official record began to include adjectives such as "courageous," "daring," and "relentless." During the siege of Atlanta he was cited for "great gallantry and spirit," and a fellow officer reported being surrounded by Confederate troops and escaping with his life only when "Captain Fetterman's command marched to my assistance with great promptness." For his contributions to the Atlanta campaign, Fetterman, along with hundreds of Union officers, received another brevet appointment, to lieutenant colonel.

By the war's end in 1865 Fetterman would decide to make the military his career, and it was with a supreme confidence that he prepared to set off for the frontier. But this was still more than a year away, and in the interim the Army was forced to overcome various blundering missteps, attributable to postwar politics, that continually impeded its Indian campaigns on the High Plains.

While the war continued and Lieutenant Colonel Fetterman was making a name for himself in the field, Lincoln and his War Department finally began to turn serious attention to the West. After General Sully's victory over Sitting Bull, the president dispatched additional columns of state volunteers from across the Midwest to man key crossings along the Missouri, Platte, and Arkansas Rivers. The Minnesota Uprising may have been the root of the Indian wars that would engulf the High Plains for most of the next decade, but those wars were also impelled by a series of almost unbelievably dunderheaded appointments of general officers on the other side of the Mississippi. Perhaps not until Vietnam 100 years hence would political and military leaders so totally misread a situation on the ground. Zachary Taylor's earlier vision of an American soldier implementing "the ax, pick, saw, and trowel" to tame the West became a blurred memory as cannons, muskets, and swords were hauled from eastern battlefields, crated, and shipped west by the ton.

Historians generally attribute this state of affairs to (or blame it on) the exigencies of the Confederate rebellion. But while it was true that the most accomplished officers were needed in the East, the Army of the Republic had undergone a subtle reconfiguration well prior to Fort Sumter. The Founding Fathers, citing ancient Rome and contemporary Europe, were convinced that a ginned-up "defence agst. foreign danger have been always the instruments of tyranny at home," as James Madison wrote. Madison added that standing armies "kept up under the pretext of defending, have enslaved the people." The Founders instead envisioned, and implemented, a "multipurpose army designed for a wide variety of functions beyond combat." Among the purposes were felling trees, building schools, delivering mail, offering medical care, and erecting hospitals and lighthouses. It was an army of surveyors and engineers—dredging canals, constructing bridges, and, by 1830, laying over 1,900 miles of road. The West Point curriculum of the early nineteenth century leaned heavily toward such skills, and the Army Corps of Topographical Engineers "became a major focus of American science . . . collecting flora, fauna, and geological specimens, and publishing their findings in prestigious journals."

However, by the late 1840s, with Europe set ablaze by revolutions, with the victory over Mexico still burnishing reputations, and with Manifest Destiny enthralling the officer class, the curriculum at the Military Academy underwent an overhaul. Imperialism and colonialism now steered the governmental policies of America's rivals, and at West Point pure science took a backseat to the study of night marches and artillery duels, of sieges and ambuscades. Nearly six decades earlier President Thomas Jefferson had warned, "Were armies to be raised whenever a speck of war is visible on our horizon, we should never be without them." But young, eager officers like Lieutenants Fleming and Grattan lived, and sometimes died, for such specks of war. For all their wrongheaded racial attitudes, the earlier generation of engineer-soldiers had attempted to administer a modicum of justice to the West's Native peoples. The officers now deployed to the frontier not only included those the War Department could spare from more important engagements against the South, but also men imbued with a sense of martial superiority, and anxious to substantiate it. They ranged from naive to obtuse to hateful, with personalities unencumbered with charisma and minds unclouded by thought.

One frontier general, for instance, was notorious for habitually confusing the names and locations of supposedly hostile tribes, and in one official dispatch he reported Indian raids west of Fort Laramie as having been carried out by the "Winnibigoshish Sioux," somehow conjuring a tribe from the name of a lake in north-central Minnesota. Another blithely admitted that he knew nothing about Indians and did not care to learn anything, and it was not unusual for his artillery batteries to conduct target practice on passing, peaceful Indian bands, or for his jumpy junior officers to order attacks on their own uniformed Pawnee scouts.* Nearly to a man these generals and their staffs showed no ability to control their raw troops, and rivalries between state volunteers threatened to escalate from fistfights into gunfights. The eastern recruits also had a farcical proclivity to go native—as would be dramatized 140 years later in the movie *Dances with Wolves.*

Perhaps inevitably, when the doomed Lieutenant Caspar Collins's company of Ohio cavalry reached Fort Laramie, its members were so influenced by the Indian-fighting tales of their Colorado and California counterparts that many began to imagine themselves frontiersmen. The transformation was hastened by the arrival of Jim Bridger, lured from his Missouri farm to become the Frontier Army's chief scout at $10 a day, more than most officers were paid. Some thought that the sixty-year-old Bridger was finally showing his age. When he was young his standard meal might include an entire side of buffalo rib. Now he was content with a jackrabbit and an eighteen-inch trout roasted on spits over a campfire and a quart of coffee to wash them down. Nonetheless officers and enlisted men alike were in awe of the mountain man's eccentric skills. He could find fresh water on the driest of alkaline flats, build and stoke a fire in a hellish winter whiteout, and safely guide a wagon team across a quicksand-laden river. He also showed the newcomers an old Indian trick: ridding their clothing of ever-present fleas and lice by spreading the garments over anthills.

On one occasion Bridger led a troop to the site of an attack on an emigrant wagon near the South Pass through the Rockies. A father and son had been killed and butchered, their bodies left splayed across the buffalo

*One unintended consequence of the Civil War was less federal protection for the harried, dwindling Pawnee. Ironically, the tribe began to see its future as lying with the whites, and many of its warriors—as much for revenge on the Sioux and Cheyenne as out of necessity—jumped at the chance to join the Army's new Pawnee scout corps.

grass near a copse of box elders. Inexplicably, the attackers had not taken the younger man's Navy Colt. Bridger dismounted and examined the mutilated corpses, which were pierced by arrows that he identified by their fletchings as Cheyenne and Arapaho. He pried the revolver, its chamber empty, from the son's hand, and walked slowly in ever-expanding circles. Soon, with a flourish, he snapped off a branch of sagebrush. There was a speck of blood on it. Bridger beamed. "The boy hit one of the scamps, anyway," he said. The dime novelist Ned Buntline could not have written a better scene.

It did not take long for somewhat of a cult to grow around "Major" Bridger and a few other former mountain men who passed through Fort Laramie. One of Lieutenant Collins's letters to his mother describes Bridger and the others in their "big white hats with beaver around it; a loose white coat of buck or antelope skins, trimmed fantastically with beaver fur; buffalo breeches, with strings hanging from ornaments along the sides; a Mexican saddle, moccasins, and spurs with rowels two inches long, which jingle as they ride. They have bridles with ten dollars' worth of silver ornaments on; Indian ponies, a heavy rifle, a Navy revolver, a hatchet and a Bowie knife." It was no wonder that many of the young enlisted men in Collins's company soon discarded their blue woolens in favor of buckskins and Spanish spurs, and purchased hardy Indian ponies out of their own base pay of $14 a month.

But something other than eastern troopers playing dress-up would constitute one of the first troubling omens for the Lakota way of life. In 1863 a single wagon train veered north off the Oregon Trail and rolled up the center of the Powder River Country. Lakota and Cheyenne scouts posted on the pine-studded foothills of the Bighorns halted the line of prairie schooners and signed a demand to speak to its leader. A tall, lanky twenty-eight-year-old and his Mexican interpreter rode out to meet them. The interpreter introduced the wagon master as "Captain" John Bozeman. Bozeman doffed his hat, revealing a thick blond mane, and told the Indians that he did not intend to settle their land but merely to pass through it en route to the new diggings beyond the mountains in western Montana. The Lakota emphatically refused. "You are going into our country where we hunt," an old chief said. "You people have taken the rest. Along the great road to the south, white men have driven away all the buffalo and antelope. We won't let you do that here. If you go into our hunting country our people will wipe you out."

Bozeman returned to the train and urged the emigrants to call the Indians' bluff, but the travelers were wary. They argued for ten days over whether or not to proceed. In the end they voted to turn back and instead follow the uncontested, if longer and more difficult, route to Montana that snaked west of the mountains. As the Indians watched the train disappear over the southern horizon, they could not have known that Bozeman, a failed gold miner from Georgia, had just taken the first step in his plan to "mine the miners" as an expedition guide along the shortened route to the gold camps. Four months earlier he and a crusty frontiersman named John Jacobs had journeyed south and east from Virginia City along this route, nearly killing themselves in the process. Bozeman was a persistent man, and not easily dissuaded by the threat of losing his handsome blond hair. The insouciance of the Lakota in dealing with him that July day would return to haunt them. From the faint wheel ruts dug by that first train would grow a beaten path known as the Bozeman Trail.

BLOOD ON THE ICE

Red Cloud's Oglalas may have been oblivious of the knife edge on which they walked, but south of the Oregon Trail the Indian situation was worsening. By the mid-1860s the traditional buffalo ranges along the Republican River were already dwindling, not least because of the first white hunting parties converging on the droves from new settlements in Missouri, Kansas, and eastern Nebraska. A solitary hunter equipped with an accurate large-bore Sharps rifle could fell up to 100 buffalo in a single stand, and this technology marked the beginning of a Plains-wide slaughter that within four decades would reduce an estimated 30 million animals to less than 1,000. It was the greatest mass destruction of warm-blooded animals in human history, far worse than what the world's whaling fleets had already accomplished, and as Sitting Bull was to lament years later, "A cold wind blew across the prairie when the last buffalo fell. A death wind for my people."

When whites killed the buffalo, the animals were skinned where they fell, everything but their hides and tongues left to rot on the prairie. The hunters considered the meat worthless, but to the tribes this was not only a criminal physical waste, but a blasphemous affront to the animals' spirits, to Mother Earth, to the Sacred Hoop of life itself. When white buffalo hunters made camp, for instance, it was a common practice to slaughter a mule some distance away to attract wolves and then spread strychnine over the carcass. The hunters never bothered to bury the poison before they moved on, which resulted in the agonizing deaths of already decimated Indian pony herds later grazing in the area. The hunters, unaware of their insult, wondered what they had done to provoke retaliation.

Meanwhile, for several years the southern branches of the Cheyenne, Arapaho, and Lakota had found themselves virtually fenced in by the Oregon Trail to the north and the Santa Fe Trail to the south. This territory was further constrained by a new branch of the overland stage that connected the East to the booming gold camps around Denver—the line's relay stations at intervals of every twenty to twenty-five miles establishing a thin ribbon of American civilization across land promised to the Indians. By the conclusion of the Civil War the tribes were forced to share even this tiny swath of territory with small regiments of buffalo hunters and with stagecoach stock competing for pasturage. Among these put-upon Oglala bands were the Bear people and the followers of Little Thunder and Spotted Tail.

By this time Spotted Tail was a changed man. He had always been an astute observer, but the sheer number of whites he had encountered during his two-year "imprisonment" as a scout at Fort Leavenworth had transformed him from fire-eater to pacifist. Fort Leavenworth was a steamboat hub on the Lower Missouri, and during those months he watched thousands of well-armed Bluecoats pass through. These were, he came to understand, just the tip of the American Army's spear. At tribal councils and in private conversations during the seven years since his return, he had urged accommodation with the Americans, citing what his Minnesota cousin Little Crow had characterized as an enemy "as numerous as the leaves in the forest."

Spotted Tail's was not a lone voice. His words were echoed by Little Thunder, gun-shy since his own encounter with Harney at the Battle of Blue Water Creek. Little Thunder foresaw nothing but calamity for his people should they take up arms against the United States. And both Lakota Head Men noted that the Ute and the Shoshones had recently signed peace pacts with the Americans. Spotted Tail and Little Thunder conveniently omitted the fact that few homesteaders or ranchers cared to settle in the Ute or Shoshone mountain realms. But in any case their arguments for moderation were mostly ignored by younger braves who viewed the older men's attitude as capitulation, if not treason. Some Dog Soldiers also had reason to suspect that Spotted Tail and other former Lakota prisoners had taken part in reprisals against Cheyenne raiders while serving as Army scouts. The most serious of these involved the execution of half a dozen Southern Cheyennes on Grand Island in southeastern Nebraska after they had thrown down their weapons in surrender.

Alone and adrift, Spotted Tail, Little Thunder, and a few other southern Lakota and Cheyenne Head Men finally acquiesced in a one-sided "treaty" forced on them by the Army. It confined their bands to an even smaller reserve between the North Platte and South Platte, and did little to stem the escalating bloodshed that by 1864 had become more brazen. Indian raids on the stage line and the lumbering emigrant and supply wagon trains traversing the corridor to the Colorado gold camps had become a regular occurrence. Over three days in early August a string of ranches along the South Platte were attacked and thirty-eight settlers were killed, nine wounded, and five captured. At the same time, farther west, the Cheyenne fell on two emigrant trains, killing another thirteen and kidnapping a girl and a boy. The raids continued throughout the fall, and one freight outfit was ambushed and burned only a few miles from Denver, the territorial capital, which now contained over 100,000 miners and attendant entrepreneurs—more people than all the Plains tribes combined. The result was a virtual closing of the Leavenworth-Denver road; all mail bound for California was rerouted across the Isthmus of Panama.

The last straw was the rout of a detachment of cavalry dispatched from Camp Sanborn, northeast of Denver. Dog Soldiers ambushed the troop and, perhaps as a retort to General Sully, beheaded the young lieutenant leading them. Rumors circulated that his head was later used in ball games at the Cheyenne camp; and hearing these rumors, the general in charge of the territory ordered a Colorado volunteer brevet colonel, the fire-breathing Methodist minister John Milton Chivington, to run the hostiles to ground.

The Army had chosen well. Colonel Chivington despised Indians. Despite a bout with smallpox in his youth, the forty-four-year-old Chivington was physically robust: he stood six feet, five inches and carried his 260 pounds with the grace of an antelope. His broad, round face was shadowed by a scraggly black beard and punctuated by a set of tiny brooding eyes disconcertingly disproportionate to his looming bulk. In his official portrait his barrel chest seems about to burst from a blue tunic sporting two rows of brass buttons shined to a glint; he resembles a meaner Ulysses S. Grant. Chivington was born in Ohio, the son of a veteran Army officer, and he had settled in Colorado following a stint on the Ohio-Illinois preachers' circuit. He had also spent time at tribal missionary posts in Kansas and Nebraska, where his low opinion of the Native inhabitants hardened. He exemplified a new breed of westerner who took a simple view of the Indian problem: in any dispute, the red man was wrong. Lost in the mists of time were the gentle persuasions of "Broken Hand" Fitzpatrick.

Chivington's booming, baritone sermons landed on his listeners like cannon fire, and although he had founded Denver's first Sunday School, the angles of his racist zeal were too sharp for even his tough frontier flock, who (as the church phrased it) "located" him into early retirement soon after he arrived. "Mr. Chivington was not as steady in his demeanor as becomes a man called of God to the work of the ministry," the religious historian James Haynes tactfully put it. But he was perfect for the job of murdering infidel Indians, and he went about it with brio. Following the incident at Camp Sanborn the settlers, emigrants, and miners along the South Platte were encouraged not to bury murdered whites and instead were asked to transport whatever remained of the mutilated corpses "stretched in the stiffness of death" to Denver. There they were put on public display, usually on the muddy wooden boardwalks that fronted saloons. One exhibition included the scalped wife and children of a slain ranch manager, Nathan Hungate. Predictably, alcohol fueled the spectators' passions. The *Rocky Mountain News* called for "a few months of active extermination against the red devils," and the *Denver Commonwealth* for the perpetrators of "such unnatural, brutal butchery to be hunted to the farthest bounds of these broad plains and burned at the stake alive." In response, the territorial governor ordered all able-bodied men to meet for military drills every morning. The governor also issued a proclamation instructing all citizens, "either individually, or in such parties as they may organize, to kill and destroy, as enemies of the country, wherever they may be found, all such hostile Indians." Colonel Chivington eagerly answered the call to vigilantism.

The Civil War had forced Congress to reorganize the western Army into three distinct services, and regulars found themselves on equal footing with state or territorial volunteers as well as local militiamen. Many of these latter "one hundred days men" who took up the governor's challenge—including cardsharps, gunfighters, drunks, and pimps—were of the opinion that any and every Indian was fit for a shroud. Since no one at the War Department, which was vexed by more immediate problems, exerted a moderating influence on these avenging crusaders, militia commanders like Chivington operated with extraordinary freedom. The "Fighting Parson" instructed his Colorado volunteers that total war was the order of the day, every day, and his detachments galloped along the South Platte and Republican annihilating whatever small bands of Cheyenne, Arapaho, and Lakota they could catch. The unlucky Indians passing through these free-fire zones were usually the peaceable, the old, and the infirm. The more agile hostiles, mounted on fast ponies, were much too savvy to face Chivington's guns head-on.

White reprisals lessened during the summer of 1862 when Colonel Chivington's Colorado volunteers were ordered south to head off a Confederate army advancing up from Texas through New Mexico. (There, these volunteers would strike a decisive blow at the Battle of Glorieta by capturing and torching a rebel supply train after which Chivington ordered the execution, by bayonet, of 500 to 600 enemy horses and mules.) The Indians took advantage of the Colorado volunteers' absence to form their largest war parties to date and to soak the Leavenworth-Denver turnpike with blood. By the autumn of 1864 the split between the tribal militants and the pacifist faction had widened to a chasm. When, at the belated urging of Washington, Colorado's territorial governor offered sanctuary to any Indians "should they repair at once to the nearest military post," two Cheyenne bands struck out for Fort Lyon on the territory's southeastern plain. One was led by the chief Black Kettle, the other by White Antelope, and they were joined by a few followers of the Arapaho Head Man Left Hand. When they reached the fort in mid-autumn they were ordered to surrender their weapons in exchange for daily food rations. By this time Colonel Chivington had returned to Denver.

Fort Lyon's new commander, Major Edward Wynkoop, was a friend of Chivington's, and far less disposed than his predecessor toward differentiating between antagonistic and friendly tribes. He looked for any excuse to declare Black Kettle and White Antelope hostiles, and when he found none he simply refused their people food; returned their old muskets, bows, arrows, and knives; and ordered them off the premises. They were, he said, free to hunt in a limited territory bordering a stream called Sand Creek that fed into the Smoky Hill River about thirty-five miles northwest of the fort. The Cheyenne sensed a trap, but they were reassured that as long as Black Kettle flew the white flag of truce above his lodge next to an old American flag the Head Man had once received as a gift, no harm would come to them.

Two days after the Indians departed, on November 28, Chivington arrived at Fort Lyon with two field cannons and 700 men of the 3rd Colorado Volunteer Cavalry. He took every precaution to keep his presence secret, throwing a ring of guards around the post to prevent anyone from leaving. That night he and the volunteers, swollen by an additional 125 Regular Army troops, rode for Sand Creek. At just past daybreak the next morning they climbed a ridge overlooking the Indian camp. Most of the warriors were absent, hunting to the east. Of the 500 to 600 Indians remaining, more than half were sleeping women and children. Chivington ordered the Indian pony herd driven off. Then his howitzers erupted and the whites charged.

Black Kettle frantically raised the two flags over his tepee as his people fell around him—including White Antelope, whose death song was silenced by a bullet to the throat. It was a slaughter. The immediate survivors staggered to the nearby frozen creek bed, where women and children huddled beneath the high banks, and the few braves who were present gouged the earth with knives and tomahawks in an attempt to dig shooting pits. They were soon surrounded, and for more than two hours Chivington's volunteers picked them off like targets in a carnival game. Afterward the colonel and his officers stood by as the usual atrocities ensued. Infants and children were butchered like veal calves—"Nits breed lice" was a saying of Chivington's—and the soldiers devoted extra attention to slicing off penises, scrotum sacks, and pudenda, which when stretched and cured would be fashioned into tobacco pouches and purses. "Barbarity of the most revolting character," an investigative committee of the U.S. House of Representatives termed it. "Such, it is to be hoped, has never before disgraced the acts of men claiming to be civilized."

The soldiers departed at dusk—Chivington had lost ten men, with another thirty-eight wounded—and as night fell the Indian survivors crawled out from beneath the dead. All told, close to 200 were murdered along Sand Creek that day, three-quarters of them women and children. Those who escaped, Black Kettle among them, spent the next several days tramping across the frozen earth toward the warriors' hunting camp on the Smoky Hill. When they reached the site, one of his band's first acts was to banish Black Kettle and his family, who eventually moved to the country south of the Arkansas. Then the survivors plotted their revenge.

THE GREAT ESCAPE

More than any other incident in the long and bloody history of red-white relations, Colonel Chivington's merciless attack at Sand Creek did more to unite the Plains tribes against the United States. While the hills were still echoing with the wails of mourning mothers, wives, and daughters, Cheyenne runners with war pipes were sent out to Lakota camped on the Solomon Fork and to Arapaho on the Republican. War councils were convened, and in preparation for an unprecedented winter campaign the Head Men of the three tribes selected nearly 1,000 braves to move on the closest Army barracks, a contingent of infantry at Fort Rankin on the South Platte in the northeast corner of Colorado. The Indians rode in formal battle columns, the Sioux warriors in the van. A place of honor was reserved for the once-pacifist Spotted Tail.

At dawn on January 7, while the main body of warriors hid behind a row of rolling sand hills south of the Army stockade, seven painted decoys descended from the snow-covered heights and paraded before the post. Predictably, a column of about fifty volunteer cavalry, strengthened by a nearly equal number of civilians from the nearby hamlet of Julesburg, poured out in pursuit. But before they could ride into the trap, some overanxious braves broke from concealment and charged. The whites recognized the ambush, turned, and fled as cannons from the fort bombarded their pursuers. They reached the post, but not before losing fourteen cavalrymen and four civilians. The enraged Head Men ordered the offending braves quirted by the *akicita*, the ultimate humiliation, and led the war party one mile east to plunder the now abandoned stage station and warehouses at Julesburg.

Over the next month the southern Lakota, Cheyenne, and Arapaho cut a bloody swath through Kansas, Nebraska, and Colorado, finally circling back to again sack Julesburg, this time with the assistance of a party of northern Strong Hearts led by Crazy Horse. Again the garrison at Fort Rankin could do nothing but watch the rebuilt stock station burn. But now the Indians recognized that time was running out. Although Colonel Chivington had resigned his commission in the face of a pending court-martial, Army troops from Denver, Nebraska's Fort Kearney, and Wyoming's Fort Laramie were already mobilizing. With certain retaliation awaiting them on three compass points, there was no other direction for the southern tribes to ride but north into the Powder River Country. No soldiers would dare follow them into the great warrior chief Red Cloud's territory.

One would expect that a plodding diaspora of nearly 4,000 Indian men, women, and children freighted with nearly 900 lodges and hauling tons of provisions and equipment through a Plains winter would be easy to locate. Amazingly, no. In moving through the densely patrolled Platte River Valley, the combined tribal force—riding in three loose parallel columns, with scouts fanned out to the front and on either side—crossed the South Platte above Julesburg without incident. A few travelers reported spotting thousands of distant campfires, or hearing the beat of war drums for miles. Yet the Army could not find them.

As they headed north the Indians looted and burned farms, ranches, and stagecoach relay stations. Precious telegraph poles, hauled to the treeless prairie and pounded into the ground four years earlier, were hacked down; their annealed wires were spooled and stolen. Supply wagons carrying food to Denver were stopped and destroyed, and the few late-starting emigrant wagon trains hoping to winter over at Fort Laramie were plundered and torched. That year the frozen carcasses of white men and women littered the "Glory Road" from eastern Nebraska to central Colorado, providing rare winter sustenance for wolves and coyotes while the citizens of Denver faced severe food shortages.

The Indian columns, swollen with herds of captured cattle as well as packhorses and mules piled with plunder, stuck to well-worn trails and buffalo fords. Yet Major General Grenville Dodge, the new Army commander of the region, was bewildered as to their whereabouts. Dodge had assumed responsibility for the Oregon Trail when the War Department, pressured by overland stage and railroad executives, finally recognized that local volunteers and militias were as much of a hindrance to progress as the hostiles. Dodge was a railroad engineer by profession and a booster of the Union Pacific, and his primary assignment was to clear and hold the North Platte corridor for the future laying of tracks toward the Rockies. In the wake of the attack at Julesburg, Dodge ordered his field commander to ride south to the Republican to punish the Indians. How the two forces moving in opposite directions across the snow-blanketed Plains managed to miss each other remains a puzzle. But the cavalry's circuitous wild-goose chase across 300 miles of empty country left the entire Platte River Valley open.

When a disgusted General Dodge finally received word that the Indians were fleeing north, he summoned to Wyoming an ambitious Indian fighter, General Patrick Connor, to finish the job. Connor was a veteran of the Indian wars in Texas and California, and had secured his reputation two years earlier when he fell on a Shoshone camp on the Bear River in Utah and slaughtered 278 men, women, and children. He would find fighting Lakota Bad Faces and Cheyenne Dog Soldiers quite another matter.

In the meantime the southern tribes crossed the frozen North Platte above Mud Springs, Nebraska, strewing shelled corn from the looted Julesburg warehouses to steady their ponies' footing on the ice. Mud Springs was the site of a telegraph station set in a bowl-shaped dell, and the Indians robbed the lightly defended outpost of its horses and a large herd of beef cattle. Before they could cut the telegraph lines, however, an operator managed to tap out a call for help. And despite the tribes' over-whelming numbers, the dozen or so whites firing from loopholes bored into the station's thick adobe walls managed to hold out. Over the next twenty-four hours 170 men from the 11th Ohio Cavalry arrived from forts on either side of the boggy swale. Many were clad in their finest "Bridger buckskins" and mounted on Indian ponies.

This suited the Indians fine; they wanted a fight, anticipating even more scalps, guns, and horses to add to their growing collection. But the officer in command of the rescue party prudently sized up their strength and instead had his troopers dig rifle pits in which to wait them out. He was a frontier veteran, and had apparently learned that this was never a bad strategy with the impatient Plains tribes. Despite a hide-and-seek skirmish that lasted for the better part of two days and nights, the braves soon grew bored. On the second night, under cover of darkness, the cara-van slipped away into Nebraska's Sand Hills and resumed its trek north toward Red Cloud's country.

When the Indian columns reached the Black Hills the Arapaho broke off toward the southwest while the majority of Cheyenne and Lakota circled north of the range and rode for the Powder. The exceptions were Spotted Tail and his band. The mercurial Brule, having undergone yet another change of heart, vowed never again to fight the Americans, and took his people east to the White River, beneath the Badlands, where, aside from occasional treks to Fort Laramie, he would remain for the rest of his life. The three columns had traversed more than 400 miles of bitter winter landscape, with the United States government having little idea of their whereabouts for most of the journey. They had also killed more soldiers, emigrants, teamsters, and ranchers than the number of Cheyenne murdered at Sand Creek.

The enraged General Dodge responded by ordering all-out war on any Indians, with no consideration given to the geographic boundaries offered by the Indian agent Thomas Twiss ten years earlier. Any red man was fair game, and a deep hole dug beneath hastily erected gallows just beyond Fort Laramie's walls began to fill with corpses. In his journal the young Second Lieutenant James Regan described watching three Lakota hanged from the crude wooden structure, "in a most barbarous manner by means

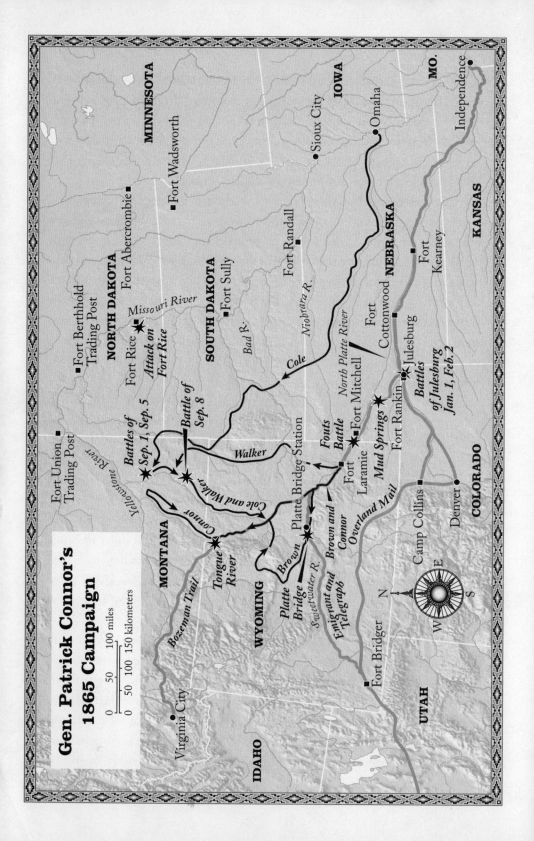

Gen. Patrick Connor's
1865 Campaign

of coarse chains around their necks, and heavy chains and iron balls attached to the lower part of the naked limbs to keep them down. There was no drop. They were allowed to writhe and strangle to death. . . . Their lifeless bodies, swayed by every passing breeze, were permitted to dangle from the cross-piece until they rotted and dropped to the ground. We could see their bones protruding from the common grave under the gallows."

Among those hanged and left to decompose were a luckless group of Laramie Loafers who were accused of riding on Fort Rankin with the southern hostiles but whose true crime may have been skinning and barbecuing a number of the post's feral cats that the quartermaster valued as mousers and ratters. Not long afterward two Lakota Head Men arrived with a white female prisoner they had purchased from a band of wild Cheyenne. Their intention was to curry favor with the whites by returning her to her people, and they assumed that this show of good faith would stand them in good stead with the soldiers. Instead the hysterical white woman accused them of rape. They were led to the scaffold by the fort's temporary commander, Colonel Thomas Moonlight, and after their execution they hung in artillery trace chains and leg irons until the putrid flesh peeled from their skeletons.

The great group of southern hostiles finally reached the Upper Powder in March 1865. Prior to their arrival the Bad Faces had passed an uneventful season; the highlight, as recorded by the Winter Count, was the capture and killing of four Crows attempting to steal horses. Now came this great group of fugitives trailing large herds of stolen cattle and pack-horses and travois piled high with looted sacks of flour, cornmeal, rice, sugar, and more. The northerners gathered goggle-eyed around strange bolts of multicolored cloth, and more than a few became nauseated after feasting on a mixture of tinned oysters, ketchup, and candied fruit. But most alluring were the repeating rifles and ammunition taken from the torched ranches and mail stations. Red Cloud's warriors and most other fighters and hunters on the Upper Powder still relied primarily on bows and arrows, and the rush to trade for these new, prized weapons was loud and raucous.

It was initially a hesitant reunion, however, despite the air of excitement. There were many northern Oglalas, not least among them Red

Cloud, who remembered well the insults that had fired the decades-long feud between the Smoke People and the Bear People. And though the Cheyenne had no such divisions, the years apart had exacerbated cultural differences between the northern and southern branches. The Northern Cheyenne, clad in rough buffalo robes and with red-painted buckskin strips plaited through crow feathers entwined in their hair, barely recognized their southern cousins, who wore cloth leggings and wool serapes. The two branches even had some trouble communicating, as the Northern Cheyenne had adopted many words from the Sioux dialect. In the end, however, turning away the ragged widows and bewildered orphans of Sand Creek would have been unthinkable. Soon enough their dramatic stories set the Bad Faces' blood boiling. The southerners described the outrage at Sand Creek in all its wretched detail, and told of the persecution of the docile Loafers as well as the hanging of the Lakota Head Men. Crazy Horse in particular was reported to have reacted to these tales of betrayal and brutality with an unconcealed rage for blood vengeance.

The more circumspect Red Cloud also recognized that the white man's war had finally arrived on his doorstep, first from the east following the troubles in Minnesota, and now from the south. There was nowhere to run. Nor, he reasoned, should his people have to run. It was time, once and for all, to fight the mighty United States and expel the Americans from the High Plains. He had long planned how to do this. The only question had been when. Sand Creek had answered that: Now.

In the early spring of 1865, not long after the southern tribes reached the Powder River Country, the leaders of the Sioux and Cheyenne soldier societies convened a war council on the Tongue. With over 2,000 braves at their disposal, Lakota war chiefs such as Red Cloud, Hump, and Young-Man-Afraid-Of-His-Horses plotted strategy with an assortment of Cheyenne counterparts including the regal Dull Knife* and the ferocious Roman Nose, who had lost kinsmen at Sand Creek. Although each

---

*It is a measure of the integration between the Northern Cheyenne and the northern Lakota that this Cheyenne chief, named Morning Star in his own language, was by now almost universally known by his Sioux name, Dull Knife.

tribe kept its own laws and customs, all were gradually coming to think of themselves as "The People." They had the Americans to thank for that.

Red Cloud was the first to address the gathering. "The Great Spirit raised both the white man and the Indian," he told his fellow fighters. "I think he raised the Indian first. He raised me in this land and it belongs to me. The white man was raised over the great waters, and his land is over there. Since they crossed the sea, I have given them room. There are now white people all about me. I have but a small spot of land left. The Great Spirit told me to keep it."

No more eloquent statement of purpose was required. For once the squabbling bands and tribes were in agreement, and it was decided that after the early-summer buffalo hunt—which would prove a particularly cumbersome affair, given the number of mouths to feed—the main force of the coalition would strike the whites at the last crossing of the North Platte on the trails west. This was the Bridge Station outpost, about 130 miles upstream from Fort Laramie. In the meantime, smaller groups of raiders who could be spared from the hunt were sent west, south, and east to keep the soldiers protecting the "Glory Road" and the South Pass of the Rockies off balance, while also gathering intelligence regarding the Army's movements.

It was a sound plan that leaped to a rousing start in April when a war party of Dog Soldiers burned out a key stage relay station west of Fort Laramie on the Wind River. The Indians killed all five of the station's defenders and staked their mutilated corpses on trees. A large detachment of cavalry under Fort Laramie's gallows-happy temporary commander, Colonel Moonlight, rode out to hunt the Indians down. But as in the Army's ineffectual response to Julesburg, Moonlight's patrol wandered in circles over 450 miles of Wind River country without seeing a hostile. Meanwhile the offending Dog Soldiers had moved east and were raiding the outpost at Deer Creek along the North Platte in conjunction with Lakota riding with Young-Man-Afraid-Of-His-Horses. Through May and June they attacked Wyoming stage stations, emigrant wagon trains, and small Army patrols, scalping and burning from Dry Creek to Sage Creek. On one humiliating occasion a platoon dispatched to chase down raiders returned to Fort Laramie at dusk and reported no Indians within twenty-five miles of the post. They had no sooner unsaddled their horses on the parade ground than a band of about thirty Lakota galloped into the fort, shooting, yelling, and waving buffalo robes. They stampeded the Army mounts through the open gates. They were never caught.

The brazen raids led General Dodge back in Omaha to again vent his spleen on the Laramie Loafers. There were at least 1,500 and probably closer to 2,000 docile Indians living within ten miles of the fort, and in June the general ordered his new field commander, the California General Patrick Connor, to wipe them out. Connor quite sensibly replied that these people were "friendlies," and reminded Dodge that if they had not risen after the atrocities on the gallows, he doubted they ever would. Further, he said, if the United States was intent on turning every Indian on the Plains against the whites, a massacre of the Loafers would be a fine start. Dodge blinked. After consulting with the War Department he telegraphed Connor to instead round up the Loafers and transport them southeast to Fort Kearney, where they would ostensibly be taught to farm. Fort Kearney was on the Lower Platte, deep in southern Nebraska: Pawnee country. The Loafers were indeed manageable, but they were not eager to be shipped into the heart of their ancient enemy's territory.

Nonetheless the Loafers were escorted under armed guard from Fort Laramie in early June, and as they passed the site of the Brule village where Lieutenant Grattan had met his end eleven years earlier, the ghosts seemed to stir them. A few nights later Crazy Horse slipped into their camp and discovered that they were already plotting an escape. He buoyed their spirits when he informed them that a war party of Strong Hearts was lurking just behind the low hills across the North Platte. The next morning, under the pretense of letting their herd graze, the Loafers lured their Army escort into an ambush. Five soldiers, including the officer in charge of the detail, were killed on the very spot where, fourteen years earlier, the Horse Creek Treaty to end all red-white hostilities had been signed. Seven more were wounded. The only Indian casualty was a Sioux prisoner, executed while still in chains.

The newly militant Indians then swam the river with their ponies as the Strong Hearts formed a defensive shield. They rode north. The next day they were pursued by Colonel Moonlight leading a contingent of 235

Ohio, Kansas, and California cavalrymen from Fort Laramie. By the time
the hard-riding American force reached Dead Man's Fork, a small creek
flowing into the White River near the Nebraska–South Dakota border,
more than a third of the troopers had been forced to turn back after their
big American steeds gave out crossing the waterless, hardscrabble tract.
The fugitive Loafers and the Strong Hearts had counted on this. They hid
themselves amid the thick sage and chokecherries that lined the stream's
steep banks. When what was left of the troop dismounted to water the
herd, the Indians sprang. They stampeded and captured the entire remuda, leaving Moonlight and his company to walk back to Fort Laramie
over 120 miles of trackless prairie. Moonlight vowed never again to enter
hostile territory without proper pickets and hobbles for his mounts, even
if it meant disobeying orders. He needn't have worried. On reaching Fort
Laramie, the colonel was relieved of command by General Connor, who
cited his incompetence, and shortly thereafter Moonlight was mustered
out of the service by General Dodge.

The Army had no idea when, where, or how the hostiles would strike
next. But old frontier hands like Jim Bridger assured the officers that it
was a long-held Indian custom to celebrate even the most minor victories
with weeks of feasts and scalp dances. There was time, he said, to amass
and mount a large enough force to ride out and surprise them. With this,
a degree of complacency settled over the forts and camps along the Oregon Trail. But for once the mountain man was mistaken because Red
Cloud was yet again one step ahead of his enemies.

BLOODY BRIDGE STATION

Buffalo and Indians had forded the North Platte at the site of Bridge Station for centuries. Sometime in the early 1840s former mountain men had begun operating crude ferries to accommodate the first emigrants crossing the river en route to Fort Laramie. And in 1859 the Missouri Frenchman Louis Guinard had opened a trading post on an oxbow near the ford. Guinard constructed a 1,000-foot bridge spanning the flow, and soon thereafter the government expanded his adobe trading post into a sturdy redoubt constructed of lodgepole pine on the river's south bank. Telegraph poles were erected, and a company of cavalry was deployed to protect the new line. It was Red Cloud's idea to attack Bridge Station. He knew that defeating its garrison and burning the fort and bridge would halt overland emigrant traffic for months. Victory at Bridge Station would also provide the Indians with an opening for further incursions against the smaller Army camps that had sprouted along the Oregon Trail.

For most of that summer the station had been manned by a feuding mix of Kansas and Ohio men, among them twenty-year-old Lieutenant Caspar Collins of the 11th Ohio Cavalry. As a child Collins had dreamed of fighting Indians, and when he came west in 1862 he was impatient for the opportunity. But after three years on the prairie his natural curiosity had tempered his bloodlust, and he had been known to ride off by himself along the Upper Powder, camping with friendly Oglalas and Brules. There were even reports that in less troubled times Crazy Horse himself had taught Collins bits of the Lakota language as well as how to fashion a bow and arrows. By all accounts Collins was an affable and capable junior officer, with a sterling reputation among the enlisted men. In July, when a large company of Kansas cavalry arrived at Bridge Station, he was bemused more than anything else. "I never saw so many men so anxious in my life to have a fight with the Indians," Collins wrote in a letter home. "But ponies are faster than American horses, and I think they will be disappointed."

Collins's reflections aside, there was bad blood between his Ohioans and the rough Jayhawkers, and not long after Collins was dispatched to Fort Laramie to secure fresh mounts, the commander of the new Kansas contingent banished most of the Ohio troops to a more isolated post farther west on the Sweetwater. Collins knew nothing of this development as he waited at Fort Laramie to join a patrol riding back to Bridge Station, and it was his bad luck to have still been there when General Dodge's new field commander General Connor arrived. Connor was yet another of the Army's hot-tempered Irishmen—he had been born in County Kerry—and in addition to his temper he possessed a constitution as hardy as a Connemara pony's. He was soon to acquire the Indian nickname "Red Beard" for the ornate copper sideburns that set off his lupine eyes set deep in a face as pinched as a hatchet blade. Connor spotted Collins apparently idling on the parade ground one day, and he tore into the young lieutenant before several witnesses.

"Why have you not returned to your post?"

Collins attempted to explain. The general cut him off.

"Are you a coward?"

Collins was shaken. "No, sir."

"Then report to your command without further delay."

Collins rode out the next day.

Connor's rebuke may have been ringing in his ears when Collins

reached Bridge Station on the afternoon of July 25 to find only a skeleton
squad of his Ohio company still remaining. It was the very day Red Cloud
had chosen to attack. The war chief's tactics were the same as the plan that
had nearly worked for the southern tribes at Fort Rankin, near Julesburg.
Earlier that morning, before Collins's arrival, the main body of Cheyenne
and Lakota—which included Oglala, Brule, Miniconjou, Sans Arcs, and
Blackfoot Sioux warriors—had concealed themselves behind the red
sandstone buttes on the north side of the river. But, taking a lesson from
the botched ambush at Fort Rankin, Red Cloud had raised a police force
from Crazy Horse's Strong Hearts as insurance in case his excitable braves
tried to break cover too early. The Cheyenne recruited members of their
own Crazy Dog Society to do the same. Red Cloud then sent a dozen or
so riders in full battle regalia out into the little valley fronting the station,
hoping to draw out most of its 119 defenders.

At first a howitzer battery seemed to have taken the bait, but after
crossing the bridge the cannoneers moved no farther, opting to dig in
on the north bank of the river and merely lob shells into the hills. Red
Cloud was restless but waited until the tangerine twilight turned to charcoal dusk before signaling for the decoys to return. That night he altered
his plan and selected a small party of Bad Faces to creep into the culvert
beneath the north side of the bridge and hide themselves amid the brush
and thick willows. At dawn he again deployed his baiting riders, who
this morning cantered even closer to the fort and taunted the soldiers by
shouting obscenities, in English, that they had learned from traders.

Again the ploy looked to have worked. The gates opened and at the
head of a column of cavalry rode Lieutenant Collins. Red Cloud had
no idea that the horsemen were coming out not to fight the decoys, but
to escort into Bridge Station five Army freight wagons returning from
delivering supplies to the Ohioans on the Sweetwater. By this time even
the rawest recruit on the frontier was aware of the Indians' repeated use
of a handful of braves to lay a trap. Collins had also been warned. Earlier
that morning, as he donned the new dress uniform that he had purchased
at Fort Laramie, several of his remaining Ohioans had tried to dissuade
him from riding out with only twenty-eight men. When he persisted they
implored him to at least request from the Kansan commander a larger

detail. Again Collins said no, and at this a fellow officer from his regiment handed him his own weapons, a brace of Navy Colts. Collins stuck one into each boot, selected a high-strung gray from the stable, and mounted up at 7:30. Before departing he handed his cap to his Ohio friend "to remember him by."

The decoys scattered as Collins and his troop crossed the bridge, followed on foot by the Ohio men and a few Kansans with Spencer carbines, eleven soldiers in all, acting as a volunteer rear guard. They watched from the riverbank as the riders moved half a mile into the North Platte Valley. The hills then erupted with painted warhorses, pinging arrows, and glinting steel. The Lakota swept down from the northern buttes, and the Cheyenne rode in from the west. On Collins's orders the little column wheeled into two ranks and discharged a volley from their carbines. A bitter-tasting fog of smoke rolled toward the river. Then Collins flinched and nearly toppled from his horse. He had been shot in the hip, and a scarlet stain seeped through his pants leg. By the time he regained his balance there were so many Indians swarming his column that lookouts on the Bridge Station parapets lost sight of the Bluecoats in the swirling dust. Except for one. Lieutenant Caspar Collins, an arrow buried deep in his forehead, was clearly visible for a moment before he and his horse disappeared into a scrum of charging braves.

Indian and American horseflesh continued to collide at close quarters, the Indians slashing with knives and spears and swinging tomahawks and war clubs to avoid firing into their own lines. The unwieldy carbines were now useless, and cavalrymen fought back with revolvers. A galloping horse broke out of the smoky haze with a wounded trooper hunched over its neck, making for the bridge. Another followed. Then another. The rear guard opened up with the Spencers, firing wildly into the melee. As if by magic the Bad Faces hidden beneath the span appeared. They threw their bodies in front of the retreating horsemen. The rear guard charged them, desperate to keep the escape route open. Riderless horses and single riders with arrows protruding from all parts of their bodies galloped back through the pandemonium. A cannon boomed from the Bridge Station bastions, and soldiers on the catwalks watched an Indian drive his spear through the heart of a dismounted cavalryman, yank it out, turn, and lunge at another, piercing his chest. But the second soldier was not dead. He fell forward, pressed his revolver against his assailant's head, and with his last cartridge blew out the Indian's brains.

Thirty minutes into the fight Red Cloud signaled the Cheyenne chief Roman Nose to break off his Dog Soldiers. They thundered up the valley toward the approaching freight wagon train. The train's five lead scouts, cresting a rise in the road that put them in sight of the fort, saw a horde of 500 Indians bearing down on them. The scouts galloped for the river and splashed their mounts into the current. Three made it across. The men at the bridge who had formed the rear guard, including the lieutenant who had given Collins his revolvers, retreated to the stockade. The lieutenant volunteered to lead a rescue detachment, reminding the post commander that the twenty wagoneers were also men from the 11th Ohio Cavalry. The Kansan refused, insisting that he needed every available body to defend the fort. The lieutenant punched him in the face, was subdued, and was taken to the guardhouse at about the time Roman Nose descended on the freighters, just reaching the same ridgeline as the scouts.

The Ohio teamsters recognized that it was suicide to try to burst through so many hostiles. They made for a shallow hollow between the road and the North Platte. They formed the best corral possible with their five wagons and a few empty wooden mess chests, and attempted to hobble their thirty mules. But an Indian captured the bell mare and led her off, the rest of the animals following. With her went their last chance of escape.

Americans dropped one by one over the succeeding four hours; but the Indians' arrows and muskets were no match for the soldiers' breech-fed, seven-shot Spencer carbines, and the survivors managed to hold off their circling attackers. By midafternoon the Indians decided to take a new tack, slithering closer on all sides through shallow trenches they scraped out of the sandy soil with knives and tomahawks, rolling logs and large boulders before them. The besieged troop, holed up below the road, could not see them. But the men on the fourteen-foot walls of Bridge Station did. They fired howitzer shells as a warning, but the meaning of the signal was lost on the teamsters. By four o'clock the Indians had crawled to within yards of the makeshift stockade. All went quiet; then came a shrill shriek. The Indians rose by the hundreds, "seeming to spring from the very ground," according to one historian. A fire broke out and soldiers on the Bridge Station walls could hear screams but could see nothing through the thick black smoke. The Indians were burning both men and wagons.

Night fell and the Lakota and Cheyenne returned to the hills while the post commander at Bridge Station counted twenty-eight men missing and presumed dead, twice as many wounded, and perhaps half left to fight. The telegraph lines east of the fort had been cut, and at ten o'clock a half-blood scout mounted a captured Indian pony and slipped through a side gate with instructions to ride for Deer Creek Station twenty-eight miles to the east. From there word could be transmitted to General Connor at Fort Laramie. The scout made it through.

On the far side of the red bluffs the day ended just as inconclusively for Red Cloud. There is no record of his losses, but the Army estimated that sixty Indians had fallen. Though this number was probably inflated, it was still a significant toll. Moreover, not only had the Native force failed to take the outpost, but a good number of Collins's cavalry had managed to make their way back through the Bad Faces and across the bridge to safety. The Cheyenne Dog Soldiers blamed the Lakota, a few even insinuating that the Lakota were cowards. The Lakota moved for their weapons but were held back at the last moment by the frustrated Red Cloud's authority.

Red Cloud and Roman Nose spent the night repairing the damaged alliance, and the next morning the great war party paraded before Bridge Station just beyond cannon range, then swung back into the hills and vanished. Red Cloud recognized that despite his superior numbers, most of his fighters, his Oglalas and Brules in particular, were far too inexperienced, ill-disciplined, and uncomprehending of tactics to lay siege to the Army outpost. Even more disturbing was the way the tribes had nearly turned on each other. The best he could hope for was that as the war progressed his followers would learn. He was probably asking too much.

THE HUNT FOR RED CLOUD

It is not recorded if, on learning of Caspar Collins's death, General Connor expressed any remorse over his verbal lashing of the young lieutenant. But it is known that when news reached Connor of the fight at Bridge Station—soon to be renamed Fort Caspar and eventually the site of Wyoming's state capital—he chafed to ride against the hostiles. The conclusion of the Civil War had finally made this possible. Though not technically a peace treaty, the surrender of Robert E. Lee's Army of Northern Virginia at Appomattox Courthouse in April 1865 marked the de facto end of hostilities, and thus of the Confederacy. It also meant that the battered Army of the Republic was able to replace the raw state militias patrolling the west with seasoned troops better capable of confronting the Indians of the Great Plains. South of the Arkansas, this meant eradicating the Kiowa and the Comanche, who were blocking movement along the Santa Fe Trail into New Mexico. North of the Platte, it meant killing Red Cloud and Sitting Bull.

General Ulysses S. Grant, the Army's commander in chief, had long planned such a moment. The previous November, the day after the Sand

Creek massacre, Grant summoned Major General John Pope to his Virginia headquarters to put such plans in motion. Despite his relative youth, the forty-three-year-old Pope was an old-school West Pointer and a topographical engineer-surveyor whose star had risen with several early successes on western fronts in the Civil War. It had dimmed just as rapidly when Lincoln placed him in command of the eastern forces; Pope was thoroughly outfoxed by Stonewall Jackson and James Longstreet at the Second Battle of Bull Run. Pope had been effectively exiled to St. Paul, Minnesota, until Grant recalled him to consolidate under one command a confusing array of bureaucratic Army "departments" and "districts" west of St. Louis. Grant named Pope the commanding general of a new Division of the Missouri, into which he enfolded three fractious geographic departments: Northwest, Missouri, and Kansas. This new division was also enlarged to include Utah and parts of the Dakotas. Pope's mandate was to execute an offensive in the summer of 1865 that would, among its prime objectives, make safe the trail stamped out by John Bozeman.

The new route went by many names: the Bozeman Trail, the Montana Road, the Bozeman Cutoff. But whatever it was called, it was the road to gold in Montana. It broke north from the great Oregon Trail and shortened the journey to the new gold fields in the rugged mountains of western Montana by some 400 weary, plodding miles. Pope had appointed General Dodge as his chief subordinate, and together the two decided on a campaign plan to crush the High Plains tribes with a large-scale pincer movement. General Connor's forces would march north out of Fort Laramie to face Red Cloud, while General Sully would lead a column northwest from Sioux City to finally finish off Sitting Bull, with whom his cavalry had been skirmishing for the better part of two years. The optimum time for such an assault was early spring, before the lush summer prairie grasses allowed the Indian ponies to regain their speed and stamina. But even with the cessation of fighting in the East, troop movements remained a cumbersome operation, and as a result through much of the spring of 1865 General Connor commanded less than 1,000 soldiers to protect the Platte corridor. This had reduced him to dispatching what were in essence rapid reaction teams up and down the "Glory Road." Their

rapidity, however, was somewhat in question. As Red Cloud had predicted, Connor's soldiers spent the first half of 1865 chasing ghosts.

The reports of these futile and frustrating excursions before and after
the debacle at Bridge Station still festered within the Army high command when additional troops were finally assigned to the new Division of
the Missouri in midsummer. General Connor's gratitude was short-lived.
The majority of the volunteers ordered into Indian Country from Civil
War battlefields felt as if they had fulfilled their duty to the Union, and
marched west with something less than zealous fervor in hopes that their
discharge papers would outpace them. Many of those hopes were realized,
and nearly half of the 4,500 reinforcements never crossed the Missouri.
Connor may have wished the same for the rest. One regiment of 600
Kansas cavalry rode into Fort Laramie and promptly mutinied, refusing
to ride any farther. Connor was forced to train his artillery on their camp
to bring them under control. Still, he was confident that the 2,500 additional men he had received—including the Kansas mutineers—were more
than enough to merge with Sully and defeat Red Cloud, Sitting Bull, and
whatever allies had been foolish enough to join them. In June 1865, he issued his infamous order to subordinate officers: find the hostile tribes and
kill all the males over the age of twelve.

The strategy faltered from the start. Rivers and streams still swollen
from heavy spring rains delayed Sully's Missouri crossing for weeks, and
when he finally managed to ferry his 1,200 troopers across the river they
rode futilely up and down its banks and tributaries for nearly a month
without finding Sitting Bull. Not finding Indians was becoming habitual
for the Army across the frontier. Sully's force of eighteen cavalry companies and four infantry companies was finally pulled back to Minnesota
when the War Department overreacted to a raid by a small party of Dakota Sioux near Mankato. By the time Sully arrived to wipe out the "hive
of hostile Sioux," the Dakotas had slipped across the border into Canada.
But he and his men were ordered to remain in the state in case the Indians returned. At faraway Fort Laramie, Connor was forced to readjust on
the run. He decided that three prongs would replace the pincers.

To that end, in early July he ordered a column of nearly 1,400

Michigan volunteers under the command of Colonel Nelson Cole to ride north out of Omaha, skirt the east face of the Black Hills until they reached the Tongue, and wipe out a contingent of the fugitive Laramie Loafers reported to be congregating near Bear Butte. Cole was then to follow the river southwest until he met and united with the regiment of Kansas cavalry dispatched from Fort Laramie. This combined troop would then provide a flanking screen against Red Cloud's multitribal forces, which Connor was confident he would locate near their favorite hunting grounds on the Upper Powder. Connor himself, meanwhile, would ride at the head of 1,000 men up John Bozeman's trail, and all three American columns were to converge on Rosebud Creek, the heart of Red Cloud's territory.

It was as fine a tactical advance as was ever drawn up in a West Point classroom. Needless to say, it failed utterly. The sulky Kansans' movement proved so desultory as to be almost worthless, and once again the grain-fed Army mounts in Cole's command withered and broke down on the desiccated South Dakota prairie. As von Clausewitz had noted, "Everything in war is very simple, but the simplest thing is difficult." Somewhere Colonel Moonlight must have felt vindicated.

Connor, freighting supplies for all three columns, remained oblivious of the difficulties his two flanking forces were experiencing when, several weeks into his own march, his Pawnee and Winnebago scouts discovered fresh tracks made by a large party of Indians moving northeast. He should have trusted his instincts; the main body of Sioux and Cheyenne were in fact still camped on the Upper Powder, hunting buffalo and celebrating the victory at Bridge Station. Instead he heeded his guides and turned his column. But the trail the Pawnee had cut belonged to a band of peaceful northern Arapaho led by a Head Man named Black Bear. Connor fell on them in north-central Wyoming near the Montana border. He raked Black Bear's camp with his howitzers before charging, killing over sixty. The Arapaho, however, surprised him by putting up a spirited defense—their women fighting as hard as their men—before vanishing into a honeycomb of red rock canyons. A few warriors, attempting to divert the Americans, led them in the opposite direction up a shallow stream called

Wolf Creek. Among the pursuing soldiers was a scout clad in buckskins whom several of the Indians recognized. They had once trapped and traded with him, and they considered him a friend. "Blanket" was his Arapaho nickname—"Blanket Jim Bridger."

Although Connor captured a third of the large Arapaho remuda and set torches to the Arapaho camp—elk-skin lodges, buffalo robes, blankets, and an entire winter food supply of thirty tons of pemmican were devoured in the huge bonfire—it is difficult to call the "Battle of Tongue River" a victory. Black Bear's son was killed in the artillery bombardment, and his death hardened the tribe's enmity toward the whites. First Left Hand at Sand Creek; now Black Bear. The Army was increasing Red Cloud's coalition for him.

Although three columns of infantry and cavalry were snaking to and fro across the High Plains searching for him—albeit reluctantly in some cases—Red Cloud appeared to have no idea that he was the object of such lusty attention. He spent his days at leisure, and whiled away long nights attending formal medicine ceremonies, feasts, and scalp dances where he, Young-Man-Afraid-Of-His-Horses, and Roman Nose were accorded places of honor. In an attempt to consolidate a popular tribal front he sent Bad Face emissaries down the Powder to take part in Sitting Bull's large Sun Dance on the Little Missouri. But the Hunkpapa chief failed to reciprocate, and this rather stunning insult was the beginning of a lifelong rift between Red Cloud and Sitting Bull.

Toward mid-August a Lakota hunting party spotted a civilian train of about twenty wagons escorted by two companies of infantry traveling west near the Badlands. Red Cloud and Dull Knife roused 500 warriors to ride out against the party. Some of the braves wore bloodied blue uniform tunics taken during the fight at Bridge Station, and at least one carried an Army bugle captured from Caspar Collins's command. On reaching the Bluecoats they cut off and killed one of the train's scouts, and at first sight of the Indians the wagons were rolled into an interlocking circle, destined to become a classic Hollywood trope. The Indians spread out on two flanking mesas, taking potshots, blowing their bugle, whooping, and taunting. The enclosed soldiers responded with howitzer fire that fell harmlessly, only gouging chunks from the surrounding hills.

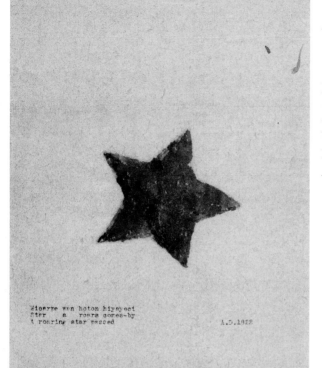

This 1821 edition of the annual Sioux Winter Count depicts "a star passed over making a noise," which probably explains how Red Cloud, born that year, received his name. *Courtesy American Museum of Natural History.*

Wyoming's Fort Laramie, a necessary stopover for wagon trains and other travelers along the Oregon Trail, as illustrated in 1853. *Courtesy American Heritage Center, University of Wyoming.*

Jim "Old Gabe" Bridger was the ultimate example of the early 1800s mountain man who blazed many a trail in his lifelong travels. *Courtesy American Heritage Center, University of Wyoming.*

The slaughter of buffalo along the Kansas Pacific Railroad line was one just of many examples of the eradication of the animal that Indian tribes depended on for food and clothing across the Great Plains. *Courtesy Library of Congress.*

This drawing from the January 24, 1863, edition of *Leslie's Illustrated Newspaper* depicts the mass hanging of thirty-eight Dakota Sioux a month earlier in Mankato, Minnesota. *Courtesy American Antiquarian Society.*

While building his Indian coalition to fight the U.S. Army, Red Cloud was the first Sioux to reach out to leaders of other tribes such as the Northern Cheyenne chiefs Little Wolf and Dull Knife. *Courtesy American Heritage Center, University of Wyoming.*

Old-Man-Afraid-Of-His Horses, a senior Oglala Head Man, hoped his son would succeed him but instead saw the warrior chief Red Cloud rise to the leadership role. *Courtesy American Hertiage Center, University of Wyoming.*

Spotted Tail, two years younger than Red Cloud, was a Brule Sioux whose fierce and spirited opposition to white expansion across the Plains was broken by a two-year stint in a U.S. federal prison. *Courtesy National Anthropological Archives, Smithsonian Institution.*

One of the very first photographs taken of the great Oglala Sioux warrior chief Red Cloud. *Courtesy National Anthropological Archives, Smithsonian Institution.*

Young-Man-Afraid-Of-His-Horses, son of Old-Man-Afraid-Of-His-Horses and a grandson of Old Smoke, fought alongside Red Cloud in the 1866–68 war. *Courtesy National Anthropological Archives, Smithsonian Institution.*

John Bozeman (*pictured here*) and John Jacobs blazed the Bozeman Trail, which in its short life provided a passage to Montana for thousands of gold seekers and settlers. *Courtesy American Heritage Center, University of Wyoming.*

Civil War hero Gen. William Te-cumseh Sherman advocated a war of extermination against the Indians of the Plains during his tenure as commander of the Missouri District, which stretched from the Mississippi River to the Rocky Mountains. *Courtesy of the American Heritage Center, University of Wyoming.*

Col. Henry Carrington, a desk-bound recruiter during the Civil War, thought establishing and maintaining forts in Wyoming represented an opportunity for action and distinction. *Courtesy Library of Congress.*

The genteel Margaret Carrington stood by her husband's side step for step across the Plains and became a comforting presence to the few other women living at Fort Phil Kearny. *Courtesy American Heritage Center, University of Wyoming.*

An 1867 sketch of Fort Phil Kearny by Lt. Jacob Paulus, as viewed from the south.
Courtesy American Heritage Center, University of Wyoming.

This photograph of a Sioux woman was taken by the ill-fated Ridgway Glover at Fort Laramie in 1866, a few weeks before he rode north to join Col. Carrington's outpost at Fort Phil Kearny. *Courtesy National Anthropological Archives, Smithsonian Institution.*

The bigamist Lt. George Grummond was looking for a fresh and heroic start by joining Col. Carrington's command in Wyoming. *Courtesy Library of Congress.*

Though pregnant, the young Frances Grummond accompanied her husband to his new posting at Fort Phil Kearny. *Courtesy American Heritage Center, University of Wyoming.*

Capt. William Judd Fetterman had a distinguished record as a Union officer during the Civil War but found Indian warfare on the Plains—and his commanding officer's tactics—very confusing and frustrating. *Courtesy American Heritage Center, University of Wyoming.*

Capt. Tenedor Ten Eyck was criticized for arriving to the massacre site too late to save Fetterman and his command. *Courtesy American Heritage Center, University of Wyoming.*

The boisterous Capt. Fred Brown, who had served with Fetterman in the Civil War, made clear his intent to personally capture or kill Red Cloud. *Courtesy American Heritage Center, University of Wyoming.*

John "Portugee" Phillips (*left*) and Capt. James Powell survived the fighting at Fort Phil Kearny in 1866. Phillips endured an exhausting journey through blizzards and bitter cold to bring word to the world of the Fetterman Massacre. Powell would later become the hero of the Wagon Box Fight. *Courtesy American Heritage Center, University of Wyoming.*

Nelson Story's historic cattle drive from Texas to Montana in 1866, in part the inspiration for Larry McMurtry's novel *Lonesome Dove*, included an "escape" from Fort Phil Kearny. *Courtesy Montana Historical Society Research Center Photography Archives.*

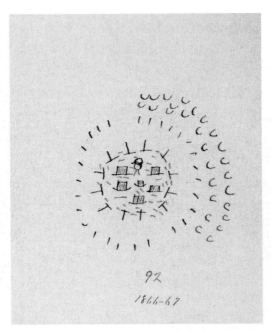

This illustration of the battle of December 21, 1866, created by the Sioux brave American Horse, depicts U.S. Army soldiers surrounded on Massacre Ridge.
Courtesy National Anthropological Archives, Smithsonian Institution.

Appalled by the Fetterman Massacre, in 1867 the U.S. government sent a peace commission to Fort Laramie to negotiate an end to what became known as "Red Cloud's War." *Courtesy American Heritage Center, University of Wyoming.*

Even after Red Cloud's victories, some docile Lakota "chiefs," confronted by Wyoming's harsh winters, continued to frequent Fort Laramie to trade for food delivered by U.S. Army supply wagons. *Courtesy American Heritage Center, University of Wyoming.*

One of several delegations that Red Cloud (*center*) led to Washington, D.C., between 1870 and the 1890s, where he met with U.S. government officials, including presidents, to advocate on behalf of the Sioux. *Courtesy American Heritage Center, University of Wyoming.*

Sitting Bull, the Hunkpapa Sioux leader, photographed in 1881, refused to travel to the Powder River Country join Red Cloud's fight against the United States in 1866. Ten years later, however, he and Crazy Horse defeated Gen. George Custer at Little Bighorn. *Courtesy Library of Congress.*

Long retired as warriors, American Horse (*left*) and Red Cloud posed for the photographer John C. H. Grabill on the Pine Ridge Reservation in 1891. *Courtesy Library of Congress.*

Henry Carrington and Frances Grummond Carrington were guests of honor at the dedication of the Fetterman monument in 1908 at the site of the former Fort Phil Kearny. *Courtesy Wyoming State Archives.*

Red Cloud late in life, uncharacteristically wearing a full headdress. He lived his last years peacefully with his wife, Pretty Owl. *Courtesy National Anthropological Archives, Smithsonian Institution.*

Soon a white flag went up; the whites wanted to parley. Red Cloud and Dull Knife personally rode out to meet with the expedition's two leaders. The civilian wagon master—an Iowa merchant who was surreptitiously surveying a trail into Montana—was joined by an Army captain commanding the infantry companies of "galvanized Yankees"—former Confederate prisoners of war who had sworn an oath of allegiance to the Union in exchange for their release. These southerners had not expected to be pressed into frontier service, and the Union officer was probably not certain whom he could trust less, the Lakota or his own troops.

Incredibly, after much palaver the two chiefs promised the train safe passage on the condition that it strike north of the Powder River buffalo grounds as well as cede a wagonload of sugar, coffee, flour, and tobacco as a toll. If this seems a curious decision for warriors who only weeks earlier had vowed to drive all whites from their territory, the explanation lay in the fact that the red man and white man did not adhere to the same concept of warfare, much less the same rules. The Sioux and Cheyenne viewed the Americans as merely a more numerous, better-armed version of the Crows, Shoshones, or Pawnee. To the Indians there was a time for battle, and a time to celebrate or mourn the results. Unlike invading soldiers, a trespassing emigrant train, even one escorted by cavalry, was more of a nuisance than a provocation.

This mind-set would eventually change, not least under Red Cloud's leadership. But that was yet to come. To the Indians the skirmish at Bridge Station had been a flawed victory, but a victory nonetheless, and Sand Creek had been avenged. Now it was natural to fall back, plan for the autumn buffalo hunt, and settle into winter camps to await next year's fighting season. There was even a notion that the lesson of Bridge Station might induce the whites to abandon the Powder River Country altogether.

As far-fetched as this seems in hindsight, war as an all-encompassing endeavor was as alien to the Indians as a naval blockade or a siege of Washington would have been. Although a few Lakota in closer contact with the whites were dimly aware of how much carnage the Americans had inflicted on each other at Chancellorsville, at Chickamauga, at Gettysburg, most had no grasp of the white man's concept of battle as a year-round industry or as what is now called a zero-sum contest. That they

had not learned from Chivington's winter ride on Sand Creek demonstrated just how ingrained was Indian custom.

As it happened, though Connor may have possessed Chivington's
ardor, he had little of the Fighting Parson's luck. After multiple delays
his two flanking columns finally met, nearly by accident, northwest of
the Black Hills on the Belle Fourche, almost 100 miles away from their
planned juncture on the Tongue. Unknowingly, Cole proceeded to march
his 2,000 men directly between Sitting Bull's Hunkpapa village on the
Little Missouri and the Lakota-Cheyenne contingent camped on the
Powder. Days of similar peregrinations followed. Cole sent out riders to
find Connor's column. They returned exhausted and bewildered. Connor
dispatched his scouts to find Cole. They could not. The Americans were,
in effect, lost in the wilderness; they were running low on supplies; and a
grumbling Kansas contingent was ready to desert at any moment. This is
how Sitting Bull and his braves found them.

BURN THE BODIES; EAT THE HORSES

S itting Bull was angry. A month earlier, about when Red Cloud fell on Bridge Station, Sitting Bull's Hunkpapas had tried to pick a fight with the garrison stationed at Fort Rice in North Dakota. The timing was serendipitous. The Indians had not planned the simultaneous raids; it was merely the season. But Sitting Bull had even less success than Red Cloud. Geography was his downfall.

A year earlier, in the wake of his victory on the Upper Knife, General Sully had ordered his engineers to construct the fort on a steep plateau overlooking the west bank of the Missouri. The plain surrounding the outpost was sketched with low, sage-encrusted bluffs broken only by dark ravines running to the horizon. As Sully had planned, the soldiers on the parapets could see for miles in every direction, and when Sitting Bull's decoys appeared before their gates the lookouts had no trouble making out the main body of 400 to 500 Hunkpapas and Dakotas trying to conceal themselves behind the distant buttes. The post commander formed a defensive skirmish line along the riverbank that furled around the stockade's cottonwood walls, but refused to allow his men to go any farther. The Sioux made one frantic charge, loosing a storm of arrows and musket balls, but fell back under an American artillery bombardment. At this post, unlike Bridge Station, there was no wagon train in need of rescue. The soldiers held their position, and their howitzers kept the Sioux well out of arrow and musket range. Sitting Bull led a sullen retreat.

When a month later his outriders spied the billowing dust clouds of Colonel Cole's force meandering not far from where the Powder empties into the Yellowstone, Sitting Bull and his frustrated Hunkpapas jumped them like angry badgers.

Cole's force outnumbered the attackers by four to one, but his men and their horses were all debilitated after marching for weeks through the low, flat heat of a baking drought that left their skin cracked and their lips, tongues, and eyeballs coated with a thin pall of fine yellow loess soil. At the first sign of Indians, Cole ordered his troop to assume a defensive position, corralling up near a grove of leafy scrub oak. Through four days and nights the Sioux probed, running off a few horses and wagon mules, with Sitting Bull personally capturing one officer's majestic black stallion. But the Indians could neither penetrate the makeshift battlements nor lure out its defenders.

It was weather that finally forced Cole's hand. On the first day of September the temperature dropped seventy degrees and a freak blizzard swept down from the north, killing over 200 of the Americans' weakened horses. After burning his extraneous wagons, harnesses, and saddles, Cole had no choice but to march his men up the Powder. Sitting Bull had sent out messengers to Red Cloud's camp, and his Hunkpapas and Dakotas were now reinforced by small parties of Oglalas as well as some Miniconjous and Sans Arcs. These Sioux kept up a steady harassment of the slow-moving Americans, albeit to little end. The farther southeast the troop drove, the more concerned Sitting Bull became over straying too far from his defenseless village back on the Little Missouri. His scouts informed him that General Sully had pulled back across the Missouri, but one never knew. The Hunkpapas harassed the column for two more days, and then fell off to ride home. It was now Red Cloud's turn.

On September 5, the Bad Face chief finally reacted to Colonel Cole's intrusion by assembling 2,000 braves to meet the beleaguered American force. He chose as his battleground a bend in the Powder marked by tall, sheer sandstone bluffs broken by winding ravines. It was an ideal site for an ambush. No one knows why Red Cloud did not ride with the war party that day; some historians contend that after days of fasting and vision quests the Cheyenne chief Roman Nose begged for the honor of leading the combined Sioux-Cheyenne contingent. Red Cloud apparently did grant Roman Nose that honor, and in his own stead sent Crazy Horse and Young-Man-Afraid-Of-His-Horses.

Without the Oglala Head Man present, however, the Indians reverted to their age-old battle tactics. Instead of ambushing the troopers from the rocky ridges, or even surprising them head-on, warriors broke into small groups according to their soldier societies, intent on stealing horses and counting coup. Some had wonderful luck. A flight of Cheyenne led by Roman Nose chased a feckless company of cavalry into a spinney of cottonwoods banking the north side of the Powder. The Indians dismounted, and using the thick leafy spurge as cover, crept in after them. Near the riverbank they broke into a clearing, where they found eighty saddled mounts tied to the bushes. Across the river the cavalrymen were emerging, dripping wet. None had fired a shot.

Buoyed by this small victory, Roman Nose attempted to rally his attackers into a coherent battle group. But by this time the main body of Cole's troops had once again formed its wagons into a hollow square, its rear against the high hills. As Roman Nose policed the Indians into a loose skirmish line between the Powder and the bluffs, Crazy Horse approached with a request. He wanted to draw out the Americans with a dare ride. This had been his signature tactic throughout the Crow wars of the late 1850s, a feat so stunningly brave that it would inspire his fellow fighters. Roman Nose of course knew all about Crazy Horse's famous dare rides, and assented. Three times a nearly naked Crazy Horse galloped the length of Cole's defensive lines, a slim, ghostly figure hunched low over his war pony's lithe neck. His sudden, darting runs resembled the lightning-quick swoops of his animal spirit, the red-tailed hawk. He taunted the soldiers to come and fight. None would, although bullets whistled past him and made tracks in the earth at his horse's hooves. Crazy Horse finally quit—his horse for once unscathed.

Not to be outshone, Roman Nose spurred his white pony across the dusty no-man's-land with its clumps of sedge and needle grass. His eagle war bonnet trailed the ground as he too raced from one end of the American position to the other, screaming insults and bellowing challenges. Again the soldiers stayed put. The Cheyenne managed three rushes before his horse was shot and killed. At this the combined tribal force charged the corral en masse. They were repelled by whistling grapeshot and the crackling reports of hundreds of Spencer carbines. As a smoky dusk fell over the battlefield the Indians predictably grew tired of the standoff. The Cheyenne were the first to depart, riding off to strike camp and move east toward the Black Hills in preparation for the fall buffalo hunt. Cole took advantage of this to set his column on the move. He drove southwest as a few Sioux continued to trail him, intent mainly on stealing horses. But the opportunity for a showdown had passed.

Three days later another arose when Cole's Pawnee scouts, trailed by a platoon of cavalry, topped a ridgeline and nearly blundered into the eastern edge of Red Cloud's huge camp on the Tongue. A band of twenty-seven Cheyenne, one of the last to depart for winter camp in the east, were the first to notice them. But the Pawnee scouts were so distant that the Cheyenne merely assumed they were either Lakota or Arapaho returning from the fight with the soldiers, and paid them no heed. The Pawnee scouts retreated and hid on top of a steep cutbank, allowing the now-moving Cheyenne to pass. Then they ambushed the Cheyenne and killed every one. When a messenger reported the situation to Cole, for once the colonel understood that he had the element of surprise. He took the offensive, organizing his troop into a European-style full frontal charge. Even the Kansas malcontents, sensing a do-or-die moment, recovered their esprit de corps.

Red Cloud, meanwhile, was unprepared for the surprise attack. With his force depleted by the departure of the Cheyenne Dog Soldiers, he organized a frantic holding action. Women and girls raced to dismantle lodges as teenage herders rounded up ponies from the surrounding grasslands. The scene at the center of the Indian camp resembled a rodeo, with armed braves lassoing and mounting any horse available. It would not be enough. Cole had the strategic and tactical advantage. Then, suddenly, as if summoned by the *Wakan Tanka* itself, the weather again intervened. The sky to the west darkened nearly to black as a succession of billowing thunderheads growled down from the Bighorns. A driving sleet pounded the prairie for the next thirty-six hours, ending the fight and turning the loamy earth into a quagmire. The Indians slipped away in the dim light, and Cole lost another 400 horses and mules to the bitter cold.

When the storm broke on September 9 the dazed Americans again set to burning the last of their expendable supplies, including their wagons. Cole's remaining animals were too weak and his men too exhausted to continue carrying the dead, and he ordered the corpses thrown onto the fires to spare them mutilation. He then led what remained of his ragtag troop southwest up the Powder River Valley. The high ridges on either side of the column teemed with hundreds of mounted Indians. But unlike Sitting Bull's Hunkpapas, or even the Southern Cheyenne—tribes whose years of warfare against the whites had resulted in the acquisition of some modern weapons—Red Cloud's Oglalas and Brules for the most part relied on bows and arrows, useless at such a distance. One of Cole's officers estimated that only one in a hundred Powder River warriors owned a good gun, and it was likely to be only a single-shot muzzle-loader. Had even a quarter of Red Cloud's braves possessed anything resembling the Army's rapid-firing Spencers and Colts, Cole's column would have been doomed. It was a lesson Red Cloud was to take to heart—bravery meant nothing in the face of repeating rifles and cannons.

For two days the Sioux flanked the line of troopers, most of whom were now on foot and weak with scurvy. They had passed nearly a month without hearing from General Connor, and appeared so pale and gaunt that daylight alone might kill them. The Lakota sensed their best opportunity to rub them out as they watched the exhausted, footsore soldiers begin to slaughter their dwindling supply of bony horses and mules and eat them raw. Unbeknownst to the Indians, the soldiers were also low on ammunition, and there was talk among them of forming a final corral and making a last stand. Such was their condition when Connor's scouts, led by Jim Bridger, found their camp.

Bridger had proved something of a curiosity to Connor on the march north. The forty-five-year-old general was not quite as awed by the veteran scout as his younger officers were, and his skin was thin enough that he took it as a challenge to his rank and reputation when Bridger warned him before the expedition that the hangings at Fort Laramie "would lead to dreadful consequences later on the trails." Now that Connor had ridden with Bridger for over a month, his negative perception of the old mountain man had hardened, and he found himself wondering if Bridger, who was sixty-one, had lost his frontier edge. The fissures and fault lines crosshatching his face could be read as a map of distress, and at times he seemed to have difficulty recalling the locations of river fords that could accommodate the column's heavy freight wagons. Further, the general found Bridger's disdain toward what he called "these damn paper-collar soldiers" far from endearing. And his guide's failure—intentional or not—to inform him that the Indians he had clashed with on the Tongue were Arapaho, not Sioux or Cheyenne, sat like a burr under Connor's saddle. Even so, no one was happier to gaze upon "Old Gabe's" leathery visage that cold, dreary day in September 1865 than Colonel Cole and his starving troop.

Bridger told Cole that General Connor's column was only sixty miles away. A short distance beyond Connor, he said, was a new fort stocked with abundant supplies. It was enough to give a jaunty step to Cole's men, who reached the rectangular log structure in late September. Why Connor had stalled his march to build the small stockade—which he dubbed Camp Connor—virtually strangling his three-pronged offensive in its cradle, he never made clear. His tussle with the Kansas mutineers may have affected his plans, as might the realization after the fight with the Arapaho that the hostiles were not the helpless savages he imagined. Moreover, while Cole's men had been marching in circles in late August, Connor had raced to rescue a road grading team that had set out from Sioux City to expand John Bozeman's trail. Eighty-two freight wagons had been pinned down for thirteen days by hundreds of Lakota led by Red Cloud himself at the Tongue River crossing near the Wyoming-Montana border. The Indians melted away at Connor's approach. But despite the relief column's apparent success the incident effectively ended any hope of opening a shorter route through the Upper Powder to the gold fields.

All told, the summer campaign had been a disaster. The United States Army spent the fighting season scouring the High Plains for hostiles and came away with nothing to show for it besides a record of bad judgment, poor discipline, and failure. The miscarried campaign to crush Red Cloud left General Connor too disgusted to even request written reports from his subordinates, and he worded his own dispatch as vaguely as possible. He minimized the number of Army casualties—between twenty and fifty—and inflated Indian losses to nearly absurd proportions, estimating between 200 and 500 killed or wounded. Meanwhile one of his own junior officers admitted, "I cannot say as we killed one." Connor made no mention of the large herds of Army mules and big American horses now mingling with Indian ponies in winter camps, nor of the surly volunteers who finally staggered back into Fort Laramie in October—their uniforms so tattered that they reminded one officer of a line of "tramps." And the general certainly did not dwell on helping to turn the neutral northern Arapaho into belligerents.

Dodge's report to General Pope, on the other hand, described the expedition as a wild success. He wrote that with Camp Connor now garrisoned by a skeleton company, the United States had finally established a foothold in the heart of the Powder River Country. He described Connor's fight with Black Bear's Arapaho as a punishment to the Indians "seldom before equaled and never excelled." He was forced to make one concession, suggesting that the Union Pacific's proposed approach to the Rockies might be better laid nearer to the South Platte than to Red Cloud's domain. Ironically, this was along roughly the same path Bridger had outlined for Captain Stansbury fifteen years earlier. Other than this, Dodge concluded, all that was needed to grind down the belligerent northern tribes once and for all and to open the Bozeman Trail was more time, funds, and matériel.

But Washington had lost its faith. One suspects that a scholarly member of Andrew Johnson's staff reminded the president of King Pyrrhus's ancient lamentation—"Another such victory and we are lost." Dodge's incessant requests for more troops and supplies was costing the government $24 million annually—$3.2 billion in today's currency—and this money might better be spent on Reconstruction. The government saw no recourse but to fall back on a tried-and-true stratagem to deal with the prairie. The United States, Congress decided, would offer the High Plains Indians a new treaty. In this matter the politicians did not consult the generals, who had other ideas.

Part IV

THE WAR

Memory is like riding a trail at night with a lighted torch. The torch casts its light only so far, and beyond that is darkness.

—Ancient Lakota saying

WAR IS PEACE

Thee pending treaty between the United States and the Sioux Indians at Fort Laramie renders it the duty of every soldier to treat all Indians with kindness. Every Indian who is wronged will visit his vengeance upon any white man he may meet."

So wrote Colonel Henry Beebee Carrington on June 13, 1866, as he rode west at the head of the 2nd Battalion of the 18th U.S. Infantry Regiment. As he was still in eastern Nebraska, Colonel Carrington had yet to meet a hostile Indian, so he could not possibly have known how right he was. He was about to find out—and, for the moment, without his second in command, Captain William Judd Fetterman.

Following the end of the Civil War both Carrington and Fetterman had decided to make the Army their career. Though Carrington was only nine years older than Fetterman, they personified the fault line between the old-school military and a new breed of soldier steeped in total war. Carrington, the well-schooled attorney fond of reading his Bible verses each morning in Greek and Hebrew, had spent the conflict overseeing the Union Army's Midwestern recruiting efforts with enough efficiency to have been credited with bringing 200,000 volunteers into the service.

He had also maintained prisoner-of-war camps, and he prosecuted the rebel Copperheads who fomented the "Great Northwest Conspiracy."* He never saw action, but these accomplishments were enough to earn him a temporary and largely ceremonial brevet promotion to brigadier general. Fetterman, on the other hand, had tactical and strategic battlefield expertise. He had also gained administrative experience in the latter stages of Sherman's Georgia campaign, including service as acting assistant adjutant general to the 14th Corps, a position in which he was responsible for more than 10,000 men. His familiarity both with field conditions and with the military procedures and protocols of every type of command made him a more attractive candidate for the postwar officer corps. Both he and Carrington lost their volunteer brevet rankings and reapplied to the Regular Army's 18th Infantry Regiment in Columbus, Ohio. Fetterman reverted to captain from colonel, and Carrington to colonel from general—a perceived slight that he felt for the rest of his life.

Carrington returned to Columbus in part to mourn the death of his infant son—the fourth of his six children to die before the age of three. He also began to lobby for a choice assignment on what he saw as the Army's next great national stage, the Frontier. At war's end, the service had been bloated with thousands of brevet colonels and generals, and Carrington—a small, gaunt, tubercular administrator—did not seem to stand much of a chance. But he was determined to will his heroic interior fictions into reality, and he had many powerful friends. He began writing letters not only to old acquaintances from the days when, as a young man, he had served as Washington Irving's secretary, but also to more recent connections such as Salmon Chase, by now chief justice of the United States. He also reached out to his former law partner William Dennison, who had been the governor of Ohio and was now the postmaster general. His contacts came through.

At the end of the war Fetterman also rode north to Columbus. His stay was shorter. Though his dossier bulged with honors and citations, he

---

*This was a bizarre attempt by a small group of rebels led by the Confederate spy Thomas Henry Hines to sneak into the United States via Canada, free southern prisoners of war near Chicago, and start an insurrection.

did not have Carrington's political clout. In the fall of 1865 Fetterman was assigned to recruiting duties in Cleveland just as Carrington with his wife, Margaret, and their two sons—six-year-old Jimmy and the younger Harry—departed for the West with 220 men of the 2nd Battalion of the 18th. The troop was undermanned by almost 700 soldiers, and the party reached Fort Leavenworth in Kansas by railroad and riverboat in early November in the midst of one of the most brutal Plains winters on record. It was the Carrington family's first time away from urban comforts, and the shock of roughing it was registered by Margaret Carrington, who noted in her journal that the mercury in her thermometer had apparently frozen at twelve degrees below zero (a physical impossibility) and "two feet of snow had to be shoveled aside before a tent could be pitched."

While the Carringtons and the 18th acclimated to this new reality, a war-weary nation was recoiling at the notion of further conflict, particularly with Indians. And vocal religious organizations, such as the Quakers, turned their attention from emancipation to the justice and wisdom of America's treatment of the western tribes. Every pulpit represented numerous voters, and eastern politicians took notice. Moreover, the preachers' public campaigns provided humanitarian cover for the new peace policy of the "Radical Republicans" taking power in Washington. The real reason for a shift in Indian policy was, of course, budgetary. Politicians in both parties were pressured by taxpayers weary of supporting the professional, and expensive, Frontier Army when the costly task of Reconstruction was only beginning. Throwing more money into another Indian campaign while paying to clean up the detritus of the last was anathema. With the western volunteer militias melting away and the Army drawing down its total number of troops from more than one million to just under 60,000—most of whom were needed to police the South—any number of congressional investigative commissions were formed to study the "Indian problem." The members of these committees tended to be both self-serving and naive, and grandstanding senators and congressmen began to personally conduct "fact-finding" missions to the West. Sand Creek was a favorite stopover for datelines and photo opportunities.

The easterners, however, were in for a surprise, for the westerners—whose population was still sparse—had no sympathy for the "savages."

Senator James Doolittle of Wisconsin, an ardent proponent of peace, was one example. In a speech at the Denver Opera House, he asked what he considered a rhetorical question: Should the Indians be placed on reservations and civilized, or exterminated? He did not receive the answer he expected, because the rest of his speech was drowned out as the audience shouted, "Exterminate them! Exterminate them!" Not long before, a similar audience at the opera house had greeted Colonel Chivington as a conquering hero. Despite such omens, Washington remained determined to reach some sort of compromise with the High Plains tribes—a clean, simple solution to avoid further bloodshed and expense. As another senator wrote to the secretary of the interior after meeting with western Indian agents, "It is time that the authorities at Washington realize the magnitude of these wars which some general gets up on his own hook, which may cost hundreds and thousands of lives, and millions upon millions of dollars."

To that end, in the fall of 1865 Indian agents approached bands of Hunkpapas, Yanktonais, Blackfeet Sioux, Yanktons, Sans Arcs, Two Kettles, and Brules living near the Missouri River with a blunt message: the raids on emigrants and settlers must cease, and a war against the United States would be unwise. But America was not heartless, the agents added, and in exchange for acceptance of Washington's latest peace offer they promised the Indians acreage, farm tools and seed, and protection against any tribes who took exception to these new agricultural pursuits.

The Sioux were naturally resistant. Living in houses, tilling fields, sending their children to school—these were white man's values and principles. But the agents were aware that the Upper Missouri tribes had to this point suffered the most from the alarming thinning of the buffalo herds, and they reminded the Indians that the fifteen-year annuity payments from the Horse Creek Treaty were about to expire, and offered a solution—a new, twenty-year deal at increased rates. All they asked in return was that the bands move permanently away from the trails and roads leading west, and vow not to molest the whites defiling their old lands with mechanical reapers, threshing machines, and barbed wire. It was a stunning demonstration of the Indians' desperation that by October enough pliable subchiefs representing over 2,000 Sioux agreed to the treaty in a ceremony at Fort Sully, located at the mouth of the Cheyenne River.

The national conscience, troubled since Sand Creek, was assuaged, and newspaper headlines declared peace with the Sioux while eastern reporters and editors, unaware that "the Sioux" came in many variations, wrote that the Bozeman Trail was now safe for travel. The government was apparently equally delusional in its belief that a similar pact could be signed with Red Cloud and his followers. Indian agents sent runners into the Powder River Country to announce that come spring the United States was willing to offer even better terms in the form of exclusive rights to the game-laden territory lying between the Black Hills, the Bighorns, and the Yellowstone in exchange for the mere right of passage along the Bozeman Trail. There was no mention of farming. The message from Washington was clear: avoid war at all costs.

The politicians and Indian agents who promoted and fostered these peace offerings had many agendas, but most were spurred by one obvious and overriding fact—the Army was small and the Plains were enormous. The generals apparently disagreed.

The political struggle for control of Indian affairs had been raging, intermittently, since 1849, two years before the Horse Creek Treaty, when tribal oversight was transferred from the War Department to the Office of Indian Affairs. The Army (correctly) considered the politicians dishonest and corrupt; the politicians (equally correctly) deemed the Army bloodthirsty and shortsighted. One proof of the latter belief had been General Connor's disastrous campaign. By rights, the bureaucrats pointed out, it should have taught the military some basic lessons, the foremost being that for all of America's industrial might, great winding columns of Bluecoats blundering across the prairie on futile search-and-destroy missions would play into the hands of a mobile, cunning enemy who knew every butte, hollow, creek, and pasture. General Sherman himself admitted that finding hostile Indians "was rather like looking for a flea in a large clover field." Yet despite his new authority as commanding general of the Army, even Grant could not alter the institutionalized hubris and Indian-hating of the War Department. By the spring of 1866 the department—as was said of the Bourbons on their return to power—had apparently learned nothing and forgotten nothing.

A year before General Grant plucked him out of obscurity, General Pope had published in the influential *Army and Navy Gazette* an indictment of what he considered America's accommodationist policy toward the High Plains tribes. This approach to the "Indian Problem" had the matter backward, he wrote. Instead of offering treaties and bribing the Natives with gifts and annuities, Pope advocated placing the burden of peace on the Indians. Were he in command of national Indian policy, he concluded, he would give the tribes a choice, take it or leave it: "an explicit understanding with the Indians that so long as *they* keep the peace the United States will also keep it. But as soon as they commit hostilities the military forces will attack them, march through their country, [and] establish military posts in it."

Now Pope *was* in command of the Department of the Missouri. In March 1866 he issued General Order No. 33, which instituted yet another Army "District," the "Mountain District." It included the route from the old Camp Connor (since renamed Fort Reno), northwest to Virginia City via the Bighorn and Yellowstone Rivers—in other words, the Bozeman Trail. The order also assigned Colonel Carrington's 18th Infantry Regiment the task of reopening and protecting the route. In order to facilitate this assignment, Carrington would need to construct a string of forts through the heart of the Powder River Country, permanent structures replacing the mule-driven supply lines that had failed so miserably in the past. For a striking illustration of the haphazard state of the postwar Army, one need look no further than the fact that on the very day General Pope issued Order No. 33, Generals Grant and Sherman decided to relieve him of command.

Grant had placed Sherman in charge of all western defenses, and he was also close to appointing a fifty-six-year-old brigadier general, Philip St. George Cooke, to succeed Pope as head of the Department of the Missouri. Sherman suggested that the role called for a younger, more vigorous general, who might actually get out into the territory to experience personally the difficulties the troops and their officers faced on the frontier. He was afraid General Cooke would be content to lead from behind,

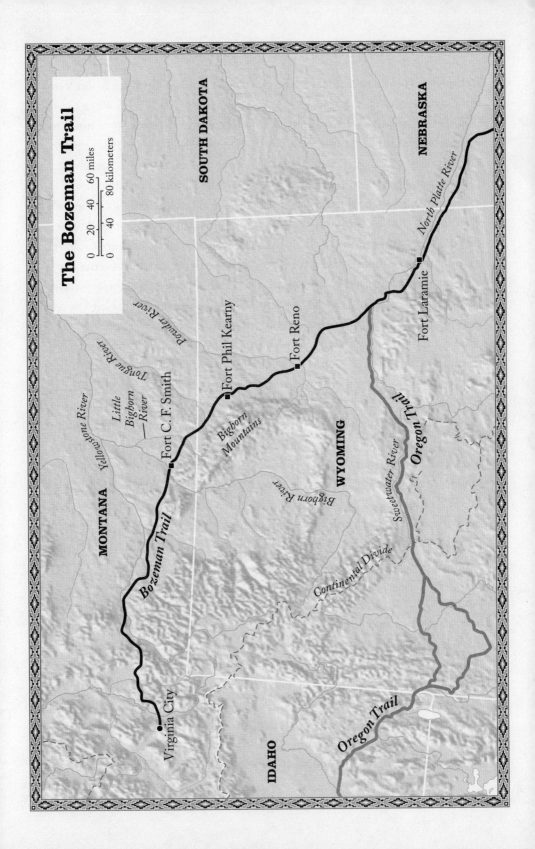

The Bozeman Trail

60 miles
40
20
0
80 kilometers
40
0

SOUTH DAKOTA

NEBRASKA

North Platte River

Fort Laramie

Powder River

Tongue River

Yellowstone River

Little Bigborn River

Fort Phil Kearny

Fort Reno

Fort C. F. Smith

Oregon Trail

Bigborn Mountains

WYOMING

Bozeman Trail

Bigborn River

Sweetwater River

MONTANA

Continental Divide

Virginia City

IDAHO

Oregon Trail

in Omaha, and he was correct. But Grant was fond of Cooke, his old Virginia dragoon who had fought so admirably against Black Hawk, against the Mexicans, and against the Mormons. (Grant may have also wanted to reward Cooke for remaining loyal to the Union when his son, his nephew, and his famous son-in-law J. E. B. Stuart went over to the Confederacy.) Grant of course prevailed, and in March Cooke assumed command.

Amid this bureaucratic confusion, Pope's General Order No. 33 stood. This meant that by virtue of the political and social contacts that had secured him command of the 18th Infantry Regiment, the obscure Colonel Henry Beebee Carrington, with no fighting experience and an attorney's approach to most military hurdles, remained in charge of the Army's most ambitious undertaking on the western frontier—the defeat of Red Cloud, the mightiest warrior chief of the mightiest tribe on the Plains. A plan to endow such an officer with the authority to build and maintain outposts throughout the very wilderness that had been ceded time and again to the Lakota by government treaty appeared not only duplicitous but idiotic. It is not known if Colonel Carrington had any idea that he was to be used merely as a placeholder, a competent fort builder who was expected to defend those outposts with untested infantrymen until a real fighter at the head of well-trained troops could complete the extermination of the western tribes. As Sherman wrote to Grant's chief of staff in the summer of 1866, "All I ask is comparative quiet this year, for by next year we can have the new cavalry enlisted, equipped, and mounted, ready to go and visit these Indians where they live." Apparently, he assumed that the Sioux would wait.

Judging from his official reports and dispatches, Colonel Carrington may have suspected that his position was tenuous when he and his battalion departed Fort Leavenworth for Nebraska's Fort Kearney. It must also have crossed his mind that the tasks lying ahead might be easier if he had a fighting cock like Fetterman at his side. Not that the 18th did not contain its share of serious soldiers. The outfit's quartermaster was a balding, brawling bachelor, Captain Frederick Brown—a hard-drinking thirty-five-year-old who during the Civil War had earned a reputation as a place where trouble started. Though both teetotalers, the Carringtons were initially fond of Brown, although it is doubtful that the colonel was aware of Brown's habit of slipping Fort Kearney's Pawnee scouts extra rations in exchange for lessons on how to skin a buffalo and scalp a man.

The officer who was to become Brown's sidekick was the battalion adjutant Lieutenant William Bisbee, battle-scarred beyond his twenty-six years. Bisbee was a city boy from Woonsocket, Rhode Island, who had enlisted in the Army of the Republic at age twenty-two and was almost immediately commissioned as a lieutenant. He shared a tent and fought side by side with Fetterman from Corinth to Atlanta, and he was devoted to the captain. Like Carrington, Bisbee brought his family—his young wife and infant son—west with him, and at first the two clans became close. But their personal friendship did not last. Carrington was appalled when he observed Bisbee's abusive behavior and language toward the enlisted men, and threatened several times to discipline him. Bisbee, who would rise through the ranks to general officer, never lost his contempt for his commander, and years later was to have his revenge.

Carrington's junior officer corps also included Captains Henry Haymond and Tenedor Ten Eyck, both hard-bitten veterans. Haymond had commanded the 2nd Battalion of the 18th through some of its hardest fighting. The laconic Dutchman Ten Eyck, whose lazy right eye lent him the appearance of a professional gunfighter, was another soldier who liked his whiskey (he would later be cited repeatedly for public intoxication). He was one of the few college-educated officers on Carrington's staff, and prior to the Civil War he had worked as a surveyor and lumberjack before catching gold fever. He was mining in Denver when the war broke out, and despite being over forty he returned to Wisconsin and enlisted as a private. Within six months he was commissioned as a captain in the 18th, and soon thereafter he was captured at Chickamauga. Tough enough to survive a bout of dysentery during the year he spent in a Confederate prison near Richmond, Ten Eyck was liberated in a prisoner exchange and returned to Wisconsin, where he had left his wife and five children when he joined the Carrington expedition.

Colonel Carrington's staff officers, well acquainted with Army routine, understood the official reasons for his absence from the front during the war. That did not mean they had to respect those reasons, or even the punctilious man himself—an attitude that the colonel would only gradually come to understand. As it was, for now he was content to spend the winter of 1865–66 at Fort Kearney, a mere 194 miles west of Omaha, and it was from there that he wrote to General Cooke that he had acquired 200 "excellent" horses from Iowa and Nebraska cavalry volunteers mustering out of Civil War service as well as scores of freight wagons with which to haul sacks of seed potatoes and onion bulbs, surveying tools, and the construction equipment for his blacksmiths, wheelwrights, and carpenters. These included hay mowers, brick- and shingle-making machines, window sashes, locks, and nails by the barrelful.

Despite this wealth of fine building materials, Carrington's unit remained woefully short of modern weaponry. The officers and sergeants had been issued Colt revolvers, but the enlisted men still carried obsolete, muzzle-loading Springfield rifles remaindered from the Civil War. These guns were in such poor condition that many would not even fire. The War Department claimed that the single-shot Springfields cut down on ammunition wasted by soldiers carrying repeating rifles, but this was nonsense. It was an open secret in Washington that kickbacks to politicians by contractors from the Springfield armory kept the guns in circulation well past their effectiveness. Carrington undoubtedly was aware of this—he was, after all, an administrator at heart—but he certainly could not voice such a complaint in his dispatches. The best he could do was hint that his mission was compromised without more men and better guns, and until they arrived he decided to wait the situation out through the harsh Nebraska winter.

From Fort Kearney Carrington also issued his own General Order No. 1, requesting from Cooke's warehouses "commissary and quartermaster supplies for one year . . . and fifty percent additional for wastage and contingencies." In spite of his inherent cautiousness, Carrington was nothing if not optimistic, as indicated by his further submission for such delicacies as canned fruit and vegetables, sewing machines, rocking chairs, and butter churns that his wife, Margaret, believed would add "a domestic cast" to their impending journey. Heading into hostile Sioux territory, he was literally trading guns for butter.

23

BIG BELLIES AND SHIRT WEARERS

In the autumn of 1865, at about the same time that government agents were finalizing their treaty with the more pliant Missouri River tribes, Lakota Head Men and warriors were convening in the foothills seventy miles northwest of Fort Laramie to revive a decades-old system of governance. It had its origins in the turn of the century, when the Western Sioux were just beginning to drive the Pawnee, Kiowa, and Crows from the High Plains. It called for seven veteran chiefs to act as an advisory war council for the tribe, concentrating on battle tactics and strategy. On the banks of an unnamed creek over a feast of buffalo tongue and boiled dog, Red Cloud was selected as the "first among equals" of these *Tezi Tanka,* or "Big Bellies"—the wise heads who would guide the tribes through what all believed was inevitable war with the whites. Notable by his absence was the belligerent Hunkpapa Sitting Bull. He was waging his own harassment campaign against the Army in eastern Montana, and whether he was envious of Red Cloud's ascendancy or preoccupied by his own battles against both the Americans and the Flathead tribe, Sitting Bull was never to be a factor in the fights for control of the Powder River Country.

It was at the Big Belly convocation that Red Cloud officially declared the 1865 fighting season over, and the Lakota agreed to reassemble for a war council in the spring. Perhaps they would even accept the white man's invitation to come to Fort Laramie for treaty talks. After all, Red Cloud reasoned, what better way to size up an enemy than to meet him in person? Before the gathering disbanded, however, he and the six other Big Bellies chose four young men to act as ceremonial "Shirt Wearers" who would keep discipline among the wild braves and lead the war parties into battle.* Among these were Young-Man-Afraid-Of-His-Horses and Crazy Horse. Red Cloud had begun to take a serious interest in Crazy Horse, the pale young warrior with the indefinable panache. He recognized in the young tribesman all the qualities required of a tactical field general. Even his name swaggered.

Now twenty-five, Crazy Horse had acquired the physical stature and mannerisms that would characterize him for life. He was slender and sinewy even for an Indian, and his lightness of carriage often left the impression than he was slighter than his five feet, nine inches. His ethereal quality was enhanced by his wavy hair, now waist length and usually plaited into two braids that framed his narrow face and his unusually delicate nose, which observers described variously as "straight and thin" and "sharp and aquiline." Whites who met him over the years were usually struck most by his penetrating hazel eyes. One American newspaperman described them as "exceedingly restless," and Susan Bordeaux Bettelyoun, the half-Brule daughter of the trader James Bordeaux, noted that Crazy Horse was a master of the sidelong glance. She wrote that he "hardly ever looked straight at a man, but didn't miss much that was going on all the same." In addition, Crazy Horse also exuded a natural melancholia, as if the humiliations and defeats he'd witnessed as a child—from Horse Creek to Harney's massacre to the defeat of the Cheyenne on the Solomon River—had scarred his psyche. It was generally assumed that if Crazy Horse could indeed make magic, some of it was black.

Red Cloud may have felt that he needed such magic. Although either

---

*The actual quilled, fringed shirts presented to these braves were woven from bighorn fleece and decorated with hair, each lock representing a coup counted, scalp taken, or brave deed accomplished. Crazy Horse's shirt had almost 250 locks.

unwilling or unable to articulate it, much less understand the reasons for it, he and most of his cohort sensed a subtle change in the land of their youth. Droughts lasted longer, grasslands had become more sparse, and even the hardy wild mustang herds, like the buffalo droves, appeared to be thinning. In fact, the middle of the nineteenth century did mark the end of a 300-year neo-boreal cooling period known as the Little Ice Age, and this was about to have a greater impact on the American West than all the Indian wars combined.

Starting around 1550, falling temperatures in the northern hemisphere had produced snowstorms in Portugal, flooding in Timbukto, and had destroyed centuries-old citrus groves in eastern China. Three centuries later, at the end of the Little Ice Age, Mary Mapes Dodge would be inspired to create a fictional character, Hans Brinker, whose silver skates carried him along frozen Dutch canals that would never again ice over. In North America the most severe repercussion from this meteorological anomaly was the desertification of buffalo ranges from the Canadian Plains to Texas. Yet the Powder River basin, because of its location between two mountain ranges and its many bountiful aquifers, escaped the environmental degradation affecting vast tracts of the West. Game proliferated in the area, cool breezes still wafted down from the mountains, and lush sweet grass scented the air. This alone made the country worth fighting for. But arguably it was not *this alone* for which Red Cloud fought: if he and his people had lived in the Mojave, or on a polar ice cap, and someone had tried to take it away, his reaction would have been the same. "If white men come into my country again, I will punish them again," he promised his tribesmen.

All of Red Cloud's plans were of a single piece—to close down the pathway into his people's verdant country, forever. He saw the world in primary colors, and if need be, he was willing to paint John Bozeman's trail blood red.

A trail becomes a Trail when it avoids alkaline flats or impassable ravines on either flank and instead meanders past water holes and through pasturage hardy enough to nourish stock; when it finds a way for wagons to wend through broken buttes and mesas while avoiding cutbanks so steep the bleached bones of buffalo litter the bottom; when it leads to fords in wild rivers where a prairie schooner carrying an entire lifetime of possessions can safely cross. Such was the nation's last great overland Trail, which John Bozeman and John Jacobs had nearly died blazing in the spring of 1863.

Before their discovery, thousands of miners had trekked west toward the Montana gold camps via two primary routes. Both were considerably roundabout. The first followed a perilous stretch of the Missouri by way of Fort Benton in north-central Montana that creased directly through Sitting Bull's territory. The second passed by Fort Laramie on the Oregon Trail before climbing through the South Pass of the Rockies at the southern end of the Wind River range. There the more traveled route to the West Coast turned southwest toward Salt Lake, forcing the Montana-bound to make a hard trek north across a vast high-country desert dotted with alkaline puddles before doubling back across the Continental Divide over even higher peaks. Game was scarce in this country, but so were Indians, and this was the route for which Jim Bridger would advocate his entire life.

The wagon road blazed by John Bozeman, on the other hand, branched north off the Oregon Trail before even reaching the mountains, and ran up the east face of the Bighorns. It rolled around the north end of the range to follow the Yellowstone corridor upriver in a northwesterly direction to the Big Bend, where it swung due west and wound into Montana's Beaverhead Valley. The 400 miles it cut from the previous routes saved one month to six weeks in travel time, and lush grasses, clean water, and fresh meat were plentiful.

In her classic book *The Bloody Bozeman,* Dorothy Johnson describes the naive, hopeful pilgrim who traversed the Bozeman Trail into the Montana wilderness. "He was a farmer eking out a living somewhere in the Middle West or fleeing the catastrophes of the War of the Rebellion. Or he was a lawyer or a doctor or a storekeeper, doing better than eking but wanting to do better still. He went west to find prosperity. This new man was not a born adventurer, but in his stubborn, sometimes cautious way he was a gambler. He gambled his life to better his condition, but he didn't really believe that *his* hair might make fringes for a Sioux or Cheyenne war shirt or that *his* mutilated body might be clawed out of a shallow grave by wolves. He preferred not to face the fact that, if he should be captured, he might scream prayers for the mercy of death for hours before that mercy came."

Ironically, were it not for the assistance of friendly Indians, Bozeman and Jacobs would probably have perished on their trailblazing journey. They almost died anyway, arriving at the Deer Creek station on the North Platte without mounts, half-naked, and nearly starved. But now that they knew the general conditions of the route, the two were confident enough to set up shop next to the Deer Creek telegraph station and sell their shortcut, offering their services as guides. The drawling, apple-cheeked Bozeman was a tireless promoter—if not exactly on a first-name basis with the bottom of the deck, he certainly put the confidence in "confidence man"—and outfitted himself in a fringed buckskin shirt and trousers to further impress prospective customers. He and Jacobs also hired a Mexican interpreter who was fluent in Sioux, and they soon attracted emigrants who were afraid of risking their wagons and stock over Bridger's more arduous road. Bozeman assured the travelers that there were no hostile Indians along his route, and on July 6, 1863, he and Jacobs led the first train out of Deer Creek and into the wild Powder River Country.

This was the train that was intercepted by the Lakota and Cheyenne near the Bighorns and voted to turn back. Undeterred, the following summer Bozeman, this time without Jacobs, led a much larger and more heavily armed caravan from the North Platte to Virginia City without incident—the first emigrants to arrive in Montana along the new trail. A week before Bozeman departed from Deer Creek another train—124 wagons led by the wagon master Allen Hurlburt—had ventured out from the North Platte along the same route. But Hurlburt's party had, proportionally, even more miners—418 men traveling with 10 women and 10 children—and Bozeman's caravan passed it when Hurlburt stopped to prospect in the Bighorns. Bozeman was already being feted in Virginia City saloons when Hurlburt finally arrived. It is by virtue of this historical quirk that subsequent overland travelers to the Montana and Idaho gold camps did not roll along the "Hurlburt Trail."

By 1866, however, word spread that traveling on the Bozeman Trail was too dangerous. This was the first year of the great post–Civil War migration west, and Bozeman's outfit was nearly out of business. One Army trooper who was part of an expedition that fought its way up the route that summer wrote to the *Army and Navy Journal,* "We thought it an impossibility to get through. There will be no more travel on that road until the government takes care of the Indians. There is plenty of firewood, water, and game, but the Indians won't let you use them."

This more or less summed up Colonel Carrington's orders—"Take care of the Indians." He got off to a rocky start. In March 1866, while he was still wintering at Fort Kearney in Nebraska, Congress ordered the printing of an official Army survey delineating Bozeman's route. The chart had been pieced together from Bozeman's own rather opaque notes, geographic reports from General Connor's expedition, aborted road-making expeditions (including the wagon train halted by Red Cloud and rescued by Connor a year earlier), and scattered newspaper clippings. When copies of this purported map reached Fort Kearney, Carrington and his officers were baffled. It resembled no chart they had ever seen, and was not much more than a squiggly dark line running vaguely northwest from the Oregon Trail through a vast, empty expanse bounded by the Black Hills to the east and the Bighorns to the west. There was no indication of elevation, nothing to differentiate desert flats from pasturage, and no mention of water holes or timbered country; and the few contoured watercourses that were outlined could have been either raging rivers or shallow streams. So spare were the map's details that someone on Carrington's staff actually dug up old copies of Lewis and Clark's reports in hopes of matching descriptions of landmarks from their diaries.

Meanwhile, the battalion's officers went about overseeing the mundane tasks common to nineteenth-century military expeditions striking out for the wilderness. The infantrymen repaired harnesses, greased axles, reshod horses and mules, and cleaned weapons, including the unit's one field howitzer and five snub-nosed mountain howitzers. They also learned to ride carrying their cumbersome Springfields. This by all accounts lent comic relief to an otherwise monotonous deployment, although Margaret Carrington noted that soon enough most of the men were able to saddle up, "and the majority actually made their first trip to water without being dismounted."

By mid-May, however, even this distraction was curtailed when a reinforcement battalion from the 18th consisting of 500 recruits arrived from Fort Leavenworth. Each unit—the one ensconced and the one arriving—assumed the other to be stocking rations, and Fort Kearney underwent a mild famine that left the men too weak to practice their horsemanship.

At least the food shortages were short-lived. By the spring of 1866 the Union Pacific had laid tracks as far as Fort Kearney, and a week after the arrival of the reinforcements a locomotive arrived hauling boxcars of commissary supplies. There were more recruits aboard as well, and riding along with them was General Sherman, making his first inspection trip to the frontier. (He had traveled as far as Omaha the previous fall.) Sherman, gaunt and hollow-cheeked, was apparently experiencing one of his manic stages. He charmed the officers' wives, posing for photographs and suggesting to each that she keep a journal of what was certain to be an important chapter in American history. He oversaw bow-and-arrow competitions between the sons of the Pawnee scouts and the American boys, including Jimmy Carrington, who was awarded an Indian pony he named Calico after winning a long-distance shoot. But when Sherman met with Carrington and his officers he exhibited uncharacteristic passivity, suggesting that, "if possible," they avoid any contest of arms with the Natives.

If Sherman felt any apprehension over sending an officer who had spent the Civil War sitting behind a desk on such a "vital mission into the most contentious territory in his command," he kept it well hidden. Dinners were jovial and at least one makeshift cotillion was arranged, with the entertainment supplied by the 18th Regiment's thirty-piece band. Carrington, who loved martial music, had insisted on bringing the musicians along, and they were his only troops outfitted with new, lighter Spencer carbines that fired .52-caliber bullets fed from a seven-round tube magazine.* After several days of relaxing under the pleasant June sunshine, Sherman bade the colonel godspeed and rode east, while Carrington marched the 18th west.

---

*Even posthumously Samuel Colt was changing the face of American warfare. His acolyte Christopher Spencer invented the manually operated, lever-action "Spencer" repeating rifle and carbine.

24

COLONEL CARRINGTON'S CIRCUS

Still short of manpower, particularly of officers, the 2nd Battalion of the 18th Regiment departed Fort Kearney in late May 1866. Over 1,000 men—700 soldiers, 11 officers, and several hundred civilian teamsters driving more than 200 wagons—followed the well-worn Oregon Trail hugging the Platte along the sage-covered Nebraska plain. Despite their new equestrian skills the infantrymen marched in the van, followed by the wagons, with at least 700 beef cattle herded by mounted officers and dragoons. Someone dubbed the long train "Carrington's Overland Circus," and though it is not recorded who coined the phrase, suspicion naturally fell on the sixty-two-year-old iconoclast Jim Bridger, who rode along as chief scout.

This was the first crossing of the endless wrinkled prairie for the majority of the eastern recruits, and it showed. Their boyish enthusiasm at the landscape's sights and sounds left the seasoned teamsters rolling their eyes. The newcomers gaped at startled pronghorns leaping in reaction to the flashes of heat lightning, and they fired potshots at skulking coyotes raising their yellow muzzles at the scent of jackrabbits the size of small dogs. They passed acres of prairie dog villages as the small rodents popped into and out of their spongy burrows like wind-up toys. And their first glimpse of the dark shape of faraway buffalo herds whose stampedes shook the earth for miles brought to mind—as one soldier noted in his journal—nothing so much as thousands of small schooners asail on a shimmering sea.

The caravan struggled through ravines clogged with shifting sands and up into crooked gorges whose rock walls narrowed to the width of a wagon. It passed cool, clear streams filled with thousands of pike, their "hard, white meat" providing a fresh and tasty alternative to the rock-like hardtack and moldy bacon. One can only imagine their thoughts when Chimney Rock rose before them, its strata of clay, volcanic ash, and sandstone erupting from the flats and tapering to a needle point that seemed to puncture the clouds. A few days later came the sight of the Scotts Bluff escarpment on the western horizon. This terraced "Gibraltar of the Plains," composed of five contiguous rock formations of crystallized magma, towers 830 feet above the prairie (and nearly half a mile above sea level), and is the highest point in Nebraska. With its rococo parapets and rain-carved stone towers it resembles nothing so much as a medieval European castle somehow dropped onto the Plains.

The troopers could hardly ignore the Indians watching them from every butte and mesa. As Lieutenant Bisbee noted, "We had no occasion to scout for Indians, they were always nearby." At first, Bridger assured the soldiers that they were friendly. But when the column approached a ramshackle Army post known as Camp Cottonwood midway between Fort Kearney and Julesburg, the old trapper's demeanor changed. He rose each morning before the reveille bugle, downed a few bites of pemmican, and brewed a pot of bitter coffee over a smoldering pile of buffalo chips—*bois de vache*, or "wood of cow" in the polite terminology of the Victorian era. He would then confer in Carrington's tent before disappearing into the vastness. No one would see him again until dusk, when he'd return to give the colonel a report.

One morning a Brule Head Man rode into camp. Carrington greeted him with military courtesy, and with one of Bridger's scouts interpreting the two parleyed over coffee and a pipe. The Brule told the colonel that many Lakota bands were camped near Fort Laramie, led by chiefs who were willing to listen to the white negotiators. With his Bozeman Trail "map" in mind, Carrington probed the Indian for geographic information on the Powder River Country. The Brule ignored the question and said, "Fighting men in that country. . . . They will not give you the road unless you whip them." Thereafter the "Circus" wagons were drawn into tight, interlocking squares each night, and Carrington issued orders reining in mounted officers who had fallen into the habit of lighting out at the sight of game.

Two weeks out of Fort Kearney the column reached Julesburg and was forced to float its gear on makeshift ferries across the mile-wide Platte running high with snowmelt. It then veered northwest, following the north fork of the river. A week later, with the temperature above 100 degrees and a rising wind ripping the canvas covers from his freight wagons, Colonel Carrington crested a cactus-studded ridge overlooking the gates of Fort Laramie. The searing heat had turned most of the prairie brown, and across the ocher flats were camped more than 2,000 Lakota, Cheyenne, and Arapaho "in assorted sizes, sexes, and conditions; dressed, half-dressed, and undressed." Carrington scanned the "menagerie" through his field glasses and was taken aback by the lax security. There were no sentries posted, and Indians and soldiers inside the stockade mingled freely. He decided to bivouac his raw troops some distance away in order to avoid accidental misunderstandings. They had, after all, been sent west to kill Indians.

That evening Carrington splashed across the shallow Laramie and entered the fort. He introduced himself to its commander, Colonel Henry Maynadier, who was serving as a member of the government's peace commission. He met the civilian negotiators, including a superintendent of the Office of Indian Affairs who was to chair the next day's treaty ceremonies. The colonel was also introduced to several Lakota Head Men. They had already learned of his mission from the Brules who had visited him, and they were cold toward the "Little White Chief." The terms of the treaty to allow Americans passage through the Powder River Country had not even been laid out or discussed, much less signed by the Indians—and already the white soldiers presumed to ride north and build forts? Carrington understood that it would be hard to dispute this point, but he intended to try nonetheless.

The following morning, while Margaret Carrington and a few other women availed themselves of the sutler's meager stock of rice, sugar, and coffee, the superintendent from the Office of Indian Affairs pulled Colonel Carrington aside and assured him that nearly all of the Brule, Miniconjou, and Oglala chiefs in attendance were ready to sign the treaty. Only a few from the Upper Powder were holding out and still needed to be convinced. But they were already in camp, and the superintendent had no doubt that they would come around. Carrington asked who these holdouts were. The superintendent rattled off a few names: Young-Man-Afraid-Of-His-Horses, Spotted Tail, Red Cloud. The latter two, Colonel Carrington was told, "rule the [Lakota] nation." This information was half right. By now the name Red Cloud was familiar to every soldier west of the Missouri. Although he was technically outranked in the Oglala hierarchy by Old-Man-Afraid-Of-His-Horses in time of peace, this was not such a time. According to an account by Colonel Maynadier, the Indian agents had made great efforts to secure the Bad Face war chief's attendance by showing more deference to him than to any other Indian. They were unaware that Red Cloud had planned to be there all along in order to take the measure of his antagonists.

Over the next few days Carrington observed the usual council formalities—introductions of tribal luminaries; a pantomime buffalo hunt followed by a grand feast; the presentation to the Indians of gifts of coffee, navy tobacco, bright bolts of calico, and sacks of brown sugar. When not monitoring the ceremonies the colonel busied himself composing ever-more beseeching dispatches to General Cooke in Omaha. Cooke had promised him fresh horses at Fort Laramie. There were none. The wagon-loads of pilot bread and hardtack he expected to take possession of would last no more than four days, and the sacks of flour marked for his com-missary were caked, musty, and brown with dry rot. Worse, he had requi-sitioned 100,000 rounds of .58-caliber ammunition for his troop's ancient rifles. The post commander could not even spare 1,000. On the outskirts of the fort he had seen Indian ponies with gunpowder kegs lashed to their saddles. No one, not even Jim Bridger, seemed to know how the Indians had come into possession of the ammunition while Carrington could not even secure shot for his men.

He was scheduled to depart in two days, and the government negotiators agreed to his request to address the Indians directly. He was certain that his opening statements of peace and amity toward the tribes would win them over, so certain that he asked his wife, Margaret, to attend. The next morning he strode poised and confident onto the parade ground in front of the post headquarters. The commission members and the Lakota Head Men sat around him in a semicircle at rough wooden tables set on a raised platform. Behind them hundreds of warriors, braves, and squaws stood or squatted under the blazing June sun. The Indian Affairs superintendent introduced Carrington, but the translator had not even completed his name before there were murmurs across the parade ground. The Indians already knew who Carrington was, and where he was going. They grew restless, squirming on the benches, and a few made guttural clucking sounds from deep in their throats.

The nervous translator suggested to Carrington that perhaps it would be prudent to allow the chiefs to speak first. The colonel nodded, and the floodgates opened. Lakota after Lakota rose to condemn and harangue the impertinent white men for daring to treat them as if they were as stupid as Pawnee children. Their way of life had been destroyed and degraded enough. The whites and their livestock had driven away the buffalo and denuded the prairie. The Indians had been crowded into smaller and smaller pockets of land to live in crude squalor until they faced starvation. And now the Americans wanted even that land? They had been invited to listen to the terms of yet another treaty that the white soldiers already considered a *fait accompli*. The presence of Carrington and his column was proof of this deceit. Young-Man-Afraid-Of-His-Horses locked eyes with the colonel and warned him that if he dared venture into the Powder River Country, "In two moons the command would not have a hoof left." The threat was followed by loud grunts and an approving chorus of *hun-huns*. Then Red Cloud rose.

The Lakota war chief stood tall, jutted his chin, and pulled his buffalo robe tight about his massive shoulders. "The Great Father sends us presents and wants a new road," he said, his voice rising to a shout. "But the White Chief already goes with soldiers to steal the road before the Indian says yes or no. I will talk with you no more. I will go now, and I will fight you. As long as I live I will fight you for the last hunting grounds." His final sentences were nearly drowned out in a welter of hoots and ululations. Carrington tried to answer, shouting over the noise that he indeed intended to build forts along the Bozeman Trail, but only for use as travelers' way stations. His words were lost in the din. The Indian Affairs superintendent banged his gavel to regain control of the meeting. Only the whites were paying attention.

As Colonel Carrington walked from the parade ground toward his horse Margaret Carrington spotted Red Cloud and another Indian breaking from the crowd. They seemed to be shadowing her husband, and gradually gaining ground. Red Cloud's right hand was at his side, his fingers gripping the hilt of a large knife. Even taking into account his not negligible temper, it is highly unlikely that a man as savvy as Red Cloud would have chosen this public moment, inside Fort Laramie, to assassinate a U.S. Army officer. Margaret Carrington's account, although no doubt accurate in its basics, must be read with caution: she was a newcomer to Indian country, and she was familiar with the era's rather feverish (and often accurate) accounts of "savage" maliciousness.

On seeing the big, angry Indian fondling his knife, Margaret shouted a warning to the colonel. Red Cloud was nearly upon him. Carrington slowed and looked sidewise at the Oglala chief, not precisely challenging him, but hitching his holster closer to his hip and resting his palm on the revolver's handle. His hand remained on his gun as Red Cloud walked past him, as if he were invisible, and continued through the post's front gates.

Later that day the commanding officer at Fort Laramie advised the Carringtons to pay no attention to Red Cloud's "tantrum," as such things were as common among Indians as with spoiled children. He even intimated that Red Cloud was not as influential a Head Man as some of the others present, including Spotted Tail. Red Cloud, he said, was no more than the leader "of the young men who they called 'Bad Faces,' always fighting other tribes and stealing their horses." Probably he would be back the next day with the rest, begging for presents. Yet when Carrington and Bridger rode back to their camp that night they noticed that Red Cloud's lodge had been struck, and that the ponies laden with the gunpowder kegs were gone. Red Cloud, observed Margaret Carrington, "in a very few days quite decidedly developed his hate and his schemes of mischief."

25

HERE BE MONSTERS

The 2nd Battalion of the 18th Infantry Regiment pushed off from Fort Laramie on June 17, 1866, the day before the peace conference formally ended. The conference was "a disgusting farce and disgraceful swindle," according to J. B. Weston, an attorney who witnessed the ceremony. Weston's prescient analysis contradicted the official report of the Indian Affairs superintendent, who wrote to Washington, "Satisfactory treaty concluded with the Sioux. Most cordial feeling prevails." In reality Red Cloud's explosion left a bitter taste all around. Some Head Men, weary of constant war, had touched the pen; these included most of the southern Lakota from the Republican River corridor. So too had Spotted Tail, who had ridden down from his territory on the White River. But none of the bolder chiefs would do so, and many braves from bands whose leaders did agree to the pact rode north from Fort Laramie with Red Cloud.

This was what now faced Carrington and his battalion as they set out across the vast hinterland. It was 150 miles to Fort Reno on the Powder, and beyond that the world as the white soldiers knew it would end. The journey through this brink of the American empire would provide

Carrington and his men with a greater understanding of just what they were to face in the months ahead.

The trail to Fort Reno, thick with prickly pear and saltbush, was punctuated by but a few lonely trading posts and ferry crossings, and the troop was watched the entire length of the march by Lakota blending into the willows in shady hollows or, concealed beneath wolf skins, lying on high rimrock. Bridger, who picked up Indian signs each day, reported to Carrington, "They follow ye always. They've seen ye, every day. And when you don't see any of them about, is just the time to look for their devilment."

Examples of such devilment were numerous. The column paused at one trading post owned by a Missouri Frenchman, Louis Gazzous, whom Bridger introduced to Carrington as "French Pete." French Pete, who was married to a Sioux woman, warned the colonel that there was already loud talk in the territory of the scalps and horseflesh of which his column would soon be relieved. At Bridger's old ferry station, now operated by a man named Mills, the colonel learned that a raiding party had emptied Mills's corrals just twenty-four hours earlier. Mills, who was also married to an Indian—an Oglala woman—was agitated. Given his wife's tribal status, he said, he had always been immune to such theft. He considered the action significant, a harbinger of a new kind of bitterness on the High Plains. When Carrington asked Mills if he had any idea who was responsible, he answered immediately: "Red Cloud." Carrington again ordered security tightened, with particular emphasis on hobbling the stock at night, and pushed on.

After the experience of Forts Kearney and Laramie, the first glimpse of Fort Reno was sobering. Set on a small rise blanketed with thistle and greasewood hard by the Powder's north bank, it overlooked a maze of arroyos and low washes, their cracked-mud beds ideal for concealing Indian raiding parties. The outpost itself was a rotting, weatherworn log structure caulked with mud; a dilapidated corral abutted a string of warehouses built into low red-shale hills. Few men or officers from the battalion had ever seen a frontier post constructed to repel a full-frontal Indian attack. This one was dominated by two defensive bastions holding two of the post's six mountain howitzers, and rifle loopholes had been bored through the adobe walls to accommodate enfilading fire. The place struck the soldiers more as a prison than a military installation. This was apt.

The previous summer General Connor had left the fort manned by a unit of Winnebago scouts and the two volunteer companies of "galvanized Yankees" that had accompanied the road-building train. The Indian scouts had only recently been ordered back to Illinois as a precaution against further inciting their ancient enemies, the Sioux. The hard winter had combined with a poor diet to leave many of the former Confederates near death from dysentery, pneumonia, and scurvy so severe that their teeth were falling out. They had the emaciated, scraggly look of shipwreck survivors. In a sense, this is what they were.

The historian Stephen E. Ambrose notes that Indian fighting on the High Plains was more akin to naval warfare than to any other type of battle. The U.S. Army "was lumbering around with battleships and cruisers, chasing pirates in sleek, fast vessels," and the forts and camps were like home ports to which large ships must return often for supplies. The Indians lived off the land much as the pirates lived off the ocean, and the soldiers deployed to the frontier had no more comprehension of their surroundings than the crews of Columbus or Magellan reading blank charts marked with the warning "Here be monsters."

Colonel Carrington, well aware of this, had originally planned to demolish Fort Reno and transport any salvageable food and construction supplies to a site closer to the Black Hills with better access to wood, water, and pasturage. But eleven hard days on the road had changed his mind. Both soldiers and emigrant travelers would need a secure post where they could lay over, and even if the unimpressive pile of wood 150 miles from Fort Laramie did not deserve the appellation "fort," it would certainly serve as a way station. Thus was "Reno Station" born as a midway stopover for resting weary stock and repairing broken wagons between the Oregon Trail and the new posts Carrington intended to build farther north. He carried with him orders mustering out the irritable "galvanized Yankees"—they immediately disappeared like ghosts in the night—and selected a company of sixty to seventy men from the battalion to permanently garrison the station. Then he and his officers set out to reconnoiter their new possession.

The warehouses—made of eight-foot cottonwood logs roofed and chinked with mud daub—had been inundated by the winter's terrible snows, and the thick slabs of bacon stocked within were so rotten that gobs of the greenish, slimy fat were sloughing off the lean meat. An infestation of mice had burrowed a network of tunnels through the flour sacks, whose contents had caked around the droppings and dead rodents. The men improvised a large sieve out of burlap sacks to separate the dead mice and the larger pieces of excrement. What remained of this unappetizing mess was dutifully repackaged and loaded onto wagons.

Carrington was further astonished to learn that three emigrant trains bound for Montana were camped a few hundred yards away over a nearby ridge, awaiting a military escort up the Bozeman Trail. A fourth train, he was told, had already departed. When he rode out to meet the travelers the following morning, he was appalled. A blinding summer hailstorm— the stones as large as pullet eggs, one trooper recorded in his journal—had transformed the camps into mud sties, and none of the expeditions' leaders had taken any precaution against Indian raids. The wagons were spread haphazardly across a gorgeous valley flecked with wild rose and pink wintergreen, and the mules and horses roamed free of hobbles or pickets. When Carrington gently chided one wagon master for his lax security, the man scoffed at him: "We'll never see an Indian unless they come to beg for sugar, flour, or tobacco."

On the ride back to Reno Station, Carrington was already formulating a set of regulations to be issued to all civilian trains passing up the Bozeman Trail. Paramount in his mind was instilling a sense of discipline in these wild, independent-minded emigrants. No trains with less than thirty armed men, he decided, would be allowed to move forward. (The number would soon be revised upward, to forty.) And each passenger on any train that did meet this quota would have to sign in at every fort along the route. If a traveler was signed in at one post but failed to appear with the train at the next, the train could not go on until the laggard caught up. This, Carrington hoped, would not only end the "constant separation and scattering of trains pretending to act in concert," but also eliminate the Indians' most tempting targets—the stragglers.

That same afternoon Carrington dropped by the sutler's rude store just north of Reno Station. It was owned and operated by A. C. Leighton, a trader who had secured a government contract to supply all the forts erected by the 18th Regiment. Before dismounting, the colonel noticed Leighton's unguarded remuda grazing in a pocket ravine on the other side of the river. Inside the store the trader, a longtime frontiersman, assured him that the animals were in no peril; he and the Lakota had always been on good terms. The words were barely out of his mouth before one of Carrington's escorts burst in, shouting, "Indians." The group rushed to the door to watch the last of Leighton's animals being stampeded over a rise by a Lakota raiding party.

Carrington's squad galloped to Reno Station, where the colonel ordered Captain Haymond to form up a party of ninety men. They were mounted and riding within thirty minutes. By midnight the patrol had not returned, and Carrington paced the battlements until, about an hour later, he spotted the exhausted detail straggling back over a dusty butte. He counted no empty saddles, but neither had the troopers recaptured any of Leighton's stock. Haymond reported that they had ridden fifty miles before losing the Indians; the only animal they could catch was a half-lame Indian pony abandoned during the chase. Carrington and his officers gathered round as Haymond emptied a bulging elk-skin sack tied to the pony's saddle. It was stuffed with bags of brown sugar and coffee, pouches of navy tobacco, and a folded length of bright calico—gifts from the treaty council.

The colonel spent nearly two weeks securing Reno Station and making ready for the next stage of his journey. There were only two incidents of note. The first was the disciplining of an infantryman for public drunkenness on Independence Day. The private, who had purchased the whiskey from the sutler Leighton, was staked to the ground, spread-eagle, for six hours as swarms of flies lapped up the alcohol oozing from his pores. The second was the departure of the civilian trains. Their impatient wagon masters decided not to wait for a military escort and formed one large train that rolled north a few days after the battalion's arrival.

Eight days later, in the predawn hours of July 16—the hottest day on record across the High Plains in the summer of 1866, with the temperature approaching 111 degrees—seven companies of the 2nd Battalion of the 18th U.S. Infantry bade farewell to the small Reno Station garrison and marched northwest. For all its heat, filth, and squalor, the soldiers would soon enough come to recall the station fondly as their last, tenuous link to civilization. The territory beyond, between the little godforsaken post on the north bank of the Powder and the gold camps of Montana, was as mysterious and terrifying as any uncharted sea.

26

THE PERFECT FORT

The transition, wrote Margaret Carrington, "was like the quick turn of a kaleidoscope." One day the flat, brown prairie had been hot enough to crack leather boots, swell mules' tongues out of their mouths, and turn the incessant grasshoppers that blanketed the earth into tiny kindling. Twenty-four hours later chilly mountain breezes forced the women to don shawls, prickly pear was replaced by luxuriant groves of leafy willow and cedar, and the cool water from mountain streams was so clear that the soldiers could count individual fish.

It took the column four days to reach the long, slim plateau that rises athwart the Bozeman Trail some forty miles south of the present-day Montana border. The grass-covered bench land—5,790 feet above sea level by Colonel Carrington's calculation—juts from a magnificent valley formed by two parallel creeks called the Little Piney and Big Piney in the shadow of the east face of the snow-crusted Bighorns. John Bozeman's maps had, of course, not done the site justice. The plentiful fresh water streaming out of the mountains had turned the surrounding acres of lush pasturage that rolled north to Goose Creek into a swaying shamrock sheen too tall and thick for a horse to canter through, and the site was only six miles from slopes covered with forests of pine, hemlock, balsam, fir, and spruce. "At last we had the prospect of finding a home," wrote Margaret Carrington. Everyone seemed satisfied except Jim Bridger.

The march from Reno Station to what was to become Fort Phil Kearny* had been tense. Trouble started a mere twelve hours out, along a nearly dry alkaline creek bed called Crazy Woman Fork. By that point nearly half the column's wagons were in need of repair, their wooden wheels so irreparably shrunk by the heat that the metal rims wobbled and finally fell off. Axles and spokes were also in poor shape, and Colonel Carrington called a halt while his wheelwrights stoked charcoal bonfires to forge new rims. When the task dragged on longer than expected the colonel marched on, leaving several companies behind under Captain Haymond to complete the work.

There were two legends regarding the naming of Crazy Woman Fork. According to the more benign story, an old, demented Indian woman had once constructed a semipermanent brush-and-grass tepee, called a wickiup, on the creek and made the site her home. The second, more gruesome, story was that an emigrant family had been ambushed there while watering stock. The husband and children were killed and mutilated before the wife's eyes, and she had been raped and had gone insane. The Indians, afraid of calling bad medicine down on themselves for killing a madwoman, allowed her to wander off, and it was said she still haunted the vicinity. The soldiers stoking the charcoal pits preferred to believe the former legend.

Not far past Crazy Woman Fork the trail descended into a long, tight ravine, and before the soldiers even reached it Jim Bridger came racing back to the main column. He and Carrington rode ahead to a spot where Bridger pointed at two small shards of a wooden cracker box, their jagged ends jammed into the dirt at the side of the road. Scrawled across the wood were messages from the consolidated emigrant train reporting that

---

*The War Department had initially ordered the post to be named Fort *Philip* Kearny after the one-armed martyr of 1862's Battle of Chantilly, who was also the nephew of the Mexican War hero Stephen Kearny. To veterans of the Army of the Republic, however, General Kearny was "Fighting Phil," and this popular usage prevailed.

here they had beaten off an attack by Indians but lost some of their horses and oxen. Carrington ordered his pickets doubled that night, but there was no sign of Indians. The next day the column reached the two Piney creeks.

Though the broken wagons and the eerie warnings had put nerves on edge, the beautiful country at the confluence of Big Piney Creek and Little Piney Creek changed everyone's mood. And by the time his horse had climbed the small plateau between the two rushing streams, Colonel Carrington was already planning. He envisioned three of his companies garrisoning this post while, the sooner the better, his four remaining companies would continue to strike north by northwest to establish two more permanent camps: one on the Bighorn and, beyond that, another on the upper Yellowstone. Jim Bridger appeared to be the only person unhappy with the arrangement.

Bridger noted that despite the plateau's proximity to forest, clean water, and rich pasturage, the site was overlooked on three sides by even taller ridges and hills, heights from which Indians could study the soldiers with impunity. Due west, a long set of foothills—Carrington named them the Sullivant Hills, after his wife's family—rolled up into the Bighorns. A separate escarpment called Lodge Trail Ridge bent around the plateau north by northeast no more than a mile and a half away. Both were excellent observation points, and Bridger urged Carrington to keep moving north to find a more suitable site somewhere on the Tongue, some fifty miles away. As Carrington led a patrol on a seventy-mile circuit to scout that area, he almost took Bridger's point. The country between Goose Creek and the Tongue teemed with game, and wild cherries, strawberries, plums, gooseberries, and currants grew in abundance. But the colonel feared that it was too remote from the forested Bighorns to haul wood for construction and winter fires.

Once the patrol returned, Carrington politely but firmly informed Bridger that construction would begin tomorrow. He noted that the gently sloped, 900-by-600-foot plateau between the Piney creeks was a natural defensive position—"an engineer would hardly make a more perfect grade for the sweep of fire." As for the Sullivant Hills and Lodge Trail Ridge, he intended to post daylight pickets on the tallest butte in the area, the nearly mile-high Pilot Knob, a mile due south across Little Piney Creek. Lookouts there would negate any Indian advantage. Bridger had stated his piece and had been overruled. He was not a man to repeat himself.

Like General Connor during the previous summer's campaign, Colonel Carrington was having a difficult time deciding what to make of Bridger. It was quite evident that the old mountain man's rough-and-ready life was finally catching up to him. He was hobbled by painful bouts of arthritis, particularly where the arrowhead had been removed from his spine, and on some mornings he looked as if he might have to be helped onto his old gray nag. Yet his instincts—and eyesight—seemed as sharp as ever. During the passage from Reno Station he had often shaded his brow with a flat hand before pointing to what he said were small groups of Indians watching their every move, although Carrington had difficulty spotting them even with his field glasses. On the day before they reached Crazy Woman Fork a small party of Lakota had met the column on the trail and, on standing orders, Bridger and his scouts had reluctantly escorted them to the colonel's tent. The Indians professed amity, telling Carrington they were going to fight Snakes "over the mountains," and the colonel rewarded them with the usual gifts of coffee and tobacco. Carrington was pleased to have made what he considered a good first impression until Bridger tactfully informed him that he had just handed over presents to a Lakota scouting party whose sole mission was to ascertain, up close, his unit's strength.

But despite Carrington's nagging doubts about Bridger, he was smart enough to recognize that he needed the old trapper at his side. This was never more evident than when he returned from his scouting mission to the Tongue to discover the first instance of what would become a persistent difficulty. Seven of his enlisted men, singly and in small groups, had deserted for the Montana gold fields. The battalion had suffered scattered desertions since Kansas, but Carrington assumed that once they had reached hostile territory no man would be so foolish as to strike out. He had not taken into his calculations the lure of what the Indians called the yellow metal that drove white men crazy, and in the coming months it was not unusual for visitors to Fort Phil Kearny to see captured AWOLs encumbered with balls and chains or wearing barrels with signs stating their offenses.

On this occasion the quartermaster Captain Brown, with Lieutenant Bisbee at his side, had pursued the deserters up the Bozeman Trail, but was stopped seven miles out by a large band of Cheyenne camped near a mobile trading post operated by "French Pete" Gazzous and his partner. Exemplifying the convoluted social and political mores of the prairie, the Cheyenne professed to be peaceable and treated Gazzous as a friend, yet warned the soldiers they would kill them if they ventured farther north. A signal from French Pete confirmed their intent, and the soldiers turned back without the deserters but with a message from a Cheyenne Head Man named Black Horse. He wanted to parley with the Little White Chief.

What followed was the same North American *pas de deux* between the white and red cultures that had been taking place since the *Mayflower* landing. By the time Black Horse and a small coterie of his subchiefs and warriors arrived at the future site of Fort Phil Kearny under white flag two days later, Carrington's surveying and engineering skills had transformed the empty grass plateau into a rectangular seventeen-acre tent city. Black Horse, seemingly impressed, told the colonel through an interpreter that his followers wanted no more war with the whites, but that other members of their tribe, allied with the Lakota and Arapaho, were determined not only to wipe out the interlopers, but to fight any Indian bands who would not join them. Throughout the daylong meeting Carrington did not need his translator to recognize the one name that was mentioned repeatedly—*Makhpiya-luta*, Red Cloud.

Red Cloud was now a Big Belly, Black Horse said, and explained what that meant. Moreover, according to the Cheyenne, Red Cloud had hundreds if not thousands of warriors riding with him. His plan was to cut off the body of the trespassing white snake between here and Reno Station, and eventually all the way south to Fort Laramie. He would then crush the weakened serpent's head beneath his moccasin heel. Carrington and his troop at Fort Phil Kearny were that head. The memory of Fort Laramie, of the daggers in Red Cloud's eyes, and of the big knife in his hand, was fresh in Carrington's mind. The colonel finally realized that Bridger had not been unrealistic with his constant warnings of being watched and studied by Red Cloud from the day they had departed Fort Laramie.

Black Horse told the soldiers that the Bad Faces knew exactly how many soldiers and horses Carrington had detached to garrison Reno Station. They had counted the precise number of troopers dispatched in the attempt to retrieve the trader Leighton's stolen remuda—which, by the way, was now in the possession of the Lakota. They knew the number of men in the smaller party still repairing wagons at Crazy Woman Fork. And Red Cloud and his braves had shadowed Carrington's patrol two days earlier when they had scouted the Tongue for alternative sites for the post. All this intelligence, Black Horse said, was in service to Red Cloud's desire for a greater understanding of the white soldiers' habits. Finally, Black Horse mentioned that many of Red Cloud's warriors were at present undergoing a Sun Dance high up on the Tongue, but there were those who had ridden south toward the Powder to begin the process of killing the white snake's body. Among the latter was Crazy Horse.

Carrington, Bridger, and the officers present remained stone-faced and seemingly unimpressed during the course of the meeting. But despite himself the colonel found the Bad Face war chief's isolate-and-destroy strategy admirably cool and calculating, a course of action worthy of Stonewall Jackson or Jeb Stuart. While they palavered Captain Haymond and the wagon repair party arrived from Crazy Woman Fork—one less worry for Carrington—but when the colonel bade good-bye to Black Horse and his party late that night he was unaware that his Cheyenne visitors were not traveling far. In fact they halted just a few miles up the Bozeman Trail to camp and trade with French Pete Gazzous.

The Cheyenne were in the process of exchanging pelts for, among other items, cheap whiskey when Red Cloud and a large party of Lakota rode in on them. Red Cloud quizzed the Cheyenne Black Horse as to the Little White Chief's intentions. Black Horse told the truth—the soldiers not only would erect a permanent fort between the Little Piney and Big Piney but also planned to build more posts farther up the trail. Then Red Cloud eyed the whiskey jugs and demanded to know why Black Horse and his Cheyenne would bother with these whites. Could the loyalty of the mighty and regal Cheyenne truly be purchased with tobacco, paltry trinkets, and the poisonous *mini wakan*? Where was their pride? "The White Man lies and steals," he said. "My lodges were many, but now they are few. The White Man wants all. The White Man must fight, and the Indian will die where his fathers died."

Black Horse offered no reply, and in a fit of rage Red Cloud and the Lakota grabbed their bows and quirted the Cheyenne across their faces, shoulders, and backs. This was unprecedented. Yes, Black Horse and his braves were outnumbered, but they were also important Cheyenne. It was the first time in their lives that these proud men had ever been treated like disobedient women. That they did not fight back against this humiliation signaled a new day on the prairie, for Red Cloud did little without calculation. This was not only a display of his contempt, but an announcement. There would be no more half measures against the whites, or against anyone who had truck with them. As the Lakota rode off Black Horse and his people immediately packed up and set a course for the mountains. Before leaving they warned French Pete and his partner that they would be wise to do the same, or at least to seek safe harbor in the soldiers' camp between the Piney creeks.

Meanwhile, several miles to the south, Colonel Carrington was discussing with Captain Haymond a change in orders. The captain had expected to start up the Bozeman Trail the following morning with four companies to scout appropriate sites to build posts. The colonel now had second thoughts about stretching his already reduced battalion so thin. Given what he had gleaned from the Cheyenne, further fragmenting his forces seemed madness, at least until reinforcements arrived. No, Haymond and his men would remain at Fort Phil Kearny, he decided. The extra hands and strong backs would not only facilitate the transformation of the fort from a tent city into a proper, permanent stockade, but also buy time to feel out Red Cloud's movements. And, with seven well-armed companies present, the Indians would not dare attempt to strike.

It was as if Red Cloud was reading Carrington's mind. He attacked the next morning.

27

"MERCIFULLY KILL ALL THE WOUNDED"

I n a move born of misplaced confidence, Captain Haymond did not bed down his four companies in the temporary tent city on the plateau after arriving from Crazy Woman Fork with the repaired wagons. He instead made camp closer to water in a rolling swale midway between Big Piney Creek and Lodge Trail Ridge. He was awakened at 5 a.m. the next day, June 17, when a picket gave a loud shout. A Lakota raiding party had slithered on their bellies down from the ridgeline, and one Indian managed to leap onto the troop's bell mare. Before Haymond or any of his men could respond, nearly 175 animals, mostly mules, were being stampeded back over the ridgeline. The easterners were to now learn their first lesson in Indian fighting—never give chase to a raiding party without a close-knit and overwhelming force.

Haymond and an aide were immediately mounted and off, but the rest of the riders had difficulty rounding up and saddling their skittish horses. Haymond was nearly out of sight by the time the troop, in scattered groups of three and four, followed the dust cloud of stolen animals. When the Indians saw the haphazard pursuit, braves began dropping back and circling around in ambush. One trooper took an arrow to his chest;

another was blasted out of his saddle by a musket ball. Reinforcements from Fort Phil Kearny eventually caught up to Haymond's party, engaged by now in a running fight stretching along a fifteen-mile length of the trail. They were too late for the two dead and three seriously wounded men in Haymond's command. Nor did the Americans manage to retrieve their mules and horses, which had vanished into the prairie.

On the slow, bitter ride back to the fort the troop trundled past the dead campfires of French Pete's mobile trading post. Half a mile up the road they found the trader and his partner splayed across the dusty saw grass. They had been scalped, their limbs hacked off, and their genitals stuffed down their throats. A few yards away, among the detritus of the traders' looted Murphy wagons, the corpses of French Pete's four teamsters were discovered similarly mutilated. The soldiers had of course heard stories of Indian atrocities, but this was their first personal encounter. One private noted in his journal that "it gave us all a most convincing lesson on what our fate would be should we fall into [their] hands." As the troop was burying the bodies a soldier heard whimpering coming from a thick copse of greasewood. He pulled French Pete's Oglala wife and her five children from their hiding spot. Whether they had been spared out of indifference or tribal loyalty, no one could say.

Over the next week Fort Phil Kearny began to rise as if by magic, a testament to Carrington's engineering skills and the hard work of his men. He dispatched woodcutters into the Bighorn foothills to establish a pinery on a small island between the two deep gorges cut by the parallel creeks. Soon, thanks to a horse-powered sawmill, mule trains were transporting logs and boards from the mountain forests by the ton and the fort's eight-foot-high walls took shape. Under Carrington the soldiers were temporarily transformed from a fighting troop into a battalion of loggers, blacksmiths, carpenters, teamsters, hay mowers, painters, and shingle makers, and the outlines of rough wooden structures appeared within the rectangle that ran roughly northwest to southeast for just over 1,500 feet.

The walls consisted of more than 4,000 logs, with firing loopholes bored through every fourth one. This stockade would soon enclose enlisted men's barracks, officers' quarters, warehouses, administration buildings, a sutler's store, an infirmary, and an underground magazine. These in turn would surround a mown parade ground complete with a gazebo bandstand from which the regiment's musicians serenaded the battalion and passing travelers during the morning's guard-mounting ceremony and again at dress parade at sunset. Such was Carrington's attention to detail that he issued orders that no one was to walk on the grass.

At the corners of the fort stood enfilading blockhouses complete with howitzer portholes; aware that the mile-high elevation would distort depths and distances to untrained eyes, the colonel had his artillerymen walk off and mark firing ranges. To the rear of the post proper a 200-by-600-foot quartermaster's yard extended southeast to Little Piney Creek. This fenced-in enclosure would eventually hold stables, civilian teamsters' quarters, mechanics' sheds, and yards for cordwood and baled hay. Big Piney Creek ran along the Bozeman Trail just before the front gate on the north. Pilot Knob, a mile to the south, overlooked the entire complex.

While construction proceeded Carrington continued to bombard General Cooke with requests for weapons and men. His eight infantry companies—now stretched along the sixty-five miles between Reno Station and Fort Phil Kearny—totaled about 700 men, more than 500 of them raw recruits with an average age of twenty-three. When not working or standing picket they required constant training, something that, given the dearth of officers, proved a difficult proposition. Even routine procedures such as target practice were curtailed because of the lack of ammunition. It was said that the 2nd Battalion of the 18th Regiment became the best knife throwers in the Army. Although they had yet to be attacked, the detachments to the pinery could feel eyes watching them from the thick forest, and each night the Indians probed for openings in the American defenses, making off with a horse here, a mule there. To make matters worse, one day a mail courier arrived from Fort Laramie with orders recalling to the States two of Colonel Carrington's officers, including Captain Haymond. The same dispatch informed the colonel that commissioned replacements were en route. He took little solace. He was not happy to trade two experienced veterans for . . . who, exactly? He had not been sent names.

Red Cloud was enraged from the first *thwunck* of ax blades gouging the trunks of the ninety-foot pines on what the Americans had dubbed Piney Island. His scouts kept up a constant surveillance of the wood-choppers, though it was hardly necessary. The whine of the sawmill and the crash of falling timber could be heard for miles—a visceral reminder of the defilement of *Wakan Tanka*. It was time for another lesson.

In the last week of June, Colonel Carrington detached a company of infantry to return to Reno Station for sacks of foodstuffs he could not haul on the initial trip north. He sent Bridger along as a precaution. Sixteen hours later the colonel's orderly and a courier covered with dust awakened him at one o'clock in the morning. Not only had his freight train been ambushed near the Clear Fork of the Powder, but three other emigrant trains in the vicinity were also under attack. Carrington was dumbfounded. Red Cloud had orchestrated four simultaneous engagements. It was unheard of. The colonel had no idea that farther south, near Crazy Woman Fork, an even larger party of Lakota had pinned down a relief column that included the battalion's five replacement officers.

The Battle of Crazy Woman Fork, as it came to be known, was notable not only for its ferocity and desperate heroism, but as one of the first recorded instances of American soldiers voting to kill each other rather than be taken by the Sioux.

The drama began at Reno Station, where on July 20 a reinforcement detachment from the 18th Regiment under the command of Lieutenant George Templeton set out for Fort Phil Kearny. The party consisted of five lieutenants, including Templeton; ten enlisted men; and an Army chaplain and surgeon reporting to Carrington. They were joined by nine teamsters contracted to drive the five freight wagons and two ambulances. One of the officers and one of the enlisted men had brought their wives and infant sons. The final member of the caravan was a dashing adventure seeker named Ridgway Glover, one of the odder characters passing through the pages of the old West.

Glover was a lanky, peripatetic thirty-four-year-old from Philadelphia with a shock of long, thick yellow hair usually tucked under a flat felt hat of the sort in vogue back east. The scion of a prominent Quaker family, he had taken up the fledgling art of photography a few years earlier, and his tintypes of President Lincoln's funeral procession had caught the eye of the director of the Smithsonian Institution, who suggested he take his talents west. Pushing and pulling an odd little handcart that was stocked with developing chemicals and that also served as his portable darkroom, Glover had crossed the Missouri lugging his slow-speed Roettger pinhole camera, bamboo tripod, brass plates, and ferrotype enamels. He also had a financial grant from the Department of the Interior, and he intended to wander through the Rockies to document the taming of the frontier. Carrington had met the photographer briefly during the treaty council at Fort Laramie, and when Glover learned of the colonel's mission he asked to accompany the battalion up-country. Carrington, against Jim Bridger's advice, had agreed. But Glover wanted more shots of the Indians at the fort, and decided to linger. He told Carrington he would join a future wagon train. Now here he was, in Lieutenant Templeton's small caravan, entertaining the two Army wives with fantastic tales of convincing his subjects that his magic box was not, in fact, stealing their souls, but merely reflecting an image caught by sunlight and transferred onto his metal plates.

The company commander at Reno Station was initially reluctant to allow Lieutenant Templeton's small party to continue up the trail. But each of the five officers as well as several of the enlisted men had experienced major combat during the Civil War, and they persuaded him to let them ride north. The party had only four saddle horses, and the officers rotated shifts between mounts and wagons. The day before reaching Crazy Woman Fork they had discovered the almost naked body of a scalped, mutilated white man, shot through with arrows. The tatters of a gray woolen blouse covering parts of his shoulders indicated that he was a soldier, probably a courier, but no one could guess from what command. Burying the bloody mess had spooked one of the lieutenants, an Indiana native named Napoleon Daniels. Unable to sleep that night, Daniels had joined Private Sam Peters on picket duty. "He said that he had a presentiment that something was going to happen to him very soon," Peters wrote not long afterward. "All efforts to discourage him from entertaining the gloomy phantasy were unavailing."

The next morning as the small caravan neared Crazy Woman Fork

the forlorn Lieutenant Daniels lifted his field glasses and spotted a herd
of buffalo meandering across a gentle slope about five miles distant. The
party needed the fresh meat, and Daniels and Lieutenant Templeton rode
ahead to turn the drove toward the trail so that by the time the wagons
reached the alkaline creek they would have the animals in a cross fire. The
two officers disappeared behind a belt of cottonwoods as the rough road
dropped into a dry arroyo leading to the fork. Here the going was slow,
the wagon wheels sinking deep into sand, and the teamsters whipped the
mules bloody. Their braying nearly drowned out the first Indian war cries,
which were followed by a dense volley of arrows.

Westerners found it difficult to convey the inchoate dread they felt toward the Plains Indians. Their Euro-American forebears were no strangers
to atrocity, and in fights against tribes from the Mohawk to the Seminoles
had both lost and taken scalps—and sometimes tanned scalps for public
viewing, as in the Dakota Little Crow's case. Old mountain men and
retired soldiers may have even remembered the Army's killing and skinning of the great Shawnee warrior Tecumseh. But these were exceptions,
and few whites were prepared for the torture almost casually meted out
by tribes like the Sioux, Comanche, and Cheyenne. These western "red
devils" were considered nearly an alien race, duplicitous and capable of inflicting suffering beyond the conception of nineteenth-century American
religious and cultural sensibilities. Even the Civil War veterans—who had
no doubt heard of, if not witnessed, bloodthirsty atrocities on battlefields
from the border states to Georgia (a fact downplayed by both sides)—
were terrified of these *others* who took such pleasure in exacting pain. Thus
one can only imagine the throat-closing fear the frontier newcomers in
Lieutenant Templeton's party felt as the rain of arrows was followed by
the shriek of eagle-bone whistles and war cries as a formation of screaming Lakota braves on war-striped ponies charged from the timber.

The soldiers, their rifles at the ready for the buffalo hunt, returned fire,
and the Indians fell back as the teamsters swung the wagons out of the
dry, sandy creek bed and made for the top of the bank, where they formed
up a loose corral. The war party made another rush; again rifle fire drove
them back. But a trooper and a teamster were wounded. A moment later

Lieutenant Daniels's riderless horse, arrows protruding from its neck and flank and its saddle twisted below its belly, galloped from the brush. It was followed by Lieutenant Templeton, slumped over his saddle pommel. An arrow was buried deep in his back and his horse, too, had wooden shafts protruding from its withers. It reached the little enclave before falling over. The surgeon hunched over Templeton and removed the arrow, but could not tarry to dress the wound. His gun was needed to repel yet another Indian charge.

The Lakota held the timbered high ground, and the remaining three officers recognized that they were in an untenable position. If they stayed where they were they would be picked off one by one. They made a decision to form up a column and make a run for a high, treeless knoll half a mile away. Twelve men covered the flanks on foot, seven more formed a rear guard, and the teamsters whipped their mules into a gallop. The Lakota recognized the maneuver, and a small party also made for the knoll in an attempt to cut them off. The Indians were too late.

The wagons barely beat the frenzied braves to the top of the rise, where again the soldiers and teamsters formed them into a square. Two more men were seriously wounded during the scramble. The little group of survivors dug rifle pits and waited for night, an interminable eight hours away. Individual Lakota warriors—one wearing Lieutenant Daniels's bloody uniform—made occasional dare rides, circling the knoll within firing range while shielding themselves behind the bodies of their ponies. One seemed particularly reckless, coming closer than the rest, close enough for the whites to notice his pale skin and long, wavy black hair. And twice more the Indians charged en masse only to fall back under rifle fire. Amazingly, during one of these forays the photographer Glover stood to set up his tripod. One of the officers knocked him down and handed him a rifle.

The situation had settled into a standoff when, seemingly from nowhere, another shower of arrows fell onto the hilltop, wounding three more men. A second volley followed before the soldiers realized that the Indians had infiltrated a skinny ravine that cut up the back face of the knoll from the creek. An enlisted man and the chaplain volunteered to clear out the ditch. Armed with rifles and an old pepperbox seven-shot pistol, they charged down the trench firing and screaming their own war cries. An arrow grazed the chaplain, but they drove the Indians off. The two dug in at the top of the cut to keep it clear.

By late afternoon the survivors were almost out of water beneath a blazing sun, and the wounded men and infants were moaning with thirst. One of the officers gathered several canteens and tapped an enlisted man, and under covering fire the two made a mad dash down the ditch to the creek. They managed to return with enough of the milky brine to ration among the children, the wounded, and the women. As the sun began to sink behind the Bighorns the Lakota made two more mounted charges, killing a sergeant and grievously wounding three more men. Half the Americans, two of them dead, were now out of action. The men's thoughts turned to the fate of the women and children if—or, as it increasingly appeared, when—they were overrun. "Our condition was now becoming so desperate that a council of war was held," wrote one enlisted man. "It was solemnly decided that in case it came to the worst that we would mercifully kill all the wounded . . . and then ourselves."

The sin of suicide and its punishment, eternal damnation, regardless of the circumstances, were too much for the chaplain. Though wounded himself, he volunteered to ride for Reno Station, twenty-six miles away. An enlisted man also stepped up. The sun was disappearing in the west as the two remaining healthy horses were saddled, and each man was handed a six-shot Colt. From the knoll, the desperate party watched as the two riders picked their way through the sandy creek bed unmolested. Then a pack of mounted Lakota burst from the cottonwoods. With a head start of several hundred yards the white men spurred their horses; the galloping Indians followed them. A moment later all were lost from view.

It was nearly dark when the men in the rifle pits noticed a large dust cloud rising from the northwest. More Indians, they were certain. The infantrymen began to loosen their shoelaces. After putting the women, children, and wounded out of their misery each man would tie one end of the shoelace to his big toe, tie the other end to his rifle trigger, and turn the gun on himself. This outcome seemed more certain when they saw a brave climb a great rocky mesa just out of rifle range. He appeared to be waving flags or banners of some sort. The whites surmised that this was a prearranged signal to the arriving Indians.

Yet as suddenly as the attack had begun fourteen hours earlier the curdling war whoops ceased. The Sioux mounted their ponies, but their precise movements were invisible in the dusk. Would they charge? Were they retreating? A rifleman cried out and pointed toward a low ridge in the direction of the dust cloud. A lone mounted silhouette appeared, a moving shadow against the last pinkish hue of the western sky. The figure reached the ravine below, a tall man in a low-crowned slouch hat wearing an old Army overcoat. He was seated on a flea-bitten gray mare. An officer shouted an order to halt. The horseman reined in.

"I am a friend."

"State your name."

"Jim Bridger."

The party on the hill let out a holler as Old Gabe's pony clambered up the incline. The dust cloud, Bridger said, was being raised by the hooves of two companies of mounted infantry hauling mountain howitzers from Fort Phil Kearny. They were no more than half a mile behind him. He apologized for the delay. The troop had been busy scattering war parties that were attacking military and emigrant trains up and down the Bozeman Trail. One corporal, foolishly riding ahead of the detail, had been killed, but otherwise all were in fair shape. Bridger's bearing and manner were as slouched and relaxed as his hat, and in his Missouri drawl he recounted riding to the rescue of soldiers and civilians as casually as if he were reeling off a grocery list to a sutler's clerk.

By the time the relief column arrived the Lakota were long gone, melted into the darkening prairie. The reinforcements put out pickets and the entire party camped across the knoll while the surgeon tended to the wounded throughout the night. The next morning a patrol discovered what was left of Lieutenant Daniels's naked corpse. His scalp had been taken, as had all ten of his fingers, and a thick cottonwood branch had been driven up his anus. Whether he was dead or alive when it happened, no one could know.

Not long afterward a detachment from Reno Station appeared on the trail, led by the chaplain and the enlisted man who had ridden for help. More excited huzzahs filled the air, although the Reno Station men seemed a bit disappointed at having been second on the scene. While they bade their fellows adios and turned back south, the bodies of Daniels and the sergeant were rolled into tarps and loaded onto a wagon next to the dead corporal from Bridger's unit. Three days later, with Colonel Carrington standing at the front gate in greeting, the ragged band rode into Fort Phil Kearny.

ROUGHING IT

Colonel Carrington's debriefing of his detail commanders, the newly arrived officers, and the civilian wagon masters gave a sense of urgency to completing the fort. Red Cloud, unlike his Indian predecessors, not only was qualified to plan and carry out multiple and simultaneous engagements, but encouraged his raiding parties to employ different tactics for each. His warriors, for instance, had ambushed the reinforcement train directly, but had attacked the first military freight column by using decoys to lure the flanking soldiers away and then falling on the main body of wagons. The raids on the civilian trains had been a combination of the two strategies. Each wagon master reported having been approached by Indians who either signed peaceful intentions or flew flags indicating as much. The leaders had ridden out to parley with them, even presenting small gifts of tobacco and the like. With the Americans' guard down, the Indians had opened fire at a signal as painted fighters poured down from stands of timber, up out of hidden gullies, and out from behind rolling buttes.

Who knew what Red Cloud would try next? It was best, Carrington noted, to have a stockade to fight from. Lieutenant Templeton's detail had carried with it a steam-powered sawmill from Fort Laramie, and Carrington organized all able bodies into dawn-to-dusk work and escort details. No freight wagons left for the pinery blockhouses, the river, or the hayfields in the little valley on the other side of Lodge Trail Ridge without a mounted armed guard. Within a week four log walls completely encased the little compound, and over 600,000 feet of four-inch plank boards and shingles were piled high next to foundations dug for work sheds, living quarters, and warehouses. Two blockhouses with multiple gun portals were also constructed on Piney Island. The new sawmill was equipped with a steam whistle, which the men found useful for sounding alarms. They were needed. The two logging camps came under serial sniping, to the point where no man even relieved himself without an escort.

Indians were not the only threat. Post butchers had begun slaughtering a few beef cattle for meat to be salted for winter, and the discarded offal drew packs of ravenous timber wolves by the score that circled the fort at night, their snarls and howls as frightening as a war cry. At first the sentries shot at the animals, but Colonel Carrington ordered the practice halted to conserve ammunition. His troopers were down to less than sixty rounds per man. The Indians noticed the change in this habit. One night a brave sheathed in a wolf pelt crawled to within a few feet of a lookout pacing a bastion and shot him dead. Soldiers on guard duty resumed firing at pretty much anything that moved in the night.

Despite the perilous environment the photographer Glover acted almost as if he were in an enormous garden laid out to his specifications. During the sweltering days he traversed the ocher buttes and ridgelines that shimmied beneath a blue dome so vast as to seem an illusion, lugging his camera equipment, overwhelmed by the striking vistas. He even ventured into the Rocky Mountains alone for days at a time with no weapon except a large Bowie knife he had picked up along the trail. He returned complaining of his inability to photograph at night, when silver moonlight bathed the snowcaps of 13,000-foot Cloud Peak, the highest of the Bighorns. Colonel Carrington warned him against such recklessness but Glover replied that with his long hair the Indians would surely take him for a Mormon and leave him alone. What effect his appearance would have on a timber wolf or grizzly bear he did not mention. When he was not out in the field he was a constant presence in and around Of-ficers' Row, joining the post wives in croquet matches on the mown pa-rade ground or regaling them with tales from the salons of Philadelphia's Main Line.

There is no record of what Carrington thought of the photographer's antics. In any case, he had more pressing problems. He had finally re-ceived a dispatch from General Cooke stating that he could expect no more reinforcements until sometime in the fall. At the same time the War Department remained anxious over the lack of forts farther up the Boze-man Trail. Carrington was in a bind. He had already sent another infantry company south to buttress the garrison at Reno Station. The thought of losing two more of his remaining six to erect a third outpost seemed foolish. His thin blue line would be stretched well over 100 miles before Red Cloud finally snapped it. Carrington's fear led him to make a risky decision—he bypassed the chain of command and wrote directly to the adjutant general in Washington, outlining his predicament and requesting assistance. Perhaps to soften this breach of military protocol he also wrote a long report to General Cooke, to be carried by the same mail courier. In it he took what he hoped was a more conciliatory tone.

"Character of Indian affairs hostile," he began. "The treaty does not yet benefit this route." He then vowed, "The work is my mission here, and I must meet it," before reiterating the long list of grievances he had been filing since his arrival at Fort Laramie. How could he be expected to build forts *and* fight Indians *and* safeguard over 500 miles of the Bozeman Trail with so few resources? His horses were weak from consuming nothing but hay, his weapons were outdated, his ammunition was rationed, his best of-ficers were being recalled, his infantrymen could barely ride, the emigrant trains were led by civilians who refused to heed his decrees, and he was acting not only as his own engineer and construction-gang boss but as a military strategist and tactician against an exceedingly shrewd enemy who picked off his men and his stock in small daily engagements yet refused to come out and fight a proper battle. "I must do all this, however arduous," he concluded, "and say I have not the men."

This was all true. The War Department had never developed any formal doctrine for dealing with a guerrilla insurgency, let alone codified it in a written guide for frontier officers. Yet however much Carrington believed he was merely stating the obvious, to the battle-tested generals who read his report he seemed to be whining and unprofessional. Rather than attempt to learn as much about their enemy as possible, Carrington's superiors, like the long, sad succession of Indian-fighting soldiers before them, were instead content to imagine what *they* would do if they were Red Cloud. It would be another ten weeks before Captain Fetterman was sent west to straighten out this mess, but by then official ignorance had already doomed Carrington's command.

As the troops in the Powder River Country awaited the arrival of the re-inforcements accompanying Captain Fetterman, the disturbing dispatches from the frontier that were reaching the War Department in Washington turned from a trickle into a flood. The reports, read today, are all the more disheartening for their terse dispassion. From Captain Ten Eyck's journal:

July 29: A "citizen train" was attacked by Indians near the South Fork of the Cheyenne and eight men were killed and two injured. One of the injured men later died from his wounds.

August 6: A train captained by an H. Merriam lost two civilians killed by Indians along the 236-mile trail between Forts Laramie and Phil Kearny. Later that night another train traveling the same route lost fifteen killed and five wounded.

August 7: Indians made their first concerted attack on the wood train on the road from Piney Island, killing one teamster.

August 12: Indians raided a civilian train near the Powder, running off a large stock of cattle and horses.

August 13: Indians attacked the Piney Island wood train again; no casualties were sustained.

August 14: Indians killed two civilians less than a mile from Reno Station.

August 17: An Indian raiding party entered Reno Station's corral and stole seventeen mules and seven of the garrison's twenty-two horses.

September 8: Under cover of lashing rain, Indians stampeded twenty horses and mules that belonged to a civilian contractor who was delivering barrels of ham, bacon, hardtack, soap, flour, sugar, and coffee to Fort Phil Kearny.

September 10: Indians returned and made off with another forty-two mules belonging to the same contractor. While the raiders led an Army patrol on a futile chase, another band took advantage of the post's weakened defenses to fall on the battalion's herd a mile from the stockade and sweep away thirty-three horses and seventy-eight more mules.

September 12: An Indian war party ambushed a hay-mowing detail, killing three and wounding six.

September 13: A combined Lakota-Arapaho raiding party, several hundred braves in total, stampeded a buffalo drove into the post's cattle herd grazing near Peno Creek. Two pickets were wounded; 209 head of cattle were lost in the buffalo run.

September 14: Two privates were killed by Indians, one while attempting to desert and the other after riding too far ahead of a hay train. Wolves made off with both bodies. Two hay-mowing machines were destroyed, and a large quantity of baled hay was burned.

September 22: The scalped, stripped, and mutilated bodies of three civilian freighters returning from Montana were discovered eleven miles from the post.

This went on through October and November until it was evident even to the Army leadership that in Red Cloud the Indians had finally found a war chief who could coordinate and sustain an effective military campaign—"a strategic chief," in the words of the historian Grace Raymond Hebard, "who was learning to follow up a victory, an art heretofore unknown to the red men." Moreover, the Bozeman Trail was an extraordinarily vulnerable supply line; every few miles offered an ideal ridgeline, draw, or mesa from which a small, swift war party could harass a cumbersome wagon train with deadly accuracy. The Indians' knowledge of the terrain was such that when Army patrols were assembled to chase them they would vanish into countless coulees and breaks. And when parties of mounted Bluecoats did cut off a large body of hostiles, the engagement left their supply wagons vulnerable to secondary attacks, a tactic that Red Cloud perfected.

As tales of the lawless, bloody Bozeman trickled back east, newspapers from St. Louis to New York eagerly published the stories. Yet still the settlers and miners came—individuals, families, entire clans—drawn by the vast swaths of free land, by the mountains veined with minerals, by the same spirit of *freedom* that had drawn their ancestors from the sclerotic kingdoms of Europe to the shores of the New World. August 1866 was the high point of emigration on the Oregon Trail, with at least one wagon train arriving per day at Fort Phil Kearny; in a single day the post's adjutant registered 979 men, 32 women, and 26 children passing through, while traveler upon traveler noted in journals surprise and delight at hearing the opening strains of the regimental band's martial songs amid the harsh, deadly environment. Many emigrants were also gratified to find women and children living at the post. Families meant civilization, if only its razor-thin edge.

Yet despite the modicum of familiarity, nothing could prepare the easterners for the difficulties of life at Fort Phil Kearny. Unlike older and more established posts such as Fort Laramie—which boasted a circulating library, a regular amateur theater, and an occasional white-gloved ball—Fort Phil Kearny was "roughing it" in the true sense of the phrase. Under the broiling summer sun the stench of human and animal sweat and dung hung over the post like an illness. And with the exception of noncommissioned officers, who were granted their own small rooms within the barracks, all enlisted men lived in an open bay heated in the winter with cast-iron stoves. The fort's buildings were stifling in summer and "breezy in winter," owing to their construction of green pine logs. As the logs and boards shrank the gaps were stuffed with sod, which was blown away by a good wind, and rain and snow—either falling through the cracks or dragged in on boots—turned the dirt floors to carpets of mud.

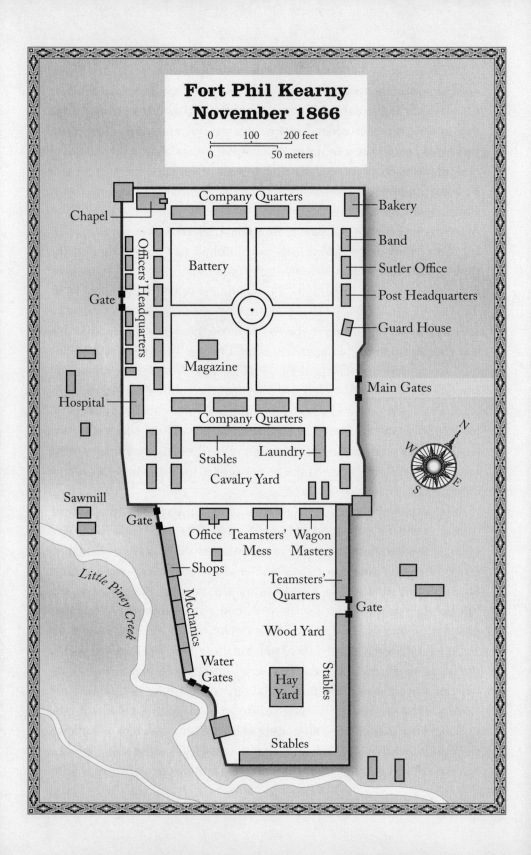

Fort Phil Kearny
November 1866

0   100   200 feet

0   50 meters

Chapel

Company Quarters

Bakery

Band

Sutler Office

Post Headquarters

Officers' Headquarters

Battery

Gate

Guard House

Magazine

Main Gates

Hospital

Company Quarters

Stables

Laundry

Cavalry Yard

Sawmill

Gate

Office

Teamsters'
Mess

Wagon
Masters

Shops

Teamsters'
Quarters

Gate

Mechanics

Little Piney Creek

Wood Yard

Water
Gates

Hay
Yard

Stables

Stables

N
W   E
S

The officers considered their individual quarters something of a step up, although these quarters were likely to horrify any women who made the grueling trek west. Along with Margaret Carrington, ten other Army wives had braved the journey to the Powder River Country. As the historian Shannon Smith notes, it was they, and in particular the officers' wives (assumed to be more educated and refined), who often set the "civil" tone for the small, isolated outpost. Although this was her first garrison, thirty-four-year-old Margaret Carrington seemed "to have been ideally suited for the task of shaping the community into a proper Victorian settlement." She exuded a "commanding presence, dignified in deportment," and was respected and well liked by the other women. The eldest of seven children, she tended to treat the other wives more as daughters than as friends, organizing sewing circles to fashion dresses and coats from calico, flannel, and linsey-woolsey—a coarse twill with a linen warp and woolen weft—purchased from the sutler's store. Nor were the troopers themselves immune to her enchantment, and they presented her with little gifts of wildflower bouquets, armloads of extra firewood, and plump rabbits for stewing. She was the first to inquire about the health of soldiers' families if word reached her that someone back east had fallen ill, and almost every night she read to the post's children (and to Old Gabe when he was on the site).

Margaret Carrington was also the fort's social matron, and before attacks on the wood trains became a daily occurrence she organized a picnic on Piney Island in celebration of the arrival of a new sutler hauling fresh vegetables "most precious and rare." It was a grand affair, with fresh elk steaks and salmon, canned lobster, and tinned oysters garnished with pineapples, tomatoes, sweet corn, peas, and pickles. Doughnuts, gingerbread, and plum cakes were served for dessert, followed by Havana cigars for the men and "Madame Clicquot" for those who imbibed. It was the last such affair. Soon enough Colonel Carrington ordered the closing of all gates to anyone without specific orders to venture outside, and the women became virtual prisoners in the stockade. Margaret Carrington and the others nonetheless attempted to impart whatever small "domestic casts" were practical.

She showed the wives along Officers' Row how to stretch canvas tarps across the underside of their sod-packed roofs as a screen against infiltrating snakes and mice, and how to sew burlap gunny sacks together to create crude carpets. She even suggested that the weeks-old, and sometimes months-old, newspapers left behind by passing emigrant trains could be hung above unglazed windows as shades—after they were passed around and read. A few of the women hired off-duty soldiers with carpentry experience to fashion double bedsteads out of pine and spruce boards, which they fitted with mattresses that were stuffed with dried prairie grass. Even these homey touches failed to overcome the maddening isolation and confinement, particularly for the eleven rambunctious children. But as every adult at the fort recognized, this situation was far preferable to the alternative.

A THIN BLUE LINE

While Fort Phil Kearny may have been gaining families, it was fast losing men. In the first week of August Colonel Carrington finally gave in to the War Department's increasingly insistent dispatches and sent two companies north to scout positions for a fort on the Bighorn. It would be named in honor of the Mexican War hero General C. F. Smith. Bridger went along to guide the expedition, but was instructed to return as soon as a suitable site was found. Another scout-interpreter, Jim Beckwourth, also rode with the detail.

Beckwourth, the son of a Virginia slaveholder and his mulatto mistress, had come west with his master in the early 1800s, was granted his freedom around the beginning of the beaver-trapping frenzy, and became one of the first mountain men to scale the Rockies. Since quitting the trapping business he had worked on and off for the Army, and he may or may not have been present at the Sand Creek massacre. He boasted that he had at least two Crow wives somewhere up in the ranges, and that the tribe treated him as a chief. Though Carrington suspected there was more rooster than Crow in Beckwourth's tall tales, he reasoned that if even a portion of what the man said was true, his in-laws might have valuable information about Red Cloud's location and plans. Other than the bits of intelligence gleaned from the Cheyenne Black Bear weeks earlier, the colonel had no clue as to the Bad Face chief's disposition.

Not long after his two companies marched north—leading a long line of civilian trains that had been awaiting an escort into Montana—the battalion was depleted of even more troops when Colonel Carrington was forced to supply a personal bodyguard to a visiting brigadier general. The general had been sent from Omaha with a small cavalry detail to inspect Army installations along the Oregon and Bozeman Trails, and he arrived at Fort Phil Kearny on August 27. Carrington was in no position to deny his request for an escort to the nearly completed Fort C. F. Smith, ninety-two miles away on the Bighorn. Two days later twenty-seven of Carrington's best mounted infantry rode out as his escort. Before departing the general assured Carrington that two companies of the 2nd Cavalry were en route from Kansas to reinforce his shrinking garrison. Whether he was mistaken or misinformed, they never arrived, although a smaller detachment of the 2nd did show up on September 4 as escort for an Army commissary train.

By early autumn the 2nd Battalion of the 18th Infantry Regiment was stretched to its limit. The wood trains to and from Piney Island required constant security details, and continuous daylight lookouts were stationed on top of the Sullivant Hills and Pilot Knob. These were in addition to regular distress calls from emigrant trains under attack. Colonel Carrington was like a chess player forced to begin his match with only eight pieces. His rolls at the fort were down to just under 350 officers and men—a fact he was certain Red Cloud knew as well as he. A few Crow Head Men had offered to lend braves to the Army to help kill their hereditary enemies, but Carrington was leery of their true intentions. Despite the successes of the Pawnee scout corps, like most officers of the era he felt that relying on Plains Indians to fight other Plains Indians would reflect negatively on his own capability. Instead he finally petitioned General Cooke to allow him to reraise the company of Winnebago scouts the Army had recalled to Omaha earlier in the spring. Their dispersal, after all, had been a sop to Sioux sensibilities. That was now pointless.

While Carrington awaited Cooke's reply he gladly hired on at Army base pay any civilians passing through the territory who asked for work. One such man was a Nebraskan, James Wheatley, traveling with his nineteen-year-old wife, Elisabeth, and two young sons. Wheatley feared that the High Plains winter would close in on his family before they could reach the Montana gold fields and requested permission to open a civilian mess outside the post's front gates. Carrington quickly agreed, and even supplied the lumber for the crude restaurant. Wheatley owned a seven-shot Spencer repeating rifle; he proved a crack shot and his wife a wonderful cook. Their wayfarers' inn with its nightly dinners of fresh antelope, buffalo, and venison steaks became a kind of clubhouse for the civilian scouts, laborers, and teamsters, who remained after dinner to nibble cheese and crackers, drink whiskey, and trade "vile jokes and curses so gloriously profane that awed bystanders gazed upward, expecting the heavens to crack open."

The Wheatleys' clientele grew when a party of forty gold miners arrived one day from Virginia City. Their leader was a frontiersman with nearly two decades of experience in the West who told Colonel Carrington that the Montana lodes were playing out. He and his men had decided to explore richer prospects along the Bighorn. But they were harassed by hostiles throughout their journey south—only two days earlier two of their number had been killed in an ambush on the Tongue—and they now wished to winter over at Fort Phil Kearny while contemplating their next move. Carrington welcomed them with open arms. Forty rugged and well-armed men with their own horses constituted nearly the equivalent of a trained cavalry company, a rarity on the frontier.*

The miners pitched a tent city just across Big Piney Creek and the next morning reported to the quartermaster, Captain Brown, for work assignments. They proved their worth almost immediately. Four days later, dawn's first light streaking Pilot Knob to the east threw into relief a war party of 200 mounted Indians on the crest of Lodge Trail Ridge. The

*The cinematic images of the standard-bearing cavalry troop riding out from a fort to fight Indians have misled generations of moviegoers. The usual population of these forts was largely mounted infantry with a few true cavalrymen for support, reconnaissance, escort duties, and mail delivery.

warriors bellowed, brandished their spears and war clubs, and charged down the slope toward the miners' camp. An officer's wife, watching from the post's battlements, recorded the fight in her diary: "Hardly three minutes had elapsed after they came into view before the smoke and crack of the miners' rifles, out from the cottonwood brush that lined the banks of the creek, had emptied half a dozen warriors' [saddles] and brought down three times as many ponies." Colonel Carrington was so excited he ordered the regimental band rushed to the parade ground to strike up a rousing battle hymn as soldiers cheered the fighting miners from the fort's walls.

The engagement was one of two that season that the colonel recorded as "victories." The other occurred about a week later when a breathless rider galloped into the stockade shouting that his wagon train was under attack not far down the trail. Carrington, following an instinct, had begun saddling and bridling the best horses at reveille each morning. The forethought now paid off. A relief detail led by Captain Brown and Lieutenant Bisbee was out of the quartermaster's gate within moments, joined by half a dozen miners. The Indians dispersed at the sight of the rescue party but not before stampeding the train's cattle. Brown and his men chased the Indians and longhorns for ten miles before overtaking them. Perhaps valuing the beef more than their lives, for once the Indians stood and fought. Brown's party dismounted, formed a skirmish line, and withstood three mounted charges. Before the Indians withdrew, the soldiers and miners killed at least five of them and wounded sixteen more. The detail, with one trooper nicked by an arrow, also recovered all of the wagon train's stock.

The small victory was noteworthy in another way. For months the prairie had rippled with rumors of white men, old mountain men, fighting alongside the Indians. The gnarled trappers, apparently as troubled as the Natives by "civilization" seeping through the Powder River Country and climbing their beloved Rockies, were even said to have planned and led attacks on the civilian trains. After this particular skirmish Captain Brown reported to Colonel Carrington that the Indian charges on his lines appeared to have been orchestrated by a white man. He was dressed in Lakota garb and was missing several fingers on his right hand, and he had ridden down on the soldiers screaming curses in English. In the final foray he was shot off his horse, but two braves scooped up his limp body. Carrington put this together with an earlier report about a "white Indian" with missing fingers—Captain Bob North—heading raids on emigrant trains. In his official dispatch to Omaha he reported the death of this Captain North.*

While the colonel reported these "significant blows," General Sherman was midway through his second tour of the frontier. The general's mood had swung again, thanks to Red Cloud, and cold fury replaced the amiable disposition he had shown four months earlier in Nebraska. During a layover at Fort Laramie he parleyed with several of the Sioux subchiefs who had signed the previous spring's treaty. When they admitted that they could not always restrain their rash young braves from joining raiding parties, Sherman's famous temper flared, his red whiskers seeming to bristle. He had heard too much of this excuse. Turning to his interpreters but pointing dramatically toward the Indians, he said, "Tell the rascals so are *mine*; and if another white man is scalped in all this region, it will be *impossible* to hold *mine* in."

Sherman then penned a letter to Colonel Carrington making his instructions clear. "We must try to distinguish friendly from hostile and kill the latter. But if you or other commanding officers strike a blow I will approve, for it seems impossible to tell the true from the false." Carrington barely had to read between the lines. The second-highest-ranking officer in the United States Army had just declared open season on all High Plains Indians, friend or foe. Such was the temper of his own troops that the order was hardly necessary.

A few days later three Piney Island woodcutters were ambushed in a thick section of forest. Two of the enlisted men escaped to the island's blockhouse with minor wounds. They told of watching their fallen comrade, Private Patrick Smith, shot through with arrows and scalped. Incredibly, Smith had not been killed, and he crawled half a mile back to the American lines leaving a trail of blood behind him. He was rushed by

---

*If in fact the raids were led by North, Brown's detail had failed to kill him, as he was hanged three years later in Kansas.

ambulance to the fort, where he died. That night at mess, graphic stories spread of Smith's death. *Scalped alive. Left for dead with the skin hanging in strips from his forehead. Arrows deliberately aimed to wound rather than to kill.* It was unusually bad timing when nine Cheyenne, professing friendship, rode up to the fort near twilight and Colonel Carrington granted them permission to camp on the Little Piney. Someone started a rumor that they were the same Indians who had killed Pat Smith. It spread rapidly through the barracks, with the troopers expressing the same conviction as Sherman: *It is impossible to tell the true from the false.*

The American conspirators waited until midnight before some ninety men crept from their bunks and scaled the post's walls. But the same chaplain who had made the heroic ride from Crazy Woman Fork got wind of the lynching party and woke Colonel Carrington. Carrington roused Captain Ten Eyck, who in turn gathered an armed guard. They arrived just in time to prevent the massacre. The mob tried to scatter, but two shots from Carrington's Colt froze them. The colonel and Captain Ten Eyck recognized among the crowd some of their best fighting men. They took a moment to confer and concluded that they could not afford to make any examples. To take the Indians' side and risk alienating the troops was too risky. The post's tiny guardhouse already held twenty-four prisoners, most of them caught deserting. The battalion was in fact averaging a desertion every other day, and harsh discipline meted out here would only spur more "gold runners." Carrington ordered the Cheyenne away, gathered the angry soldiers, and settled for a "brief tongue lashing" before marching them back to their quarters. It must have crossed Colonel Carrington's mind that had the decision to stop the killings been Sherman's, the general may not have been so quick to intervene.

The colonel was still contemplating this incident when Bridger returned from Fort C. F. Smith. He and Beckwourth had met with the Crows, who told them that Red Cloud was camped along the headwaters of the Tongue not seventy miles away with about 500 lodges of Lakota, Arapaho, and a few Gros Ventres. This meant anywhere from 500 to 1,000 warriors, counting the soldier societies that invariably staked separate villages. Bridger said that hostile Northern Cheyenne were also in the vicinity, camped along Rosebud Creek, and that the Crows had told him it took half a day to ride through the villages. All told, it was the largest combined Indian force Bridger had ever heard of, and there was talk of destroying the white soldiers' two forts. For once "Old Gabe" looked concerned. His rheumatism was bothering him, and he paced along the compound's battlements, "constantly scanning the opposite hills that commanded a good view of the fort as if he suspected Indians of having scouts behind every sage clump or fallen cottonwood."

FIRE IN THE BELLY

Moments past daybreak on Monday, September 17, Red Cloud struck again. A large war party of Lakota and Arapaho rode down into the little valley east of the fort at the juncture of Big Piney and Little Piney Creeks. They moved on what was left of the battalion's withered cattle herd—only 50 cows remained out of the 700 that had begun the trip through Nebraska. The pickets, no strangers by now to surprise attacks, were nonetheless confused to find the Indians firing revolvers. The raiders stampeded the animals, but the post was prepared. Brown and Bisbee, alert to any action, immediately mounted a detail. Quartermaster Brown was in charge of the fort's stock, and over the weeks the job of chasing Indians had naturally devolved to him. He did it so often that the Indians had come to recognize him from his haircut—a friar's tonsure—and gave him the nickname Bald Head Eagle. Fortunately, Brown thrived on the assignment—so much so that, with Colonel Carrington's tacit approval, he was stalling transfer orders to Fort Laramie that he had received a week earlier.

As Brown's detail charged from the corral, Carrington ordered his twelve-pound field howitzer fired. The shells burst among the Indians, driving them back into the hills and scattering the cattle. Within minutes Brown had recaptured the herd and was driving the cattle back toward the fort when they crossed paths with an Army freight train coming up the Bozeman Trail. It had just delivered ammunition to Reno Station and was carrying another 60,000 rounds for the Fort Phil Kearny garrison. Among the train's passengers were two civilian surgeons contracted to the battalion as well as a replacement officer, Second Lieutenant George Washington Grummond. Grummond—dashingly handsome, with the posture of a telegraph pole, and sporting the luxuriant facial hair typical of the era—had fought with the Michigan volunteers during the Civil War and was traveling with his pregnant wife, Frances.

Grummond was an odd case. On the one hand, at thirty years old he was the kind of experienced fighter you wanted by your side in Indian country. On the other, he was frightening. A stormy-tempered alcoholic who had worked on Great Lakes merchant ships since childhood, he had risen from sergeant to lieutenant colonel during the war for his aggressive, if reckless, tactics. His junior officers lived in fear of him and eventually petitioned the adjutant general to investigate several incidents in which, they claimed, his whiskey courage had imperiled the troops. He was subsequently court-martialed and found guilty of threatening to shoot a fellow officer while in a drunken rage. But the Union Army needed officers, and Grummond was soon back in the saddle, leading a company of Michigan volunteers through General Robert Granger's Tennessee campaign. He was finally relieved of field command when he jumped the gun during a precisely coordinated offensive against General Joe Wheeler's Confederate forces on the heights of Kennesaw Mountain. His actions not only allowed Wheeler's army to escape a pincer-like trap but also imperiled his own company, which was surrounded and nearly wiped out. "Not even a semblance of company organization" was one of the many negative performance reviews filed in his military jacket.

His personal life was equally chaotic. At the war's onset Grummond had left behind in Detroit his pregnant wife, Delia, and his five-year-old son, George Jr. Three years later, while stationed in central Tennessee, he began courting a naive southern belle, Frances Courtney, the nineteen-year-old daughter of a slaveholding tobacco farmer. Grummond abandoned his Detroit family, which now included an infant daughter, and in September 1865 married Frances. The two Mrs. Grummonds remained unaware of each other's existence for the rest of his life. Postwar Victorian America was unlikely to accept Grummond's tangled marital situation, and frontier service was an inviting alternative. So he applied for, and accepted, a commission in Colonel Carrington's command. That was how a pregnant and somewhat bewildered Frances Grummond came to be seated in a freight wagon pulling into an army outpost in the terrifying middle of nowhere.

When the Grummonds' train neared the fort's main gate it was forced to halt in order to make way for an ambulance wagon racing in from Piney Island. Frances Grummond—who moments earlier had been nearly overcome with relief at seeing the picket atop Pilot Knob waving a welcome flag, followed by the sight of the sturdy, walled stockade—now recoiled, sickened. It is said that terror is dry and horror is wet, and the blood-soaked torso in the open bed of the ambulance was indeed dripping wet. It was also naked, and next to the body a severed head rolled back and forth with each bump in the road. The head had been scalped, and the victim's back was cleft with a tomahawk gash so deep it exposed the man's spinal column. Frances Grummond had no way of knowing that somewhere on the prairie, a warrior was adorning his tepee with the thick yellow mane of the photographer Ridgway Glover.

Some of the troopers had considered Glover's fate only a matter of time. Glover had seemed to consider himself invulnerable, wandering alone through the mountains to record his tintype "views." Lately he had been camping with the woodcutters on Piney Island, and the day before he had announced his intention to return to the fort despite the fact that it was a Sunday, when no wood trains were scheduled. Glover had no horse, and he mentioned to one soldier that he considered it a fine day for a six-mile walk with his portable darkroom. The woodcutters warned him that this was insanity; he did not even carry a gun. But despite all he had seen, he had convinced himself that his civilian status conferred on him an immunity that the Lakota or Cheyenne would recognize and respect.

The next morning, just prior to the Grummonds' arrival, the regular wood train heading to the pinery discovered his body on the road two miles from the post. His head was found a few yards away. In addition to the tomahawk wound, he had been disemboweled, and a fire had been lit in the cavity of his belly. Looking at the bloody, mangled form positioned on its stomach, one officer claimed that the Indians had sent a message. Glover, he said, "had not died brave."

Frances Grummond would later write, "My whole being seemed to be absorbed in the one desire, an agonized but unuttered cry, 'Let me get within the gate!' That strange feeling of apprehension never left me." She spent a restless first night at Fort Phil Kearny, finally falling asleep sometime after midnight. When she and her husband awoke the next morning their tent was buried beneath a foot of snow.

In October 1866 the rift between Lakota moderates and militants widened. Indian agents were again putting out feelers regarding treaties, and with winter approaching and more gifts in mind, some Oglalas were inclined to listen. One of them was Old-Man-Afraid-Of-His-Horses. Although technically still a Big Belly, he had lately reverted to subtle calls for diplomacy, and as a result the most hostile tribal factions were gravitating to Red Cloud, now recognized as the supreme Lakota war chief, the *blotahunka ataya*. It may have been tempting, at this moment, for Red Cloud to side with Old-Man-Afraid-Of-His-Horses. The banks of the prairie creeks were crusting over with ice, and Red Cloud was now forty-five, and in earlier days he would have been free to rest on his reputation as a warrior who had proved himself again and again and enjoy life—to grow fat hunting deer, buffalo, and antelope; to sire more children; to instruct his children and their children in the old ways.

Instead, when the Little White Chief had sent his Bluecoats north to the Bighorn to build a second fort, it was Red Cloud who sponsored a formal war-pipe council among the Lakota and Northern Cheyenne. He proposed a major offensive against the original fort between the Piney creeks once the snows completely cut off communications among the whites. Red Cloud had attracted a large contingent of Miniconjou, Sans Arcs, and Brule fighters to his cause, and he had personally recruited warriors from formerly neutral Arapaho bands, citing the injustices to Left Hand at Sand Creek and the killing of Black Bear's son the previous summer by General Connor's "guns that shoot twice." Further, in late August he swept aside a century of blood enmity to lead a delegation across the Bighorns to parley with the Crows. At the main Crow village he asked his hereditary enemies to join his war against the whites. As part of the bargain he offered to return to the tribe a portion of its old hunting grounds east of the mountains.

The bid was unsuccessful. Although several Crow braves were eager to don war paint against the whites, their Head Men remained noncommittal, promising only to reciprocate with a visit to the Bad Face camp. But the fact that Red Cloud dared to break long-standing tradition, and that some Crows had considered fighting alongside the Lakota, was evidence of the desperate High Plains Indians' extraordinary existential crisis. One concession Red Cloud did receive from his longtime enemies was a series of one-day truces between the Lakota and the Crows that allowed each tribe to conduct trade fairs on the Bighorn. There, his braves were able to swap pelts, robes, and horses for Crow guns, mostly revolvers. Although the Northern Cheyenne possessed a few repeating rifles, Sioux and Arapaho warriors still made do with lances, war clubs, tomahawks, and arrows. A few Oglalas carried into battle single-shot muskets and percussion Hawken long rifles, but they were a distinct minority.

It was for this same reason, the need for firepower, that Red Cloud encouraged visits from the new generation of Laramie Loafers who had signed the white man's treaty the previous spring. Though these Loafers, predominantly Brules, were forbidden to own more than one rifle (and were certainly unwilling to trade away their personal weapons), they were allowed to buy boxes of ammunition from white traders in exchange for the buffalo robes that Red Cloud supplied by the pack train. This was better than nothing. When the Loafers arrived in camp Red Cloud did not even bother to try to persuade them to fight with him. But taking the long view, he did pump them for information about the strength and movements of the soldiers along the Oregon Trail. He even swallowed his pride and sent emissaries to Sitting Bull's Hunkpapas far to the northeast, asking about the possibility of acquiring weapons from Canadian traders. Nothing much came of that.

Red Cloud had also begun to draw into his inner circle the maturing

Crazy Horse, the leader of a cohort of young fighters who increasingly looked to the *blotahunka ataya* for guidance and direction. The gruff, physically imposing Big Belly and the slight, diffident warrior nineteen years his junior made an unlikely pair. It was common knowledge among the Lakota that Crazy Horse still pined for Black Buffalo Woman, whom Red Cloud had casually promised to another warrior. Still, there was no question that Crazy Horse and his Strong Hearts had been responsible for most of the destruction along the lower Bozeman Trail through the summer. The Strong Hearts had marauded as far south and east as Fort Laramie, and Crazy Horse had led the raiding party that sneaked into the Reno Station corral to run off the horses and mules one week before he ambushed the white soldiers at Crazy Woman Fork. As the weather turned and the emigrant trains thinned, the Strong Hearts had moved north to harass the woodcutting and hay-mowing details from Fort Phil Kearny, and when Crazy Horse intermittently returned from these forays there was always a seat awaiting him at Red Cloud's council fire. Crazy Horse had never shown interest in mundane tribal politics—the elections of subchiefs, the planning of hunts, the debates over future campsites— but now that the talk centered on killing whites, he was often present, though he hardly ever spoke.

Meanwhile, as the last civilian trains of the season made haste for Montana before winter snows blocked the north country's valleys and passes, two commissary caravans pulled into Fort Phil Kearny from Nebraska. Together they had hauled nearly 180,000 pounds of corn and over 20,000 pounds of oats, enough grain to carry the post's weakened mounts through midwinter. Despite the feed delivery, however, when Colonel Carrington and Captain Brown inspected their remuda they determined that only forty horses were strong enough for the pursuit of the Indians.

The supply trains also carried a cache of much-needed medical supplies; but, as with the horse feed, Carrington realized that these would not last until spring. The medicine consisted of the usual assortment of nineteenth-century remedies from the cure-all school of castor oil in the spring, mustard plaster in the fall. According to Army manifests the shipment also included tincture of peppermint oil, "for nausea and flatulence"; an ammonial liniment (obtained as a by-product from the distillation of tar, coal, and animal bones), for treating sore muscles; malt barley for digestive troubles; Epsom salts as a laxative; a fetid resinous herbal gum called asafetida, used to expel digestive gases; and ferrous iodide syrup to combat "consumption." For the surgeons' infirmary there were forty-five yards of adhesive plaster; 3,600 roller bandages; chlorinated soda and zinc sulfate for use as an antiseptic on arrow and gunshot wounds; and several cases of porter for, it was said, "restoring invalids."

More good news arrived late that October with the return of the visiting general's mounted infantry escort. There had been no news from Fort C. F. Smith since Bridger's report, and the escort detail's lead officer reported that the northern post, situated so close to friendly Crow country, had yet to be attacked. The escort had lost one scout killed and one trooper wounded riding through Sioux territory. In addition, three soldiers had deserted when the party skirted the Montana gold camps. Colonel Carrington took those desertions stoically. But desertion was not only a military problem; he also found himself dealing with civilians who had gone missing from Army freight trains. Teamsters signed round-trip government contracts in Omaha, counting on strength in numbers to get them up the Bozeman Trail with their hair intact. Once they reached Fort Phil Kearny, though, they might suddenly develop gold fever. Carrington dutifully listened to the contractors' loud complaints before dispatching details to round up the wayward mule skinners. It was a waste of time, energy, and manpower. It was also part of his job.

Another issue was that the approaching High Plains winter appeared to be driving some people stir crazy. In mid-October a courier brought word from Omaha that the garrison commander whom Carrington had left in charge at Reno Station, a captain with whom Carrington had no more than a passing formal relationship, had arrested the lieutenant serving as his second in command. The young officer's crime apparently consisted of allowing the Indians to make off with most of the post's mules and horses during the August raid. Carrington was beside himself, not only because of what he considered unjust discipline, but even more because he had to learn of his own command's turmoil from General Cooke. Fort Phil Kearny was still in too precarious a state for Carrington to journey the sixty-five miles to Reno Station to investigate the matter himself—he had sent an artillery battery with one of the mountain howitzers to camp on Piney Island, but the Indians were still picking off his men one by one. He was instead left to request that Cooke forward the indictment to him in the next mailbag.

Perhaps it was such humiliations, combined with the stress of frontier command, that contributed to the colonel's own state of mind, which seems to have been bordering on paranoia. He began to fear that his junior officers were plotting against him, and he took to sleeping in his uniform and making his own nightly inspection rounds "to secure personal knowledge of deportment of guards and condition of post." Moreover, the same courier who delivered news of the arrest at Reno Station carried another disturbing letter from Cooke. In it the general seemed to be assuming that a company of the 2nd Cavalry had recently arrived to reinforce Fort Phil Kearny—although in fact none had. Cooke "strongly recommended" that, since Carrington now possessed an abundance of mounts, he send his surplus horses to Fort Laramie to aid in its defense. A company of cavalry? Surplus horses? Was Cooke out of his mind? Between this order, the Reno Station incident, and Carrington's own Queeg-like suspicions, it was as if some virulent strain of madness was infecting the U.S. Army's officer corps.

And then the cowboys arrived.

31

HIGH PLAINS DRIFTERS

Nelson Gile Story was one of those larger-than-life Old West characters. The youngest son of Ohio corn farmers of flinty New Hampshire stock, Story was eighteen when his parents died in 1856 and soon thereafter he lit out for the Colorado Territory, finding work as a bullwhacker and freight driver. He was a handsome if hollow-cheeked young man with a shock of bear-greased black hair and a thick goatee that hung like Spanish moss. Story met and married his wife, Ellen Trent, around 1860, during a timber-hauling run to Missouri. Back in Denver, in 1863 he purchased an oxen team and a string of pack mules and dragged Ellen over the Rockies to the Montana gold fields. Quick with his Navy Colt and not shy about using it—though according to family lore he preferred pistol-whipping to shooting—he joined a vigilante committee that hanged at least twenty-one criminals, and he once blew the gun hand off a claim jumper who was holding a hostage as a human shield. In the meantime he washed $30,000 worth of dust and nuggets out of a placer claim in Alder Gulch—part of the "Fourteen Mile City" that included the boomtowns of Bannack and Virginia City.

Grubstake in hand, Story looked south to cattle country. Leaving his wife in the care of a local preacher's family, he struck out for Texas. The Civil War had just ended, the North was clamoring for beef, and south Texas had an overabundance of both wild cattle and rancheros across the Mexican border virtually begging to be rustled. "Beeves" of both varieties eventually found their way to Fort Worth, the preeminent cow town on the Old Chisholm Trail. So did Story. He arrived in April 1866 with $10,000 sewn into the lining of his overcoat, purchased 1,000 longhorns, and hired a trail crew of twenty-seven cowboys. His destination was the busy railhead at Sedalia, Missouri.

On reaching the Kansas line, however, his drive was blocked by armed vigilantes who feared that their herds would contract Texas fever, a parasitic cattle disease that killed almost all other breeds coming into contact with the hardier longhorns. There were too many Kansans for even Story's crew of rough cowpunchers to fight off, and he faced a decision—double back through the Indian Territory of present-day Oklahoma, or turn northwest along a route no cattlemen had ever before taken. Recalling his yearning for a good beefsteak in the stark, cold Montana mining camps, Story pushed the herd northwest. He had already covered over 300 miles and barely lost a cow. Virginia City was only another 1,000 miles away.

On their trek west Story and his cowboys lay over at Fort Leavenworth, where he stocked fifteen oxcarts not only with supplies for the drive but with crates of tools and bolts of calico to sell in gold country. The drovers then traced the Oregon Trail across Nebraska and into Wyoming until they reached Fort Laramie, where soldiers informed Story that Red Cloud had turned the Powder River Country into a bloody obstacle course. They would be fools to continue on, they were warned; the Lakota, Arapaho, and Cheyenne would raid them and stampede their herd. Moreover, the Fort Laramie garrison commander told Story that the colonel in charge of the Mountain District—another Ohio man, by the name of Carrington—had banned any civilian parties with fewer than forty armed men from overland travel. Story ignored him, purchased thirty new Remington breech-loading rifles and thousands of rounds of ammunition from the local sutler, and spurred his outfit up the Bozeman Trail.

Two days shy of Reno Station they were hit. A war party of Sioux boiled up over a frost-rimmed slope, stampeded the herd, and cut out several hundred cows. Two of the drovers suffered serious arrow wounds. That afternoon Story and his men rounded up the bulk of the cows and set a guard to protect them and the wounded men. He then led fifteen or so of his cowboys on a counterattack. The little posse of seasoned trackers followed the Lakota to a camp on the Powder River, where the stolen longhorns had been enclosed by a ring of tepees. They surprised the Indians with a night charge, the barrels of their Remingtons and Colts flaming as the startled braves panicked and fled. They recovered the animals, and one of Story's hands later said that they wiped out the entire camp, although this seems unlikely. Actually, the cagey Story would never admit to any killing (although years later he did tell his son he had never killed an Indian before that night).

Leaving the two wounded cowboys at Reno Station, the party pulled into Fort Phil Kearny in mid-October. There, Colonel Carrington counted heads and said that Story did not have the requisite forty armed men to move north. Story argued that he and twenty-five cowboys armed with Remingtons equaled the firepower of at least 100 emigrants. The colonel stood firm and offered to purchase the beef at set Army prices. Both men understood that Story could command four or five times that amount from hungry Montana placermen. Story declined to sell. The colonel then ordered the Texans to graze their longhorns some distance from the post and wait to join the next civilian train bound for Virginia City. Story protested against the security arrangements; he did not like camping so far from the fort. Carrington coldly explained that he needed to conserve the prairie grasses on the nearby bottomlands for his own reduced Army herd. Story, perhaps admiringly, sensed a setup. He knew that this late in the season no other emigrant train was likely to roll up the Bozeman Trail, and he suspected that the fussy colonel really wanted to keep his stock in the area until winter iced them in and the Army could buy them cheap.

On the night of October 22 he called his trail crew together and put the matter to a vote—aye to leave, nay to stay. Only one man voted to remain; Story had him covered with his revolver almost before the word was out of his mouth. He hog-tied the dissenter, tossed him into a wagon, and the Texans hitched their oxen. The herd moved out in the dead of night. The next morning the naysayer was turned loose, given a horse and his gun, and told he could return to Fort Phil Kearny. He decided to keep riding for the brand.

Colonel Carrington was apoplectic when he discovered the cow camp vanished. His first instinct was to form a large pursuit detail—and it would have to be large, given the Texans' firepower. But his legal training got the better of his temper and he instead spent the morning weighing his options. On the one hand he could dispatch a detail to overtake the drovers and force them to return. Story had disregarded a direct order issued by the commanding officer of the territory, the only law in the land. But would the headstrong trail boss obey? Or would the confrontation lead to a shootout between white men that could go either way and could also require an explanation before a military tribunal and lead to embarrassing newspaper headlines? On the other hand, his overriding mandate was the protection of civilians passing through the Powder River Country. In the end, whether from personal prudence or a sense of duty, Colonel Carrington dispatched fifteen mounted infantrymen to find Story and his herd and accompany them to Montana. It was a superficial gesture. The colonel knew as well as the cowboys that the soldiers and their single-shot rifles added little to the endeavor. But with their presence, technically, Story's expedition satisfied Carrington's forty-man decree.

The outfit—trailing by night, grazing by day—fought off two more attacks by Sioux raiders, and a cowboy was killed during a battle with Crows. But on a snow-muffled morning in early December the residents of Virginia City, Montana, awoke to find two dozen Texas cowboys flashing Mexican spurs and silver saddle pommels as they guided more than 900 longhorns down the muddy main street. It would be four more years before anyone else dared drive a herd from Texas that far north, and the expedition made Story rich. He became the north country's first cattle baron, with his Paradise Valley herd growing to over 15,000 head, and soon afterward he was the Montana Territory's first millionaire. He did not stop pistol-whipping claim jumpers or hanging alleged outlaws; and he also swindled government Indian agents, bribed federal grand juries, and even investigated the mysterious murder of his friend John Bozeman. But meanwhile, like most scoundrels of the Gilded Age, he smoothed his grifter edges by founding a legitimate bank, building a string of flour mills, endowing a hospital, and becoming the town of Bozeman's largest real estate holder.

For all of his achievements, however, Story is best remembered for his epic cattle drive, which was one inspiration for the author Larry McMurtry's Pulitzer Prize–winning saga *Lonesome Dove*. The fact that Story made it from Fort Worth to Montana is said to be no less remarkable than the fact that he tried in the first place. In any case, if Story's exploits contributed in some small way to McMurtry's characters Woodrow F. Call and Augustus "Gus" McCrae, that may be his true legacy.

Not long after Nelson Story made history, a courier from Omaha rode into Fort Phil Kearny with orders from General Sherman officially abolishing the Army's Mountain District. The directive was in the main benign. Colonel Carrington remained in command of the 18th Regiment with the same responsibility to make the Powder River Country safe. The order's only real impact was to eliminate reams of redundant paperwork. But it served to highlight one crucial difference between the colonel and his primary antagonist. Unlike Carrington, Red Cloud not only executed policy, but made it as well. Generals hundreds if not thousands of miles from Fort Phil Kearny concocted the strategy and tactics to be used against him, and expected their agent on the scene to carry them out. Red Cloud was on the scene, a strategic and tactical genius running circles around the Little White Chief. Although he never mentioned it or wrote of it, Colonel Carrington was probably aware of this.

In part to show his command that the dissolution of the Mountain District was by no means a slight on their (and his) performance, and in part to celebrate the return of the visiting general's escort detail, the colonel declared the last day of October a holiday. That morning was unusually balmy, and the first order of business was a formal battalion inspection. A day earlier the troopers had been issued new uniforms from the quartermaster's store to replace the patched, mended rags some had been wearing since the Civil War, and every man, weapon, and mount was lined up for review on the small plain between the stockade and the Big Piney. The soldiers in their smooth new blue blouses and trousers, burnished boots, and spit-shined brass buttons met all the tests. But the remuda left something to be desired; and more than 100 of the old Springfield rifles were found to be "unserviceable," including twenty of twenty-seven in one company alone.

Still, these problems did not dampen the festivities. Throughout the day the band played, poems were read aloud, Margaret Carrington was hostess at a tea social, cannons were fired, and a moment of silence was observed for those who had lost their lives. When a great luncheon on the parade ground was complete the chaplain stepped forward to offer a prayer and Colonel Carrington signaled to his flag bearers. It was time for the *pièce de résistance*.

For the past week a pair of enlisted men—one a former ship's carpenter, the other an expert woodworker—had been putting the finishing touches on the garrison's crowning achievement, a 124-foot flagpole. It was constructed of two lodgepole pine trunks, each as straight as a ruler, which had been shaved into octagons, painted black, and pinned together like a tall ship's mast. Now the two enlisted men approached the pole and the regimental band played "Hail Columbia" as they unfurled an enormous American flag, twenty by thirty-six feet; gathered the halyards; and hoisted the Stars and Stripes, to a loud cheer. It was the first United States garrison flag to fly between the North Platte and the Yellowstone, and the vibrant red, white, and blue waving high above the prairie would serve as a beacon to travelers coming up the Bozeman Trail. After the official ceremonies, for the first time since their arrival at Fort Phil Kearny 110 days earlier, the 360 officers and enlisted men of the 2nd Battalion of the 18th U.S. Infantry Regiment were given permission to loaf the rest of the afternoon.

Two hours later they were recalled to their general-quarters posts when Indians flashing mirror signals appeared on Lodge Trail Ridge. Among the Indians were Red Cloud and Crazy Horse.

Part V

THE MASSACRE

Never interrupt your enemy when he is making a mistake.

—Napoléon Bonaparte

32

FETTERMAN

It was the incessant cannon reports that attracted the Indians. Crazy Horse was already in the surrounding hills probing for raiding opportunities when the soldiers ran up their flag and lit off their big guns. He sent messengers to the Tongue with word of this strange behavior, and Red Cloud joined the large, curious group riding south to see what the commotion was about. It was pure chance that so many Indians arrived on the bluffs overlooking Fort Phil Kearny hours before the last emigrant train of the season pulled into the post.

Red Cloud had not sent any war parties south to Reno Station for weeks, supposing the whites were done traveling for the season. For precisely this reason the train had rolled up the Bozeman Trail unscathed, and its security measures were lax. That night, after the wagon master conferred with Colonel Carrington, the emigrants dutifully circled their prairie schooners on the little plain 100 yards from the fort—where, earlier in the day, the garrison had been inspected—cinching them wheel to wheel with hemp ropes and enclosing the stock within. But the travelers' guard was down. A few of the miners lit campfires and sat around the flames playing cards as a party of Strong Hearts crept close and let loose a volley.

One man was killed instantly by an arrow; two more were wounded. The Lakota vanished by the time the panicked emigrants began firing blindly into the darkness. It was good to kill the white trespassers, but the attack so close to the fort also served another purpose. Afterward the Indians lit their own bonfires on the hills overlooking the post and danced furiously, brazenly flitting into and out of shadows cast by the flames. It was a reminder to the soldiers of whose territory they dared occupy. It was also a mistake. The Bluecoats hauled out their guns that shoot twice and bombarded the dancers with grapeshot. Several Indians were killed or wounded.

After the shelling, angry warriors argued that now was the time to strike the Americans in force, to wipe out the post and all within it. The autumn buffalo hunt was completed. The Upper Powder tribes were strong and united. What was Red Cloud waiting for? The *blotahunka ataya* asked for patience. Not yet, he said. But soon enough. There were, his scouts had informed him, more white soldiers on the way.

Captain William Judd Fetterman crested Pilot Knob at the head of Lieutenant Horatio Bingham's company of the 2nd Cavalry on the morning of November 3, 1866. It was two days after the attack on the last civilian wagon train bound for Montana and, in Margaret Carrington's words, his return to his old battalion had been "looked for with glad anticipation." The snowbound ravines and coulees the party had just traversed were nearly impassable, and Fetterman may have been puzzled as to why the outpost spread before him at the foot of the Bighorns was merely dusted with snow, and why even less was accumulated on the surrounding hilltops and ridgelines. Actually, just four miles to the west of Fort Phil Kearny four feet of powder covered the lower slopes of the mountains. Despite his unfamiliarity with the frontier, however, he surely admired what he saw. Inside the stout pine walls dozens of buildings had been completed or were nearing completion, and from the top of Pilot Knob the post gave the impression of a good redoubt from which to conduct his hunt for Red Cloud.

Once through the main gate Fetterman, Bingham, and the sixty-three horsemen were greeted with sighs of relief. The incessant Indian attacks over the previous months had left the post's inhabitants on edge, and the mounted reinforcements led by one of the regiment's most decorated officers were a welcome sight. Before Fetterman even dismounted he was hailed warmly by his Civil War comrades Fred Brown and Bill Bisbee, his old quartermaster and adjutant from the Atlanta campaign. He had also become close to Captain James Powell on the journey from Omaha, and soon the feisty lieutenant George Grummond fell into his orbit. Together with scores of enlisted men who had followed him through some of the war's bloodiest battles they would form a clique. These men felt they could clear the hostiles from the territory in a snap if only the ineffectual garrison commander would unleash them.

It did not take Fetterman long to identify the obstacles. Like all the officers deployed to the Powder River Country, Captain Brown and Lieutenant Bisbee could recite the disturbing statistics from memory and were anxious to do so for their old commander. Since the Army's arrival in July there had been fifty-one attacks on the post and its environs. One hundred fifty-four soldiers and civilians had been killed, and at least three times that number had been wounded. Not a single wagon train had reached Montana without violent loss of life. Over 800 head of Army livestock had been stolen, in addition to an untold number of emigrants' horses, mules, cattle, and oxen. And though it was not yet winter, the government had already ordered the Bozeman Trail closed for the following summer, as too unsafe for civilian traffic. In that time Colonel Carrington had not undertaken one offensive operation against the hostiles. This inaction was embarrassing to the junior officers at Fort Phil Kearny; worse, to the sensibility of the nineteenth-century U.S. Army, it reflected dishonorably on the post and the garrison.

Accompanying Captain Fetterman and Lieutenant Bingham had been two additional officers. Captain Powell, an infantry company commander, was a veteran of the 18th who still carried two musket balls in his body from the Battle of Jonesboro. Major Henry Almstedt was the regiment's paymaster. Almstedt had come west carrying a satchel of greenbacks, the battalion's back pay, and James Wheatley's little restaurant saw an immediate increase in customers. All told, the influx of new men raised the strength of the garrison to some 400 effective troops; but despite the almost 200 additional armed civilian teamsters, hay mowers, and pinery workers, this was a modest number of able bodies, and it surely struck Fetterman as too few to police the vast territory he had just crossed.

Meanwhile the Crows, through the old "chief" Jim Beckwourth, had again offered the Americans their services—250 mounted warriors to join the war against their old enemies the Lakota. These braves knew the countryside intimately; it had once been theirs. They were also wise to the ways of Red Cloud. Colonel Carrington declined. It was not merely a question of expense, although the Crow Head Men would undoubtedly want a hefty fee for their services. Carrington had received no word from General Cooke in Omaha about his request for the return of the Winnebagos, but he still hoped. He reasoned that fifty Winnebagos with rifles trumped five times as many Crows with bows and arrows. The logic seemed sound given the era's military ethos. If only to a white easterner.

Captain Fetterman outranked Captain Ten Eyck by several months' service, and immediately replaced him as Carrington's principal tactical officer. As part of this role Fetterman conducted his own troop inspection shortly after his arrival, and he was appalled at the condition of the garrison, particularly the inadequate weaponry. Bingham's cavalry company had been issued a mixture of passable Starr carbines—single-shot, but at least breech-loading—and obsolete Enfield rifles. Though the majority of Carrington's infantry were equipped with the ancient Springfields, the musicians in his band had managed to hold on to their Spencer rifles until now, when the colonel ordered them turned over to Bingham's command. This meant at least two-thirds of the horsemen now had proper arms, which lifted their spirits considerably. It was a needed boost, for the trek from Omaha had worn out Company C's mounts, and by the time they reached the post they were not much more serviceable than the weary remuda in Quartermaster Brown's corral. Corn and oats were already strictly rationed, and there was nothing that could be done about it.

Before his departure from Omaha Fetterman had been informed that the Frontier Army was planning yet another reorganization, scheduled for January 1, 1867. On that date the 2nd Battalion would become the nucleus for the new 27th Regiment and, General Cooke hinted strongly, Fetterman would replace Carrington as the battalion's commanding officer. Fetterman was a hungry soldier, eager for advancement, and not a man to allow his cordial prewar relationship with his superior to stand in the way of his own ambition. To that end he moved quickly to make his presence known, both to Red Cloud and to the War Department. He got his chance on his third day at the fort.

That evening Fetterman approached Carrington after dinner with a plan to turn the Indians' own tactics against them. He proposed to hobble a string of mules to serve as decoys near a thicket of cottonwoods along the Big Piney about a mile from the post. He and a company of infantry would conceal themselves in the nearby trees and fall on any Indians who took the bait. He said he had talked over the idea with Brown and Grummond, who wanted to join the ambush. Carrington granted him permission. Fetterman, Brown, Grummond, Bisbee, and about fifty enlisted men settled into the cottonwood stand shortly after dusk. Their rifles were primed and cocked, but the only movements they saw all night were meteors creasing the sky. Near dawn, as they were getting ready to return to the post, they heard shots from the opposite side of the stockade. A mile away from their position Indian raiders, aware of the ruse from the outset, had stampeded a small herd of cattle belonging to Wheatley. It was Fetterman's first such lesson, and last such effort. A few days later fifty of Bingham's cavalry departed, ten men escorting a mail rider to Fort Laramie and forty riding with the paymaster to Fort C. F. Smith, where they would remain. With their departure Carrington deemed his troop too stretched for any more ambush schemes. Fetterman seethed.

Despite the failed trap, in hindsight it is apparent that Fetterman's arrival had the War Department's intended effect on Carrington. Two days later, in a dispatch to General Cooke, Carrington described Red Cloud's increasing strength and concluded, "I hope to be yet able to soon strike a blow." He had never expressed such a desire before. Meanwhile, as Fetterman acclimated to life at the fort his disdain for Carrington's passivity intensified into nearly open contempt, and he wrote to his old friend Dr. Charles Sully, "We are afflicted with an incompetent commanding officer." Yet despite his and the others' "disgust" with the colonel, the era's code of conduct, both military and social, prevented open insubordination. One officer noted that "the feeling was not harmonious" between

Carrington and the Young Turks, "but there was no open rupture." At least for the moment.

Following the attack on the emigrant train camped on the Big Piney, Red Cloud intensified his harassment of the post itself, turning loose Crazy Horse and the Strong Hearts to darken the snow-covered ground with American blood. A beef contractor driving a herd up the Bozeman Trail was attacked, and the raids on the wood trains to and from Piney Island escalated. Red Cloud had taught his young warriors that the best time to strike at the whites was either early in the morning, when their minds were still hazy with sleep, or late in the afternoon, when they were exhausted from a day of chopping wood or ice. Crazy Horse followed through with a series of ambushes and hit-and-run forays, which left the fort's contract surgeons running perilously low on zinc sulfate and roller bandages.

Red Cloud was satisfied with the physical damage he was inflicting, though he was probably not aware of the psychological toll his guerrilla tactics were taking on the isolated garrison. With every dead or wounded trooper, with every stolen horse or mule, with every whistle of an arrow and crack of a Hawken, the tension at the fort heightened. Bickering among soldiers has gone on since man invented war. But this was different. The troop at Fort Phil Kearny was disintegrating under the weight of petty feuds and traded insults. Even relatively mundane annoyances—the paltry pay, the dearth of promotions, the usurious cost of full uniforms ($100) and new boots ($17)—could set off a quarrel or fistfight. The underlying problem stemmed from Carrington's refusal to take the fight to the Indians. When the colonel appeared to ignore a direct order* from General Cooke to do just that, the grumbling increased and the post was further split. Indian attacks continued as the snow piled high; and as the

---

*"You are hereby instructed that as soon as the troops and stores are covered from the weather, to turn your earnest attention to the possibility of striking the hostile band of Indians by surprise in their winter camps," Cooke wrote to Carrington. "An extraordinary effort in winter when the Indian horses are unserviceable, it is believed, should be followed by more success than can be accomplished by very large expeditions in the summer."

diversion of emigrant trains ceased and the arrival of couriers with news of the outside world grew rare, the remote stillness of Fort Phil Kearny—interrupted only by shrieking war cries—began to fray men's nerves.

The soldiers could not know that after five months of raids and ambushes the Indians were nearly as weary of Red Cloud's slow, fitful campaign. By this time of year the three tribes should have been ensconced in comfortable winter camps, the Sioux and Cheyenne in sheltered wooded hollows near the Black Hills, the Arapaho off toward the Rockies. There men would sleep late after trading stories well into the night around warming fires and pass the dreary afternoons fashioning new bows and arrows in a fug of pipe smoke while boys collected firewood and women and girls attempted to augment the winter larders by adding rose berries, acorns, and even old horsemeat to the buffalo and dog stews. Instead, the warriors now spent their days greasing their limbs against the bitter cold in preparation for creeping around the open prairie or forested hills wrapped in stinking wolf skins and inverted buffalo robes, their high-topped buffalo-fur moccasins soaked through and freezing—all in the hope of running across a straggling Bluecoat and putting an arrow through his throat.

Ironically, it was now the formerly quiet Crazy Horse whose voice was loudest at the council fires. He exhorted the war chiefs to attack in force, to strike a single, final blow against the soldiers. But Red Cloud was hesitant. He knew exactly how much food and winter fodder the garrison had stored, and he planned to starve and weaken it to a point of impotence that would make its inhabitants as easy to kill as newborns. On the other hand, he recognized that it might not be wise to ignore the words of his best fighter. He had always respected Crazy Horse's tactics; perhaps it was time to heed his young lieutenant's strategy as well. Perhaps it was time to test the Americans where they lived.

33

DRESS REHEARSAL

On December 3, 1866, an elegant horse-drawn carriage arrived at the White House to carry President Andrew Johnson through the marbled canyons of Washington, D.C., to the Capitol, where he would deliver his second State of the Union address. The hour-long speech was lofty, oratory as gilded as the president's coach, extolling and thanking "an all-wise and merciful Providence" for restoring "peace, order, tranquility, and civil authority" to the war-ravaged nation. Johnson managed to spare 38 of his 7,134 words for the frontier, in remarks wedged between his report on payments to Army pensioners and his listing of the number of patents issued the previous year "for useful inventions and designs." He assured the political luminaries in attendance, "Treaties have been concluded with the Indians, who, enticed into armed opposition to our Government at the outbreak of the rebellion, have unconditionally submitted to our authority and manifested an earnest desire for a renewal of friendly relations."

Three days later, on the morning of December 6, Red Cloud mounted his finest war pony and left his camp on the Tongue at the head of several hundred angry warriors. The temperature was below freezing, creeks flowed beneath thick ice, and wispy gray clouds scudded down from the Bighorns on a biting wind that scoured the prairie. When the Indians reached the small, flat valley carved by Peno Creek on the far side of Lodge Trail Ridge from Fort Phil Kearny, about 100 braves broke west, circled behind the edge of the ridge, and descended into the timber around Piney Island. With ferocious screams and shrieking whistles they immediately fell on a wood train and its escort returning from the pinery. A messenger made the dangerous four-mile ride back to the post to alert Colonel Carrington, who ordered every serviceable horse saddled. If General Cooke wanted offensive action, Carrington would give it to him. What occurred next was a farrago of bravery, recklessness, confusion, cowardice, and stupidity—timeless elements that compose the fog of war.

Colonel Carrington directed Captain Fetterman and Lieutenant Bingham to lead the cavalry and a squad of mounted infantry, just over fifty men, due west up the wood road to relieve the train and drive the attackers back across the creek. In the meantime he and Lieutenant Grummond, at the head of another squad of twenty-four horsemen, would ride north up Lodge Trail Ridge to intercept the retreating Indians, trapping them in the Peno Creek valley. As Carrington galloped up the south bank of Big Piney Creek he saw Indians above him lining the crest of Lodge Trail Ridge to his right. He signaled his squad to cross Big Piney, but his own mount slipped and floundered on the ice sheet and threw him from the saddle. He remounted and made the crossing, and he and Grummond led the troopers up the steep slope.

They were greeted at the crest by four Indians, their ponies straddling the wagon ruts of the Bozeman Trail several hundred yards away. More were trying to conceal themselves in thick stands of chokecherry and scrub oak, but Carrington had reached the ridgeline sooner than they expected and he spotted them, counting at least thirty-two. Instead of attacking, he concentrated on the wood road below him to his left, where at this moment he saw another fifty or so hostiles galloping out of the timber. Fetterman's and Bingham's detail was in hot pursuit. The colonel drove off the four taunting braves with a volley and pointed downslope. After many frustrating months, it was time to spring his own trap.

Carrington cautioned his inexperienced riders against scattering, and ordered them to pick their way slowly down the face of the serrated ridge that descended into the Peno Creek valley. As if to prove the military proverb that no plan survives the first contact with the enemy, Lieutenant Grummond ignored him and spurred his mount to a gallop. Events deteriorated from there. Grummond put so much distance between himself and Carrington's squad that the fuming colonel sent his best rider to overtake him with orders to either halt "or return to the post." The messenger could not catch Grummond, who disappeared into the valley's tangle of ravines and draws. The colonel's anger increased when he reached the bottom of the incline and came across fifteen dismounted cavalrymen from Bingham's command looking thoroughly confounded. He ordered them folded into his squad and took off at a trot without bothering to look back and see if they had actually saddled up.

They had not. A quarter mile later he reached a small hill, the only way around it being a thin trail. He expected to find Grummond and Bingham somewhere on the other side. Instead, when he rounded the rise his path was blocked by several dozen Indians on horseback. He turned to give skirmish orders. Only six of his inexperienced riders were still with him. One of them was Bingham's bugler, a German immigrant named Adolph Metzger. Carrington sputtered to the little bugler, "Where is Lieutenant Bingham?" Metzger, whose command of English was limited, pointed past the Indians. Carrington immediately surmised that the hostiles had doubled back, hidden in the folds of the hill, and allowed Fetterman's and Bingham's larger party to ride on in order to confront him. The trap had been turned.

The Indians whooped and charged, and at the same moment a few straggling soldiers caught up to Carrington. One trooper's mount was shot out from under him. The man lay trapped beneath the horse as an Indian rushed at him with a raised war club. Carrington swung his horse toward the scene and got off several shots with his Colt. The Indian either fell or turned away; the colonel could not tell which. Indian ponies enveloped his small group, and he ordered the soldiers to dismount and form into a circular defense. Gun barrels and ramrods glistened in the pale December light as Carrington directed a steady stream of bullets and balls into his attackers. He made certain that the men staggered their fire, allowing every other trooper time to reload. Though they rarely appeared to hit either Indians or ponies, the hostiles could not break through. Carrington finally turned to the bugler Metzger. The language barrier was not too great for the little German to understand Carrington's frantic demand to sound recall. Metzger pursed his lips and blew for his life. The cracked notes carried on the cold wind and echoed off the hills and ridges, and the Indians inexplicably quit. Carrington turned to see his stragglers riding to his rescue. Moments later Captain Fetterman appeared from out of the timber with his fourteen mounted infantrymen.

The colonel hurriedly briefed Fetterman, informing him that Lieutenants Grummond and Bingham were missing. He guessed that they might be off near Peno Creek, and led the combined troop in that direction. They heard the drumming of hoofbeats before they saw the riders. Grummond and three enlisted men broke through a spinney of scrub oak, galloping straight for them. Seven screaming Indians were a few yards behind them. The Indians veered off, shaking their lances and war clubs as they vanished into a cutbank. Grummond, gulping air, reined in his frothing horse beside the colonel's and the two seemed to shout at each other. What they said is not known, although Lieutenant Bisbee testified later that Grummond told him he had demanded to know if Carrington was a "coward or a fool" to allow his command to be cut to pieces.

They were still short an officer. Lieutenant Bingham was undoubtedly in trouble. When Grummond regained his composure he told a troubling tale. He and Bingham were following the raiding party into the valley when hundreds of Indians streamed out of gullies and surrounded them. Grummond said he watched Bingham turn in his saddle, shout, "Come on," and gallop ahead with four men. But most of his raw, frightened troopers froze in their tracks in the face of the Indian onslaught. A few had begun to turn their mounts to make a run for the fort when Grummond, Captain Brown, and another officer leveled their guns to check the retreat. By the time they re-formed and scattered the Indians, Lieutenant Bingham had disappeared down a narrow, twisting trail that led to the flats along the frozen Peno Creek. Grummond rode after him alone. He caught him and his small patrol two miles away, stalking a single warrior. Then, he told Carrington, he joined the hunt.

What occurred next encapsulated everything that went wrong for the U.S. Army during Red Cloud's War.

It may have struck Crazy Horse as too easy. Had these naive American officers never fought an Indian before? Red Cloud had taught his warriors to differentiate officers from enlisted men by the strange symbols they wore on the shoulders and sleeves and the long knives the officers carried at their sides. These two had simply taken his bait as if they were trout. Crazy Horse dismounted and pretended to examine his pony's hind leg, acting as if he were digging a stone from its hoof. On either side he could see the puffs of vapor expelled from the mouths of the Strong Hearts concealed in the shallow draws.

A soldier fired at him. Crazy Horse did not move. He allowed the little group of Bluecoats, six in all, to come close enough for one of them to draw his saber and charge. He leaped on his pony and rode hard. They followed. And then the Strong Hearts jumped from their hiding places and surrounded them. A gunshot sounded, shattering the face of the officer with the drawn saber. There was supposed to be no shooting.

Lieutenant Bingham slumped over his pommel and was yanked from the saddle. An Indian scalped him; another grabbed his horse. There were no more arrows or gunshots. They wanted the horses. That was what saved the rest.

Except one. The Indians surrounded the little group and tried to lasso the soldiers and pull them off their mounts. Sergeant Gideon Bowers, a grizzled Civil War veteran, shot three dead with his Colt before they pulled him to the ground. Warriors swarmed him and hacked repeatedly with tomahawks and knives. In the fighting at close quarters the Indians attempted to loop their bowstrings over the remaining four soldiers' heads. The enlisted men used the butt ends of their rifles as clubs, and Grummond slashed with his saber. He could hear a repulsive click with every skull he cleaved. Finally, he jammed the sword into his horse's withers. The animal reared up and kicked its forelegs, creating an opening. Grummond broke from the surround and galloped back toward the ridge, the three enlisted men following him. Half a dozen Indians jumped onto their ponies and raced, screaming, after them. They quit the chase, however, at the sight of Carrington's and Fetterman's column.

Then, suddenly, as if by magic, the Indians were gone. Patches of crusty snow up and down Lodge Trail Ridge were smeared with blood, which grew thicker at the site where Bingham and Bowers had fallen, but the Indians had carried off their dead. Carrington ordered a search for the Americans' bodies. Within the hour they found Sergeant Bowers, his skull split in half but, astonishingly, still alive. However, he died moments later. Not far away Lieutenant Bingham was impaled on a tree stump in a clump of brush, his body bristling with over fifty arrow shafts. By midafternoon the troop was back at the post, where Carrington tried to make sense of the blunder-filled fight.

The cowardice of the inexperienced recruits was at least explicable, if still disgraceful. But Lieutenant Grummond had disobeyed a direct order and, for whatever reason, Lieutenant Bingham had abandoned his men to ride off recklessly to his death—and now the cavalry had no officers. Even Fetterman was at a loss to explain the actions of Bingham, a decorated Civil War commander. "I cannot account for the movement of such an officer of such unquestionable gallantry," he wrote in his report. Nor had Carrington covered himself with glory when he had outpaced his own squad and led them into an ambush. Given all that had gone wrong, it was a near miracle that Bingham and Bowers were the only men killed. Another sergeant and four privates had been wounded, and five horses had been so badly injured that they needed to be put down. More amazingly, Captain Fetterman for once appeared chastened. "This Indian War has become a hand-to-hand fight," he told Carrington when he delivered his written report. In his own dispatch the colonel generously estimated that at least 10 Indians out of 300 attackers were killed, one by a bullet from his own Colt, and perhaps twice as many wounded.

The apprehension that had seized Frances Grummond from the moment she arrived at Fort Phil Kearny "deepened from that hour. No sleep ever came to my weary eyes, except fitfully, for many nights. And even then in my dreams I could see [my husband] riding madly from me with the Indians in pursuit."

For President Johnson, beset with the task of piecing together a sundered nation, the skirmish was a minor incident on a treeless prairie so distant it might as well have been the moon.

For Red Cloud it was a dress rehearsal.

34

SOLDIERS IN BOTH HANDS

Red Cloud was convinced: these foolish soldiers were ready to be slaughtered. He had watched the previous day's fighting, and even directed some of it from a high tor in Peno Creek valley, marveling at the dull-witted behavior of the Bluecoats. They were like spoiled, ignorant children—dangle a piece of hard molasses in front of them and they would do anything, no matter how stupid, to grab it. Back at the Indian camp on the Tongue, Crazy Horse described in detail the parts of the battle Red Cloud had not personally witnessed. The young warrior told of twice luring officers—first Bingham, then Grummond—away from their troops, as easily as separating an old cow from a buffalo herd. When Red Cloud summoned the Lakota subchief Yellow Eagle, who had led the initial attack on the wood train, he boasted of baiting Fetterman's and Bingham's larger relief detail and allowing them to ride past him while he lay in wait for the Little White Chief's smaller patrol.

If it had worked once, why not a second time with a larger force? Red Cloud conferred with his allies. The Miniconjou Head Men High Backbone and Black Shield agreed, as did the Cheyenne war chiefs Roman Nose and Medicine Man. Two Arapaho—Little Chief and Sorrel

Horse—also said their seventy-five braves were prepared to fight. All told there were over 2,000 warriors. And thus it was decided. On the first auspicious day after the next full moon the Lakota, Cheyenne, and Arapaho would ride south. They would again feint toward the soldiers' wood train, and again work the decoy trick along the ridge. But this time they would lure as many men as possible out of the fort, kill them all, and burn the American outpost.

Red Cloud had come to the same conclusion as Jim Bridger, who told Carrington morosely after the December 6 fight, "Your men who fought down south are crazy. They don't know anything about fighting Indians."

Three days later they buried Lieutenant Bingham and Sergeant Bowers. Little imagination is required to place yourself in the cracked, toe-numbing split-leather boots of the reinforcements newly arrived at Fort Phil Kearny as they watched the tin-lined pine coffins being lowered into the frozen earth. It was Sunday, December 9, and none of the forty-three infantrymen had been involved in the fight. Nor had their commanding officer, twenty-five-year-old Lieutenant Wilbur Arnold. Colonel Carrington had deemed the newcomers too raw, and while the rest of the 2nd Battalion chased Indians up and down the rambling trails across Lodge Trail Ridge and into the Peno Creek valley, Lieutenant Arnold and his men had been busy constructing their own housing along the post's barracks row. Arnold had come closest to the action when he led an ambulance detail to retrieve the bodies of Bingham and Bowers. Even this tangential task was cause for concern. Carrington had expressly directed Captain Powell to bring the ambulance to the site. But Powell had disobeyed the written order, remained at the post, and sent the green Arnold instead.

As the new men looked around they would have noticed the fresh graves dotting the little cemetery beneath Pilot Knob. It was filling rapidly, and not one death could be attributed to natural causes. They doffed their caps when Lieutenant Grummond and six other members of the Masonic lodge accorded their brother Bingham the Masons' final honors; they remained bareheaded in the biting wind while the post chaplain prayed over the site. Before the caskets were closed they watched Captain

Brown pin his treasured Army of the Cumberland badge to the sergeant's uniform breast. Brown had fought with Bowers from Stones River to Atlanta. At the conclusion of the rite the newcomers helped cover the graves with mounds of frozen dirt and piled small boulders on top of them to keep the wolves out.

The same afternoon the troop also bade farewell to Lieutenant Bisbee, who had been transferred to Omaha. With Colonel Carrington's permission, Bisbee had refitted a coach with double boards to transport his wife and young son. The temperature had fallen below zero, but the canvas-topped wagon was equipped with a small sheet-iron camp stove whose pipe protruded through a hole in the roof. Bisbee, who would ride beside it, was nearly unrecognizable beneath layers of woolen and buffalo-hair shirts and pants, gloves, and a hat. He also wore "buffalo-lined hip boots over two pairs of woolen socks." Seven cavalrymen were selected to escort the Bisbees as far as Fort Laramie, and before the detail departed Captain Fetterman handed Bisbee a package to be delivered to Lieutenant Bingham's sister, Stella, in St. Charles, Minnesota. It contained his unsent letters, sword, sash, and epaulets. His other effects, as was the Army custom, were sold at auction, with the proceeds sent to the adjutant general to be placed in the War Department's general fund. "Your brother was much esteemed by all who knew him," Fetterman wrote to Stella Bingham, "and his death is severely felt by all."

Not least by Colonel Carrington, who was down to six officers to maintain control of an edgy garrison. He decided to start from square one. Captain Fetterman and Captain Powell, who replaced Lieutenant Bingham as cavalry commander, were ordered to drill the entire battalion each morning and evening in military basics such as mounting and dismounting, loading and firing weapons on command, and forming columns of twos and fours. It was fortunate for the drillmasters that the Indians also appeared to be regrouping. In the two weeks following the December 6 fight not a single hostile incident was recorded, although the Lakota scouts remained ever-present on distant hills, signaling with mirrors, smoke, and flags. Carrington also used the lull to lay in as much winter wood as possible, as well as to personally oversee the construction of a forty-five-foot wagon bridge spanning Big Piney Creek from Piney

Island to the wood train road. The fact that remedial military courses were necessary in hostile territory was disturbing, although Captain Fetterman and Captain Brown apparently did not think so.

After supper on the evening of December 19 the two called on Colonel Carrington in his private quarters. Quartermaster Brown, who sported two Colt revolvers on his hips, had ostentatiously hung his spurs from the buttonholes of his greatcoat. He did the talking. The Indians had broken the thirteen-day quiescence that morning, again raiding the wood train, but were driven off by Captain Powell's relief detail. Before Powell left, Carrington had explicitly directed him to "heed the lessons of the Sixth. Do not pursue Indians across Lodge Trail Ridge." This time Powell obeyed his orders, and neither side had inflicted or sustained any casualties. This, Brown said now, was a perfect example of the sort of pinprick hostilities that were demoralizing the men. But there was a solution.

He said that he and Fetterman had spoken to the miners, and all forty as well as an additional ten civilians had agreed to join an equal number of the battalion's most able troopers to ride against the hostiles in their camp on the Tongue. Appealing to the colonel's proprietary and meticulous engineering mind, Brown added that destroying the Indian village would ensure a peaceful winter during which construction of the fort could be completed without interruption. It would also be likely to augur the reopening of the Bozeman Trail come spring. Brown had stalled his transfer orders all he could and was scheduled to leave for Fort Laramie the day after Christmas. He remembered the thrill of defeating the combined Lakota-Arapaho raiding party presumably led by Captain North back in September, and wanted one more crack at the savages. Fetterman said nothing.

Carrington showed polite interest while hearing out his quartermaster. When Brown was finished the colonel rather nonchalantly ticked off the reasons he could not allow it. Fifty seasoned veterans were the core of his troop. With them gone his pickets and escorts would be stretched to their limits with untested recruits, and the mail riders would have to cease. He handed Brown that morning's duty report. Only forty-two horses had been deemed serviceable (as Brown well knew). Were his two officers proposing to leave Fort Phil Kearny without mounts? He intended, Carrington said, to continue his defensive policy until more re-inforcements arrived. As if to buck up their spirits, he read to the officers the contents of a dispatch he had sent by special courier that day to Fort Laramie to be telegraphed to General Cooke: "Indians appeared today and fired on wood train, but were repulsed. They are accomplishing noth-ing, while I am perfecting all details of the post and preparing for active movements."

Their time would come, the colonel implied, if unfortunately not for the departing Brown. The visibly dejected quartermaster said good night. On his way out the door he turned to Carrington and added that, as im-possible as it sounded, he felt that he could kill a dozen Indians himself. Fetterman still said nothing.

Had Colonel Carrington agreed to the plan, the chances are excellent that Fetterman's and Brown's 100-man troop would have ridden directly into 2,000 warriors camped just over Lodge Trail Ridge.

They had arrived that morning, a large war party consisting of Lakota, Cheyenne, and Arapaho. On the ride south from the Tongue they had ob-served the same formalities as before the attacks on Julesburg and Bridge Station—official Pipe Bearers formed a van ahead of Red Cloud and the other war chiefs leading the column, while Strong Hearts and Cheyenne Crazy Dogs kept discipline on its flanks. They made camp about ten miles north of the American post, and following the brief skirmish with Powell's force, they dug in for the night. A snowstorm swept in on a bitter north wind. By dawn on December 20 the snow was still falling, a feathery pow-der that blanketed the prairie, and the Head Men agreed to postpone any more fighting for at least a day while their warriors erected small, mobile tepees in three abutting circles, one for each tribe, and constructed wind-breaks out of their red Hudson Bay blankets. They lit warming fires and around midday a few hunting parties returned with fresh deer and buffalo meat, but it was not nearly enough to feed the entire camp, and most of the braves gnawed on hunks of frozen pemmican. Scouts were posted on the hills overlooking the fort. They reported that the weather had also kept most of the soldiers indoors.

Red Cloud and his fellow war leaders decided that the best place to

lay their ambush was on the forks of Peno Creek, about halfway between
the Indian camp and the American fort. They would trap the Americans
on the flats of the little valley carved by the creek, attacking from the
breaks and leafless dogwood thickets dense enough to hide a large force.
But what if the soldiers again refused to cross the Lodge Trail Ridge en
masse and ride down into the valley? The previous feint on the wood train
had been to gauge the Bluecoats' reaction. Young braves on fast ponies,
including Crazy Horse, had been planted on the ridgeline to again lure
the soldiers on. That Powell's detachment had ignored the decoys after
scattering the raiding party was worrisome. Perhaps the Americans were
not as stupid as they looked. The tribes needed an omen.

When a hermaphrodite, or "half-man," was born into a Lakota band the
child was believed to have special powers of divination. Sioux and Cheyenne warriors put such faith in the ability of a hermaphrodite to predict
the future that battles were often postponed on his advice. On this day
Red Cloud summoned the most powerful Lakota half-man, a Miniconjou, to the top of a butte overlooking the forks of Peno Creek. The
war chief waved his arm across the potential battlefield, and the diviner
mounted his sorrel pony, threw a black blanket over his head, and made
three wild, zigzagging runs over the cuts and mesas, nearly to Lodge Trail
Ridge. Each time when he returned he fell from his mount and rolled in
the snow before sitting up and claiming that he had Bluecoats in his con-
vulsing, balled fist: first ten, then twenty, and finally thirty. On each occasion the war chiefs told him that it was not enough. He returned from his
frenzied fourth gallop, fell to the frozen earth as if in a trance, and when
he came out of it said that he now had American soldiers in both hands.
When asked how many, he opened his fists and declared that there were
over one hundred. A raucous shout echoed through the hills.

As evening dissolved into night the weather turned again, and a tem-
perate breeze blew up from the Southern Plains to melt most of the snow,
although it remained deep in the mountains and shaded gulches. It was
decided at the council fire that the next morning would be a good day to
fight.

35

THE HALF-MAN'S OMEN

December 21, 1866, dawned glorious, the winter sun bursting like a red dahlia over Pilot Knob. It was the kind of crisp morning that often follows a storm in the Powder River Country, with the air cold and dry and the wind still. It was a dramatic turn from the previous night's unseasonable warmth, and a harbinger of a colder storm front moving in. Most of the snow around the post had melted, but Colonel Carrington knew that the powder would still be deep in the pine forests. He delayed the wood train's morning departure until he was convinced that the weather would hold at least for the day.

On the far side of Lodge Trail Ridge Red Cloud was also grateful for the snowmelt. His warriors could now hide themselves in the draws and ravines of the Peno Creek valley without leaving tracks. A mile-long section of the Bozeman Trail followed the creek on a thin saddle connecting two buttes; it was called the High Backbone, and its edges fell off precipitously on either side into wending cutbanks thick with bushes and tall scrub. Red Cloud would position his force in these thickets while Yellow Eagle would again lead a smaller raiding party of perhaps forty warriors toward the pinery; the soldiers might find that number more enticing.

When Yellow Eagle departed, the Oglala, Cheyenne, and Arapaho formed up to the southwest of the High Backbone, and the bulk of the Miniconjous and a few scattered Sans Arcs concentrated below the saddle's bank on the northeast. Red Cloud and his battle chiefs rode about another quarter-mile down the valley and climbed the tallest hill. From here, with his captured field glasses, Red Cloud could see both the ambush site and the wood train road winding toward the new bridge onto Piney Island.

At 10 a.m. Colonel Carrington ordered the woodcutters to set out from the fort, this time with an extra guard attached to the usual mounted escort. All told there were perhaps ninety soldiers and civilians in the detail, about double the usual number. Less than an hour later pickets on Pilot Knob waved their coded flags, signaling that a raiding party was attacking the wood train. Bugles sounded inside the post and two Indians appeared above the fort across Big Piney Creek on the south slope of Lodge Trail Ridge. They dismounted, wrapped their red Hudson Bay blankets tight about them, and sat beneath a lone serviceberry tree watching the activity inside the log walls.

Carrington was later to say that he had sent for Captain Powell to lead the relief detail, because Powell had demonstrated common sense and restraint two days earlier. He was surprised when Fetterman arrived on the steps of his headquarters at the head of a company of infantry and a detachment of Company C's cavalry, fifty-three men in all. Fetterman reminded Carrington that, as with Captain Ten Eyck, he outranked Powell in length of service, and asked to be the one to take out the relief detail. Carrington was in a bind. Men were under attack several miles up the road and he did not have time to waste arguing the finer points of command with his obstreperous number two. He acquiesced, but—he was to testify—not before issuing these orders to Fetterman: "Support the wood train. Relieve it and report to me. Do not engage or pursue Indians at its expense. Under no circumstances pursue over . . . Lodge Trail Ridge." No one else heard Carrington give these orders.

Fetterman's infantry, flanked by the horsemen, had nearly reached the south gate when Carrington sent his adjutant running to intercept the captain and have him repeat the orders back. Fetterman allegedly did this before exiting the post. The colonel then summoned Lieutenant

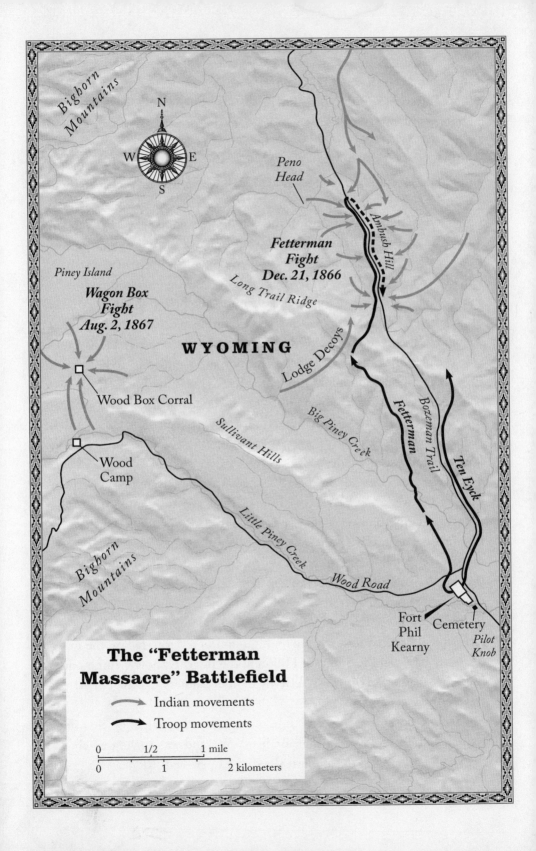

Bighorn
Mountains

*Peno
Head*

Ambush Hill

**Fetterman
Fight
Dec. 21, 1866**

Long Trail Ridge

Piney Island

**Wagon Box
Fight
Aug. 2, 1867**

WYOMING

Lodge Decoys

Wood Box Corral

Big Piney Creek

Bozeman Trail

Fetterman

Ten Eyck

Wood
Camp

Sullivant Hills

Bighorn
Mountains

Little Piney Creek

Wood Road

Fort
Phil
Kearny

Cemetery

*Pilot
Knob*

The "Fetterman
Massacre" Battlefield

→ Indian movements
→ Troop movements

0   1/2   1 mile
0   1   2 kilometers

Grummond and directed him to muster the remainder of the cavalry and follow Fetterman up the road. The riders would undoubtedly overtake the marching infantry, and Grummond was to fall in with Fetterman's troop "and never leave him." Carrington inspected Grummond's twenty-three cavalrymen, each outfitted with a Spencer rifle, and reiterated the orders forbidding Grummond to cross Lodge Trail Ridge. To this exchange there were witnesses.

Before Grummond rode out, the colonel was approached by Captain Brown and a private named Thomas Maddeon, who asked to join the detail. Maddeon had somehow requisitioned the last fit horse in the stables, and a jubilant Brown was leading Jimmy Carrington's mottled little mount, Calico, the pony the boy had won in the arrow-shooting contest at Nebraska's Fort Kearney—it seemed a lifetime ago. Carrington granted them permission and checked his pocket watch; it was nearly 11:30. Outside the post the innkeeper James Wheatley and a miner, Isaac Fisher, fell in with the mounted detail, bringing it to twenty-seven men. These two civilians were former Union Army officers who apparently had a hankering to kill Indians and had just purchased new sixteen-shot Henry rifles. Although the lever-action Henry was not as effective as a Springfield at long range, it was quite deadly up to 200 yards.

Carrington climbed the post's sentry walk and watched Fetterman veer off the wood road, cross Big Piney Creek, and turn onto a trail running west along the south slope of Lodge Trail Ridge—the same ascent he himself had taken two weeks earlier. Perplexed and angry, he turned toward the pickets on Pilot Knob. They were signaling that the wood train was no longer engaged, had broken its defensive corral, and was rolling onto the pinery. Carrington knew that Fetterman, perhaps a mile from the post, could also see the flagmen and he calmed down, supposing that Fetterman had decided to reach the high ground in order to fall on the raiding party between the Sullivant Hills and the ridge. By now Grummond's horsemen had swung in with Fetterman's foot soldiers, and together they traversed the slope.

Carrington noted with a mixture of unease and anticipation that Fetterman had deployed skirmishers on his flanks "and was moving wisely up the creek and along the southern slope of Lodge Trail Ridge, with good promise of cutting off the Indians as they should withdraw." He also saw that Fetterman's position offered "perfect vantage ground" should the raiders turn and attack the wood train again. Simultaneously, Carrington noticed the two Indians huddled beneath the tree across Big Piney Creek. He ordered Captain Powell to direct the artillerymen to lob several spherical case shots toward them. Much to everyone's surprise the whistling shell fragments flushed from the brushy cuts another thirty Indians. The hostiles fled back up the ridge. One pony was riderless.

It was with a sense of relief that Carrington, "entertaining no further thought of danger," climbed down from the bastion. Fetterman and Grummond were apparently obeying his command to engage only the war party that had attacked the wood train, and his big guns had scattered any hostile rear guard. He walked back to his headquarters with his mind, he would later write, already elsewhere. Fort Phil Kearny's infirmary was nearly complete—only a portion of the roof remained to be laid on—as were the barracks for the reinforcements, and the post's company was secure enough that well-attended church services were held on the parade ground each Sunday morning. To call Carrington a meticulous builder was to say that the Ancient Mariner just needed a moment of your time. It was the first day of winter, and in a mere six months his architectural exactness had produced a frontier outpost to stand up to any Army bivouac in the nation. Every board, jamb, and shingle had been fashioned with mathematical precision. He was proud of his accomplishments, regardless of the feeling in Omaha.

By noon Grummond's cavalry were slightly outpacing Fetterman's infantry, providing point and flank support, and had ridden about halfway up the slope of Lodge Trail Ridge. Awaiting Fetterman, Grummond halted his men just below the site where the Bozeman Trail ran northwest through a cut in the ridgeline. The sky had darkened, again thickening for snow, and against the skyline Grummond could make out individual braves, perhaps ten, racing their ponies near the crest. They waved red blankets to try to frighten his horses, and their wolflike yips and howls echoed off the buttes and hills rising from Big Piney Creek. Within moments Captain Fetterman's force had caught up to Grummond, and with his big coal eyes loaded with thunder the captain ordered a volley fired at the impertinent savages. The Indians quirted their ponies out of rifle range, but before the gun smoke cleared they had danced back and were daring the soldiers to chase them farther up the incline. Among them was Crazy Horse.

Fetterman continued climbing in skirmish formation, but he was hesitant. Below the crest of the ridge he held his position for a good twenty minutes, and the lookouts on Pilot Knob who were tracking his advance signaled to the post that he had halted the troop. Despite Colonel Carrington's directive, every Civil War officer understood the glory to be gained by seizing opportunities based on rapidly shifting battle scenarios—as long as the risk proved successful. The flamboyant Confederate cavalry commander General Jeb Stuart had won fame raiding Union lines against his superiors' wishes. But Stuart's delayed arrival at Gettysburg was also an egregious example of what could happen to a man's career and reputation if such decisions backfired or, as in his case, were perceived to have failed. Also, this was not the Civil War. Where were the enemy's rifle pits? His battle lines? His artillery bunkers? Fetterman knew that the wood train he had been sent out to protect was safe. *Support the wood train* had been the colonel's primary directive. That had been accomplished. *Do not engage or pursue Indians at its expense.* With the wood train safe, he could now either turn back toward the post, or teach the redskins a hard lesson about fighting real soldiers. It was Crazy Horse who forced his hand.

The wispy brave with the wavy hair dashed to and fro before the Bluecoats on his favorite bay racer, distinguished by its white face and stockings. He tried every trick he knew. He taunted the soldiers in English with vile curses. He dismounted within rifle range, again pretending that his horse had pulled up lame. He waved his blanket and stood tall with obvious disdain as bullets pocked the dirt at his feet. He even dismounted and started a small fire, acting as if his horse was so injured that he had given up and was ready to submit to a Black Heart warrior's suicide. Still Fetterman would not budge. Crazy Horse, clad in only a breechclout and deerskin leggings, with a single hawk's feather twined in his hair and a lone pebble tied behind his ear, was down to his final ploy. He turned his back toward the soldiers, flipped his breechclout up over his back, pulled down his leggings, and wiggled his naked ass in their faces.

The pickets on Pilot Knob shifted their field glasses from the taunting Indian to Captain Fetterman, who was pacing before his infantrymen. They saw him unsheathe his saber and appear to shout. The lookouts blinked, and the soldiers were gone.

In the dogwood defiles the steam of the concealed Strong Hearts' breath mingled with that of their ponies as they caressed the animals' snouts to keep them from whinnying. Not far away along frozen Peno Creek, Lakota, Cheyenne, and Arapaho braves flexed their bowstrings and tightened their grips on their lances.

36

BROKEN ARROWS

Captain Fetterman's Bluecoats topped the crest of Lodge Trail Ridge, and for once no warrior bolted to give the ambush away. A cold, damp wind had risen, bracing the foot soldiers as they flowed down the north slope following Crazy Horse and the yipping decoys. They reached the butte where the High Backbone began, the rise overspread by a jumble of flat-topped rocks deposited by an ancient glacier. They continued about 800 yards across the land bridge, firing as they walked. A few taunting Indians fell, and Lieutenant Grummond, riding in front of Fetterman and to Fetterman's left, spotted what appeared to be a small village with a herd of Indian ponies milling in a dell perhaps half a mile to the northwest. Without consulting Fetterman he ordered a charge, and the cavalry spurred into a gallop, the civilians Wheatley and Fisher out ahead with five troopers riding point.

At a few minutes past noon Crazy Horse and his decoys skidded their horses across the ice of Peno Creek and out of rifle range, the infantry still marching double-quick after them. Suddenly the Indians halted, formed up into two single files, and streamed back toward the whites. Not far from the creek the two files crossed in a perfect X. It was the end of the beginning, the prearranged signal to the hidden war party.

Two thousand warriors rose as one. A trembling war cry borne by the wind echoed through the hills, a curdling primal scream evoked by half a century of white indignities, lies, and betrayals. The Indians rolled toward the soldiers like a prairie fire. From the left, Cheyenne horsemen charged from clusters of dogwoods and cottonwoods. From the cutbank on the right, Lakota and Arapaho on foot scrambled from the tall grass and shot out from behind ash and box elders. Arrows blackened the sky, killing and wounding both friend and foe. Fetterman's commands could barely be heard amid the shrieks and shrill whistles.

The post bugler was about to sound the noon mess call when sentinels on the walls of Fort Phil Kearny heard firing, "continuous and rapid," from beyond Lodge Trail Ridge. At the first gunshots Colonel Carrington climbed to a lookout station on top of his quarters and scanned the ridgeline with his field glasses. He saw neither soldiers nor Indians. The colonel had received word from the woodcutters that they had reached the blockhouses on Piney Island with no casualties, but he knew that an Indian raiding party was still lurking somewhere between the fort and the Sullivant Hills. No one at the post was alarmed by either the gunshots or Fetterman's disappearance. Hostiles would not dare attack so strong a force, "the largest," the new arrival Lieutenant Arnold noted, "that had ever been sent out from the garrison."

Carrington assumed that his officers had decided to clear out the decoys near Peno Creek before coming back over the northernmost crest of the ridge and flanking the war party near the pinery. It was what he would have done; it was what he had attempted to do on December 6. He was slightly concerned that both Fetterman and Grummond had disregarded his orders not to cross the ridge, but even as an administrator who had rarely seen action he understood the necessity of making tactical decisions in the field. As a precaution he directed Captain Ten Eyck to assemble a detail and march for the sound of the rifle reports. Ten Eyck gathered the last forty infantrymen with working weapons and reported to the colonel.

Carrington told him that after he had merged with Captain Fetterman's troop, all soldiers were to return to the post. Ten Eyck's infantry marched out on the double-quick but slowed while fording Big Piney Creek. The ice had partially melted and had not completely refrozen, and the men removed their socks and boots to wade across. At the creek a handful of mounted civilians fell in with them.

Meanwhile, Colonel Carrington called for what was left of the Company C cavalry and ordered the teamster wagonmasters to gather all armed civilians still at the post. The detail came to about thirty men, some of whom piled into three mule-drawn ammunition wagons and an ambulance in order to catch up to Ten Eyck. There were no more serviceable horses at the fort.

Fetterman somehow managed to form up his surrounded troops and march them back across the High Backbone through the rain of arrows until they reached the flat-topped rock pile. From there they could go no farther. The air palled with powder smoke as Fetterman ordered his men into two loose, outward-facing skirmish lines twenty paces apart—a formation ideal in Civil War battles to determine an enemy's position and provide cover for the maneuvers of larger forces or reinforcements. But there were no reinforcements within striking distance, and these tactics meant little to the marauding Indians.

Far below Fetterman, Lieutenant Grummond realized too late what had happened. As he neared the pony herd he, too, was nearly enveloped by warriors; his stunned cavalrymen reined in their panicked, rearing mounts, awaiting orders that would never come. Grummond and a veteran sergeant were among the first to fall, with dozens of Cheyenne arrows penetrating their bodies. Without an officer the cavalry retreated in terror, ignoring Fetterman's plight and making for the crest of Lodge Trail Ridge. They also abandoned the civilians Wheatley and Fisher and the little patrol of point riders, who were too far out in front and were quickly cut off. This group dismounted and formed a small circle; the concentrated fire from their Henrys felled so many braves that within moments a great pile of dead Indians and ponies, mixed with their own slain animals, formed a natural barricade. But there were too many hostiles. They kept coming until it was knives and tomahawks against bayonets and swinging rifle butts. No one knows in what order the white men died.

Back at the rock pile Fetterman was also fast losing soldiers. His skirmish lines had devolved into two loosely concentric rings rapidly collapsing in on themselves—a tightening noose with the captain in its center. Their position at the top of the rise bought them some time, but daring Indians burst through the defenses on horse and on foot, first singly, then by twos and threes, and finally a second storm of arrows preceded a wave of thrusting lances and swinging war clubs. Warriors in front were pushed ahead by a surge from behind. The soldiers fired their old Springfields, but the Indians were so close that there was no time to reload.

Captain Brown broke away from the surviving cavalry troops who were scrambling up Lodge Trail Ridge and somehow made it through the mass of bodies at the rock pile. He dismounted beside Captain Fetterman, set loose Jimmy Carrington's pony, and stood back to back with his old commander, blasting away with his Colts. Brown fought off one charging Indian while another, a Lakota named American Horse, rushed his war pony into the rocks and brained Fetterman with his nail-studded club of solid bur oak. American Horse leaped from his saddle onto Fetterman's body and slit his throat, nearly severing Fetterman's head. The dwindling infantry fought hand to hand, some from their knees, swinging the shards of their shattered rifles. When several soldiers broke from the rocks and made a run for the cavalry, howling Indians rode and sprinted after them.

Brown was still standing, surrounded by an orgy of butchery. Eyeballs were gouged and noses and tongues torn from the wounded, screaming men. The Indians severed chins, sliced off fingers at the joints, and forced mouths open to chop out teeth. Skulls were cleaved open and brain matter was scooped out and set on rocks next to severed arms, legs, and feet. Uniform pants were pulled down or cut away and penises were hacked off and shoved into mouths. Brown had one cartridge left in his revolver. He put the barrel to his temple and pulled the trigger.

Up on the slope of Lodge Trail Ridge the frantic, terrified cavalrymen led their mounts by the reins. The climb across the icy hollows of the boulder-strewn hillside was slow and hard, and some horses skittered and broke away. One horseman walked backward, a lonesome rear guard continuously pumping the lever of his seven-shot Spencer, reloading, and firing again. The few infantrymen who had escaped the rock pile rushed past him up the incline. He covered them until an arrow tore through his heart.

When the first cavalrymen reached the summit, a narrow, slippery forty-foot shelf, they could see Fort Phil Kearny less than four miles away on the plateau beyond Big Piney Creek. They also saw Yellow Eagle's raiders, reinforced with at least 100 braves, charging up the south slope on snorting war ponies. The troopers' escape was blocked. They released their horses and dug into a cluster of boulders. There was a lull in the savage howls, and for a moment they dared to hope that reinforcements had overtaken the war party. The Indians had indeed broken off the attack, but only to collect the Army horses. A shower of arrows signaled their return.

Now spotters watching the fort flashed mirror signals to Red Cloud that more soldiers—Captain Ten Eyck's detail—were crossing Big Piney Creek. This news was at first greeted eagerly, until the scouts signaled that the soldiers were riding in wagons. Red Cloud was certain this meant the guns that shoot twice. He knew that, even hauling heavy howitzers, the soldiers would crest the ridge in less than thirty minutes—was this enough time to kill every last white still caught in the ambush? Red Cloud signaled back from the tall hill, and the warriors surrounding the cavalry crawled as close as they could to the boulders. At a second signal they stood and ran into the teeth of the Bluecoats' last volley, vanishing in clouds of gun smoke. The attackers suffered heavy casualties as they jabbed their lances and swung their war clubs and tomahawks, scalping soldiers alive. Crazy Horse was said to have been among these fighters, killing with his steel hatchet.

The little German bugler Adolph Metzger was one of the last to die. He found a crevasse between two large rocks, burrowed in backward, and fired his Spencer until its magazine was empty. Then he swung his bugle until it was a shapeless hunk of metal smeared with blood and war paint. For his bravery he was accorded the highest honor his enemies could bestow—he was the only soldier not scalped. His bleeding, battered body, wounded in a dozen places, was covered with a buffalo-robe shroud as a sign of respect.

If true, Metzger was the exception.* The official Army report, suppressed for twenty years, noted that many of the soldiers were probably still alive when their "eyes, ears, mouths and arms [were] penetrated with spearheads, sticks, and arrows; ribs slashed to separation with knifes; skulls severed in every form, from chin to crown; muscles of calves, thighs, stomach, breast, back, arm, and cheek taken out. [There were] punctures upon every sensitive part of the body, even to the soles of the feet and the palms of the hand." From decoys to depredations, it had taken a mere forty minutes. Eighty-one Americans lay dead.

---

*Or so reported the civilian from Colonel Carrington's burial detail who claimed to have recovered Metzger's corpse. Not long afterward, Crow Indians related a similar story to a fur trader, but with a different ending. According to the Crows, for his bravery Metzger was indeed accorded the highest honor his enemies could bestow—by being carried off alive and tortured to death back at the hostiles' camp. Years later Northern Cheyenne warriors gave Metzger's misshapen bugle to a Buffalo, Wyoming, store owner. It remains on display at the store.

37

"LIKE HOGS BROUGHT TO MARKET"

On the southern slope of Lodge Trail Ridge the firing from the other side grew louder. But instead of following Captain Fetterman's path directly up the Bozeman Trail, Captain Ten Eyck ordered his troops east and then north, aiming for the ridgeline's highest point. He wanted to be certain he controlled the high ground for whatever he would face on the other side of the ridgeline. The route added fifteen to twenty minutes to his mission.

At 12:45 Ten Eyck's lead skirmishers were just topping the crest some 200 yards east of the battlefield when all gunshots from the Peno Creek valley ceased. One of the civilians riding just ahead of Ten Eyck's troop thought he heard groans and screams. Within minutes the entire column had reached the summit. The Peno Creek valley stretching before them was aswarm with thousands of painted warriors, more than any man in the garrison had ever seen. Many seemed to be concentrated on either side of the High Backbone. When the Indians spotted the relief detail they jeered, shrieked, and waved their weapons toward the sky, daring the Americans to come down and fight. Others were running down saddled American horses and recovering some of the 40,000 arrows that had been shot, 1,000 for every minute of the fight. Still others were loading their dead onto makeshift travois or tending to the wounded.* And a group of about 100 were clustered around a pile of boulders half a mile or so to the west along the crest of the ridgeline. A dog darted out from the scrub, and some of the soldiers recognized it as one of the hounds from the fort. An Indian put an arrow through its brain.

Ten Eyck was confused. Where was Fetterman? Where was Grummond's cavalry? He dispatched his only mounted messenger back to the fort and continued to stare at the vista before him, trying to make sense of what he was seeing. Meanwhile the wagons arrived, and the Indians slowly withdrew from the little valley. Suddenly, a trooper cried, "There's the men down there, all dead." From a distance the naked white bodies could have been mistaken for patches of snow.

Back at the fort Colonel Carrington paced his small lookout tower, watching as Captain Ten Eyck's relief party topped the ridge. Below him, on the front porch, Mrs. Wheatley and the wives of officers and enlisted men gathered with Margaret Carrington. The women stared wordlessly at the heights across the Big Piney. "The silence," wrote Frances Grummond, who was five months' pregnant, "was dreadful." At a little past one o'clock they spotted a lone horseman riding furiously down the slope. Within moments he had galloped through the main gate and skidded to a halt before the colonel's headquarters. "Captain Ten Eyck says he can see or hear nothing of Captain Fetterman," the courier reported. "The Indians are on the road challenging him to come down."

There were Indians as far as the eye could see, he said, and Ten Eyck had requested reinforcements and a mountain howitzer. Then the messenger lowered his voice. "The Captain is afraid Fetterman's party is all gone up, sir." There were no more fit horses to replace the messenger's exhausted

---

* Reliable estimates of Indian casualties at the Fetterman fight are difficult to come by. The figures for deaths range from 11 to 60. The wounded are said to have numbered between 60 and 300, of whom an estimated 100 died soon thereafter. All the figures were recounted many years later by various old Indians who claimed to have taken part in the battle. In any case, most historians concur that the Indians' heaviest losses came from their own arrows.

mount, and Carrington ordered one of his personal horses, a big sturdy gray, retrieved from the stable. He scrawled a message on a piece of paper, informing Ten Eyck that reinforcements and ammunition were on their way. He was unaware that these had already reached him. And as if doubting either the captain or his messenger, he also ordered Ten Eyck to find Fetterman, unite with him, collect the wood train, and return to the post. Perhaps he also anticipated the public outcry should the courier's aside be true, for before handing the message over he jotted a sentence reprimanding Ten Eyck for his roundabout route up the slope. "You could have saved two miles toward the scene of action if you had taken Lodge Trail Ridge." If it was the lawyer-turned-colonel's purpose to plant the first seed of blame elsewhere for whatever had happened on the other side of that ridge, it was a move well played.

Captain Ten Eyck waited until the entire huge war party had departed over a string of distant buttes before he advanced cautiously down the north slope of Lodge Trail Ridge. He reached Peno Creek and turned west, following the wagon ruts of the Bozeman Trail. The knoll with the flat-topped rock pile loomed before him. Bodies covered the stones. The corpses formed a ring about forty feet in diameter. The harsh wind had scattered much paper—maps, unsent letters, journal pages—a common sight in the aftermath of frontier warfare. Some soldiers recognized fellow infantrymen from scraps of uniforms that the Indians had not shredded or stolen.

It was difficult to identify individuals, although "Bald Head Eagle" Brown, with a powder burn on his temple and a bullet in his brain, was recognizable. The Indians had "scalped" his tonsure. He was the only trooper killed by a gunshot. Dead Indian ponies and American horses littered the blood-soaked ground, the snouts of the Army animals pointing toward the fort. In the cuts and draws below, on the rises above, and in the scrub and among the trees they found more men—scalped, mutilated, the blood frozen in their wounds. Some soldiers who fanned out to search through the tall yellow saw grass recoiled when they realized that the greasy material they were slipping on was the organs and entrails of their comrades. They had yet to discover Grummond's troops on the ridge.

Though a mule is far less likely to spook than a horse, it was well known throughout the West that mules shied more from the smell of blood, and now they brayed and reared at the scent of so much of it. The temperature was falling, the corpses were rapidly stiffening, and Ten Eyck ordered as many loaded into the four wagons as could fit. It was rough, slow work, and they did not reach the gates of Fort Phil Kearny until dusk. In the gloaming the dove-gray sky had the macabre formality of a steel engraving. "We brought in about fifty in wagons," wrote the post surgeon, "like you see hogs brought to market."

As night fell the temperature dropped below zero, the wind picked up, and Fort Phil Kearny was locked down and braced for the next attack. Nearly a third of its garrison had abruptly vanished—closer to half, taking into account the armed soldiers and teamsters on Piney Island. Colonel Carrington certainly did, and he sent for them immediately. He also ordered all civilians brought into the fort, released every prisoner from the guardhouse, and placed the entire post under arms, such as they were. The howitzers and mounds of grapeshot and case shot were pulled to the battlements, rifles were stacked across the parade ground, and orders were passed to bar every door and window. Three troopers were assigned to each of the stockade's firing loopholes, but most of the Spencers had been captured in the fight and Springfield ammunition was so short that each man was issued only five rounds. The balls jangled in their haversacks like marbles. Every man understood that the fort could not hold out long against a full-bore assault. Survivors recalled that the men assumed their posts without expression in their eyes, as if coming from no past and having no future.

When the wagons arrived from the pinery Colonel Carrington had the beds removed and upended to form three concentric circles girding the post's underground magazine. As he studied the Indian signal fires on the hills and ridges ringing the fort, his wife knocked on Frances Grummond's door along Officers' Row to break the news that her husband was still missing. Given the "horrible and sickening" condition of the forty-nine bodies carried back to the post—these were being sorted through and identified in the emptied guardhouse—neither woman held much hope that he was still alive. Margaret Carrington insisted that the lieutenant's wife move into her quarters—tellingly, no similar offer was made to the innkeeper James Wheatley's wife and children—and as Frances gathered a few belongings, another knock sounded on her door. She pulled it open to find a dark, wiry civilian with a pointy black beard and "bright, piercing eyes" filling her small door frame.

Mrs. Grummond knew this man's name although they had never before spoken to each other. He was John "Portugee" Phillips, the mining partner of Isaac Fisher. Phillips had been born in the Azores to Portuguese parents, and in a lilting accent he told her that he had been out hauling water when Fisher and Wheatley joined her husband's troop, or else he would have surely ridden with them. Now, he said, Colonel Carrington had called for volunteers to ride to Fort Laramie for help, and he had stepped forward. He had come, he said, to say good-bye. Frances Grummond was flustered. She barely knew the man.

Phillips glanced at Grummond's distended stomach. "I will go if it costs me my life," he said with tears in his eyes. And though still in shock and taken somewhat aback by the stranger's familiarity, she finally understood his words to mean that Phillips was following his own Code of the West, whereby the safety of a pregnant woman in danger was paramount. Phillips removed the wolf-skin robe from his shoulders and handed it to her before departing. "I brought it for you to keep and remember me by if you never see me again," he said. Then he turned and left.

Throughout all this—the preparations for an attack, the identification of the bodies stacked in the guardhouse, the mourning, the fear and confusion—memories of Captain Fetterman and his eighty dead hovered over the little outpost like ghosts. No one slept well that night.

Colonel Carrington hunched over his lamplit writing desk and scratched out two messages: one for General Cooke in Omaha and one for General Grant in Washington. They were nearly identical. He described what little he knew of the day's battle—"a fight unexampled in Indian warfare"—and informed his superiors that though only forty-nine bodies had been recovered, he suspected that the missing thirty-one troopers and their

officer Lieutenant Grummond were also dead. Without immediate reinforcements armed with Spencer rifles, he wrote, a retaliatory "expedition
now with my force is impossible." He assured both generals that he was
prepared to defend Fort Phil Kearny to the last man, and concluded with
perhaps his first realistic assessment of his position since arriving in the
Powder River Country in July. "The Indians are desperate; I spare none,
and they spare none."

As with his note to Ten Eyck, it must surely have occurred to the savvy
citizen-soldier that the Army, indeed the nation, would soon be looking
for scapegoats. It was likely with this in mind that he added a personal
comment to General Grant's dispatch:

> I send a copy of dispatch to General Cooke simply as a case when in un-
> certain communication, I think you should know the facts at once. I want
> all my officers. I want men. Depend upon it, as I wrote in July, no treaty
> but hard fighting is to assure this line. I have no reason to think otherwise.
> I will operate all winter, whatever the season, if supported; but to redeem
> my pledge to open and guarantee this line, I must have re-enforcements
> and the best arms up to my full estimate.

Carrington had his adjutant make two copies of both letters. In addition to "Portugee" Phillips, he had recruited two more couriers—a miner
named William Bailey and the wagon master George Dillon—to ride
separately for Horseshoe Station, the closest telegraph office, 196 miles
away. But the Horseshoe Station line was frequently down, so he asked
all three to continue on to Fort Laramie, another forty miles south. It was
Phillips in whom he had the most confidence.

It was nearing midnight on December 21 when Colonel Carrington
met Phillips in the quartermaster's stables. He led Phillips to his own
stalls, where the miner selected one of the colonel's personal mounts, a
white Kentucky thoroughbred. Phillips crammed his saddlebags with
hardtack and tied a quarter-sack of oats to his pommel. The thermometer
read eighteen degrees below zero, and the air smelled of a gathering storm.
Phillips cinched his buffalo-hair coat, wrapped tight the wool leggings beneath his thigh-high buffalo boots, pulled his beaver hat low over his ears,

and jammed his hands into sheepskin mittens that stretched to his elbows. He then led the horse to the southeast water gate of the quartermaster's yard, Carrington walking beside him. The first threatening bits of swirling sleet and snow pricked the men's faces.

The three enlisted men posted at the gate were jumpy. At the sound of boots crunching on the frozen ground a private called out a challenge. Carrington moved close enough to be recognized and the sergeant of the guard shouted, "Attention!"

"Never mind, sergeant," Carrington said. "Open the gate."

Two soldiers pushed open the heavy log sally port and stood silent. Carrington gave Phillips brief final instructions before reaching out to shake his hand. "May God help you," he said, and the horseman led his charger out, mounted, wheeled, and trotted away.

Carrington and the three guardsmen stood wordless for half a minute, the colonel's head cocked as if he was listening for the hiss of an arrow. Then the hoofbeats went silent. "Good," he said. "He has taken softer ground at the side of the trail." The snow began falling harder.

38

FEAR AND MOURNING

His wife, the post surgeon, and his four surviving junior officers tried to talk him out of it. They all agreed it was a terrible idea. Colonel Carrington insisted. He would not allow the hostiles to sense any weakness. But the more powerful reason was that he had to see for himself. It was midday and bitterly cold on December 22 when he mounted the sturdy gray he had lent to Captain Ten Eyck's messenger twenty-four hours earlier. Eighty-three soldiers and civilians, the best he could select, followed him through the front gate toward Lodge Trail Ridge. Storm clouds scudded down from the north, and enough spitting snow had already fallen to muffle the footfalls of the marchers and the creaking of the mule-drawn wagons.

Carrington was surprised that the Indians had not followed up the massacre with a sunrise attack. When the bugle blew reveille and the report of the morning gun echoed back from the hills, he had expected the sound to be met with howls, eagle whistles, and arrows. But as the pale sun rose farther over Pilot Knob not an Indian was visible on the ridges and hills. This, Carrington knew, did not mean the Indians were not there. It was, however, unlike them to refrain from ostentatiously exhibiting their joy at the outcome of yesterday's fight. Perhaps the reason was the blizzard that everyone sensed was coming.

While his troop assembled he had whispered to Mrs. Grummond a promise to retrieve her husband's body. Then he'd handed Captain Powell two written orders. Captain Ten Eyck would be accompanying him over the ridgeline, and Powell was left in charge of the post. The first order concerned communications. On his departure, Carrington wrote, Powell was to run a white lamp up the flagstaff; if Indians appeared, he was to fire the twelve-pounder three times and substitute a red lantern for the white one. The second directive was more confidential, and Carrington pulled Powell aside to issue it orally as well: "If in my absence, Indians in overwhelming numbers attack, put the women and children in the magazine with supplies of water, bread, crackers, and other supplies that seem best, and, in the event of a last desperate struggle, destroy all together, rather than have any captured alive."

To remove any doubt Carrington himself strode through the circular wagon fortification, pulled open the magazine door, cut open a sphere of case shot, and laid a train of black powder that would ignite at the touch of a match.

Jim Bridger's failing eyesight and the biting cold may have made him less of an asset to the battalion—the old mountain man's arthritis barely allowed him to walk, much less mount a horse and ride for any length of time. But he had been proved correct in one observation: these "paper-collar" soldiers did not know anything about fighting Indians. Bridger had pulled himself out of bed that morning and limped out into the day. Despite the intense pain in his joints he volunteered to ride as a scout. He, too, expected an attack at any moment, and he'd decided that when it occurred it would be as fine an occasion as any to end his career and his life. Once through the main gate, Bridger set about directing skirmishers to key sites on the column's flanks and positioned pairs of infantry pickets on successive outcrops and ridges, creating a chain that reached all the way back to the fort. He made certain that each set of the guards standing higher and higher along the route would never be out of sight of the men below.

The temperature remained around zero, and darker storm clouds blotted out the sun as the detail trod silently past the rock pile and reached the high ground strewn with boulders. The rocky earth along the ridgeline was streaked with frozen pools of blood, and the bodies were so stiff that one civilian likened the task of loading them onto the wagons to stacking cordwood. The mules again huffed and kicked at the smell of blood and offal, and soldiers were assigned to hold their heads and reins to keep them from bolting. One team of mules threw off the flailing handlers and dumped a half-filled wagon. Corpses frozen into grotesque contortions tumbled across the slope. "It was," wrote a witness, "a terrible sight and a horrible job."

The men on the ridge, like Fetterman's soldiers, had been butchered, but cavalrymen in the detail recognized infantry insignia mixed among the dead. One horseman, John Guthrie, noted, "Some had crosses cut on their breasts, faces to the sky, some crosses on the back, faces to the ground. . . . We walked on top of internals and did not know it in the high grass. Picked them up, that is their internals, did not know the soldier they belonged to, so you see the cavalry man got an infantry man's gutts [*sic*] and an infantry man got a cavalry man's gutts."

From the ridgeline the wagons rolled slowly down to Peno Creek, where Lieutenant Grummond and Sergeant Augustus Lang were discovered. Grummond's head had been severed and his body had suffered the usual mutilations. Not far away from him lay the frozen hulk of Jimmy Carrington's pony, Calico. The horse, too, had been scalped. Someone remarked that such was the Indians' contempt for the quartermaster Captain Brown that they had even scalped his horse. A few hundred yards down the creek bed lay the bodies of James Wheatley, Isaac Fisher, "and four or five of the old long-tried and experienced soldiers." Piles of spent Henry rifle cartridges littered the little ring created by their slain horses and an additional ten dead ponies. Outside the defensive circle a soldier counted sixty-five smudges of dark, clotted blood, perhaps indicating where an Indian had fallen.

It was dark before the column moved back over the crest of Lodge Trail Ridge. Excited word was passed from front to back that the white lantern still swung from the top of the flagstaff. Back inside the fort Colonel

Carrington handed Frances Grummond a sealed envelope containing a lock of her husband's hair. Not long afterward, the blizzard that had threatened all day began. The temperature dropped to twenty below and by daylight on December 23 snowdrifts had crested so high against the west wall of the stockade that guards could walk over it. Bridger assured Colonel Carrington that not even Red Cloud was bold or crazy enough to attack in such weather. Even so, all through the day before Christmas Fort Phil Kearny was tense. A triple guard remained at every loophole.

If any scintilla of holiday spirit still breathed it was smothered by the steady whine of handsaws and a clanging of hammers on nails as carpenters worked around the clock constructing pine coffins—two men to a coffin except for the dead officers. Captain Fetterman, Lieutenant Grummond, and Captain Brown had separate caskets. The coffins were numbered to identify each occupant, and Colonel Carrington dispatched a grave-digging detail to break the frozen earth beneath Pilot Knob. He hoped for a solemn Christmas Day service. But even continuous half-hour work shifts could not accomplish that. The snow was too high, the ground was too hard, and the threat of another attack was too overwhelming to spare enough men. So a day late, on December 26, forty-two pine boxes were hurriedly interred in a shallow fifty-foot-long trench. No words were spoken over the graves.

Following the somber ceremony there was nothing to do but batten down Fort Phil Kearny and wait. For what, only God and Red Cloud knew.

The blizzard gave the Indians time to mourn. For three days the wives, sisters, mothers, and daughters in the great village on the Tongue made their way to the bluffs to cut their fingers and arms and chop their hair in memory of the dead. Snowdrifts five and six feet deep ran with blood. And then, on the fourth day, the victory dances commenced to celebrate the fight the Indians would call—referring to the half-man's augury—the "Battle of the Hundred-in-the-Hands."

Paeans were composed to Yellow Eagle for leading the raids on the wood road, and decoys such as Young-Man-Afraid-Of-His-Horses and American Horse, Fetterman's slayer, were feted at feasts. A wan Crazy Horse was dragged into the firelight and for once not allowed to back away. To him were rendered honors for his deft disciplining of the decoy party, and old men sang of the fearlessness he had shown while standing unflinching against the American guns. It was a turning point in Crazy Horse's life. Never again would he be able to remain silently aloof in the shadows of the council fires, a lone-wolf warrior-hunter responsible to no one but himself. Like his friend Young-Man-Afraid-Of-His-Horses, he would now be groomed for tribal leadership, and the Cheyenne and Arapaho as well as the Lakota would look to, and depend on, his wisdom in both war and peace. Given their familiarity with the ways of the whites, however, there were few on the Tongue in the last week of December 1866 who believed that peace had been achieved.

And then there was Red Cloud. To him went "all the honor" for the stunning victory. His strategic planning, so often questioned, had proved a masterstroke—everything he had foreseen, from the victory at Bridge Station to the warnings that accompanied his verbal explosion at Fort Laramie, had indeed occurred. He had held together his Indian coalition while balancing older, more experienced voices urging accommodation with the whites against young warriors too eager to strike too soon. His forward thinking and his keen military judgment in choosing lieutenants such as Crazy Horse had inspired the disparate tribes with a sense of unity. He had told his people that their cause, his cause, was just, and that "The Heart of Everything That Is" was worth fighting for and, if need be, dying for. Best of all, in the end it was the Bluecoats who had done the dying.

At the grand celebrations that followed the Peno Creek fight Red Cloud's political rivals, Old-Man-Afraid-Of-His-Horses in particular, deferred to him. He graciously returned their praise while modestly accepting the accolades. If he seemed subdued, there was good reason. He fretted that his warriors had failed to destroy the despised fort between the Pineys. And he knew that this war was far from over. The Battle of the Hundred-in-the-Hands had been a fine start, perhaps even a signal to the Americans that they should leave the Powder River Country and never return. It was what he hoped, but Red Cloud could hardly have believed it. He knew his enemy. The Americans would be back, and he would fight them again—and only on his terms. But he also understood the ways of his own people and the allied tribes. Despite the victory, it would be difficult to rally them again so soon. His braves needed time to fill their bellies over warm winter fires while the war ponies recovered their strength. It would be a short cold season, and when the new grass sprouted from the prairie he would reveal his next step.

To that end he had decided that the Lakota bands would forgo their annual trek east to stake individual winter camps near the Black Hills. Instead they would move west en masse into the old Crow lands in the valley of the Little Bighorn to prepare for a spring offensive. He was certain that warriors from other bands would seek him out to swell his fighting force. He would use these numbers wisely; the Americans would not know what hit them. Already the details were forming in his mind, like a set of tumblers clicking into place. First he would simultaneously attack the two most northern garrisons, Forts Phil Kearny and C. F. Smith, and kill everyone in them. That would leave Reno Station isolated, and either the Army would abandon it or he would burn it. This was an audacious plan, but Red Cloud was certain it would work.

What to do about Fort Laramie, Red Cloud was not certain. By then the Americans might well have left the territory forever. Of this eventual outcome he was certain. Then, after it was all over, after the Indians had won his war, he would find rest in his lodge.

Portugee Phillips was half dead, and his mount was in even worse shape. He rode by night and hid by day through one of the most vicious northers ever recorded on the High Plains. He rationed his hardtack and supplemented his horse feed with the odd tuft of prairie grass dug out from under thigh-deep snow. He reached the Horseshoe Station telegraph office late Christmas morning. Somewhere along the trail he had met up with William Bailey and George Dillon, and the three arrived together, exhausted, hungry, and freezing, Bailey and Dillon too spent to go on.

John Friend, the telegraph operator, tapped out a synopsis of Colonel Carrington's dispatches. But he told the three that he had received no messages that day, and he feared that either the storm or the Indians had cut the line. Without saying a word Phillips began rebinding his legs with burlap sacks. Bailey and Dillon, collapsed in a heap by the fire, begged Phillips not to risk it. He ignored them, threw on his buffalo coat and beaver cap, saddled his horse, and rode. By noon the blizzard had blown north, behind him, and he traveled all afternoon across a landscape so white that by dusk he was snow-blind. Sunset brought relief but also the arrival of another storm. He rode by feel, always tracking south, the new sheets of snow thicker with his mount's every footfall.

The temperature was twenty-five degrees below zero when Phillips reeled through the main gate of Fort Laramie late on Christmas night, his mount drawn as a moth to flame by the lighted and gaily decorated windows of the main officers' quarters. A full-dress garrison ball was in progress, and the strains of the band wafted over his head as he slumped in his saddle and fell from his horse. Snow and ice matted his pointy black beard. Icicles hung from his coat and hat. The officer of the guard, a young lieutenant, rushed from his sentry box and helped him to his feet. Phillips was too weak to walk by himself, and his vocal cords were so frozen that his voice was a tinny croak when he said he needed to see the post's commanding officer.

The lieutenant slung Phillips's arm over his shoulders and half-carried him to the ballroom, where the officers were about to select partners for the next dance. People gasped when he staggered through the door. The band fell silent and Lieutenant Colonel Innis Palmer, Fort Laramie's commanding officer, rushed to his side. Earlier that afternoon Palmer had received a telegram from Horseshoe Station reporting an Indian massacre. But the communication was so garbled and incomplete—it did not say who had been massacred, or where the incident had occurred—that he took it as just another of the many rumors that flew across the High Plains.

Now Phillips reached under his buffalo coat and woolen shirts and pulled out Colonel Carrington's dispatches. Lieutenant Colonel Palmer's face whitened as he read them. He looked at Phillips, who had just ridden 236 miles in four days through raging blizzards—a feat that would become equal in western lore to Paul Revere's famous ride. Palmer turned back to the cold papers in his hands. He was wearing white kid gloves. He handed the messages to an aide, who ran to the post's telegraph office, and directed two soldiers to carry Phillips to the post infirmary. On the way they passed Colonel Carrington's white Kentucky thoroughbred charger, lying dead on the parade ground.

• • •

The Fort Laramie telegraph operator relayed the dispatches word for word to both General Cooke in Omaha and General Grant in Washington. It was 3:15 p.m. on December 26, 1866, when Grant and the War Department received the first news about what would soon be known nationwide as the "Fetterman Massacre."

The next morning the *New York Times* provided brief details of the "horrid massacre" in the distant Dakota Territory, noting that it accounted for 8 percent of all Army deaths in half a century of Indian fighting west of the Mississippi. And though what would later be referred to as "Red Cloud's War" was far from over, this was the moment when Grant came to the realization that the United States had been defeated for the first time by an Indian opponent.

Red Cloud never spoke to any whites of his great victory, so we are left to imagine his thoughts as the Bad Faces led the Lakota push west into the Bighorn Valley. Perhaps he recalled his orphaned childhood, or his first lethal coup against the Pawnees, or even the suicide of the tragic Pine Leaf. What we do know is that the boy shunned by so many and the man feared by all had accomplished what no other Indian ever had before.

The son of an alcoholic Brule had taught himself to lead, to suppress his snarl and his personal rage and remain still when he wanted to strike out. He had developed a steely self-discipline, and it had enabled him to become the first warrior chief to transfigure an Indian military culture that had stood for centuries, if not millennia. He had not only united the fractious Lakota, enticing Oglalas, Brules, Miniconjous, and Sans Arcs to fight as one, but had also drawn to his banner the Cheyenne, Arapaho, Nez Percé, and Shoshones. It was the only way, he knew from the beginning, to defeat the Americans, to humble a people so strong, so numerous, so intent on taking his land when they already had so much of their own. And he had shown the United States; he had achieved, in a sense, what more exalted generals such as Cornwallis and Lee had been unable to do.

The irony, of course, lay in the fact that Red Cloud did not even know who those men were.

The white man made me a lot of promises, and they only kept one.
They promised to take my land, and they took it.

—Red Cloud

I f Red Cloud's fame was not already established in America—though it certainly was among whites on the frontier—the Battle of the Hundred-in-the-Hands secured it. "Red Cloud's War" would go on for more than another year before the United States would admit it was beaten and sue for peace—for the first time on Indian terms.

Following the Fetterman fight Red Cloud allowed the remainder of the winter of 1866–67 to pass uneventfully, helping to ensure the survival of those who remained at Fort Phil Kearny. But his harassment of the three American forts in the Powder River Country began anew as soon as the first spring grass of 1867 began to renourish Indian ponies. In August, the "Moon of Black Cherries," the powerful Lakota war chief's alliance launched its next full-scale attack. That battle, on August 2, came to be known as the Wagon Box Fight. It would prove to be significant for both the Oglala Head Man and the U.S. government—but for completely different reasons.

The first reinforcements arrived at Fort Phil Kearny on December 27, 1866, five days after the victorious Indians had begun moving west toward winter camp. The detail consisted of twenty-five men commanded by Captain George B. Dandy, who pushed through the snow after word of the disaster reached Reno Station. Dandy and his men marched into a demoralized and frightened post that was still waiting for the next arrows to fall.

As the news of Fetterman's defeat spread east from Wyoming, the U.S. military and political bureaucracy was set into motion. After digesting Colonel Carrington's dispatch, General Cooke wrote to General Grant that given "the completeness of the massacre," it was probable that there had been 3,000 Indians involved. Cooke also reported that he was about to relieve Colonel Carrington of the command of Fort Phil Kearny and order him to Fort McPherson in Nebraska, where the new 18th Regiment was to be headquartered. He then asked Grant's permission to name Colonel Henry W. Wessells as the garrison commander at Fort Phil Kearny. Grant agreed.

The next day General Sherman, writing from St. Louis, reiterated to Grant, "We must act with vindictive earnestness against the Sioux, even to their extermination, men, women and children. Nothing less will reach the root of this case." For weeks afterward telegrams and letters flew among Grant, Sherman, officials at the Bureau of Indian Affairs, and congressional leaders. General Cooke was quietly "retired" as Senate hearings were opened and an Army commission was formed to officially investigate the disaster. Unofficially, the politicians and the generals were looking for scapegoats. Carrington, who in mid-January 1867 bade farewell to the tidy fort he had built in the heart of the Powder River Country, was naturally called to testify before both the Senate hearings and the Army commission. The Little White Chief would spend the rest of his life defending his actions and, with the aid of his first and second wives, shifting the blame for the Fetterman Massacre to the man whose name it bore.

When Carrington departed the post between the Piney Creeks and retraced the trek he had taken the previous spring he was accompanied by his wife, Margaret, and by Frances Grummond, who had agreed to the arduous journey in a jolting wagon despite her pregnancy. She traveled with a pine box containing the remains of her husband, exhumed from the trench. It was not an easy trip. Snowdrifts and below-zero temperatures made for slow going, and several members of the escort detail suffered from frostbite that later necessitated the amputation of their hands and feet. On the route between Reno Station and Fort Laramie, Carrington's revolver misfired, shooting a bullet into his thigh. When he arrived at Fort McPherson to reassume command of the reconstituted 18th Infantry, he was in an ambulance.

After picking up details of the battle from smaller newspapers throughout Montana and Nebraska, reporters and editors from St. Louis to the Eastern Seaboard presented to their shocked readers lurid and often erroneous reports of the fight and its aftermath. On March 14, 1867, the *Montana Post* reported, "Eighteen hundred lodges of Sioux, numbering three warriors in each lodge, under the Chiefs Red Cloud, Iron Plate and White Young Bull, are encamped on the Big Horn River, about thirty-five miles from Fort Smith. The Crows, Bloods, Peguins, Grosentres [*sic*] and Sioux have made peace among themselves in league against the whites. About 800 lodges are yet north of the Missouri River, but will cross over and camp near Muscle Shell River as soon as Spring opens, and after concentrating their forces the confederation will wage war against the whites."

This, though far from accurate, got the Army's attention. In his annual report to Grant regarding "operations within my command," Sherman lamented that the army had failed "to follow the savages and take a just vengeance" for the Fetterman massacre. He added that he had personally "passed over 455 miles of finished railroad west of Omaha," and that the laying of track was proceeding apace. Sherman was slow to recognize that the progress of civilization would be more effective in subduing Indians than any act of war. In any event, newspaper readers and politicians alike remained confused as the spring thaw brought no further news of grand battles with this large Indian force. Behind the scenes, however, officials from the Bureau of Indian Affairs were already putting out treaty feelers to Red Cloud through more manageable Lakota like Spotted Tail. They were met with silence.

As he had planned all along, Red Cloud returned to the environs of Fort Phil Kearny in June 1867 to begin a series of vicious skirmishes with Colonel Wessells's troops. The post had been resupplied and there were fresh herds of cattle and horses to raid. The attacks became so intense that by July, Wessells, fully comprehending Carrington's predicament of a year earlier, was forced to assign entire companies to guard the woodcutters and hay mowers. All this was a prologue to the events of the first week of August.

In late July the war chiefs from the tribal alliance had again convened on the Tongue, and Red Cloud and the other Big Bellies laid plans to attack two of the white man's forts almost simultaneously. On the morning of August 1 a large war party of Cheyenne led by Dull Knife and Two Moons surrounded a civilian hay-cutting detail protected by nineteen soldiers about two miles from Montana's Fort C. F. Smith. Two troopers and a civilian were killed as the beleaguered Americans, holed up in a makeshift corral, withstood a daylong assault. It was only when howitzers from the post arrived near dusk that the Cheyenne melted away with the captured Army mounts.

The next morning, August 2, a loaded wood train and its Army escort set off from Piney Island for Fort Phil Kearny, and at about the same time an empty wood train consisting of fourteen wagons left the post for the pinery. Among the civilians working in the latter detail was Portugee Phillips. All of the soldiers in the field were under the command of Captain James Powell, who, along with Captain Tenedor Ten Eyck, was a holdover from Carrington's command. Once again Red Cloud, leading about 1,000 Oglala and Miniconjou warriors, climbed a high hill west of the fort to observe the action. Once again Crazy Horse and the Miniconjou warrior High Backbone were his field commanders. However, Red Cloud was unaware that only a few weeks earlier the garrison at Fort Phil Kearny had received a shipment of 700 new Springfield-Allin conversion rifles with trapdoor breechloaders, along with 100,000 rounds of .50-70-450 Martin bar-anvil, center-fire primed cartridges. The guns and ammunition had been delivered by a reinforcement company of the 27th Infantry. This time, the Indians would not be fighting soldiers who had only outdated muzzle-loaders.

At 9 a.m., as the two wood trains were about to converge three miles from the fort, troopers spotted the Indians. Powell immediately ordered the fourteen empty wagons to form an oval. This could not be readily done with the incoming train, which was laden with logs and planks, and the Sioux fell on it and burned every wagon. They then regrouped to attack the oval of empty wagons. In overwhelming numbers they charged the makeshift corral on horseback and on foot; this was perhaps the only time in the history of the West that an Indian offensive involved sacrificing a large number of lives in order to take a position. They absorbed the volley they were expecting and assumed they had the usual thirty seconds to swoop in while soldiers reloaded. Instead they were shocked and repelled by steady fire from the Springfield-Allins.

For the next five hours they came in waves, but they never breached the American defenses. Six soldiers were killed, including Captain Powell's second in command, Lieutenant John Jenness. Jenness had been warned to keep low behind cover. He had shouted back, "I know how to fight Indians." Then he rose to fire and was shot through the head. Indian losses were much more severe, Powell claimed: about 60 dead and over 100 wounded. In this case the Army estimates do not appear to be exaggerated. Red Cloud had seen the future, and it was shaped by a Springfield-Allin.

But the U.S. government lacked this foresight. To the Americans the synchronized incidents on the outskirts of two forts ninety miles apart burnished Red Cloud's reputation as the leader of a large hostile force to be reckoned with. That his imposing personality had held together a large intertribal alliance for over two seasons of hard fighting was literally awesome, and his influence showed no signs of abating. His overall leadership, his organizing genius, and his ability to persuade contentious tribes to band together and direct their hatred against the whites had enabled perhaps the most impressive campaign in the annals of Indian warfare. One general ominously informed the War Department that he would need 20,000 soldiers to defeat Red Cloud's forces. This perceived siege of the mighty United States of America was what forced the country to the negotiating table.

The first step took place in October 1867, when Captain Dandy, now the quartermaster at Fort Phil Kearny, held a meeting within sight of the post's bastions with representatives from the Lakota, Arapaho, and Cheyenne. They conveyed Red Cloud's insistence that the Bozeman Trail be closed forever and the three forts built along it abandoned before he would even consider peace. The Army was staggered by Red Cloud's effrontery. But in Washington the Reconstruction of the South and the protection and completion of the Union Pacific were deemed higher priorities than control of the Powder River Country.

It was not until April 1868 that another peace commission arrived at Fort Laramie. Red Cloud would not legitimize the council by his presence and instead sent a message reiterating his original message: begone. A month later the concessions were agreed to. Major General Christopher C. Auger, representing General Sherman on the commission, ordered the Bozeman Trail closed to all emigrants and miners, and issued a proclamation to abandon "the military posts of C. F. Smith, Phil Kearny and Reno, on what is known as the Powder River route."

Still Red Cloud waited. He had heard too many white promises in his lifetime. This time he intended to see the results *before* signing anything. Thus it was with a sense of grim finality that the contents of Fort C. F. Smith were sold to a Montana freighting company, and anything that could be hauled from the two lower outposts was loaded onto wagons bound for Fort Laramie. In the final weeks of August the last train rolled out of Reno Station and Fort Phil Kearny. Whether the departing troops felt anger or relief as they struck the colors from the latter's towering flagpole for the final time is unrecorded. An eerie silence fell over the little plateau between the two Piney Creeks, broken the following dawn when Red Cloud led his warriors down from the hills and burned the forts to the ground.

On November 6, 1868—after making the increasingly nervous white commissioners and Army officers wait until the conclusion of the autumn buffalo hunt—the forty-seven-year-old Bad Face warrior chief rode into Fort Laramie and triumphantly signed the treaty whereby the United States conceded to him and his people the territory from the Bighorns eastward to the Missouri River, and from the forty-sixth parallel south to the Dakota-Nebraska boundary. It was understood, at least by the whites, that the Indians would live in the eastern section and reserve the western section, the Powder River Country, as hunting grounds open to all tribes and bands. In the center of this tract, like a glittering jewel, lay the Black Hills. *Paha Sapa*. The Heart of Everything That Is.

It was the proudest moment of Red Cloud's life. That sentiment lasted a mere twelve months. For the Lakota were not finished dying.

In the fall of 1868, from the far side of the Black Hills, Sitting Bull sent word to both Red Cloud and the American peace commission that he would have nothing to do with, nor would he abide by, any treaty with the United States. Though the concessions Red Cloud was able to wring from the government were "unprecedented in the history of Indian Wars," the Hunkpapas and their dwindling Dakota allies would continue to wage war. Even some of the younger, more militant faction of Red Cloud's own Oglalas, most notably Crazy Horse, would later ride east to join the fight.

Meanwhile, the man whom General Sherman appointed to oversee the High Plains, the Civil War hero General Philip Sheridan, viewed the latest Fort Laramie peace pact as an opportunity. One of its seventeen articles contained a nebulously worded clause requiring the disparate tribes to live, and remain, on specified pieces of land anchored by Bureau of Indian Affairs trading posts. Red Cloud quite naturally interpreted this as referring to the entire Powder River Country, the Black Hills, and the western swath of present-day South Dakota for which he had just fought, and won, a war. If the whites wanted to keep tabs on him, and if the whites offered guns and ammunition, he would be more than happy to resume trading at Fort Laramie.

General Sheridan saw it differently, and began to formulate a long-range plan that would force the Indians, particularly the Lakota, onto reservations well east of the Powder River Country. This would serve the dual purpose of keeping the enemy under observation as well as gradually making him more reliant on government goods and services. Whereas Red Cloud was thinking of weapons, Sheridan was thinking of plows. As part of his strategy Sheridan closed Fort Laramie to Indian trading. The Lakota were told that if they wished to trade, they were free to do business at Fort Randall on the Missouri in distant southeast South Dakota, about as far from *Paha Sapa* as one can travel and still be in the state. To salt the wound, Sheridan placed none other than the retired General

Harney, the presumed "hero" of the fight at Blue Water Creek, in charge
of the post. Red Cloud was insulted and said that he and his people would
have nothing to do with the vicious old "Mad Bear."

With their trading post closed, the Laramie Loafers had no choice but
to relocate to Fort Randall. But Red Cloud and his followers stubbornly
resisted all government efforts to move them closer to the Missouri. And
though Red Cloud stopped short of declaring war, he could not contain
his more militant braves—no Indian chief could do that. Skirmishes
between Army units and Sioux and Cheyenne warriors broke out, particularly on Sitting Bull's Hunkpapa lands on the Upper Missouri and in
the Republican River basin to the south of the Oregon Trail. And though
Red Cloud does not seem to have taken an active part in the fights, at
one point he sent word to the whites that if they refused to reopen Fort
Laramie as an Indian trading post, it should be closed altogether, just as
the Army had abandoned the Upper Powder forts. When the Army ignored this veiled threat, Red Cloud appeared unexpectedly one morning
in March 1869 before Fort Laramie's gates at the head of 1,000 mounted
warriors. It was a political show. Instead of attacking, his party slowly rode
off to hunt in the Wind River country. He did, however, leave lobbyists
behind in the form of mixed-blood traders to argue his cause.

The generals running the U.S. Army could be as headstrong as any Indian warrior chief. When Red Cloud, ever the politician, recognized this,
instead of starting a new war he decided to take his arguments directly to
the top. In June 1870, he and Spotted Tail accepted a long-standing invitation to visit Washington, D.C., and traveled east at the head of a delegation of Oglalas and Brules. There they were given tours of the Capitol and
Army and Navy facilities, with special emphasis on the War Department's
arsenal, where huge coastal cannons and howitzers were lathed and stored.
For the first time Red Cloud saw the true military might of the United
States. Ulysses S. Grant, who had been elected president two years earlier,
gave a reception for him and the others at the White House. There and in
subsequent meetings with government officials the provisions of the treaty
were debated, with the plain-spoken Red Cloud acting as lead negotiator.
"As a consequence," wrote R. Eli Paul, the editor of Red Cloud's memoirs,
"he became stunningly famous. The head-warrior-turned-statesman and

his entourage took the country by storm. Newspapers recounted his every word and deed, and large crowds of onlookers gathered at every public sighting of the celebrated group."

The adulation continued in New York City when the Indian delegation arrived there later in the month. Thousands of people lined Fifth Avenue to catch a glimpse of the celebrated warrior chief who had bested the U.S. Army, and Red Cloud was invited to deliver a speech at the Cooper Institute in Manhattan. In it he reiterated his belief that the treaty he signed protected the territory he had fought for. "No one who listened to Red Cloud's speech yesterday can doubt that he is a man of great talents," wrote the editors of the *New York Times*, describing him as "a man of brains, a good ruler, an eloquent speaker, an able general and a fair diplomat." This did not mean that those in power were prepared to meet his demands.

It was during this journey that Red Cloud, a quick learner, ultimately realized the futility of his aspirations. Though he managed to wrangle minor concessions from the government—a new trading post forty miles north of Fort Laramie was promised, for instance—and he may have considered himself the equal of any white man he encountered on his trip east, he had finally recognized the limitations of the Western Sioux nation as an entity. As he told Secretary of the Interior Joseph P. Cox, "Now we are melting like snow on the hillside, while you are growing like spring grass." Or, as one still militant Lakota warrior put it on his return, "Red Cloud saw too much."

The beginning of the end for Red Cloud's Lakota, and all Plains Indians, had actually arrived one year earlier, in 1869, when the Union Pacific Railroad was completed across southern Wyoming and northern Utah, with a spur line running north to the western Montana goldfields. Once the final spike was driven the old overland trails—the Oregon and the Mormon, the Santa Fe and the Bozeman—were obsolete. And with the railroad arrived an army of buffalo hunters, whose deadly accurate .50-caliber Sharps rifles would soon wipe the prairie clean and do what no battle commander had ever been able to accomplish—drive the starving, destitute Lakota onto the white man's reservations.

On his return from the East, Red Cloud and his Bad Faces continued to roam the Powder River Country, but the end of their lifestyle was as inevitable as the end of the buffalo. Using the last of his dwindling influence, in early 1872 Red Cloud again traveled to Washington and persuaded the government to set aside a rolling swath of land along the White River in northwestern Nebraska as a new "Red Cloud Agency," the first version of which had briefly been located on the North Platte. The site was visually breathtaking, a partially wooded tract marked by high bluffs that overlooked a green, rolling prairie veined with streams and creeks. Red Cloud, who had played his last card, moved there that same year. He was fifty-one. From this new home, he declared, "I shall not go to war any more with whites."

In 1874 gold was discovered in the Black Hills. That *Paha Sapa* had been guaranteed to the tribes was of little consequence to the whites. After the financial Panic of 1873, extracting the gold became a national priority. As usual, Washington concocted a rationalization for violating a treaty and taking Indian land. The Grant administration decided that it would no longer block miners from entering the Black Hills, and that the Lakota and Cheyenne still roaming freely on both sides of the range would have to be forced onto reservations, ostensibly for their own safety. Runners were sent out that winter to inform the Indians of this decision, made over 1,600 miles away. It was little more than political cover. Both sides recognized that no such directives would or could be obeyed, and an American military campaign was already being planned. This suited the cantankerous, hard-drinking General Sheridan.

"Little Phil," who stood barely five feet, five inches, had come out of the Civil War with a reputation for courage, daring, and a propensity to employ the new "scorched earth" battle tactics that were coming into use around the world. To him, and to his equation of good Indians with dead Indians, we owe perhaps our most often quoted line from the decades of Indian wars. Sheridan's main target was Sitting Bull, who was amassing his own intertribal force to defend the territory. For all his hatred of the red man, however, Sheridan, unlike Carrington and so many officers whose thinking was influenced by racial prejudice, did not hesitate to employ Native allies. The Crows, Shoshones, Rees, Pawnee, and Ute, trampled beneath Sioux hegemony for decades, eagerly signed up to fight for the Americans.

When Sitting Bull's agitators approached Red Cloud, he stuck to his promise. Like a surgeon who had grown weary of blood, he saw no point in shedding more of it. Taking to the warpath against the United States, he knew, would lead to a grimly waged campaign of attrition that would wear down the Indians day after insufferable day. The white soldiers who saw no evil in exterminating his people regardless of age or gender would never give them rest, and their territory would shrink until they were boxed in and forced to choose annihilation or surrender.

General George Armstrong Custer's blunder into the large Lakota and Northern Cheyenne camp on the Little Bighorn in June 1876—the Indians called it the Battle of the Greasy Grass, and one that his Crow scouts had warned Custer against—was the Sioux's last hurrah. The shocking slaughter of Custer's entire immediate command intensified the national fervor to eradicate the Northern Plains tribes. Ironically, what the Indians lacked was a strategist on the order of Red Cloud to follow up their great tactical victory at the Little Bighorn. America struck back hard, and the Army's mopping-up operations continued through the spring of 1877, when even Crazy Horse recognized the futility of the fight and turned himself in to soldiers at the Red Cloud Agency. Four months later Crazy Horse was bayoneted to death by a guard at the agency while allegedly trying to escape from so-called protective custody. Controversy still surrounds his death.

With Crazy Horse dead and Sitting Bull a fugitive in Canada, what was left of the hostile tribes became resigned to their fate: on the reservation. Once again, sadly, Red Cloud had been prescient. In 1878 the Red Cloud Agency, Red Cloud along with it, was relocated to southwest South Dakota and renamed the Pine Ridge Reservation.

Few men have the ability to completely deviate from their life's philosophy, particularly in old age. Red Cloud was one of them. His attitude toward the reservation, once the symbol of a caged life unworthy of living, altered once he was established at Pine Ridge. He would adhere to the white man's lifestyle, live in a house, wear a white man's clothes, engage in white people's commercial activities, and send his children to their schools. He had once been a man of a certain place and time; now he was a man of another place and time. His political gifts were numerous and ingrained, and he wielded them to remain the physical and spiritual leader of the Oglalas. Red Cloud had not changed, but he had adapted, and unlike Sitting Bull and Crazy Horse and the others who fought on, he had seen his people's future. He understood that he, and they, had been overcome by historical forces.

Over the decades Red Cloud made several more trips east to plead for better conditions for his people, especially the next generation of Lakota. Unlike his military forays, his political aims were destined to fail, though not for lack of effort. In a remarkable address to President Rutherford B. Hayes on September 26, 1877, he complained about the dry, dusty, infertile soil of the Pine Ridge Reservation and declared, "God made this earth for us and everybody; there is good streams, good lands; and I wish you to take me to a good place to raise my children. The place where I am now was selected with the advice of the Great Father. I also want schools to enable my children to read and write so they will be as wise as the white man's children. I have the same feelings as all the white men have for their families; they love their children, as I do mine, and I would like to raise my children well."

He was also quick to point out that he had not supported Sitting Bull's uprising, shrewdly distancing himself from the Custer massacre. But this sop to the Americans did not sit well with the more militant members of his tribe, and accusations persist to this day that he had a hidden hand in the death of his onetime protégé Crazy Horse. Nonetheless as the years passed Red Cloud remained a respected if increasingly distant figure on the Pine Ridge Reservation. His children had children, and his oldest son, Jack, would succeed him as the tribe's Head Man. (Jack Red Cloud would in turn be succeeded by his son James; his son, Chief Oliver Red Cloud, died at ninety-three on July 4, 2013, 110 years to the day after his great-grandfather stepped down as chief.) Red Cloud and Pretty Owl lived quietly, though from time to time he would still advocate on behalf of the Lakota and protest against intrusions in the Black Hills and conditions on the reservation. His last journey to Washington, D.C., was in 1897.

On July 4, 1903, the eighty-two-year-old Red Cloud, nearly blind, made his final public address to a gathering of Lakota. "My sun is set," he said. "My day is done. Darkness is stealing over me. Before I lie down to rise no more, I will speak to my people. Hear me, my friends, for it is not the time for me to tell you a lie. The Great Spirit made us, the Indians, and gave us this land we live in. He gave us the buffalo, the antelope, and the deer for food and clothing. We moved our hunting grounds from the Minnesota to the Platte and from the Mississippi to the great mountains. No one put bounds on us. We were free as the winds, and like the eagle, heard no man's commands."

The white men had changed all that. They were too numerous and too powerful, and their arrival marked the passing of an era as surely as the disappearance of the buffalo. "Shadows are long and dark before me," Red Cloud concluded. "I shall soon lie down to rise no more. While my spirit is with my body the smoke of my breath shall be towards the Sun, for he knows all things and knows that I am still true to him."

On December 10, 1909, Red Cloud died peacefully in his sleep at the age of eighty-eight. His death prompted headlines around the country. In a lengthy appreciation, the *New York Times* noted, "When Red Cloud fought the whites he did so to the best of his ability. But when he signed the first peace paper he buried his tomahawk and this peace pact was never broken." It was, of course, broken many times—by the U.S. government.

Red Cloud's grave is in a cemetery atop a hill on the Pine Ridge Reservation, a short walk from the Red Cloud Heritage Center. From there, on a clear day, you can almost see the sacred *Paha Sapa*.

A frontier fort was named after William Judd Fetterman. There was no such honor for Henry Beebee Carrington, yet he persevered. In July 1908, for the first time since the Battle of the Hundred-in-the-Hands forty-two years earlier, Carrington returned to the site of the outpost he had painstakingly constructed on the desolate plateau in northwest Wyoming. Only the outline of its foundation remained. The few men and women still living who had occupied Fort Phil Kearny had been invited to mark the Independence Day weekend by visiting the rocky knoll in the Peno Creek Valley where Fetterman had fallen and where a monument was to be erected consecrating the battle. Today the stone marker rises from the yellow sweet clover and the purple Canada thistle only a few yards from a short section of the Bozeman Trail still rutted from wagon wheels; most of the rest of the old trail has been paved over for highways and county roads, plowed under by dryland farmers, or set aside as open grazing land.

On that day in 1908, Carrington, who was eighty-four, wore his blue colonel's uniform and was accompanied by his wife, the former Frances Grummond. Margaret Carrington had died, probably from tuberculosis, in 1870. Her husband was out of uniform by then, having accepted a position as a professor of military science at Wabash College in Indiana. Meanwhile Frances Grummond had returned to her hometown, Franklin, Tennessee, where she buried her husband, George. When she tried to collect her husband's military death benefits she discovered for the first time that George Grummond had another wife. When Frances learned of Margaret's death, she wrote a note of condolence to Henry. The two continued to exchange letters, a romance bloomed, and they were married in 1871.

With Frances at his side Carrington continued to vigorously reject contentions that he bore responsibility for the Fetterman Massacre. His efforts included revisions of the ensuing six editions of Margaret's memoir, *Absaraka: Home of the Crows*, which was published in 1868. When Frances's own book was published in 1910, Fetterman's reputation was further sullied. (Fetterman's good friend William Bisbee, who retired in 1903 as a brigadier general, was one of the few who defended him, in his own book.) Those attending the 1908 reunion were surprised by the vigor of the old soldier as he delivered an extemporaneous, hour-long speech that once more defended his actions of half a lifetime ago. Like Red Cloud's final public utterance, this would be Carrington's last hurrah. The Carringtons returned east, where Frances died in October 1911 at sixty-four. Henry, defiant to the end, died almost a year to the day later in Boston, like Red Cloud at age eighty-eight.

The military historian Peter Maslowski, attending a guest-lecture series at the U.S. Army Command and General Staff College, was puzzled when a general from the Chinese People's Army casually mentioned that the

United States had fought the longest war in history. America had never fought a Thirty Years' War, let alone a Hundred Years' War. What was the visiting general talking about? The answer came with the foreigner's next breath. He explained that he was referring to America's nearly 300-year war against its Indians. Much of the world beyond North America considered it to have begun in the early seventeenth century and to have lasted until the late nineteenth.

"From the perspective of military historians this was a dubious assertion," Maslowski writes in an essay he contributed to the book *Between War and Peace: How America Ends Its Wars*. "Few of them viewed the Euro-Americans' struggle against the indigenous peoples as a single, continuous war of subjugation."

After Maslowski digested the idea, however, what he had at first found "implausible" struck him as more and more valid. "And yet the general had a point: Euro-Americans did wage a protracted war to conquer Indian nations in order to acquire their land and its resources." The proof lies in the figures. In 1866, at the height of Red Cloud's War, fewer than 2 million whites populated the West; twenty-five years later, with a grid of iron rails crisscrossing the prairie, the number had risen to 8.5 million. Today it is 86 million. Yet whether this was one war or many, the fact remains: the great warrior chief Red Cloud was the only Indian ever able to claim victory over the United States.

In the end, despite his proximity to the new settlers and his many journeys across America, Red Cloud may never really have come to comprehend these whites—their motives, their greed, their insatiable desires. If he could read he might have had his answer, although it is still doubtful that he would have understood. Years later, William H. Bisbee attempted to come to grips with an overriding rhetorical question of that bygone era—for what purpose did the United States fight Red Cloud?

"My only answer could be," General Bisbee wrote, "we did it for Civilization."

ACKNOWLEDGMENTS

This book would not have been possible without the courtesy and expertise of curators, researchers, historians, and all those others who staff the centers where so much information—some of it proving quite difficult to unearth—was found and generously shared with us. In particular, we are grateful to the American Antiquarian Society and Jackie Penny; American Heritage Center, University of Wyoming, and Rick Ewig, John Waggener, and Hailey Kaylenne Woodall; American Museum of Natural History and Barry Landua, Kristen Mable, and Mai Reitmeyer; Bozeman Trail Association; Center for Western Studies and Elizabeth Thrond; East Hampton Public Library; Eli Ricker Collection; Fort Phil Kearny State Historic Site and Christopher Morton; John Jermain Memorial Library; Library of Congress and Frederick Plummer and Courtney Pruitt; Montana Historical Society and Rebecca Kohl and Zoe Ann Stoltz; Nebraska State Historical Society and Andrea Faling; Smithsonian Institution and Megan Gambino, Daisy Njoku, and Gina Rappaport; South Dakota Historical Society and Patti Edman; South Dakota State Archives and Matthew Reitzel; Western History Association; The Wyoming Room, Sheridan County Public Library, and Judy Slack; and Wyoming State Archives and Cindy Brown.

We want to give a special mention to the eminent historian Robert Utley, who kindly agreed to review a draft of this manuscript for omissions and any errors in both judgment and fact. His remarks and guidance were, and are, greatly appreciated. He made our book better.

Similarly, we send special thank-yous to Mary Anne Red Cloud and the other members of the Red Cloud family, as well as the residents of the Pine Ridge Indian Reservation and the hardworking staffers at the Red Cloud Heritage Center, for their insights and recollections.

From the beginning of this project we received enthusiastic support from Jofie Ferrari-Adler, Jonathan Karp, Sarah Nalle, and everyone at Simon & Schuster. We are very grateful to them for it. And however many times we thank Nat Sobel and the crack staff at Sobel-Weber Associates, it is never enough—but here is one more thank you anyway.

As with any long and involved writing project, this book benefitted by the authors having the encouragement and support of family and friends. Our gratitude goes to Denise McDonald and Leslie Reingold; Michael Gambino, David Hughes, and Bobby Kelly; and our children, Brendan Clavin, Kathryn Clavin, and Liam-Antoine DeBusschere-Drury.

NOTES AND BIBLIOGRAPHY

The names Sitting Bull and Crazy Horse rank with Smith and Wesson as symbols of adversity and calamity in the old West. Red Cloud may have been more feared than either, but it did not benefit his historical or popular reputation that the majority of his victorious raids, fights, and battles took place against fellow Indians and went, for the most part, unrecorded. Moreover, when Red Cloud did defeat American soldiers—in particular Captain Fetterman's command—in most of these cases none were left alive to testify to his military prowess. So the fact that Red Cloud was credited with an astonishing eighty coups during his fighting career— Sitting Bull claimed forty-five—would probably have been lost to history if not for the re-rediscovery of his little-known autobiography. It allows us to add flesh, bone, and blood to a mythic shadow.

In fact, it is something of a miracle—or more precisely, a series of small miracles—that an autobiography of Red Cloud actually exists. The narrative of the twists and turns the manuscript took before its publication rivals any switchback mountain trail Red Cloud ever rode. It is because of this rare look into the opening of the West from the Sioux point of view that one does not have to guess at heretofore hidden Indian motivations. In this overlooked journal Red Cloud presents his appraisal of daily Indian life, his intimate descriptions of battle tactics and strategies in a succession of intertribal wars, and his brutal account of his time on the prairie.

The story of the "lost memoir" begins in the spring of 1893, when the old trader Sam Deon and the newspaperman Charles Wesley Allen, the newly appointed postmaster for the Pine Ridge Indian Reservation, hatched a plan to bring Red Cloud's life and times to the page. Red Cloud, who was seventy-two, had known Deon for four decades and was related to him by marriage; and the editor Allen, originally from Indiana, had also married a mixed-blood Lakota woman with whom he fathered nine children. This made his presence on the Pine Ridge Reservation more palatable to the Oglala chief.

By the 1890s all three men were living on the "rez," and Deon had fallen into the daily habit of accompanying Red Cloud to the post office to pick up his mail. The two old friends would afterward repair to a bench outside the building, sit in the sun, and swap stories. It occurred to Allen that this was a perfect opportunity to record a swath of history before it disappeared forever, and he prepped Deon with leading questions about Red Cloud's life before the arrival of the whites. The wise warrior chief was reluctant to address his battles against the United States. Despite the passage of nearly three decades, such reminiscences could still get him killed. But he was open about all other aspects of life on the High Plains, and each day after their talks Red Cloud would walk home while Deon relayed the old Head Man's recollections as best he could to Allen, who hand-copied them into a ledger. As the concept of an "as told to" Indian autobiography was still in its developing stages, Allen wrote in the third person. (A translator had published the memoirs of the Sauk chief Black Hawk half a century earlier, but it would be twelve and forty years, respectively, before Geronimo and Black Elk would write best sellers.)

As the summer days of 1893 shortened into autumn, Allen considered the narrative complete enough to publish. But Sitting Bull and Crazy Horse, more recently at the center of the news for the Battle of the Little Bighorn, had eclipsed Red Cloud's fame. There was little interest in the work. A South Dakota literary magazine excerpted portions of "Life of Red Cloud," but book publishers passed it up. After several futile attempts to self-publish the book, Allen swallowed his pride and appealed to a former rival newspaper editor, Addison Sheldon, who had since been elected a Nebraska state legislator. Sheldon, who would soon become the head of the Nebraska State Historical Society, agreed to look at the material. Allen turned it over. The proposed book then vanished.

Apparently Sheldon was initially intent on incorporating Allen's work into a broader biography of Red Cloud. But he never got around to this. The manuscript was stuck in a drawer and forgotten. Then, in 1932, the work was rediscovered and Allen's handwritten narrative was typed up. Allen and Sheldon both died before anything more came of the project, and once again the Red Cloud manuscript—now a 134-page, double-spaced typescript—languished at the Nebraska State Historical Society. There it was unearthed in the 1990s by the historian R. Eli Paul, who added introductory overviews to each of Red Cloud's tales and eventually published an annotated version. The manuscript is recognized by scholars of the American West as a significant historical document containing details about Sioux life, in particular that of the tribe's greatest warrior chief, never before known. Its reappearance is better late than never.

Similarly, we are also grateful to the late-in-life decision by the descendants of Crazy Horse to speak publicly about their famous forefather's life in general, and in particular his role in the Fetterman Massacre. Previously published accounts of the event by respected historians and authors such as John D. McDermott, George Hyde, and Shannon Smith place Crazy Horse at the scene in the position of the lead decoy who set the battle events in motion.

On a trip to the site of the fight in northeast Wyoming, we were fortunate to meet with Christopher Morton, a National Parks Department historian who is also on the board of the Fort Phil Kearny National Historical Site. Morton directed us to the little-known DVD titled *The Autobiography of Crazy Horse and His Family*, which contains interviews with Floyd Clowe Crazy Horse, Don Red Thunder Crazy Horse, and Doug War Eagle Crazy Horse, the grandsons of Crazy Horse's half-sister, Iron Cedar. Moreover, Morton recalled, only months earlier the three men had visited with Morton at the battle site. When they reached Lodge Trail Ridge they all described how their grand-uncle—whom they referred to as "Grandfather"—finally lured Fetterman over the ridge by mooning him. While some academics might not consider this information sufficiently scholarly, we think it would be wrong to discount, or disrespect, the strong oral history tradition of the Crazy Horse family.

It is said that history is fable agreed on. And Henry Beebee Carrington, who outlived William Judd Fetterman by forty-six years, certainly worked hard to gain agreement for his side of the story. The primary conduit for his public relations campaign was the memoir by his first wife, Margaret, who published *Absaraka: Home of the Crows* in 1868. For years the book was a bible for historians and western writers chronicling Red Cloud's War. In quite a few passages a reader detects not only the hidden hand of her husband, Henry, but perhaps also that of Captain Tenedor Ten Eyck. The Carringtons were friends of Ten Eyck, who had little use for his contemporary officers Fetterman, George Grummond, and Frederick Brown. Many of Mrs. Carrington's anecdotes—Quartermaster Brown vowing to personally take Red Cloud's scalp, for instance—would logically seem to have come from a "source" aside from her husband and outside her small social circle at Fort Phil Kearny. Ten Eyck, who quit the Army after being accused of dereliction of duty and cowardice by fellow officers for his delay in reaching the Fetterman battlefield and who spent his final years in an alcoholic haze, is a very likely candidate. Further, throughout her book Mrs. Carrington stresses, contra much evidence, Fetterman's impatience to "summarily" punish Indians. "He permitted this feeling and contempt of the enemy to drive him to hopeless ruin," she writes, "where a simple deference to the orders and known policy of the commander"—who just happened to be her husband—"would have brought no loss of life whatever."

Whatever Margaret Carrington's motives—and it is fairly obvious that she was essentially deflecting criticism away from Henry Carrington—the smear campaign worked. The influential writer Dee Brown, for one, is squarely in Colonel Carrington's corner. In his book *The Fetterman Massacre,* he lumped Mrs. Carrington's gossip and hearsay together in a litany of "reckless boasts" that she (or her husband, or Ten Eyck) allegedly overheard being made by Carrington's junior officers. "A single company of regulars could whip a thousand Indians" is one example. "A full regiment would whip the entire array of hostile tribes" is another.

Brown concluded the list with Fetterman's famous, if dubious, declaration that "with eighty men I could ride through the whole Sioux nation." It is hard to believe that an author as judicious as Brown was unaware that grandiosity and boastfulness were fairly common personal traits among the United States' aristocratic nineteenth-century officer corps. Yet his conclusion belies this fact. "This was the beginning of a schism between Carrington and his officers which would grow deeper and more dangerous with each passing week," he wrote.

Only in recent years, thanks to the efforts of scholars including Shannon Smith and John Monnett, has a more accurate and balanced view of Fetterman been presented, overturning the familiar portrait of the arrogant fire-eater contemptuous of the Indians' fighting ability. Monnett notes that Fetterman's bravura statement about riding through the entire Sioux nation with eighty men—conveniently, the exact number of soldiers who died with him—did not appear in Margaret Carrington's memoir, or anywhere in print, until 1904, "38 years after it was allegedly uttered." And even if Fetterman had made such a boast, Monnett contends, in this "golden age of windbags," particularly those who had yet to encounter Indians in battle, it was quite natural for Civil War veterans to engage in what he calls "parlor bluster."

Moreover, given the racial attitudes of the era, few of Fetterman's contemporary detractors bothered to factor Red Cloud into their equations. The idea that a mere savage could have outsmarted and outfought an officer of the U.S. Army was too great a leap. Thus biased authors such as Margaret Carrington and, later, Frances Grummond Carrington in *My Army Life and the Fort Phil Kearny Massacre* attempt to pin responsibility solely on Fetterman. Luckily, for them, Red Cloud could not read.

Finally, a personal note about the delightful habit of nineteenth-century letter-writing and journal-keeping as well as our methodology in using such research materials: it was not just the Army officers, their wives, and the upper classes of the 1800s who remarked incessantly upon the vicissitudes of life on the prairie with evocative diary entries. In our previous book collaborations, writing about conflicts from World War II to Vietnam, we had the good fortune to supplement our research with interviews with the men, and sometimes women, who had lived through the events we chronicled.

In this case, we were astounded by the detailed journals and diaries kept, it almost seemed to us, by every other teamster's wife and preserved across the West by university libraries and state historical societies. In some cases we were not even allowed to physically handle these frayed and fragile journals; instead they were presented to us by friendly librarians and state historians in Plexiglas cases, and we could only turn the pages with tong-like implements lest the oil from a human hand further degrade them.

With this plethora of research—the entire narrative, in essence, constructed of information found in books, letters, journal and diary entries, and contemporaneous newspaper and magazine accounts—we found that nearly every sentence of the book could have been sourced. Since we are primarily interested in telling a good yarn, however, and did not want cumbersome sourcing to get in the way of the story, we decided to use "trailing phrases" rather than footnoted numbers in the text, and to list specific sources only when we quote from a letter, journal, or another author, or took his or her words as an indisputable "fact." Anything that is not cited specifically in the Notes comes from the sources listed in the Selected Bibliography that follows the Notes. That said, as always the responsibility for any inaccuracies herein is ours and ours alone.

NOTES

Prologue: Paha Sapa

PAGE

2   *Company C was nominally:* Monnett, *Where a Hundred Soldiers Were Killed*, p. 96.

4   *"this dangerous snake":* Red Cloud, speech to government treaty negotiators at Fort Laramie, June 1865.

4   *"The White Man lies":* Ibid.

4   *"Noble Savages":* Billington, *Land of Savagery, Land of Promise*, p. 129.

5   *"They will make many a poor white man":* Letter from Frank Elliott to his father, May 1867, Frank Elliott Papers.

6   *"Imagine: soldiers who had recently outfought":* Christopher Morton interview.

7   *"a strategic chief":* Hebard and Brininstool, *The Bozeman Trail*, Vol. 2, p. 121.

7   *Sioux braves slithering:* F. Carrington, *My Army Life and the Fort Phil Kearny Massacre*, p. 214.

7 *"Scarcely a day or night passes":* Letter written by Henry Beebee Carrington, July 30, 1866, Henry B. Carrington Papers.

9 *"Indian warfare in the Powder River Country":* National Archives and Records Administration, letter written by General Philip St. George Cooke.

10 *"We are not going to let":* Papers of General William T. Sherman, University of Notre Dame.

10 *"Where you have been, General":* Ibid.

14 *He had been cited for his leadership:* U.S. War Department, *The War of the Rebellion,* Official Records, Ser. 1, Vol. 38, Part 1, 94, 527, 586–88.

14 *"Few came [to Fort Phil Kearny] from Omaha":* Indian Hostilities, Executive Document No. 33, 1.

15 *"an arrogant fool":* Smith, *Give Me Eighty Men,* p. 198.

Part I: The Prairie

Chapter One: First Contact

PAGE

20 *"The fisheries are spoken of":* Parkman, *The Oregon Trail,* pp. 108–9.

21 *"totally out of their element":* Ibid., p. 103.

21 *In 1850 alone an estimated 55,000 California-bound:* Hafen and Young, *Fort Laramie and the Pageant of the West,* p. 164.

22 *A conservative estimate of trailside deaths:* Mattes, "Platte River Narratives," p. 3.

23 *Called "Broken Hand" by nearly all the tribes: Jefferson* (Missouri) *Inquirer,* December 25, 1847.

23 *Among the Lakota bands:* Ambrose, *Crazy Horse and Custer,* p. 17.

24 *also present was the eleven-year-old:* Bray, *Crazy Horse,* p. 80.

24 *His formal name was:* Ibid., p. 2.

24 *On the whole he projected:* Franklin Welles Calkins, *Weekly Review* 3, No. 14 (1905).

25 *And though he had yet to do battle:* Parker, "Journal of an Exploring Tour," p. 99.

25 *He undoubtedly observed:* Marshall, *The Journey of Crazy Horse,* p. 35.

26 *"very graphic and descriptive":* Hafen and Young, p. 177.

27 *"My chief would'er killed him":* Lowe, "Five Years a Dragoon," pp. 79–81.

27 *"while braves and boys dashed about":* Hafen and Young, p. 183.

28 *Reported a correspondent for the* Missouri Republican*:* Ibid., p. 182.

28 *There were perhaps 2 million wild mustangs:* Dobie, *The Mustangs,* pp. 108–09.

28 *"Each nation approached":* Correspondence of B. G. Brown, American Heritage Center, University of Wyoming.

30 *Even the men—and they were:* Paul, *Autobiography of Red Cloud,* p. 147.

31 *More than a week was spent:* T. Powers, *The Killing of Crazy Horse,* p. 112.

31   *And the famous Belgian Jesuit priest:* Hafen and Young, p. 192.

31   *"spout bits of Christian doctrine":* Robinson, "The Education of Red Cloud," p. 162.

31   *"No epoch in Indian annals":* Ibid., p. 194.

32   *"I would be glad if the whites would pick":* Hafen and Young, p. 190.

33   *"lasting peace on the Plains forevermore":* Algier, *The Crow and the Eagle,* p. 136.

Chapter Two: Guns and Badlands
PAGE

36   *Later, when he handed the scalp:* Hassrick, *The Sioux,* p. 99.

37   *The Sioux referred to themselves:* W. K. Powers, *Oglala Religion,* pp. 3–16.

38   *The Scottish explorer Alexander Mackenzie:* Alexander Mackenzie, *Journals: Exploring Across Canada in 1789 and 1793,* p. 89.

39   *the pioneering Brules and Oglalas:* Hyde, *Red Cloud's Folk,* p. 8.

40   *Nearly every tribe called itself "The People":* Moten, *Between War and Peace,* p. 135.

44   *Three great epidemics:* Hyde, *Red Cloud's Folk,* p. 17.

48   *The Indians would merely cut:* Calkins, *Weekly Review.*

48   *they mocked their Brule cousins:* Hyde, *Red Cloud's Folk,* p. 22.

Chapter Three: The Black Hills and Beyond
PAGE

50   *"And do you know why":* Author visit to Pine Ridge Reservation, August 2011.

50   *Thus it seems to "exhale":* Ostler, *The Lakotas and the Black Hills,* p. 4.

51   *Sensing a captive and untapped market:* Cohen, *Conquered into Liberty,* p. 26.

51   *Succeeding iterations grew:* Black Hills Visitors Center.

52   *the fleet Spanish mustang traced its lineage:* Hispanic American Historical Review 23 (November 1943).

52   *Within two decades:* Gwynne, *Empire of the Summer Moon,* p. 29.

53   *Describing a buffalo hunt, Coronado wrote:* The Journey of Coronado, pp. 111–12.

54   *Once New Mexico was cleared:* Humanities 23, No. 6 (November–December 2002).

54   *"Great Horse Dispersal":* Fehrenbach, *Comanches,* p. 87.

54   *They were the first tribe to perfect:* Gwynne, pp. 28–36.

55   *"arrogance born of successful conquest":* Hassrick, *The Sioux,* p. 71.

55   *and by 1803 had cleared the Kiowa:* Hyde, *Red Cloud's Folk,* p. 23.

56   *In recognition of the horse's transformation:* Paul, *Autobiography of Red Cloud,* p. 122.

56 *In other words, the arrival: The Works of Hubert Howe Bancroft*, Vol. 1, p. 595.

56 *"a reclining female figure":* Brown, *Bury My Heart at Wounded Knee*, p. 4.

57 *Yet the Lakotas seemed to tolerate:* Larson, *Red Cloud*, p. 21.

57 *Although thoroughly outgunned:* Denig, *Five Indian Tribes of the Upper Missouri*, p. 145.

58 *Contemporaneous accounts, however:* Ibid., p. 155.

59 *Following a parley:* Hyde, p. 29.

60 *At this time the Northern Plains:* Larson, p. 25.

Chapter Four: "Red Cloud Comes!"
PAGE

61 *This was probably an undercount:* Larson, *Red Cloud*, p. 23.

63 *"the future residence of these people":* La Vere, *Contrary Neighbors*, p. 55.

63 *Red Cloud may have witnessed his father:* Robinson, "The Education of Red Cloud," p. 158.

63 *Red Cloud abhorred:* Paul, *Autobiography of Red Cloud*, p. 156.

63 *He recognized her as a "sister":* Robinson, p. 156.

64 *"unusually headstrong impulses":* Larson, p. 36.

67 *Young males were continually showered:* Ambrose, *Crazy Horse and Custer*, p. 15.

68 *This ensured that each male:* Hassrick, *The Sioux*, p. 319.

69 *Its owner would train it:* Walker, *Lakota Society*, p. 80.

69 *"They could hit a button":* Brown, *The Fetterman Massacre*, p. 45.

71 *This philosophy of security:* Paul, p. 24.

71 *"When I was young":* New York Times, June 11, 1870.

72 *"Red Cloud comes!":* Paul, p. 35.

Chapter Five: Counting Coup
PAGE

77 *Red Cloud, true to his word:* Paul, *Autobiography of Red Cloud*, p. 103.

77 *Some whites who observed:* Hassrick, *The Sioux*, p. 294.

78 *As medicine men uttered prayers:* Ewers, *Indian Life on the Upper Missouri*, pp. 152–53.

Chapter Six: "Print the Legend"
PAGE

84 *"Do you see that high blue ridge":* Paul, *Autobiography of Red Cloud*, p. 58.

87 *The Indians were not sticklers:* Ibid., p. 64.

89 *"You are the cause of this":* Ibid., p. 69.

Part II: The Invasion
Chapter Seven: Old Gabe
PAGE

93 *A charcoal-hued pictograph:* Hassrick, *The Sioux*, p. 349.

93 *The Indians, equally cynical:* W. K. Powers, *Oglala Religion*, p. 99.

94 *as many as 400 million beavers:* Ferry, "Leave It to Beavers," p. 24.

97 *"rough and violent":* Hafen, *Mountain Men and Fur Traders of the Far West*, p. 255.

97 *"that one would back water":* Spring, *Caspar Collins*, p. 148.

97 *He wore his mop of long brown hair:* Dodge, "Biographical Sketch of Jim Bridger," pp. 5–6.

98 *They had the scalp of a Blackfoot:* Hafen and Young, *Fort Laramie and the Pageant of the West*, pp. 54–56.

98 *By this time Bridger was a legend:* Parkman, *The Oregon Trail*, p. 103.

98 *"extracted an iron arrow":* Parker, "Journal of an Exploring Tour Beyond the Rocky Mountains," pp. 80–81.

99 *Meanwhile Fitzpatrick and his men:* Bonner, *The Life and Adventures of James P. Beckwourth*, pp. 60–61.

100 *According to the well-traveled:* Father De Smet: *Life, Letters and Travels of Father Pierre-Jean De Smet*, pp. 210–13.

100 *"promises fairly":* Hafen, p. 261.

101 *"with one third of the continent":* *American Spectator*, March 15, 2004.

Chapter Eight: The Glory Road
PAGE

103 *made famous by Kit Carson:* Sides, *Blood and* Thunder, p. 1.

103 *So great was their thirst:* Hyde, *Red Cloud's Folk*, p. 61.

104 *"The ax, pick, saw, and trowel":* *New York Times*, November 11, 2010 (op-ed).

105 *When the soldiers:* U.S. Department of the Interior, Fort Laramie Historic Site.

105 *From 1849 to 1851:* Ibid.

106 *The whites refused and stood by:* Dary, *The Oregon Trail*, p. 146.

106 *The sullen "savages":* Hafen, *Mountain Men and Fur Traders*, p. 247.

107 *names such as McQuiery:* Wagon Box Fight Historic Site.

Chapter Nine: Pretty Owl and Pine Leaf
PAGE

108 *Red Cloud's "unexcelled":* Hassrick, *The Sioux*, 14.

110 *He looked over the ponies casually:* Paul, *Autobiography of Red Cloud*, p. 80.

110 *"You are mine":* Parkman, *The Oregon Trail*, p. 90.

110 *The two retired to their lodge:* Paul, p. 82.

111 *Red Cloud fathered five children:* Larson, *Red Cloud*, p. 43.

119 *But many other Sioux bands were decimated:* Dary, *The Oregon Trail*, p. 245.

119 *On one of his surveying expeditions:* Larson, p. 63.

120 *Red Cloud is reported:* Hyde, *Red Cloud's Folk*, p. 64.

121 *"ugly as Macbeth's witches":* Parkman, p. 90.

121 *"The whites had one truth":* Marshall, *The Journey of Crazy Horse*, p. 63.

121 *He knew well that aside:* Ambrose, *Crazy Horse and Custer*, p. 55.

Chapter Ten: A Blood-Tinged Season

PAGE

122 *All were awaiting delivery:* Hyde, *Red Cloud's Folk*, p. 70.

123 *"quarrelsome and predatory" factions:* Denig, *Five Indian Tribes of the Upper Missouri*, p. 24.

123 *"The Indians no more look smiling":* Hyde, p. 71.

123 *"most terrible butcheries":* J. B. Weston, testimony to the Sanborn Commission, 1867.

124 *One of the soldiers who fell:* "Disunion," *New York Times*, April 2, 2012.

124 *He became a constant drinking partner:* Hyde, p. 72.

126 *A provision of the Horse Creek Treaty:* Ibid., p. 73.

127 *He eyed the clusters:* Paul, *Autobiography of Red Cloud*, p. 4.

127 *Still, on nearing the Miniconjou camp:* Hyde, p. 74.

128 *He later died from his wounds:* Council Bluffs Bugle, p. 1.

128 *The rest were engulfed:* Bray, *Crazy Horse*, p. 32.

128 *Odds are Red Cloud killed:* Robinson, "Education of Red Cloud," p. 164.

128 *One of them was the fair-skinned:* Ambrose, *Crazy Horse and Custer*, p. 65.

129 *"calling him a squaw":* Council Bluffs Bugle.

130 *The raiders were led by a half-Brule:* Hyde, p. 77.

130 *clean out the "savage" menace:* Ostler, *The Lakotas and the Black Hills*, p. 44.

Chapter Eleven: A Lone Stranger

PAGE

132 *to serve as an "altar":* Paul, *Autobiography of Red Cloud*, p. 109.

134 *During the melee:* Hafen and Young, *Fort Laramie and the Pageant of the West*, pp. 238–39.

135 *He himself had escaped:* Bliss letter, Briscoe Center for American History.

135 *The resultant embarrassment:* Ibid.

135 *Twiss's first official proclamation:* Hyde, *Red Cloud's Folk*, p. 78.

136 *His final instructions to his men:* Adams, *General William S. Harney*, p. 118.

137 *"the heart-rending sight—":* Wyomingtalesandtrails.com.

137 *The soldiers, bent on revenge:* Ambrose, *Crazy Horse and Custer*, p. 73.

137 *When the abandoned Indian campsite:* Utley, *Frontiersmen in Blue*, p. 117.

137 *a popular Army marching song:* Hyde, p. 80.

138 *"shared out among the soldiers":* W. K. Powers, *Oglala Religion*, p. 100.

138 *He stated that when he moved:* Hyde, p. 79.

139 *As word of Harney's testimony:* Larson, *Red Cloud*, p. 69.

139 *"They are split into different factions":* Denig, *Five Indian Tribes of the Upper Missouri*, p. 22.

140 *Gradually the dark speck:* Johnson and Smith, *Tribes of the Sioux Nation*, p. 43.

Chapter Twelve: Samuel Colt's Invention

PAGE

142 *By some estimates as many as 10,000:* Ostler, *The Lakotas and the Black Hills*, p. 60.

146 *Soon enough, in mid-July:* Utley, *Frontiersmen in Blue*, p. 122.

148 *"Thus," writes the Sioux historian:* Larson, *Red Cloud*, p. 75.

Chapter Thirteen: A Brief Respite

PAGE

149 *White settlers had converted:* Hyde, *Red Cloud's Folk*, p. 83.

150 *No longer could he afford:* Paul, *Autobiography of Red Cloud*, p. 141.

152 *The area around Pikes Peak:* Ostler, *The Lakotas and the Black Hills*, p. 48.

152 *by 1860 the newly formed Pony Express:* Hafen and Young, *Fort Laramie and the Pageant of the West*, p. 270.

152 *The buffalo had disappeared:* Price, *The Oglala People, 1841–1879*, p. 30.

152 *"a swath of stinking refuge":* Ibid.

152 *As late as 1852 Jim Bridger had been sighted:* Alter, *Jim Bridger*, p. 262.

153 *"Old Gabe" was tried:* Ibid., p. 263.

154 *Marcy recorded that among:* Ibid.

154 *It took six wagons:* Algier, *The Crow and the Eagle*, p. 132.

154 *Though greenhorn Army officers:* Robinson, "The Education of Red Cloud," p. 165.

Chapter Fourteen: The Dakotas Rise

PAGE

156 *"the frontier army suddenly ceased":* Utley, *Frontiersmen in Blue*, pp. 212–13.

156 *Even the detachment at Fort Laramie:* Hafen and Young, *Fort Laramie and the Pageant of the West*, p. 303.

158 *In addition, the Dakotas agreed:* Monnett, *Where a Hundred Soldiers Were Killed*, p. 6.

159 *the advocacy of a local Episcopal bishop:* Carley, *The Dakota War of 1862*, p. 4.

159 *"inefficiency and fraud":* Price, *The Oglala People, 1841–1879*, p. 51.

159 *A merchant named Andrew Myrick:* Carley, p. 6.

160 *Also at the Baker homestead:* Anderson and Woolworth, *Through Dakota Eyes*, p. 36.

160 *"The white men are like locusts":* Ibid.

161 *The Dakotas claimed they were promised:* Ibid.

162 *His tanned scalp, skull, and wrist bones:* Brown, *The American West*, p. 83.

162 *A short, wiry man:* Paul, *Autobiography of Red Cloud*, p. 13.

162 *The ruddy-faced Deon:* St. Paul (Minnesota) *Press*, January 4, 1863.

163 *Red Cloud was fresh from:* Monnett, p. 6.

165 *"The Lost Children":* Paul, *The Autobiography of Red Cloud*, p. 165.

166 *the Indians' "lifeless bodies":* St. Paul (Minn.) *Press*, January 4, 1863.

166 *It was the largest mass execution:* Ibid.

Part III: The Resistance

Chapter Fifteen: Strong Hearts

PAGE

170 *The last anyone saw:* Hyde, *Red Cloud's Folk*, p. 125.

170 *"I am not a coward":* Soule, *Wild West* Magazine, December 1996.

171 *Bears Ribs's 250 ragged followers:* Price, *The Oglala People, 1841–1879*, p. 49.

173 *One relief party of troops:* Hafen and Young, *Fort Laramie and the Pageant of the West*, p. 336.

173 *"We know Crazy Horse better":* Bray, *Crazy Horse*, p. 72.

174 *His fellow fighters were also struck:* Ambrose, *Crazy Horse and Custer*, p. 134.

174 *"[He] was good for nothing":* Bray, p. 84.

175 *"gave permission for the women":* Hyde, *Red Cloud's Folk*, p. 115.

Chapter Sixteen: An Army in Shambles

PAGE

176 *when he applied in 1853:* Smith, *Give Me Eighty Men*, p. 19.

177 *"refinement, gentlemanly manners":* M. Carrington, *Absaraka*, p. 244.

177 *despite suffering more casualties:* McDermott, *Portraits of Fort Phil Kearny*, p. 81.

178 *"courageous," "daring," and "relentless":* Ibid.

178 *"great gallantry and spirit":* Ibid.

178 *"Captain Fetterman's command marched":* Ibid.

178 *"defence agst. foreign danger":* Madison, *Notes of the Debates of the Federal Convention, 1787*.

179   *The Founders instead envisioned:* Ibid.

179   *"became a major focus":* Dominic Tierney, *New York Times*, November 11, 2010.

179   *"Were armies to be raised":* Jefferson, Sixth Annual Message to Congress.

179   *"Winnibigoshish Sioux":* Hyde, *Red Cloud's Folk*, p. 103.

180   *The transformation was hastened:* McGinniss, *Counting Coups and Cutting Horses*, p. 101.

180   *One unintended consequence:* Alter, *Jim Bridger*, p. 311.

181   *"The boy hit one of the scamps":* Ibid, p. 299.

181   *One of Lieutenant Collins's letters:* Spring, *Caspar Collins*, p. 124.

181   *The interpreter introduced:* Bray, *Crazy Horse*, p. 74.

181   *"You are going into our country":* Johnson, *The Bloody Bozeman*, p. 63.

Chapter Seventeen: Blood on the Ice

PAGE

183   *"A cold wind blew":* Geist, *Buffalo Nation*, p. 101.

185   *The most serious of these involved:* Bray, *Crazy Horse*, p. 46.

185   *The raids continued throughout:* Ibid., p. 74.

185   *Dog Soldiers ambushed the troop:* Grinnell, *The Fighting Cheyennes*, pp. 134–36.

186   *"Mr. Chivington was not as steady":* Haynes, *History of the Methodist Episcopal Church in Omaha and Suburbs*, p. 44.

186   *One exhibition included:* Hafen and Young, *Fort Laramie and the Pageant of the West*, p. 319.

186   *The* Rocky Mountain News *called:* Ibid., p. 324.

187   *The governor also issued:* Report of the Committee on the Conduct of the War on the Massacre of Cheyenne Indians, U.S. House of Representatives, January 10, 1865.

187   *Colonel Chivington eagerly answered:* Sides, *Blood and Thunder*, p. 369.

187   *There, these volunteers would strike:* Ibid., p. 374.

187   *"should they repair at once":* Report of the Committee on the Conduct of the War.

189   *Infants and children were butchered:* Sides, p. 470.

189   *"Such, it is to be hoped":* Ibid.

Chapter Eighteen: The Great Escape

PAGE

190   *A place of honor:* Ostler, *The Lakotas and the Black Hills*, p. 50.

191   *Over the next month:* Larson, *Red Cloud*, p. 82.

191   *Although Colonel Chivington had resigned:* Ibid., p. 81.

192   *In the meantime the southern tribes:* Encyclopedia of Indian Wars, p. 165.

193 *James Regan described watching three Lakotas:* Wyomingtalesandtrails.com.

195 *The northerners gathered goggle-eyed:* Ambrose, *Crazy House and Custer*, p. 146.

196 *Crazy Horse in particular was reported:* Bray, *Crazy Horse*, p. 84.

196 *Although each tribe kept its own laws:* Matthiessen, *In the Spirit of Crazy Horse*, p. 94.

197 *"The Great Spirit raised":* U.S. Commission of Indian Affairs 1871 Report, p. 439.

198 *A few nights later Crazy Horse:* Ambrose, p. 157.

199 *Moonlight vowed never again to enter:* Encyclopedia of Indian Wars, p. 177.

Chapter Nineteen: Bloody Bridge Station

PAGE

201 *There were even reports:* Ambrose, *Crazy House and Custer*, p. 147.

201 *"I never saw so many men":* Spring, *Caspar Collins*, p. 115.

201 *Connor spotted Collins apparently idling:* Monnett, *Where a Hundred Soldiers Were Killed*, p. 2.

201 *"Are you a coward?":* Soule, *Wild West* Magazine, December 1996.

202 *But, taking a lesson:* Bray, *Crazy Horse*, p. 79.

202 *The Cheyenne recruited:* Hyde, *Red Cloud's Folk*, p. 124.

202 *Earlier that morning:* Soule, *Wild West* Magazine, December 1996.

203 *"to remember him by":* Ibid.

203 *The unwieldly carbines:* Utley, *Frontiersmen in Blue*, p. 320.

205 *"seeming to spring":* Ibid.

Chapter Twenty: The Hunt for Red Cloud

PAGE

208 *In June 1865, he issued:* Monnett, *Where a Hundred Soldiers Were Killed*, p. 9.

208 *By the time Sully arrived:* Utley, *Frontiersmen in Blue*, p. 322.

209 *The Arapaho, however, surprised him:* Matthiessen, *In the Spirit of Crazy Horse*, p. 108.

210 *"Blanket" was his Arapaho nickname:* Ibid., p. 109.

210 *Although Connor captured a third:* Ibid.

210 *Some of the braves wore:* Ibid., p. 104.

Chapter Twenty-One: Burn the Bodies; Eat the Horses

PAGE

214 *Through four days and nights:* Matthiessen, *In the Spirit of Crazy Horse*, p. 112.

217 *The Indians slipped away:* Hyde, *Red Cloud's Folk*, p. 132.

218 *"would lead to dreadful consequences":* Alter, *Jim Bridger*, p. 310.

218 *Further, the general found:* Ibid., p. 313.

219 *"I cannot say as we killed one":* Utley, *Frontiersmen in Blue*, p. 332.

219 *a line of "tramps":* Hyde, p. 133.

219 *"seldom before equaled":* Utley, p. 332.

Part IV: The War

Chapter Twenty-Two: War Is Peace

PAGE

221 *Memory is like riding a trail:* Marshall, *The Journey of Crazy Horse*, p. 57 (Part IV epigram).

224 *He had also gained:* Smith, *Give Me Eighty Men*, p. 20.

225 *"two feet of snow":* M. Carrington, *Absaraka*, p. 37.

225 *study the "Indian Problem":* Gwynne, *Empire of the Summer Moon*, p. 223.

225 *Sand Creek was a favorite:* Utley, *Frontiersmen in Blue*, p. 309.

226 *"It is time that the authorities":* Ibid., p. 313.

227 *Indian agents sent runners:* Price, *The Oglala People, 1841–1879*, p. 59.

227 *"was rather like looking":* Moten, *Between War and Peace*, p. 143.

228 *"an explicit understanding":* Army and Navy Journal and Gazette of the Regular and Volunteer Forces, April 1864.

230 *"All I ask is comparative quiet":* Ambrose, *Crazy Horse and Custer*, p. 228.

232 *These included hay mowers:* Brown, *The Fetterman Massacre*, p. 21.

232 *"commissary and quartermaster supplies:* Colonel Henry Carrington testimony, 1867 hearings, U.S. Senate, p. 2.

232 *"a domestic cast":* Brown, *The Fetterman Massacre*, p. 21.

Chapter Twenty-Three: Big Bellies and Shirt Wearers

PAGE

233 *It called for seven veteran chiefs:* Ambrose, *Crazy Horse and Custer*, p. 135.

233 *On the banks of an unnamed creek:* Bray, *Crazy Horse*, p. 93.

234 *Among these were Young-Man:* Ambrose, p. 136.

234 *His ethereal quality:* Bray, *Crazy Horse*, p. 72.

234 *"hardly every looked straight":* Ibid.

235 *"If white men come":* Matthiessen, *In the Spirit of Crazy Horse*, p. 115.

236 *In her classic book:* Johnson, *The Bloody Bozeman*, pp. 3–4.

236 *"He was a farmer":* Ibid.

238 *"We thought it an impossibility":* Brown, *The Fetterman Massacre*, p. 15.

238 *"and the majority actually made":* M. Carrington, *Absaraka*, p. 37.

239 *He charmed the officers' wives:* Smith, *Give Me Eighty Men*, p. 25.

239 *But when Sherman met with Carrington:* Brown, *The Fetterman Massacre*, p. 24.

239 *If Sherman felt:* Smith, p. 25.

Chapter Twenty-Four: Colonel Carrington's Circus

PAGE

240 *Someone dubbed the long train:* Brown, *The Fetterman Massacre*, p. 25.

241 *It passed cool, clear streams:* M. Carrington, *Absaraka*, p. 71.

241 *"We had no occasion":* Bisbee, *Through Four American Wars*, p. 162.

242 *"Fighting men in that country":* Indian Hostilities, Senate Executive Document No. 33, pp. 3–4.

242 *"in assorted sizes":* Bisbee, p. 166.

243 *The latter two:* Larson, *Red Cloud*, p. 90.

244 *"In two moons the command":* Indian Hostilities, p. 18.

244 *The threat was followed:* Brown, *The Fetterman Massacre*, p. 43.

244 *"The Great Father sends us presents":* Brown, *The American West*, p. 85.

245 *Carrington tried to answer:* Monnett, *Where a Hundred Soldiers Were Killed*, p. 27.

245 *Later that day the commanding officer:* F. Carrington, *My Army Life*, pp. 124–25.

245 *Red Cloud, he said:* Ibid.

246 *Red Cloud, observed Margaret Carrington:* M. Carrington, *Absaraka*, p. 79.

Chapter Twenty-Five: Here Be Monsters

PAGE

247 *"a disgusting farce":* Special Commission Investigating the Fort Philip Kearny Massacre, July 29, 1867.

247 *Satisfactory treaty concluded:* Ambrose, *Crazy Horse and Custer*, p. 229.

248 *"They follow ye always":* M. Carrington, *Absaraka*, p. 83.

248 *When Carrington asked Mills:* Brown, *The Fetterman Massacre*, p. 50.

249 *"was lumbering around":* Ambrose, p. 291.

250 *A blinding summer hailstorm:* Brown, *The Fetterman Massacre*, p. 57.

250 *"We'll never see an Indian":* M. Carrington, p. 95.

250 *"constant separation and scattering":* Brown, *The Fetterman Massacre*, p. 60.

251 *The words were barely:* Ibid., p. 58.

Chapter Twenty-Six: The Perfect Fort

PAGE

253 *"was like the quick turn":* M. Carrington, *Absaraka*, p. 26.

254 *"At last we had the prospect":* Ibid., p. 67.

256 *The Indians professed amity:* Bisbee, *Through Four American Wars*, p. 168.

259 *"The White Man lies":* Ibid.

Chapter Twenty-Seven: "Mercifully Kill All the Wounded"

PAGE

261 *One private noted in his journal:* Brown, *The Fetterman Massacre*, p. 78.

262 *His eight infantry companies:* Fort Phil Kearny plaque, Wyoming Historical Society.

264 *"He said that he had a presentiment":* F. Carrington, *My Army Life and the Fort Phil Kearny Massacre*, p. 74.

267 *"Our condition was now becoming":* Hebard and Brininstool, *The Bozeman Trail*, p. 91.

268 *"I am a friend":* F. Carrington, p. 80.

Chapter Twenty-Eight: Roughing It

PAGE

272 *"Character of Indian affairs hostile":* Indian Hostilities, Executive Document No. 33, pp. 12–13.

272 *"I must do all this":* Ibid.

274 *"a strategic chief":* Hebard and Brininstool, *The Bozeman Trail*, p. 121.

275 *August 1866 was the high point:* Brown, *The Fetterman Massacre*, p. 145.

275 *"breezy in winter":* Fort Phil Kearny plaque, Wyoming Historical Society.

277 *As the historian Shannon Smith notes:* Smith, *Give Me Eighty Men*, p. 42.

277 *seemed "to have been ideally suited":* Ibid.

277 *"commanding presence":* Ibid.

277 *The eldest of seven children:* Brown, *The Fetterman Massacre*, p. 151.

277 *"most precious and rare":* Fort Phil Kearny plaque.

277 *Doughnuts, gingerbread:* Ibid.

Chapter Twenty-Nine: A Thin Blue Line

PAGE

281 *"vile jokes and curses":* F. Carrington, *My Army Life and the Fort Phil Kearny Massacre*, p. 121.

282 *"Hardly three minutes":* Brown, *The Fetterman Massacre*, p. 122.

283 *If in fact the raids were led:* Papers of William T. Sherman.

283 *"Tell the rascals":* Indian Hostilities, Executive Document No. 33.

283 *"We must try to distinguish":* Fort Phil Kearny plaque, Wyoming Historical Society.

284 *The post's tiny guardhouse:* Brown, *The Fetterman Massacre*, p. 127.

284 *"brief tongue lashing":* F. Carrington, p. 121.

285 *"constantly scanning":* Ibid.

Chapter Thirty: Fire in the Belly

PAGE

286 *He did it so often:* Guthrie, "The Fetterman Massacre," p. 717.

287 *He was finally relieved:* Monnett, *Where a Hundred Soldiers Were Killed*, p. 117.

287 *His actions not only allowed:* U.S. War Department, *Official Records*, Ser. 1, Vol. 98, Part 1, pp. 495–507.

288 *The two Mrs. Grummonds:* Smith, *Give Me Eighty Men*, p. 68.

289 *"had not died brave":* Bisbee, *Through Four American Wars*, p. 170.

289 *"My whole being seemed":* F. Carrington, *My Army Life*, p. 154.

291 *Crazy Horse had never shown interest:* Bray, *Crazy Horse*, p. 72.

291 *Together they had hauled nearly:* Brown, *The Fetterman Massacre*, p. 129.

291 *According to Army manifests:* Ibid., p. 137.

292 *"restoring invalids":* Ibid.

293 *"to secure personal knowledge":* M. Carrington, *Absaraka*, p. 172.

Chapter Thirty-One: High Plains Drifters

PAGE

294 *Quick with his Navy Colt:* Gail Schontzler, *Bozeman Daily Chronicle*, January 23, 2011.

295 *On reaching the Kansas line:* Ibid.

296 *Actually, the cagey Story:* Brown and Schmidt, *Trail Driving Days*, p. 118.

298 *But the remuda left:* Brown, *The Fetterman Massacre*, p. 141.

Part V: The Massacre

Chapter Thirty-Two: Fetterman

PAGE

304 *"looked for with glad anticipation":* M. Carrington, *Absaraka*, p. 245.

307 *"I hope to be yet able":* Monnett, *Where a Hundred Soldiers Were Killed*, p. 103.

307 *"We are afflicted":* 1867 hearings, U.S. Senate, Bisbee testimony, p. 4.

307 *Yet despite his and the others' "disgust":* Ibid., Arnold testimony, p. 5.

307 *"the feeling was not harmonious":* Indian Hostilities, Executive Document No. 33.

308 *Even relatively mundane annoyances:* Brown, *The Fetterman Massacre*, p. 154.

308 *"You are hereby instructed":* Indian Hostilities, Executive Document No. 33.

Chapter Thirty-Three: Dress Rehearsal

PAGE

312 *"or return to the post":* Indian Hostilities, Executive Document No. 33.

312 *Carrington sputtered:* 1867 hearings, U.S. Senate, Wands testimony.

313 *a "coward or a fool":* Ibid., Bisbee testimony, p. 79.

314 *He could hear a repulsive click:* Hebard and Brininstool, *The Bozeman Trail*, p. 99.

314 *Finally, he jammed the sword:* F. Carrington, *My Army Life*, p. 134.

315 *"I cannot account":* Indian Hostilities, Executive Document No. 13, pp. 37–38.

315 *"This Indian War has become":* Brown, *The Fetterman Massacre*, p. 166.

315 *"deepened from that hour":* F. Carrington, p. 134.

Chapter Thirty-Four: Soldiers in Both Hands

PAGE

318 *"Your men who fought":* Vestal, *Jim Bridger,* p. 270.

318 *It was filling rapidly:* Hebard and Brininstool, *The Bozeman Trail*, p. 99.

319 *"buffalo-lined hip boots":* Bisbee, *Through Four American Wars*, p. 176.

319 *"Your brother was much esteemed":* Old Travois Trails 3, no. 3 (1942), 65.

320 *"heed the lessons":* F. Carrington, *My Army Life*, p. 135.

321 *On his way out the door:* Vestal, *Jim Bridger*, p. 273.

322 *When a hermaphrodite:* Hyde, *Red Cloud's Folk*, p. 147.

322 *The war chief waved his arm:* Brown, "Red Cloud of the Sioux," p. 91.

322 *When asked how many:* Hyde, p. 147.

Chapter Thirty-Five: The Half-Man's Omen

PAGE

324 *From here, with his captured:* Brown, "Red Cloud of the Sioux," p. 90.

324 *He acquiesced:* Indian Hostilities, Executive Document No. 33.

326 *"and never leave him":* F. Carrington, *My Army Life,* p. 143.

326 *To this exchange:* Wands testimony, 1867 hearings, U.S. Senate, p. 8.

326 *"and was moving wisely":* Indian Hostilities, Executive Document No. 33.

327 *"perfect vantage ground":* Ibid.

327 *"entertaining no further thought":* Henry Carrington's testimony, in Monnett, *Wild West* Magazine (October 2010).

328 *The wispy brave:* Bray, *Crazy Horse*, p. 96.

329 *He turned his back:* Christopher Morton interview.

Chapter Thirty-Six: Broken Arrows

PAGE

331 *"continuous and rapid":* Brown, *The Fetterman Massacre*, p. 12.

331 *"the largest":* Arnold testimony, 1867 hearings, U.S. Senate.

335 *It remains on display:* Smith, *Give Me Eighty Men*, p. 119.

335 *The official Army report:* Indian Hostilities, Executive Document No. 33.

Chapter Thirty-Seven: "Like Hogs Brought to Market"

PAGE

336 *One of the civilians:* J. B. Weston testimony, 1867 hearings, U.S. Senate, p. 5.

337 *"There's the men down there":* Brown, *The Fetterman Massacre*, p. 12.

337 *"The silence":* Ibid., p. 186.

337 *"Captain Ten Eyck says":* Indian Hostilities, Executive Document No. 33, p. 46.

337 *"The Captain is afraid":* Ibid.

338 *Perhaps he also anticipated:* Brown, *The Fetterman Massacre*, p. 190.

338 *"You could have saved":* Ibid., p. 185.

338 *He was the only trooper:* Horton testimony, 1867 hearings, U.S. Senate, p. 4.

339 *"We brought in about fifty":* Indian Hostilities, Executive Document No. 13, p. 15.

339 *"horrible and sickening":* F. Carrington, *My Army Life*, p. 149.

340 *"bright, piercing eyes":* Brown, *The Fetterman Massacre*, p. 192.

340 *"I will go if it costs":* F. Carrington, p. 149.

340 *Then he turned and left:* Ibid.

340 *Throughout all this:* Brown, *The Fetterman Massacre*, p. 191.

341 *Without immediate reinforcements:* Indian Hostilities, Executive Document No. 33, pp. 49–50.

341 *I send a copy of dispatch:* Ibid.

342 *"Good," he said:* Ostrander, *An Army Boy*, p. 194.

Chapter Thirty-Eight: Fear and Mourning

PAGE

344 *"If in my absence":* F. Carrington, *My Army Life*, p. 151.

345 *"It was," wrote a witness:* Brown, *The Fetterman Massacre*, p. 197.

345 *"Some had crosses cut":* Guthrie, "The Fetterman Massacre," p. 717.

345 *Someone remarked that such:* Brown, *The Fetterman Massacre*, p. 199.

345 *A few hundred yards:* Indian Hostilities, Executive Document No. 13, p. 65.

345 *Piles of spent Henry rifle cartridges:* Bray, *Crazy Horse*, p. 101.

345 *Outside the defensive circle:* Ibid.

347 *"all the honor":* Rocky Bear 1902 statement, Addison Sheldon Papers, Nebraska State Historical Society.

350 *"horrid massacre":* Murray, *The Bozeman Trail*, pp. 45–46.

Epilogue

PAGE

352 *"the completeness of the massacre":* Momett, *Where a Hundred Soldiers Died*, p. 96.

352 *"We must act":* Report of the Secretary of War to the Senate, Document No. 15.

353 *"operations within my command":* National Archives and Records Administration, Papers Accompanying the Report to General-in-Chief, p. 3.

353 *"passed over 455 miles":* Ibid.

355 *"I know how to fight":* Wyoming Historical Society interpretive sign at Wagon Box Fight site.

355 *"One general ominously informed":* Larson, *Red Cloud,* p. 115.

356 *Major General Christopher C. Auger:* Brown, *The Fetterman Massacre,* p. 224.

357 *"unprecedented in the history":* Yenne, *Sitting Bull,* p. 50.

358 *"As a consequence":* Paul, *Autobiography of Red Cloud,* p. 7.

359 *"No one who listened":* New York Times, June 17, 1868.

359 *"Now we are melting like snow":* Larson, p. 132.

359 *"Red Cloud saw too much":* Ibid.

360 *"I shall not go to war":* Ibid., p. 150.

362 *"God made this earth":* Eli Ricker Collection.

363 *"Shadows are long and dark":* Red Cloud Heritage Center.

363 *"When Red Cloud fought":* New York Times, December 11, 1909.

365 *"From the perspective":* Moten, *Between War and Peace,* p. 150.

365 *"And yet the general":* Ibid., p. 151.

365 *"My only answer":* Bisbee, *Through Four American Wars,* p. 166.

BIBLIOGRAPHY

Books

Adams, George Rollie. *General William S. Harney: Prince of Dragoons.* Lincoln: University of Nebraska Press, 2005.

Algier, Keith W. *The Crow and the Eagle: A Tribal History from Lewis and Clark to Custer.* Caldwell, OH: Caxton, 1993.

Alter, J. Cecil. *Jim Bridger.* Norman: University of Oklahoma Press, 1962.

Ambrose, Stephen E. *Crazy Horse and Custer: The Parallel Lives of Two American Warriors.* New York: Anchor, 1996.

Anderson, Gary Clayton, and Alan R. Woolworth, eds. *Through Dakota Eyes: Narrative Accounts of the Minnesota Indian War of 1862.* St. Paul: Minnesota Historical Society Press, 1988.

Andrist, Ralph K. *The Long Death: The Last Days of the Plains Indians.* New York: Collier, 1969.

Athearn, Robert G. *William Tecumseh Sherman and the Settlement of the West.* Norman: University of Oklahoma Press, 1956.

Bancroft, Hubert Howe. *The Works of Hubert Howe Bancroft,* Vol. 1.

Barnes, Jeff. *Forts of the Northern Plains.* Mechanicsburg, PA: Stackpole, 2008.

Billington, Ray Allen. *Land of Savagery, Land of Promise: The European Image of the American Frontier.* New York: Norton, 1981.

Bisbee, William H. *Through Four American Wars.* Boston: Meador, 1931.

Bonner, T. D. *The Life and Adventures of James P. Beckwourth.* Lincoln: University of Nebraska Press, 1981.

Brady, Cyrus. *Indian Fights and Fighters.* New York: McClure, Phillips, 1904.

Bray, Kingsley M. *Crazy Horse: A Lakota Life.* Norman: University of Oklahoma Press, 2006.

Brininstool, E. A. *Fighting Indian Warriors.* Mechanicsburg, PA: Stackpole, 1953.

Brown, Dee. *The American West.* New York: Touchstone, 1994.

———. *Bury My Heart at Wounded Knee.* New York: Holt, Rinehart and Winston, 1971.

———. *The Fetterman Massacre.* London: Pan, 1974.

Brown, Dee, and Martin Schmidt. *Trail Driving Days.* New York: Scribner, 1952.

Burt, Struthers. *Powder River.* New York: Farrar and Reinhart, 1978.

Carley, Kenneth. *The Dakota War of 1862.* St. Paul: Minnesota Historical Society, 2001.

Carlos, Ann M., and Frank D. Lewis. *Commerce by a Frozen Sea: Native Americans and the European Fur Trade.* Philadelphia: University of Pennsylvania Press, 2010.

Carrington, Frances. *My Army Life and the Fort Phil Kearny Massacre.* New York: Lippincott, 1910.

Carrington, Henry B. *The Indian Question.* Boston: De Wolfe and Fiske, 1909.

Carrington, Margaret. *Absaraka: Home of the Crows.* New York: Lippincott, 1878.

Carroll, John M., ed. *Papers of the Order of the Indian Wars of the United States.* Fort Collins, CO: Old Army Press, 1975.

Chiaventure, Frederick J. *Moon of Bitter Cold.* New York: Forge, 2002.

Chittenden, H. M., and A. T. Richardson, eds. *Life, Letters and Travels of Father Pierre-Jean De Smet.* New York, 1905.

Cohen, Eliot A. *Conquered into Liberty.* New York: Free Press, 2011.

Dary, David. *The Oregon Trail: An American Saga.* New York: Knopf, 2004.

Denig, E. T. *Five Indian Tribes of the Upper Missouri: Sioux, Arickaras, Assiniboines, Crees, Crows.* Norman: University of Oklahoma Press, 1961.

Dobie, J. Frank. *The Mustangs.* Lincoln, NE: Bison, 2005.

Dodge, Grenville. *Biographical Sketch of Jim Bridger.* Kansas City, MO: R. M. Rigby, 1904.

Doyle, Susan Badger. *Bound for Montana: Diaries from the Bozeman Trail, 1863–66.* Helena: Montana Historical Society, 2004.

Eder, Tamara. *Animal Tracks of the Great Plains.* Edmonton: Lone Pine, 2001.

Etulain, Richard W. *Chiefs and Generals.* Golden, CO: Fulcrum, 2004.

Ewers, John C. *Indian Life on the Upper Missouri.* Norman: University of Oklahoma Press, 1968.

Fehrenbach, T. R. *Comanches: The Destruction of a People.* New York: Knopf, 1974.

Geist, Valerius. *Buffalo Nation: History and Legend of the North American Bison.* Stillwater, MN: Voyageur, 1996.

Goble, Paul. *Brave Eagle's Account of the Fetterman Fight.* Lincoln: University of Nebraska Press, 1992.

Goodyear, Frank H., III. *Red Cloud: Photographs of a Lakota Chief.* Lincoln: University of Nebraska Press, 2003.

Grant, Ulysses Simpson. *Personal Memoirs of U. S. Grant.* New York: Dover, 1995.

Great Western Indian Fights. Garden City, NY: Doubleday, 1960.

Greene, Jerome A. *Indian War Veterans: Memories of Army Life and Campaigns in the West, 1864–1898.* New York: Savas Beatie, 2007.

Grinnell, George Bird. *The Fighting Cheyennes.* New York: Scribner, 1915.

Gwynne, S. C. *Empire of the Summer Moon.* New York: Scribner, 2010.

Hafen, LeRoy R., ed. *Mountain Men and Fur Traders of the Far West.* Lincoln: University of Nebraska Press, 1982.

Hafen, LeRoy, and Francis Young. *Fort Laramie and the Pageant of the West, 1834–1890.* Glendale, CA: A. H. Clark, 1938.

Hagan, Barry J. *"Exactly in the Right Place": A History of Fort C. F. Smith, Montana Territory, 1866–68.* El Segundo, CA: Upton, 1999.

Hagan, William T. *Quanah Parker.* Norman: University of Oklahoma Press, 1993.

Hassrick, Royal B. *The Sioux: Life and Customs of a Warrior Society.* Norman: University of Oklahoma Press, 1964.

Haynes, James. *History of the Methodist Episcopal Church in Omaha and Suburbs.* Omaha: Nebraska Printing Company, 1895.

Hebard, Grace R., and E. A. Brininstool. *The Bozeman Trail: Historical Accounts of the Blazing of the Overland Routes into the Northwest, and the Fights with Red Cloud's Warriors.* Cleveland: A. H. Clark, 1922.

Hyde, George E. *Red Cloud's Folk: A History of the Oglala Sioux Indians.* Norman: University of Oklahoma Press, 1937.

———. *Spotted Tail's Folk.* Norman: University of Oklahoma Press, 1961.

Jensen, Richard E. *Voice of the American West: Interviews of Eli S. Ricker, 1903–1919.* Lincoln: University of Nebraska Press, 2005.

Johnson, Dorothy M. *The Bloody Bozeman: The Perilous Trail to Montana's Gold.* New York: McGraw-Hill, 1971.

Johnson, James R., and Gary E. Larson. *Grassland Plants of South Dakota and the Northern Great Plains.* Brookings: South Dakota State University, 2007.

Johnson, Mark W. *That Body of Brave Men: The U.S. Regular Infantry and the Civil War in the West.* Cambridge, MA: Da Capo, 2003.

Johnson, Michael, and Jonathan Smith. *Tribes of the Sioux Nation.* Oxford, UK: Osprey Publishing, 2000.

Jones, Douglas C. *The Treaty of Medicine Lodge: The Story of the Great Treaty Council as Told by Eyewitnesses.* Norman: University of Oklahoma Press, 1966.

Kavanagh, James, and Raymond Leung. *Wyoming Trees and Wildflowers.* Dunedin, FL: Waterford, 2009.

Keenan, Jerry. *The Wagon Box Fight: An Episode of Red Cloud's War.* Conshohocken, PA: Savas, 2000.

Lamar, Howard R. *Dakota Territory, 1861–1889.* New Haven: Yale University Press, 1956.

Larson, Robert W. *Red Cloud: Warrior-Statesman of the Lakota Sioux.* Norman: University of Oklahoma Press, 1997.

La Vere, David. *Contrary Neighbors: Southern Plains and Removed Indians in Indian Territory.* Norman: University of Oklahoma Press, 2001.

Lazar, Jerry. *Red Cloud: Sioux War Chief.* New York: Chelsea House, 1995.

Lazarus, Edward. *Black Hills/White Justice: The Sioux Nation Versus the United States, 1775 to the Present.* New York: HarperCollins, 1991.

Lowe, Percival Green. *Five Years a Dragoon.* Kansas City, MO: F. Hudson, 1906.

Mackenzie, Alexander. *The Journals of Alexander Mackenzie: Exploring Across Canada in 1789 and 1793.* Torrington, WY: Narrative Press, 2001.

Mann, Charles C. *1491: New Revelations of the Americas Before Columbus.* New York: Vintage, 2005.

Marshall, Joseph M., III. *The Journey of Crazy Horse.* New York: Viking, 2004.

Mattes, Merrill J. *Platte River Road Narratives.* Champaign: University of Illinois, 1988.

Matthiessen, Peter. *In the Spirit of Crazy Horse.* New York: Viking, 1983.

McDermott, John D. *Circle of Fire: The Indian War of 1865.* New York: Stackpole, 2003.

———, ed. *Portraits of Fort Phil Kearny.* Banner, WY: Bozeman Trail Association, 1993.

———. *Red Cloud's War: The Bozeman Trail, 1866–68.* Norman, OK: Arthur H. Clark, 2010.

McGinnis, Anthony. *Counting Coups and Cutting Horses.* Evergreen, CO: Cordillera Press, 1990.

McLaughlin, Morie L. *Myths and Legends of the Sioux.* Charleston, SC: Nabu Press, 2010.

McMurtry, Larry. *Boone's Lick.* New York: Simon & Schuster, 2000.

Michno, Gregory F. *Encyclopedia of Indian Wars: Western Battles and Skirmishes, 1850–1890.* Missoula, MT: Mountain Press, 2003.

Monnett, John H. *Crazy Horse: A Life.* New York: Viking, 1999.

———. *Where a Hundred Soldiers Were Killed.* Albuquerque: University of New Mexico Press, 2008.

Moten, Matthew, ed. *Between War and Peace: How America Ends Its Wars.* New York: Free Press, 2011.

Murray, Robert. *The Bozeman Trail: Highway of History.* Portland, OR: Westwinds Press, 2000.

Neihardt, John G. *Black Elk Speaks: Being the Life Story of a Holy Man of the Oglala Sioux.* Lincoln: University of Nebraska Press, 1961.

Nichols, David A. *Lincoln and the Indians.* Urbana: University of Illinois Press, 2000.

Olson, James C. *Red Cloud and the Sioux Problem.* Lincoln: University of Nebraska Press, 1965.

Ostler, Jeffrey. *The Lakotas and the Black Hills.* New York: Viking, 2010.

Ostrander, Alson B. *An Army Boy of the Sixties.* Yonkers, NY: World Book, 1924.

Page, Jake. *In the Hands of the Great Spirit.* New York: Free Press, 2004.

Parker, Samuel. *Journal of an Exploring Tour Beyond the Rocky Mountains.* Whitefish, MT: Kessinger, 2006.

Parkman, Francis. *The Oregon Trail.* New York: Library of America, 1991.

Paul, R. Eli. *Autobiography of Red Cloud.* Helena: Montana Historical Society Press, 1997.

Powers, Thomas. *The Killing of Crazy Horse.* New York: Knopf, 2010.

Powers, William K. *Oglala Religion.* Lincoln: University of Nebraska Press, 1975.

Price, Catherine. *The Oglala People, 1841–1879: A Political History.* Lincoln: University of Nebraska Press, 1996.

Pringle, Catherine Sager. *Across the Plains in 1844.* Whitefish, MT: Kessinger, 2009.

Sajna, Mike. *Crazy Horse: The Life Behind the Legend.* New York: Wiley, 2000.

Sandoz, Mari. *Crazy Horse: Strange Man of the Oglalas.* New York: Knopf, 1942.

Smith, Shannon D. *Give Me Eighty Men: Women and the Myth of the Fetterman Fight.* Lincoln: University of Nebraska Press, 2008.

Spring, Agnes Wright. *Caspar Collins: The Life and Exploits of an Indian Fighter of the 60s.* New York: Columbia University Press, 1927.

Straight, Michael. *Carrington: A Novel of the West.* New York: Knopf, 1960.

Utley, Robert. *Frontier Regulars: The United States Army and the Indian, 1866–1891.* New York: Macmillan, 1973.

————. *Frontiersmen in Blue.* New York: Macmillan, 1967.

Vestal, Stanley. *Jim Bridger.* New York: Morrow, 1946.

————. *Warpath: The True Story of the Fighting Sioux.* Boston: Houghton Mifflin, 1934.

Viola, Herman J. *Diplomats in Buckskins: A History of Indian Delegations in Washington City.* Washington, DC: Smithsonian Institution Press, 1981.

Walker, James R. *Lakota Society.* Lincoln: University of Nebraska Press, 1982.

Washburn, Wilcomb E. *The Indians in America.* New York: Harper and Row, 1975.

Webb, Walter Prescott. *The Great Plains.* Lincoln: University of Nebraska Press, 1981.

Wissler, Clark. *North American Indians of the Plains.* New York: American Museum of Natural History, 1934.

Yenne, Bill. *Sitting Bull.* Yardley, PA: Westholme, 2008.

Articles

Belish, Elbert D. "American Horse: The Man Who Killed Fetterman," *Annals of Wyoming* 63, no. 1 (spring 1985), 28–47.

Carrington, James B. "Across the Plains with Bridger as Guide," *Scribner's Magazine* 85 (January 1929), 66–81.

Doyle, Susan Badger. "Indian Perspectives of the Bozeman Trail," *Montana: The Magazine of Western History* 40, no. 1 (winter 1990), 56–57.

Ellison, R. S. "John 'Portugee' Phillips and His Famous Ride," *Old Travois Trails* 2, no. 1 (1941).

Ferry, David. "Leave It to Beavers," *Atlantic*, May 2012.

Glover, Ridgeway. Letter to the Editor, *Philadelphia Photographer* 3 (1866).

Greene, Jerome A. "The Hayfield Fight: A Reappraisal of a Neglected Action," *Montana: The Magazine of Western History* 22, no. 4 (autumn 1972), 30–43.

————. "Lt. Palmer Writes from the Bozeman Trail," *Montana: The Magazine of Western History* 28, no. 3 (summer 1978), 16–35.

Grouard, Frank. "An Indian Scout's Recollections of Crazy Horse," *Nebraska History Magazine* 12 (January–March 1929), 24–29.

Guthrie, John. "The Fetterman Massacre," *Annals of Wyoming* 9 (October 1932), 714–18.

Hagan, Barry. "Prelude to a Massacre: Fort Phil Kearny, Dec. 6, 1866," *Journal of the Order of the Indian Wars* 1 (fall 1980), 1–17.

Hyer, Joel R. "Just Another Battle? The Significance of the Hayfield Fight," *Annals of Wyoming* 79 (summer–autumn 2007), 2–13.

McCaig, Donald. "The Bozeman Trail," *Smithsonian Magazine* 7 (October 2000), 88–100.

Monnett, John H. "The Falsehoods of Fetterman's Fight," *Wild West* (December 2010).

O'Hara, Cleophas C. "Red Cloud and Rapid City," *The Pahasapa Quarterly* 4, no. 3 (April 1915).

Olson, James C. "The Interview as a Source of Indian History," Nebraska State Historical Society.

Palmer, H. E. "History of the Powder River Indian Expedition of 1865," *Transactions* 2 (1887), 197–229.

Richardson, E. M. "The Forgotten Haycutters of Fort C. F. Smith," *Montana: The Magazine of Western History* 9, no. 3 (July 1959).

Robinson, Doane. "The Education of Red Cloud." Collection of the South Dakota Department of History, XII (1924), 156–78.

Shockley, P. M. "Fort Phil Kearny: The Fetterman Massacre," *Quartermaster Review* 11 (May–June 1932), 27–32.

———. "The Wagon Box Fight: The Last Important Event of Fort Phil Kearny's Short Existence," *Quartermaster Review* 11 (September–October 1932).

Soule, Doris. "11th Ohio Cavalry—Ohio in the Civil War," *Wild West Magazine* (December 1996).

Utley, Robert M. "The Bozeman Trail Before John Bozeman: A Busy Land," *Montana: The Magazine of Western History* 53, no. 2 (summer 2003), 20–31.

Villard, Henry. "Recollections of Lincoln," *The Atlantic Presents the Civil War* (Special Commemorative Issue, 2011), 34–37.

White, Richard. "The Winning of the West," *Journal of American History* 65 (September 1978), 321.

Young, Will H. "The Journal of Will H. Young," *Annals of Wyoming* 7 (1930), 402–24.

Archives and Other Sources

American West Heritage Center (awhc.org).

Bozeman Trail Association: Papers at Fulmer Public Library, Sheridan, Wyoming.

Christopher Morton, U.S. National Parks Department Historian, Board of Fort Phil Kearny National Historic Site.

Eli Ricker Collection: Nebraska State Historical Society.

Fort Phil Kearny State Historic Site: Banner, Wyoming.

Frank Elliott Papers: Montana Historical Society.

Fulmer Library, Sheridan, Wyoming.

Henry B. Carrington Papers: Sterling Memorial Library, Yale University.

Heritagecenter@redcloudschool.org (Pine Ridge Indian Reservation, South Dakota).

Jefferson, Thomas: Sixth Annual Message to Congress, December 1806.

Library of Congress.

Madison, James: *Notes of the Debates of the Federal Convention, 1787.*

National Anthropological Archives, Maryland.

National Archives, Maryland:

- Official Records of Fort Phil Kearny.
- U.S. War Department, Department of the Platte. Letter Book No. 1, 1866.
- U.S. War Department, 18th Infantry Regiment. Muster Rolls and Record of Events, April 1866–July 1867.
- Board of Survey Orders, September 1866–July 1867.
- Still Pictures Archive.

Nebraska State Historical Society, Lincoln.

Omaha Weekly Herald.

Omaha Weekly Republican.

Rocky Mountain News, 1865–66.

Report of the Committee on the Conduct of the War on the Massacre of Cheyenne Indians, U.S. House of Representatives, January 10, 1865.

Report of Lieutenant General Sherman, October 1, 1867.

South Dakota Historical Society.

Special Commission Investigating the Fort Phil Kearny Massacre, U.S. Senate, 1867.

Tenedor Ten Eyck Diary: University of Arizona.

University of Nebraska, Lincoln.

Western History Association: University of Missouri, St. Louis.

U.S. Congress, 40th, 1st Session, Senate. *Indian Hostilities* (Executive Documents No. 13 and No. 33). Washington, D.C., 1868.

American-tribes.com.

Oglala Sioux College, Kyle, South Dakota.

Wyomingtalesandtrails.com.

INDEX

Page numbers that are *italicized* indicate illustrations.

ABOUT THE AUTHOR

BOB DRURY is the author/coauthor/editor of nine books, the last three in collaboration with Tom Clavin. His last solo book, *The Rescue Season,* was adapted into a documentary by the History Channel. He has written for numerous publications, including *The New York Times, Vanity Fair, Men's Journal,* and *GQ.* He is currently a contributing editor and foreign correspondent for *Men's Health* magazine, and has reported from Iraq, Darfur, Liberia, Afghanistan, Sarajevo, and Belfast. He lives in Manasquan, New Jersey.

TOM CLAVIN is the author or coauthor of sixteen books. For fifteen years he wrote for *The New York Times,* and he has contributed articles to many magazines, including *Golf, Men's Journal, Parade, Reader's Digest,* and *Smithsonian.* He is currently the investigative features correspondent for *Manhattan Magazine.* He lives in Sag Harbor, New York.

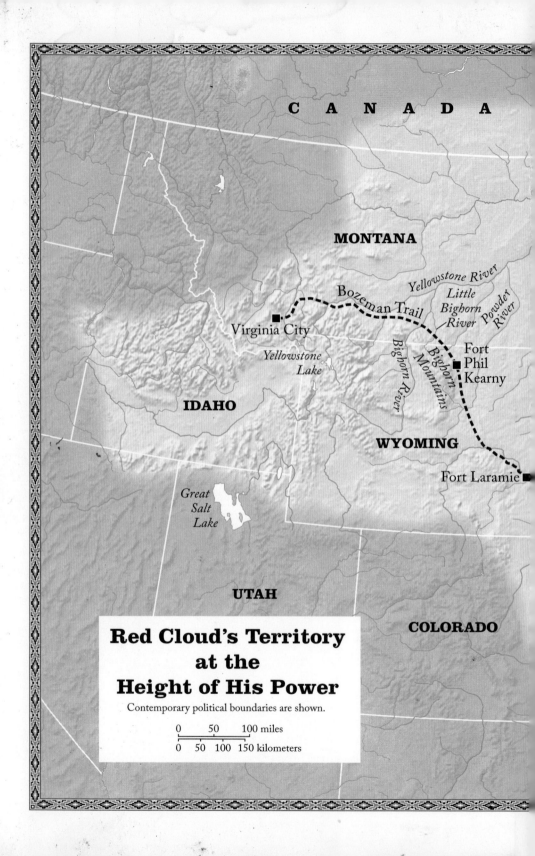

Red Cloud's Territory
at the
Height of His Power

Contemporary political boundaries are shown.

```
0      50     100 miles
0   50  100  150 kilometers
```

CANADA

MONTANA

Bozeman Trail

Yellowstone River

Little
Bighorn
River

Powder
River

Virginia City

Yellowstone
Lake

Bighorn River

Bighorn
Mountains

Fort
Phil
Kearny

IDAHO

WYOMING

Fort Laramie

Great
Salt
Lake

UTAH

COLORADO